ART BOOKS

FROM CRESCENT MOON PUBLISHING

Bellini
By Jennie Ellis Keysor

The Life of Michelangelo Buonarroti
By John Addington Symonds

Dante Gabriel Rossetti
By Esther Wood

Rodin: The Man and His Art
Edited by Judith Cladel

Rodin
By Rainer Maria Rilke

Fra Angelico
By James Mason

The Madonna In Art
By Estelle Hurll

The Venetian School of Painting
By Evelyn Phillipps

Boucher
By Haldane McFall

Leonardo da Vinci
By Maurice Brockwell

Famous European Painters
By Sarah Bolton

Delacroix
By Paul Konody

DANTE ROSSETTI
AND THE PRE-RAPHAELITE
MOVEMENT

DANTE ROSSETTI
AND THE PRE-RAPHAELITE
MOVEMENT

BY ESTHER WOOD

CRESCENT MOON

First published 1894. This edition © 2018.

Printed and bound in the U.S.A.
Set in Book Antiqua 10 on 14pt.
Designed by Radiance Graphics.

Thanks to the authors and publishers quoted.

British Library Cataloguing in Publication data

ISBN-13 9781861716392

CRESCENT MOON PUBLISHING
P.O. Box 1312, Maidstone, Kent, ME14 5XU
Great Britain, www.crmoon.com

CONTENTS

in Painting – Ideals of Womanhood – "The Girlhood of Mary Virgin" and "Ecce Ancilla Domini" – The Problem of Suffering – "Christ in the House of His Parents," "The Passover in the Holy Family," "The Shadow of Death," "The Scapegoat" – Hunt's Symbolism – "The Light of the World" – Rossetti's Symbolism – "Mary Magdalene at the Door," and "Mary in the House of John" – The Idea of Victory through Suffering – Bethlehem Gate" – "The Triumph of the Innocents" – The Spirit of Inquiry – "Christ in the Temple" – The Atonement – "The Infant Christ Adored" – Comparison with Madox Brown and Burne-Jones – "The Entombment" – "The Tree of Life"

NOTE ON THE TEXT

The text is from *Dante Rossetti and the Pre-Raphaelite Movement* by Esther Wood, published by Sampson Low, Marston and Company, Ltd, London, in 1894.

Footnotes are in square brackets, thus: [*1]

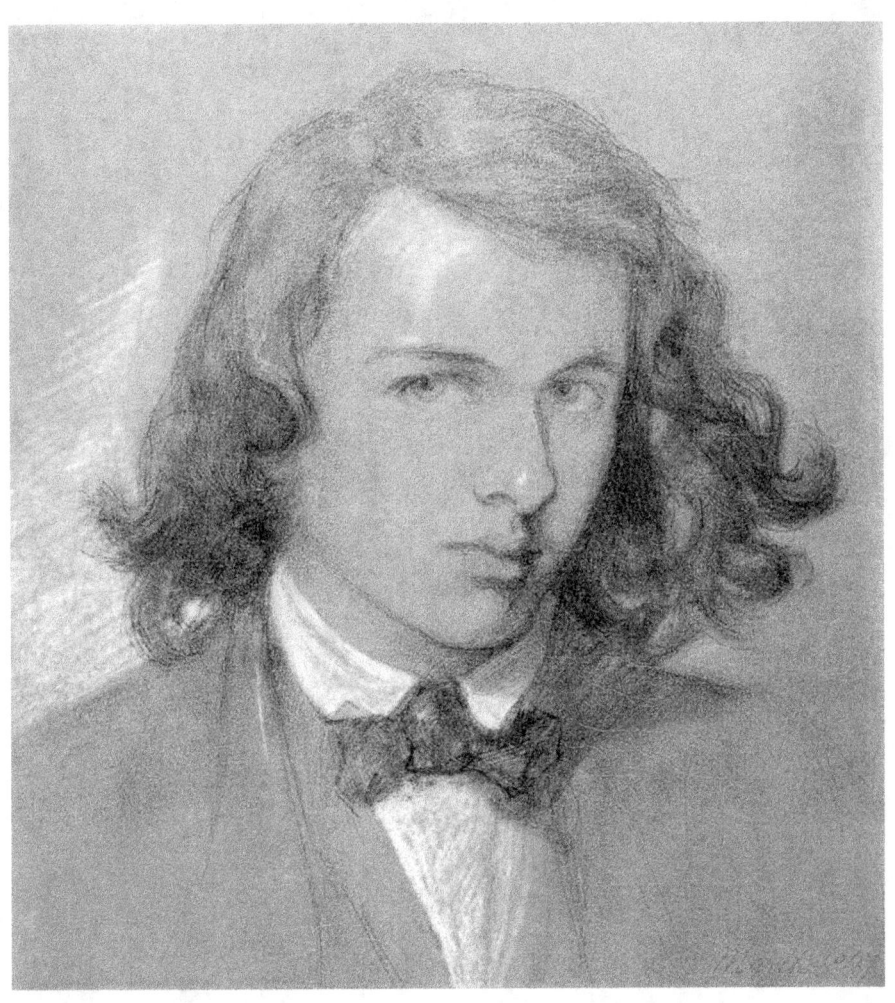

Dante Gabriel Rossetti, Self-Portrait, 1847,
National Portrait Gallery, London

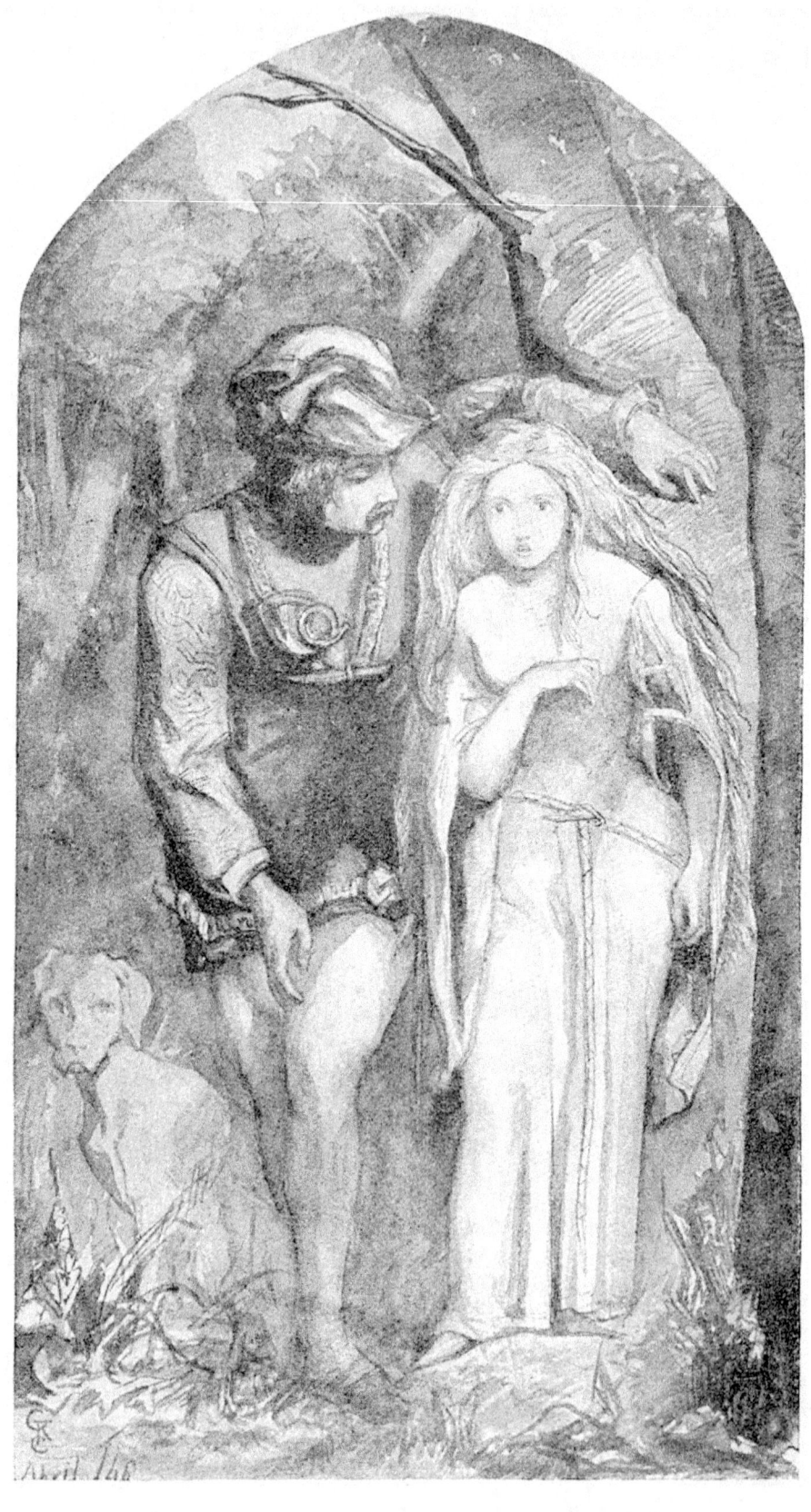

Dante Gabriel Rossetti, La Belle Dame Sans Merci, 1848

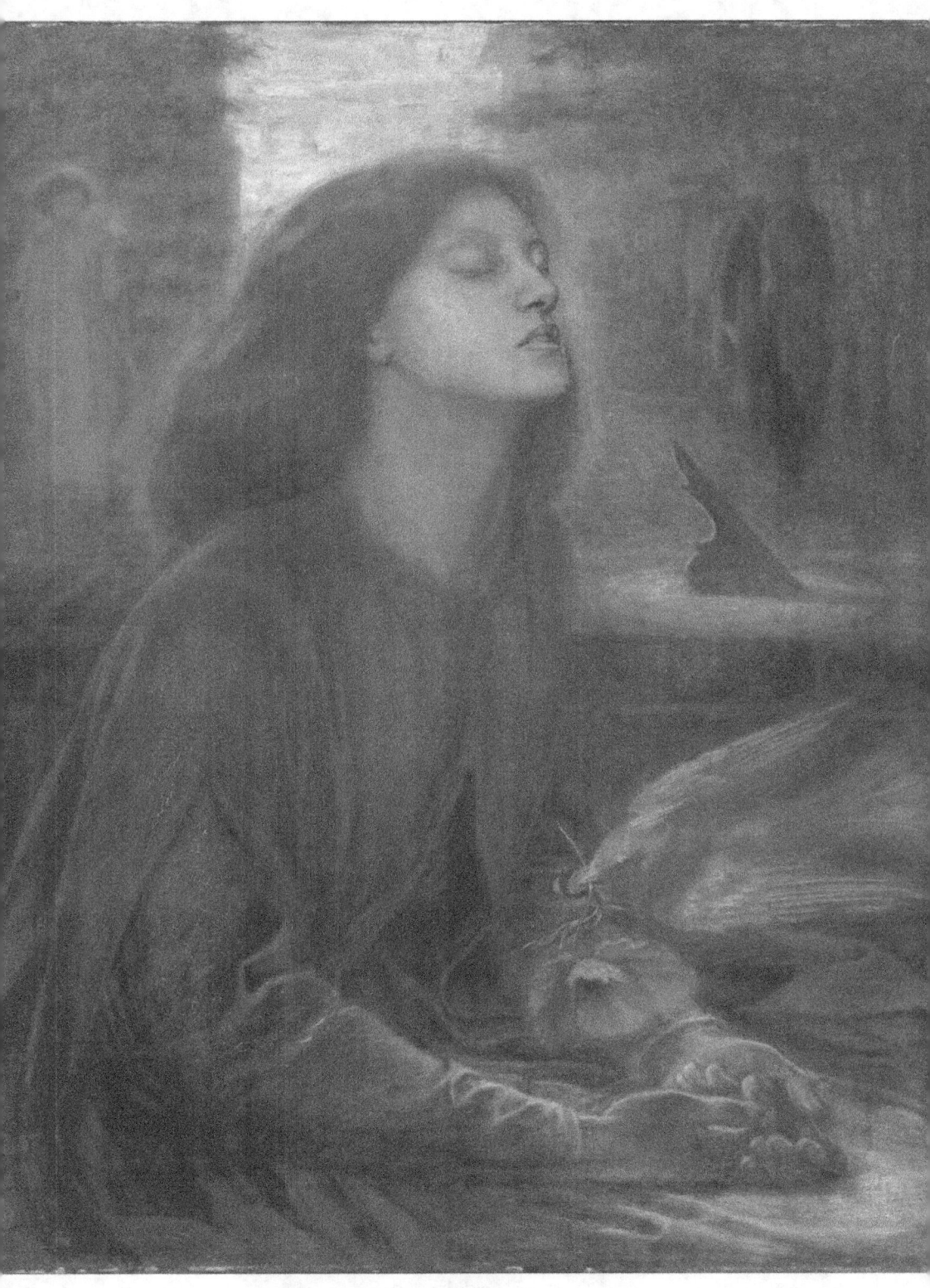

Dante Gabriel Rossetti, Beata Beatrix, 1864-70, Tate Britain

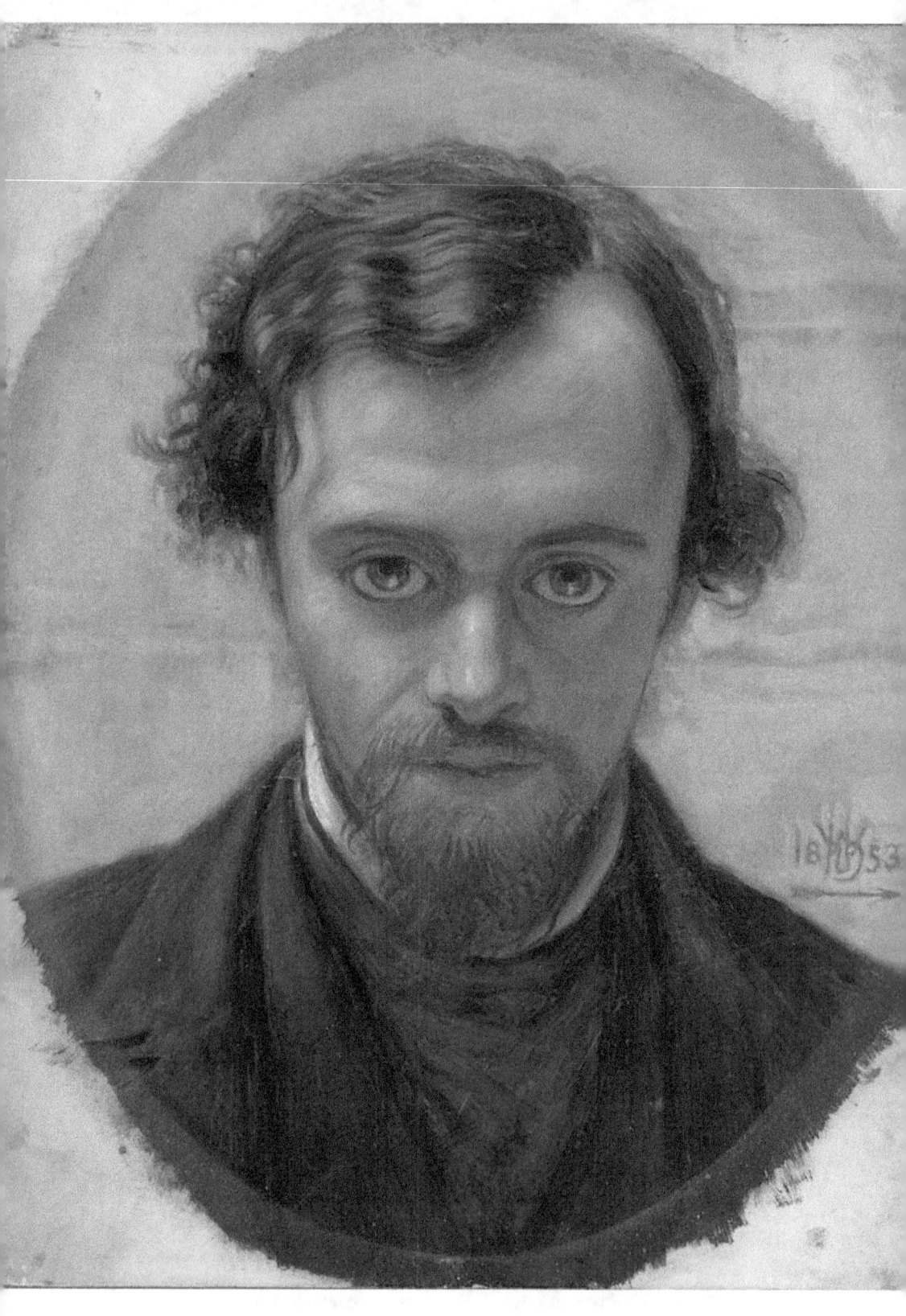

Holman Hunt, Dante Gabriel Rossetti, 1882-83, Birmingham

PREFACE

The following pages do not afford any material additions to what is already known of Dante Rossetti, or of the history and purpose of the Pre-Raphaelite Brotherhood. The authoritative biography of Rossetti has yet to be written; and while availing myself fully of such new details as may cast fresh side-lights upon the dominant personalities of the Pre-Raphaelite movement, my aim has rather been to present the main features of that movement in their relation to the larger intellectual tendencies of the age, and to the moral principles which have determined the growth of taste and feeling in the nineteenth century. To this end I have avoided as far as possible the proper domain of the art critic, and endeavoured to deal with the Pre-Raphaelite movement more as an ethical than an æsthetic revolution.

"It was always known to be Rossetti's wish," says Mr. Hall Caine in his interesting and graphic "Recollections of Rossetti,"

> "that if at any moment after his death it should appear that the story of his life required to be written, the one friend who during many of his later years knew him most intimately, and to whom he unlocked the most sacred secrets of his heart, Mr. Theodore Watts, should write it; unless indeed it were undertaken by his brother William. But though I know that whenever Mr. Watts sets pen to paper in pursuance of such a purpose and in fulfilment of such charge, he will afford us a recognizable portrait of the man, vivified by picturesque illustration, the like of which few other writers could compass, I also

know from what Rossetti often told me of his friend's immersion in all kinds and varieties of life, that years (perhaps many years) may elapse before such a biography is given to the world."

In the meantime, the present writer is indebted to Mr. J.A. Vinter, Rossetti's fellow-student at the Royal Academy Schools, for some interesting reminiscences of class-room and studio life, and to the Rev. Walter Tuckwell, rector of Stockton, Rugby, for personal recollections of the Pre-Raphaelites at Oxford. Mr. Gerald Massey has also assisted with suggestions and notes.

Through the courtesy of present owners of Rossetti's pictures, several important drawings and studies are here engraved for the first time. Lord Battersea and Overstrand has kindly permitted a photograph to be made from the sketch in his possession, "Mary Magdalene at the Door of Simon the Pharisee." A similar privilege has been granted by the Corporation of Birmingham in regard to their monochrome, "The Boat of Love," and the beautiful unfinished study of "Our Lady of Pity." I have also to acknowledge the kindness of Mr. Moncure D. Conway, in giving access to the fine study of the "Head of Christ" in his collection, and, by no means least, of Mr. Theodore Watts, in the matter of his two superb crayons, "The Day-dream" and "Pandora." The "Beata Beatrix" and "Ecce Ancilla Domini" are from the now familiar paintings in the National Gallery.

Esther Wood.
Hampstead,
February, 1894.

CHAPTER I.

THE PREPARATION
FOR REFORM IN ART.

Constable prophesies the Decay of English Art – The new Impulse from Italy – The English Renaissance of 1850 – Rossetti and the Specialistic Temperament – Classicism of the Eighteenth Century – Influence of the French Revolution – Revival of Romance – Distinction between Mediæval and Modern Romance – Pessimism in Pre-Raphaelite Painting – Nature as a Background – Moral Significance of the Change.

A study of the Pre-Raphaelite movement in England at the zenith of the nineteenth century opens up perhaps a wider field for controversy in the ethics of art than is afforded by any other phase of modern painting. Between the ridicule which, for the most part, greeted Rossetti's first picture, "The Girlhood of Mary Virgin," in 1849, and the enthusiastic homage which exalted him, thirty years later, to the dominance not merely of a school, but almost of a religion, lies a ground of infinite question and dispute, still awaiting the historian who shall adjust the issues of the strife to the main thought-current of the period.

"In thirty years," said Constable in 1821, "English art will have ceased to exist."

The words were significant of that first stirring of weariness and discontent which precedes either a collapse or a revolution. It was impossible that the conventions of the eighteenth century, persisting in pictorial art long after they had been cast off by literature, should suffice for an age which had wholly outgrown the conceptions of life on which they were founded. Landscape and portraiture, however enriched by the last gleams of a flickering classicism in the genius of a Turner, a Lawrence, or a Constable, were still in the "bondage of corruption" to traditional schools. Turner, indeed, is too great to be bracketed with his contemporaries, or with the pioneers of the Pre-Raphaelite movement. He stands as much alone as Titian. But the thrall of the conventional, of the accepted canons of what should be perceived and conceived, and how things ought to look in pictures, lay yet upon English art. One other painter, a solitary and uncouth herald of the new day, holds a unique position in that transition period. Blake alone, working his fantastic will like a sanctified Rabelais run riot in all supernal things, discerned weird glimpses of the coming light; such glimpses as Chatterton, in the world of poetry, caught brokenly before the neo-romantic dawn.

Posterity may decide that the catastrophe thus prophesied by Constable was only averted by the grafting of an Italian genius upon English stock, and that to the country of the Great Renaissance England owes – at least in the field of painting – her own Renaissance of the nineteenth century. Spontaneous as was the impulse of revolt in kindred minds, and worthily as it issued in the hands of others, the supreme achievement of the Pre-Raphaelite movement abides with Dante Gabriel Rossetti. Without him there might have been – and indeed was already begun – a breaking up of the old pictorial conventions; an experiment both significant and fruitful in contemporary art. Failing this ready soil, the genius brought over by Rossetti from a Latin race could hardly have been naturalized as it was in early life by interchange of thought and method with fellow-schismatics from the English schools. But whether that vital change of spirit which found its fullest expression in the Pre-Raphaelite movement would have produced anything like its present results independently of Rossetti, is a question still entangled in that injudicial partisanship of opinion from which no contemporary judgment can quite shake itself free. A final estimate of Rossetti's debt to his comrades, and of the original and intrinsic merit both of their own work and of his, is beyond the reach of the present century. Meanwhile, a verdict of no inconsiderable weight is available in the words of Ruskin: "I believe Rosetti's name should be placed first on the list of men who have raised and changed the spirit of modern art; raised in absolute attainment, changed in the direction of temper."

Probably, if one were called upon to name a score of typical pictures of the Pre-Raphaelite School, the first rough catalogue rising to the lips would be strangely inadequate to the question. Rossetti's "Girlhood of Mary Virgin," "Ecce Ancilla Domini," "Found," "Beata Beatrix," "Dante's Dream," and "The Blessed Damozel;" Madox Brown's "The Last of England," "The Entombment," and "Romeo and Juliet;" Holman Hunt's "Christ in the Temple," "The Scapegoat," and "The Light of the World;" Millais's "Eve of St. Agnes," "A Huguenot," and "Ophelia;" – these, if among the most familiar to English eyes, are but a small fraction of the product of that fruitful thirty years, leaving altogether out of count the later and important work of G.F. Watts and E. Burne-Jones, to say nothing of such worthy adherents as Arthur Hughes, James Collinson, Henry Wallis, Walter Deverell, J.M. Strudwick, and others who fairly claim the shadow of the Pre-Raphaelite wing. Yet even in so imperfect a group the student may read at least the dominant features of the painting, and especially in the work of Dante Gabriel Rossetti. Here for the first time in English art is *colour* supreme, triumphant, as in Titian; *form* ethereal and chastened, like the visions of a Fra Angelico; *subjects*, rather than objects, set forth in so direct and often crude an imagery; not figures merely, but symbols; fragments of human history, actual and urgent, full of problems and wonders, weighty with meanings and desires. The draped and ordered models of the past – the Ladies Sophia, Elizabeth, and Lavinia as the three Graces, and the Countess Agatha as a species of Muse – have given place to a new "dream of fair women," not posing or self-conscious, but as if caught and painted unaware; knights like young monks, sad-eyed but alert in a rapt sobriety; Madonnas more human than angelic, with the sweet cares of womanhood upon them all; Christs neither new-born nor dying, but seen in full child-life and manhood, artless and simple and strong. Here, certainly, is the utterance of men who if they have not looked broadly over life have at least seen deeply into it, and concerned themselves not so much with its rare crises as with the permanent conditions and problems of human experience.

It is easily argued that all criticism, all appreciation even, resolves itself ultimately into a question of temperament. To some minds, and these not the least discriminate, the very limitations and extravagances of Pre-Raphaelitism appeal with a peculiar force. There are whole aspects of life which Romance, if it touch, can never transfigure. The passionate, brooding loveliness of Rossetti's women, the remote and subtle pathos of Holman Hunt, the dreamy and yet vivid tenderness of Millais's earlier style, – these are not qualities of universal charm: they are the outcome of special moods and conditions which find neither voice nor answer save in the channels they themselves create. It is only given to a rarely catholic genius – a Shakespeare, a Handel, or a Raphael – to move, as it were, the broad currents of common feeling, and to command the general sympathies of the educated world. Artists of more distinctive and personal quality – a Shelley in poetry, a Chopin in music, or a Rossetti in painting – will rather gain each an elect circle of interpreters through whom to sway less immediately the thought of their generation; the more so since in the realm of the fine arts is felt most potently the growing tendency to specialize both thought and utterance in the tension of modern life. "Our age," it has been aptly said, "has seen a specialization of emotions as well as of studies and industries. Let us not then expect all things from any man. Let us welcome the best representative of every mood of the mind."[*1]

The private life of Dante Gabriel Rossetti, though leaving to those who loved him an inexhaustible harvest of tender and pathetic memories, was outwardly uneventful enough, save for the one romance and tragedy of his early manhood by which he is vaguely known to the outer world. But behind the veil of recordable history, few artists have suffered greater mental vicissitudes in a lifetime of half a century, or have lived at such high spiritual pressure and imaginative strain. London-born and London-bred though he was, the force of his Italian parentage and temperament isolated him – save for a very few congenial spirits – in an alien world; and though his work in painting and poetry was largely Saxonized by training and environment, the man himself was oppressed with the burden of an imagination steeped in the very soul of mediæval Florentine romance. His whole nature was overstrung and at the mercy of physical and social "weather." Memory, daily experience, his own conceptions and creations in design and poetry, small incidents of life woven by his own feverish brain into actual calamity, possessed him with a power simply incomprehensible to the average mind. Like Sir Bedevere, striding from ridge to ridge in Lyonness, –

"His own thought drove him like a goad."

At the last, his death, it has been affirmed by Mr. Theodore Watts, was due but indirectly to physical disease; primarily to the prolonged and terrible fervour of writing "The King's Tragedy." Out of such conditions of artistic expression came a depth and intensity of feeling incompatible with wide versatility or range of vision. Such a temperament must either specialize or achieve nothing.

But it is the business of the historian to look behind temperament towards the deep and primal impulses of a nation and a century. To him the sum of temperaments becomes the spirit of an age; or rather, the nation itself, in the grasp of the age, is conceived as a living, thinking, struggling personality; complex, problematic, self-contradictory, but strong to inspire the same loyalties, the same aspirations, as the old world found in Rome, or mediæval Europe in the great mother-cities which were at once her burden and her pride. To study a temperament like Rossetti's in its relation to the intellectual life of the age, and to ask how such a temperament was in its turn brought to bear upon some of the problems of that life, is to be confronted with much more than a personality or a career; is to deal with a wide and crucial phase in the history of a people.

For the Pre-Raphaelite movement was much more than a revolution in the ideals and methods of painting. It was a single wave in a great reactionary tide – the ever rising protest and rebellion of our century against artificial authority, against tradition and convention in every department of life. It broke out, socially, with the French Revolution; it found voice in the poetic impulse which followed it in Coleridge, Shelley, and Keats; it spread from ethics to politics, it touched all morality and all knowledge, and it affected the whole literature of Europe from philosophy to fiction and from the drama to the lyric poem. Schumann and Chopin breathed it into music; Darwin, re-forming the world of science, laid in the doctrine of evolution the foundations of the new cosmogony. It remained for painting, the youngest of the arts, to enter last into the van of progress and take its stand against the classic and orthodox scholasticism now discredited and void.

Not that the classicism of eighteenth century art was without a beauty and a meaning of its own. It was at least the relic of a noble ideal, the outworn garment of a spirit once vigorous and sincere. The true classic temper – the mental ordering of the visible world into types and models according to academic rule – is the natural outgrowth of man's effort to select and classify those objects around him which it gives him pleasure to contemplate.

The "choosing-spirit" of an age – its preference for certain aspects of life and indifference to other aspects – embodies itself in set forms and modes of artistic expression which are accepted by that age as sufficient and final, and stereotyped by common usage into conventions from which, in the progress of a growing people, all vitality gradually ebbs away. Just as in science or philosophy the theories and methods of authoritative men are established as "classic" till fresh facts and fresh problems come to light, so in literature, in music, and in painting, certain types and modes are adopted by general consent as the fit vehicles for the thought to be expressed, and these persist, by force of authority and usage, into a new age bringing new ideas into play and seeing the *subject-matter* of all art – namely life itself – in a new light. Thus the accepted canons of art, which were at first the natural reflection of the highest culture of the period, become at last the barren dogmas of an outgrown habit of mind. The thought of the people has outrun the language of the schools. The strife of the new thought with the old language is begun.

Such a strife it was that came upon the western world under the outward turmoil of the French Revolution. Europe was in the mood for great reactions. The vast and sordid materialism of the eighteenth century, with its prodigious hypocrisies and its flippant sensuality, – its sentimentality even, which, as Heine reminds us, is always a product of materialism – was rudely broken up. The disruption of the settled order of worldly things awoke men's dormant questions as to the divine order of things, the moral government of the universe. Or rather, the rejection of external authority was but the evidence of the rejection of authority within – the rejection of traditional standards of right and wrong, beauty and happiness, wisdom and truth; and the demand for new standards for the criticism of life, for new ethics, new ideals, new gods.

Now the pure and lofty classicism of the seventeenth century, as exemplified supremely in the poetry of Milton, was saved from materialism by the robust piety of a Puritan world. It was not until the beginning of the eighteenth century, when the accession of imperial and commercial power brought with it a certain coarsening of the moral fibre of the nation, that the "grand" style became petrified, as it always tends to do, into the grandiose. A people nurtured in the somewhat tawdry luxury of the Hanoverian period was not likely to take very serious views of life, but was well content with superficial philosophies. In the blaze of outward prosperity the inward vision grew dim. Art became the slave of tradition instead of the handmaid of a living will.

Then the great wave of rebellion, surging through the life of Europe, swept into the deep backwaters of imaginative and creative thought. Men born into the storm and stress of revolution, and confronted with the great problems of practical life, were driven back to question ultimate things; were thrown once more upon the spiritual world. And as the outward struggle spent itself, its full significance weighed more upon the peoples. The deep charm of the contemplative, the reflective, the critical, fell once more upon the European mind.

So the "classic" temper – the love of order and authority (degraded at last into mere acceptance of tradition and rule) – gave place to the "romantic" temper, – the temper of enquiry and experiment, the sense of the mystery and the reality of life, the openness of the mind towards spiritual things. And with this new consciousness of the invisible world and all its significance upon the life of man, comes the utter discarding of *self*-consciousness; the repudiation of "pose." Life has become too real for attitudinizing.

The first result of this change of spirit upon the art of a nation appears in the choice of subject for artistic treatment. The painter begins to portray not merely things and persons but incidents and conditions; to picture men and women as they are in actual life; in short, to *state the problems* fairly; to see facts and examine circumstances, in order to reach the solutions and the meanings, vaguely guessed and earnestly desired by the soul awakened to the perception of the supernatural and the divine. This was the initial task of the neo-romantic revival; in this lay the primary significance of the new school of painting which appeared soon after the year 1845 on English exhibition walls.

And to do this it became necessary to set out, as it were, the *terms* on which life is lived; to deal not merely with the beauty which man loves and the joy which he desires, but also with the stern conditions of their attainment. The struggle between the present evil and the recognized good, the conflict of the soul with earthly bonds, Love baffled in dire cross-currents of fate and duty, or wasted and despoiled in sin, Faith shaken by the storms of circumstance, Hope bowed down before the closing doors of death; and, on the other hand, the glory of consummated joys (though never without the under-thought of their transiency), or the strength of human fidelity and endurance – these are the themes of the second renaissance.

It is hardly surprising that the considerable class of critics (more numerous in the eighteen-forties than to-day) to whom all seriousness is melancholy and all mystery painful, should have dismissed much of the Pre-Raphaelite work under the inaccurate label of "pessimism." To bring the mood of awe, of sadness, of perplexity, into art at all, and more especially to present serious themes with the directness of familiar life, and without the stage-craft glamour of the heroic and the exceptional, is, in the judgment of such persons, to be indisputably a pessimist. Yet from this standpoint we should have to exclude no small part of the greatest art the world has ever seen. If we accept Heine's dictum that no man is truly a man until he suffers, we shall call no nation great in art until it is great in tragedy. There comes with every awakening of an age (whether in ancient Greece, Elizabethan England, or mediæval Italy) to problems new to the world at large, or which the preceding age had lost sight of, a straining of the vision towards ultimate meanings and purposes. And the cry for light is answered often by a lurid dawn.

But the temper of Pre-Raphaelitism differs both from that of

Greek tragedy (in being essentially romantic and ascetic), and from the mediæval mysticism of which it is to some extent a revival. However sincerely Rossetti and his comrades may have found their inspiration in the early and purest period of the Italian Renaissance (as we shall have to consider in examining the name "Pre-Raphaelite"), it was impossible, in the middle of the nineteenth century, to return absolutely to the mediæval habit of mind. All that was best in the romance of the middle ages, the passionate idealism, the abiding sense of the reality of the unseen, the self-abandonment of devotion to the transcendental and the super-sensuous life, the exquisite childlikeness of spirit which comes of the highest maturity – all these indeed were regained, but with a difference. For the enigma of the universe, regarded by the mediæval world as a mystery of faith, has come upon our own age rather as a mystery of doubt. The silence of the natural world towards man's eagerest questionings of the Power behind it, was to those pious souls only the holy reticence of an all-wise and all-sufficient God. They accepted with a brave resignation what the modern world endures with a no less courageous but far less trustful mind.

Therefore the much-debated mysticism of the Pre-Raphaelite School carries with it a deeper sombreness than that of a purely mediæval type, and makes the relations between man and external Nature more problematic and obscure. The sense of the impassive irony of Nature behind the little drama of man's life on earth comes again and again into the dim vistas of landscape behind Rossetti's loveliest women, and into the mingling of scenic grandeur with an atmosphere of desolation in some of the backgrounds of Holman Hunt. Even Millais, the least subjective of the Brotherhood, achieves, in "The Vale of Rest," something of that subtle contrast, half discord and half harmony, between the glory and absolute peace of sunset and the dumb unquestionable night of death foreshadowed in the open grave. The classic method of rendering natural background to human tragedy is rather to adjust the mood of Nature to the subject in hand; to depict natural forces either as warring (as in Turner) in the blind anger and fury of the elements against man, or assuming an aspect in harmony with his own pain. But the romantic method finds more tragedy in the ironic beauty and indifference of Nature in the face of human vicissitude, and comes nearer to tears than the affectation of dramatic sympathy; just as, in great crises of suffering and doubt, no anger wounds us so deeply as a smile.

Of this special phase of nature-feeling, a later artist, of strong affinity of spirit with certain undercurrents of Pre-Raphaelite thought – Frederick Walker – is perhaps a greater exponent. But the old-world Nature-worship, independent of human interest and moral significance, is as dead in art as it is in science. Unconsciously perhaps, but surely, art in all its forms has cast off the yoke of the old cosmogony which the implacable Time-Spirit has overthrown. The criticism of life has passed from the self-satisfied, the confident, the epicurean, to the reflective, the questioning, and the experimental stage.

Where, then, is the secret of the changed attitude of English culture towards the Pre-Raphaelite Brotherhood? What was it that was actually accomplished by this little band of young reformers with their visions of a world of beauty and meaning undreamed of in Royal Academy philosophy? The controversy that raged for years round the work of the leaders – least of all round that of Millais, more round that of Holman Hunt, and most bitterly round the work of Rossetti – was it primarily over a technical question, a matter of pigments and perspective, of anatomy and composition? If so, the house was divided against itself and should have fallen, for Millais soon forsook (if indeed he ever adopted) the path of his early comrades, and a total divergence in method and manner finally separated Rossetti from Holman Hunt. Or was it concerned with underlying principles and purposes with which English culture had not for three hundred years been troubled? Was it essentially an ethical revolt; the first impulse towards that fusion of ethics with æsthetics which will be the task of the twentieth century; the inmost stirring, at the nation's heart, of a new life which the intellect still fails to lay hold of, and the laggard will, for the most part, yet resists?

CHAPTER II.

THE RENAISSANCE OF THE NINETEENTH CENTURY.

Childhood of Rossetti – Religious and Literary Influences – Art Training – Conflict between Imagination and Technique – Friendship with Millais and Holman Hunt – The Westminster Competitions – Ford Madox Brown – Influence of Ruskin's "Modern Painters" – The Early Italian Masters – The Renaissance in Mediæval Europe – Relation of Paganism to Christianity – Revival of Hellenism, and blending of Classic with Romantic Art – Growth of Technique and Return to Convention – The Rule of the Raphaelesque.

Into this atmosphere of revolt and aspiration, charged as with electric forces of long-gathering change, a little band of young painters and poets came, when the time was ripe, to play their part in the great *Aufklärung* of the century. Students they were in more than the conventional significance of the word; men of widely different endowments, and of the most diverse mental quality, but sensitive at all points to the drift of thought beneath the surface of the life around them. Their task it was to translate into art the message already proclaimed in poetry, and to make, even of the poetic vehicle, a finer and more exquisite setting for the new evangel.

The greatest poet of their company, if not in a literal sense the greatest painter also, was born within a year of Blake's death, – on the 12th of May, 1828, at 38, Charlotte Street, Portland Place, London: the successor of Blake in English romance, yet an alien in the land of his birth. Rossetti suffered, as M. Gabrièl Sarrazin has aptly expressed it, a double banishment; remote alike from his country and his age. Essentially Italian by heritage and temperament, he belonged no less to the fifteenth century than to Tuscany, and bore about with him, though perhaps unconsciously, the burden of the exile as well as of the reformer and the pioneer. He was as one born out of due time; or rather, let us say, reborn; a spirit anew-incarnate from the golden age; brought back, indeed, from a still earlier re-birth, so that men almost deemed, as they saw his work and dimly understood its purport, that one of the prophets was risen from the dead.

Beyond his inheritance from the far-off past, from the dormant but undying influences of the Italian Renaissance, Rossetti held from his immediate ancestry no mean estate of talent and of character. His mother, half Tuscan and half English (on her mother's side), was sister to the "Dr. Polidori" known to history as Byron's travelling companion and friend. These were the children of Gaetano Polidori, an accomplished and successful *littérateur*. Gabriele Rossetti, the father of Dante Gabriel, was wholly Italian, of Neapolitan family. He also was a man of high literary tastes and achievements; a poet of genuine quality, and a patriot exiled for his political faith. His popular lays, as well as his personal activities, fanned the flame of democratic insurrection under Ferdinand of Naples in 1820, and three years later he found himself compelled to flee in disguise. He left Italy, never to return; but, happily, not without honour in his own country, for, a quarter of a century later, a medal was struck in recognition of his services, and a statue subsequently erected to his memory in the chief piazza of Vasto, Naples, which also bears his name. In 1824 Gabriele Rossetti settled in England. He married in 1826, and was shortly appointed professor of Italian at King's College, London; in which adopted city – the great foster-mother of so much of the world's best genius – his four children, Dante Gabriel and his brother and sisters, were brought up.

Trained from the first in the Protestant faith, though inheriting on both sides the mental bias of Roman tradition, the children entered early into the age-long conflict between the tender mysticism and spiritual glamour of catholic piety and the robuster spirit of intellectual truth. Herein lay the key to that strange mingling of rationalism and superstition which, both in his poetry and in his painting, has perplexed many critics of Dante Rossetti's philosophy. Hence came his insatiable symbolism, and his acutely realistic detail; his remoteness of vision, and his keen alertness to present and actual things. His own perpetual struggle between the real and the ideal, his ceaseless strivings to reconcile the inward spirit with the outward sense, – or rather, to set them in their right relations to each other, the sense as the instrument and vehicle of the soul, – these were but the epitome, in his own many-sided nature, of the larger strife that ceases not from age to age; only the battle-ground and the weapons of the fight are altered.

To the simple Christian creed which they professed, was added in the Rossettis' household the religion of an ardent and unwavering patriotism. From their earliest childhood the little ones were accustomed to hear around their own fireside high talks of national liberty and the popular cause. Their home, unpretentious but hospitable as it always was, became the resort of many a political refugee; a gathering-place for kindred souls oppressed with the same misfortunes, or fired with the supreme enthusiasm of a common ideal. Hither came Mazzini, the greatest patriot of the century, and one of her truest seers. All that was best in the young democracy of the mid-century, its eager idealism, its narrow but profound hero-worship, its poetry, its self-devotion, was here brought before the children's eyes; its coarser elements eliminated by the personal distinction of such men as

Gabriele Rossetti loved to gather to his side. The little circle was thus open, in those crucial years, to influences more potent upon art than was then apparent, since the humanitarian impulse first manifested in political and social life had not yet adjusted itself to pictorial expression.

Nor was the literary side of Dante Rossetti's genius less sympathetically nurtured in the home atmosphere. His father was an enthusiastic student and commentator of Dante, after whom he named his eldest son, – a baptism strangely prophetic of his destiny; of that fortuity of fate by which, in after years, bereft of love, maligned by criticism, robbed of health and power, he was made partaker in the sufferings as well as in the glory of the great Florentine poet. Thus was fostered in the young Dante of a later day that love of old romance and noble allegory which remained both with him and with his younger sister – perhaps the choicest of our women-poets – as an abiding passion and an inspiration to the highest artistic service.

At the age of fifteen Rossetti passed from King's College School to Cary's Art Academy in Queen Street, Bloomsbury, and thence to the Antique School of the Royal Academy; there to pursue the artistic training to which a strong inclination and evident talent had long called him. Rossetti, however, was a very wayward pupil, and extremely irregular in his attendance. A fellow-student with him at that time, Mr. J.A. Vinter, well recalls one morning when the truant was taken to task for his absence on the previous day. "Why," said Mr. Cary, "were you not here yesterday?" Rossetti answered coolly, "I had a fit of idleness." But when the master's back was turned, an interesting explanation of the avowed idleness was soon forthcoming. Rossetti pulled from his pocket a bundle of manuscript sonnets, which he proceeded, with impartial generosity, to paste inside all his friends' hats! Fortunately for the subsequent peace of the hyper-sensitive and fastidious author, none of these early effusions seem to have been preserved. Mr. Vinter's impression of Rossetti was – like that of many who knew him in youth – that beneath a certain brusquerie and unapproachableness of bearing there lay an unbounded warmth of affection and a ready generosity and kindliness of heart. But his delight in practical jokes, his high spirits and his boisterous hilarity in the classroom sometimes put Mr. Cary (the son, by the way, of the eminent translator of Dante) to considerable embarrassment. There was one song in particular which Rossetti was never tired of singing; and he sang it with all the vigour of his strong young voice, almost to the nauseation of his classmates, – in praise of a certain "Alice Gray." One morning Mr. Cary, entering the room, besought him to abate his tune awhile, for a clergyman had called with his son to see the school, with a view to enrolling the lad as a pupil. Rossetti lowered his voice, but only for a moment. When the visitors appeared on the threshold, his thrilling notes were heard again in passionate protestation of his willingness to die for "Alice Gray."

The school was visited on Saturdays by Mr. Redgrave, R.A., who speedily observed Rossetti's favourite amusement of drawing grotesque caricatures of antique figures round the margin of his board, and protested that "such liberties were hardly consistent with the dignity of the antique."

Rossetti's outlining is said to have been very beautiful in effect, though produced in a highly unconventional manner. Mr. Cary forbade charcoal outlines altogether, but Rossetti, who obeyed no rules, invariably made a thick, solid charcoal line which he gradually pared away on either side with pellets of bread till he had reduced it to the desired minimum. It is noticeable that one at least of Rossetti's friends of this period, and intimately associated with him in the movement which he subsequently led, has always retained the hardness of outline which Rossetti afterwards outgrew.

Yet it must be admitted that with all his ardour, his real though very fitful diligence, and his sincere delight in his chosen profession, Rossetti never fully conquered that imperfection of technique in draughtsmanship which has been the stronghold of hostile criticism throughout the Pre-Raphaelite movement, but which in fact arose from the inevitable deficiency of a mind too impatient for ideas, too eager for subject-matter, to be steadfastly concerned with the science of expression.

That neither Rossetti nor any other of the Pre-Raphaelites *as such* have attained to technical greatness, still less to technical perfection, is a charge weightily preferred, and not without reason, but hardly of so fatal an import as at first appears. It must be remembered that no new message comes to the world ready-clothed in the full grace of accurate and harmonious speech. The voice crying in the wilderness is apt to be harsh and unmusical. The visions of the seer are at first too vivid, too bewildering in the fresh glory of revelation, to be told (if he would set them forth on canvas) in any but broken lights and shadowy images. In every art, the gospel of a new epoch has been proclaimed with faltering speech and stammering tongue. The torrent of denunciation outpoured on Wagner's transgressions of strict form, yet powerless, as it has proved, to drown his music, was not more sweeping than the judgment of authority against the metrical solecisms of Walt Whitman's poetry; nor has the storm still raging round the modern Scandinavian drama been less fierce than that which overtook the leaders of the Pre-Raphaelite van.

Obviously a certain measure of the faculty of expression is necessary if the meaning is to be intelligible at all. Our judgment of an artist, though determined primarily by the nature of his message, must ultimately rest on his ability to deliver it. In Rossetti's case it must depend upon the degree in which the greatness of his material can create a technique of its own, and take the imagination by storm, as Rossetti does, with those exquisite surprises of design, those marvellous *tours-de-force* among his earlier pen and ink drawings, or those southern, almost tropical colour-triumphs of his maturity, which were perhaps rather the divine accidents of genius than its habit, either natural or acquired. They were, in truth, inspirations of utterance, wielding the imperfect instrument to their own high purposes. The verdict given upon such achievements by the thoughtful world outside the charmed circle of the initiate – by that unlearned but not unworthy 27"outer circle," as it were, who, approaching art with intelligence and sympathy, are yet without the knowledge to assess its technical worth – will always, as we have already suggested, be decided by the temperament of the spectator – whether he be as peculiarly sensitive to beauty of idea as his neighbour is to beauty of expression. And after all, the supreme mission of art is to the great world of the *un*initiate. By the authority of its priests and prophets must its form and practice be directed and controlled; but the final test of its greatness is not satisfied until the exquisite consolations of beauty, the moral significances of artistic truth, the proclamation of noble ideals, are "understanded of the people."

But the new gospel, when Rossetti entered the Academy Schools, had only reached the initial stage of a "gospel of discontent." It was still negative, indefinite, unpromising. Yet even in that early phase, the old, simple instincts of the missionary spirit are often potent, and fruitful in the development of ideas. "Andrew ... first findeth his own brother Simon," and "Philip findeth Nathaniel," – not designedly, perhaps, but rather by the spontaneous attraction of kindred souls; not necessarily with the deliberate aim of a propagandist, for it would be pretentious to credit a group of nineteenth-century young Britons in their teens with a very exalted conception of their artistic mission. There is every evidence that they were as unaffectedly boyish, and even school-boyish, as the most orthodox Englishman could wish them. It was well that they should not yet know the meaning of their own rebellion, or guess the effect to be wrought upon English art by Rossetti's meeting with the first fellow-student who can in any sense be called his disciple. Probably it was an impulse of purely personal affection, or that magnetic charm of character which Rossetti exercised over almost all impressionable natures around him, rather than any deep affinity of purpose and ideal, that won to his side a younger and in many respects more brilliant aspirant, John Everett Millais, who had passed through his two years' elementary training at Cary's at a very early age, and in technical proficiency was already far ahead of his new friend. Born on the 8th of June, 1829, in Portland Place, Southampton, the first five years of his life were chiefly spent in Jersey (his father's ancestral home), and the succeeding four at Dinan, in Brittany. In 1838, at the age of nine, he was entered at Cary's Academy, then under the direction of Mr. Sass, where his drawing from the antique soon won a silver medal from the Society of Arts. In 1840, at the age of eleven, he entered the Royal Academy Schools; the youngest pupil ever admitted within their walls. Here he won a silver medal in 1843, and four years later a gold medal for historical painting with "The Benjamites Seizing their Brides," shown at the British Institution in 1848. In 1846 his first exhibited picture, "Pizarro before the Inca of Peru," appeared at the Royal Academy, where "Elgiva Seized by Odo" was shown in 1847.

Millais himself, meanwhile, had made acquaintance with an older and still more earnest student not yet pursuing the Academy curriculum, but for whom the future had in store a place second only to Rossetti's in the movement which united and inspired them in their youth. William Holman Hunt, indeed, may claim to have been earlier than any of his Pre-Raphaelite brethren upon the field of reform; for in the hard solitude of mercantile life, under the stress of poverty and amid the most uncongenial surroundings, he had already thought out and pursued those methods of direct and veracious artistic expression which were afterwards enforced by Pre-Raphaelite rule. Born in London on the 27th of April, 1828, and destined by his father for commercial life, the lad secured from chance companions some occasional help in the artistic studies which he loved. He took a few lessons from a city portrait-painter, and at last gave up his business career, and threw himself upon his own artistic resources for a livelihood.

Admission to the schools of the Royal Academy at that time was by a test as arbitrary and inadequate as the teaching to which it led. Each student was required to produce a drawing from the antique, in chalk or charcoal, laboriously stippled in the conventional style; and in this task the half-trained and inexperienced Hunt very pardonably failed on two successive occasions. It was not until the year 1846 that he was at last admitted as a student, and at almost the same time secured a place on the Academy Exhibition walls, where he was represented by a small picture entitled "Hark!" – a little child holding a watch to her ear. It was in the antique galleries at the British Museum, while toiling forlornly at his trial-drawing among a host of similar candidates, that he came across the more successful but sympathetic and genial Millais. The story of Millais's friendship with the poor and struggling student somewhat older than himself, and of the generous pecuniary help afforded from his own private resources to Hunt at a moment when the magic portals of Art seemed closed for ever against him, has already been told by Mr. Harry Quilter in his history of those early years.

In the autumn of 1845 Mr. Cary sent up five students, including Rossetti and J.A. Vinter, for admission to the Academy Schools. His classes were held in high esteem as a means of introduction to that orthodox fold, already regarded by many neophytes with impatience and distrust, but offering at that time the only possible entrance to professional life. Both the competitors just mentioned were successful, and the admission of Holman Hunt was independently gained soon afterwards. Mr. Vinter has a characteristic reminiscence of the opening day of the ensuing term, when the freshmen were assembled in a class-room, and required to give their names to the keeper, Mr. Jones. When it came to his turn, Rossetti, who was rather proud of his mellifluous designation, greatly amused his companions and impressed the venerable official by slowly rolling out, in his rich, sonorous tones, "Gabriel – Charles – Dante – Rossetti!" "Dear me, sir," stammered Mr. Jones, in confused amazement, "Dear me, sir, you *have* a fine name!"

A probation of three months was necessary, however, before the candidates were finally accepted as students in the Royal

Academy Schools. It is doubtful whether Rossetti ever finished his probationary drawings: at all events he never entered the Life School, and does not appear to have passed beyond the elementary stages of the Antique. But whatever may have been the deficiencies of their early training in art, a result of ample significance was now realized by the intercourse which united in close friendship the illustrious trio – Rossetti, Millais, and Holman Hunt – who were shortly to be recognized as the prime movers in the Pre-Raphaelite revolt.

There was yet, however, another reformer at work, unknown to them, upon the same problems as perplexed themselves, stirred with the same restless discontent with the vain canons of conventional art, and pursuing, in his own obscure studio, methods which came upon the younger trio as the revelation that they needed. Ford Madox Brown, with whom they now became acquainted, was seven years older than Dante Rossetti, having been born at Calais, of English parents, on the 16th of April, 1821. He studied first under Van Hanselaer at Ghent, and afterwards spent two years under Baron Wappers at the Antwerp Academy (1837–1839), three in Paris, (1841–1844), and one in Rome (1845). In his twentieth year he married his cousin, Miss Elizabeth Bromley, who died in 1846. His experiences of the foreign schools seem to have kindled in him the same dissatisfaction with current standards of perfection as was gaining ground among his contemporaries at home. At all events, when Rossetti was vaguely casting about for kindred spirits aflame with revolutionary fire, Madox Brown was the poor and unknown painter of a few decorative cartoons exhibited during the eighteen-forties in Westminster Hall, for a competition organized by the government with a view to selecting the best available fresco-work for the ornamentation of the new House of Lords. The competition was carried over several years, and served in a great measure to define and organize the growing revolt against the tyranny of the Academy, under which, as early as the year 1840, the younger generation of painters was already beginning to writhe. The leading Academicians of that time were men whose names, as far as the outer world is concerned, have scarcely outlived their owners. Etty, Mulready, Maclise, Leslie, Herbert, Chalon, Cooper, Collins, Eastlake, Howard, Hart, Jones, Unwins, Patten, Charles Landseer, Redgrave, Shee, – who knows them now beyond the student and the connoisseur? Webster, indeed, has earned a more enduring fame, and gained a secure if unpretentious rank in the portrayal of village life, fairly comparable to that of Mrs. Gaskell in fiction. But for the rest, even the few gifted and sincere aspirants outside the Academy, but still in the thrall of conventional methods, such as Cope, Dyce, Ward, Egg, Elmore, Goodall, Pickersgill, Hook, Poole, Stone, Martin, Haydon, and David Scott, were but a heterogeneous group, without clear aims or common aspirations. The Westminster competition attracted and developed new talent from independent quarters. It was the first deliberate effort of English art to shake itself free from academic control. Its effect was to revive, for the time being, a decorative method noble in itself, but still more valuable as a training in breadth and dignity of expression, especially for the young artist to whom the fresco was practically a foreign language, full of latent possibility and charm. Practice in fresco-work had a directly good effect on the technique of new and unknown men at the precise stage of their studies at which it was afforded them. Madox Brown's style in particular was strongly and permanently influenced by such exercise, and the competitions evoked from him a series of historical and dramatic *genre* paintings which won Rossetti's special admiration. Chief among them were "The Body of Harold brought before William the Conqueror," which still ranks with the artist's finest productions of its kind, "Justice," a widow pleading before a Norman baron, "Adam and Eve after the Fall," "Wiclif reading his Translation of the Bible to John of Gaunt," "Our Lady of Good Children," and "The Infant's Repast." One fine cartoon from the hand of another artist also drew Rossetti's delighted attention, "Caractacus led Captive in Triumph through the Streets of Rome," by G.F. Watts, a painter worthily representative of the noblest phase of Pre-Raphaelite work, though never openly associated with the movement. He too had vainly traversed the desert of academic studentship, as we may gather from his own naïve record: "Finding there was no teaching, I very soon ceased to attend." His picture of "Caractacus," however, was now rewarded with a first-class prize of £300. Millais also competed in the exhibition of 1847; taking for his subject "The Widow bestowing her Mite."

In the spring of 1848, Rossetti, deeply impressed by the originality and power of Madox Brown's designs, wrote to the artist and begged permission to enter his studio as a pupil. Mr. Brown did not receive pupils professionally, but, with a generosity which he showed to many an eager votary at that period, he welcomed Rossetti to his studio as a friend, and from that time became one of his kindest and most valued counsellors.

At the date of Rossetti's self-introduction to Madox Brown, the latter was engaged upon a somewhat elaborate picture, "Chaucer reading the Legend of Custance before the Court of Edward III."; and Rossetti was invited to sit to him for the head of the poet. Hunt and Rossetti were now working together in a studio which they shared in Cleveland Street, Fitzroy Square; whither soon came Madox Brown to encourage their tentative efforts, and to aid them both with practical and friendly instruction.

And now a new influence from the world of literature came upon the little student-band. It was the inspiration and stimulus of Ruskin's "Modern Painters." For Ruskin also was at war with the old conventions that lay chill and heavy upon English art; he too was weary of the dead level of triviality and scholasticism to which painting had sunk, and saw with prophetic eyes, through the murk of present life and the shadowy vistas of history, a higher and attainable ideal.

"Modern Painters" struck the keynote of the coming change. A fellow-student lent the volumes to Holman Hunt, who in his turn shared them with his friends; and reading together, they found therein, not only a sympathy for their own revolt, but a definite guidance for their aspirations. With the authority of the trained draughtsman and *connoisseur* as well as with the force and fascination of the literary artist, Ruskin declared for originality and truth in design, as against the imitations and artifices of degenerate schools, in a voice that would brook no compromise. Like Carlyle, his whole being was possest with that passionate scorn of pretensions and shams, that hatred of formalism and of every species of cant, which swept like a cleansing wind over Europe after the French Revolution, and which, if its immediate results were iconoclastic and disruptive, was so much the better preparation for the reconstruction to follow.

Ruskin bade men turn, from the Art of the past, to Nature, and seek fresh inspiration at its primal source. Through Nature alone, he said, they would reach truth, and finding it, gain also the power to interpret and reveal. And Nature was a jealous mistress; only to a faithful lover would she unveil the exquisite mysteries of her beauty; unto his ear alone would she whisper the high secrets of her soul; she would endure no translator, no partial and distorted reflection of her face: the man himself must worship at her inmost shrine, and learn her lesson there direct and clear.

– A truism, it seems to us, who have seen the swinging of the pendulum still further in the naturalistic direction, since the reaction in divers quarters against convention and precedent has carried many to the opposite extreme. Yet, in the history of the world, the demand for precedent and conformity, the love of imitation, the morbid hatred of novelty and the dread of original experiment, which appear in almost every crisis of man's development, exhibit one of the most curious phases of the human mind. Psychologists might argue at length as to the relation between indolence and cowardice in the strange game of "follow-my-leader" played by humanity from age to age, – and might attribute both to a vague and deep sense of the bitter cost of all knowledge, and a consequent and not wholly vain tenacity towards things apparently knowable and known.

Ruskin, with a vision large enough to retain all that was

eternally precious in the past, began by recognizing the elements of real vitality even in the outworn classicism which was the occasion of his readers' revolt; and led them thence to the higher places of refreshment and advance. "We must be careful," said he, "not to lose sight of the real use of what has been left us by antiquity, nor to take that for a model of perfection which is, in many cases, only a guide to it. The young artist, while he should shrink with horror from the iconoclast who would tear from him every landmark and light which has been bequeathed him by the ancients, and leave him in a liberated childhood, may be equally certain of being betrayed by those who would give him the power and the knowledge of past time, and then fetter his strength from all advance, and bend his eyes backward on a beaten path; who would thrust canvas between him and the sky, and tradition between him and God."

Again, Ruskin insisted continually upon the essential and supreme moral purpose of art as a "criticism of life" – as a later authority has called it. He made clear the relation between *thought* and *language* in painting, wherein lies for ever the crux of art; and pointed to examples of the contrast and the conflict between those two principles whereof the right adjustment is art's final aim. "Most pictures," said Ruskin, "of the Dutch school, for instance, excepting always those of Rubens, Vandyke, and Rembrandt, are ostentatious exhibitions of the artist's power of speech, the clear and vigorous elocution of useless and senseless words; while the early efforts of Cimabue and Giotto are the burning messages of prophecy, delivered by the stammering lips of infants. It must be the part of the judicious critic carefully to distinguish what is language and what is thought, and to rank and praise pictures chiefly for the latter, considering the former as a totally inferior excellence, and one which cannot be compared with, nor weighed against thought in any way or in any degree whatsoever. The picture which has the nobler and more numerous ideas, however awkwardly expressed, is a greater and a better picture than that which has the less noble and less numerous ideas, however beautifully expressed."

Thus the author of "Modern Painters" did for his readers what was more helpful than all precept, – he showed them the high paths trodden aforetime by men of like aspirations after a similar revolt. He led them back to an age which had seen the same struggle between the old art and the new; an age in which the difficulty of presenting human life and its environment in faithful colours and in natural images had already been met, and in some measure overcome. That age was the mother of modern art in Europe. The fourteenth century, waking from mediævalism, felt the first quickenings of the Renaissance in Italy.

To that momentous impulse of new life wherein lay, deep-rooted in the laws of reaction and development, the destinies of modern Europe, the historian of the Pre-Raphaelite movement must turn if he would read aright the motive and the message of to-day. For the impulse sought in the records of the past by the reformers of a later age was of a spirit kindred with their own, though grappling with its problems under a somewhat different guise. It was a revolt, not from materialism as we commonly understand it, namely, the acceptance of matter as the sole and ultimate reality, and a tacit or open disavowal of the spiritual life; but rather from that more subtle and insidious form of materialism so often mistaken for its opposite – the asceticism of mediæval Christianity. To deny the dignity and sanctity of the physical as the garment of the spiritual world is surely as blank a materialism as that which makes the physical sufficient and supreme. To see no spirit in the flesh is to be no less blind than they who see no spirit *beyond* the flesh. The innate cynicism of the monastic idea – its radical *faith*lessness, its utter distrust of the Spirit's power to transfigure and ennoble the noble life of man – is sufficiently evidenced by the fact that the results of that idea upon the art of the nation were almost identical with the results wrought upon England by the materialism of the eighteenth century. Art became a fashion instead of a mission, a cult instead of a worship; it became the prerogative of a ruling class which conventionalized – as such must ever do – the spontaneous utterance of the many into the vain repetitions of the few. That class in modern England was the *bourgeoisie*: in mediæval Italy it was the priesthood. Herein arose the narrow religiosity of the early Italian painters, no less than the ascetic barrenness of the dark ages which preceded them. Art had been subsidized by a ruling class, however beneficent, for its own purposes, however sincere and high. The gradual establishment of Christianity as the state religion of the later Roman period involved the repudiation – or at least the effort to repudiate – the whole intellectual or æsthetic heritage of the Græco-Roman world.

There is a curious pathos in the attempt of every vigorous outgrowth of human endeavour to disown the prior activity which gave it birth. The ancient fable of the chick and the egg-shell is of perennial meaning and pertinence. Militant Christianity marched forward wholly unconscious of its own vast debt to the very paganism upon which it thrust itself in holy war. The novel fervour of asceticism had extinguished science before the end of the third century, art in the sixth and seventh, and the Greek language by the ninth. But the transition of Italy from paganism to Christianity was not a substitution of wholly new ideals for old. It was the gradual absorption of all the permanent elements in pagan culture into a religion of which the germ only was brought from the Hebrew world, and which owed most of its strength and much of its weakness to the rich and heterogeneous soil in which it was planted. The extravagances of mediæval Christianity – its austere intolerance and contempt of the natural and obvious, its demand, in the first strenuous tension of novelty and triumph, for the subjective and the transcendental life – breaking up, when the strain was relaxed, into a hard formalism of thought and practice – these were but the inevitable reaction from the grossness of a degenerate paganism whose vital force was spent. The immense lapse of time occupied by the transition from paganism to Christianity, as Mr. Bernard Bosanquet ably points out in dealing with the issues of that change, gave room for as many secondary waves of action and reaction within itself as did the movement of the Renaissance which succeeded it. "From the first distinct breach in naïve or natural paganism to the assumption of a definitely doctrinal and orthodox form of Christianity, there is an interval which cannot be reckoned at less than seven hundred years, from the death of Socrates to the triumph of Christianity under Constantine. So far from being a new thing, contrasting with the degradation of the pagan world, the establishment of Christianity was the issue of the advance of that world during four centuries, and it was not thoroughly completed until, in a further development of five centuries, it had adopted from paganism the germs of almost all permanently valuable elements that the latter contained.... The Dark Ages are not a proof that the great classical culture had lost its power for human welfare; they prove only how long a discipline was needed by the mass of humanity before it could appreciate more than the first stammering misapprehension of its great inheritance."[*2]

The dawn, then, of the Renaissance in Italy, was the waking of the mediæval world to the sense of this lost inheritance, yet to be regained; this hidden dower of beauty and gladness, and of strong and abundant life. The old message of the Galilean Christ had to be re-translated, as it has to-day: "I am come that they might have life, and that they might have it more abundantly," – not a one-sided life, not a spiritual life at the cost of the body, any more than a bodily life at the cost of the soul, but a life robust, many-sided, catholic; harmonized at all points with what is good and sweet and fair in the physical world as well as what is high and pure and noble in the life within. And that message led men back to the great first principles of conduct and consciousness, till they were confronted afresh with the want of equipoise between physical instinct and moral law which is the root-problem of human history. The struggle for *existence* in the animal world rises in humanity from a physical to a moral sphere, and passes into a struggle for *life*.

"History," says Buckle, "is a record of tendencies, not of

events." The first tendency of the people thus waking, as we have said, to the sense of their own birthright and heritage, partook rather of the first of these two impulses. It was a revolt against the spiritual exclusiveness of the monastic ideal, and a recoil upon Nature, – especially upon the apotheosis and worship of Nature already achieved for them in the Hellenic world. The imperious demands of the physical life, so long starved and neglected, drove men back upon external things; slowly to re-discover, through outward and visible realities, the deeper meanings of which they were in search. The end of the twelfth and the beginning of the thirteenth century saw a new turn of the current of feeling towards liberty and expansion of the whole life of man. The painters set themselves to humanize religion; to bring it into relation with the vital interests of the so-called secular sphere. And as the fine arts became emancipated from sacerdotal control, the spirit of free culture spread into other departments of intellectual activity. In the next century, the revival of learning followed upon the emancipation of art. Literature, religion, painting and sculpture, were infused with the same spirit of experiment and research. Art was brought into touch with scholarship, and scholarship in its turn graced and dignified by art. The essence of romance lies in its utter fidelity to immediate and present life. Its concern is with particular instances, not with abstractions and generalities. Romance is primarily analytic and experimental; classicism, synthetic and positive. Romance is inductive, classicism deductive in its reasoning. Herein romance – deemed for the most part antagonistic to reason and science, approaches more nearly to the scientific spirit than any canons of classic art. Its root and base is in that patient observation of actual things, that sure simplicity and directness of vision, which is the narrow way to knowledge. Hence comes the realism of romance, – the realism both of the early Renaissance and of its later maturity. A dominant characteristic (for instance) of Michaelangelo – the greatest and most fascinating personality of the whole Renaissance period – was, as his latest biographer, Mr. John Addington

Symonds, has pointed out, that "he invariably preferred the particular to the universal, the critical moment of an action to suggestions of the possibilities of action." This feature of the highest Renaissance work, though it seem at first sight to disprove the general theory of romance as the meditative, contrasted with the classic or dramatic form of art, is really consonant with it, since one example of one action is more analytic and reflective in quality than the suggestion of action generally. Our assertion, then, that the first manifestation of the break-up of the monastic system was a return to Nature as revealed and worshipped in the Hellenic ideal, must be qualified by a recognition of another tendency modifying and chastening the first.

The second tendency was towards the reconciliation of the superb naturalism of Grecian art with the Christian spirit of self-discipline and heroic denial. It was an effort after that ultimate balance and harmony prophesied (to bring a modern instance) in Ibsen's "Third Kingdom;" the kingdom in which the realism of the flesh and the idealism of the spirit shall be blended into one perfect humanity. "It was a movement," to quote again from Mr. J.A. Symonds, "towards that further point outside both Paganism and mediæval Christianity, at which the classical ideal of a temperate and joyous natural life shall be restored to the conscience educated by the gospel." The vision of this union was the inspiration of Pre-Raphaelite art. It quickened the hands of the painters to great tasks; it stirred the scholars to a new energy of labour and of hope. The poets, interpreting its meaning for the life of a future Italy, began to speak one to another across the mediæval gloom, as waking birds call and answer, while it is yet dark, with a sure instinct prophetic of the dawn.

Thus the unruffled calm and dignity of Hellenism was troubled, in its re-birth, with a sense of moral conflict and perplexity unknown to the ancient world. A peculiar mysticism resulted upon literature from that revival of the Platonic spirit which was initiated by Pico della Mirandola and his successors in metaphysical thought. Throughout the Pre-Raphaelite epoch, from

Cimabue (1240) to Perugino, the master of Raphael (1446), the impulse of naturalism is seen adjusting itself, through much crudeness of expression, through many blunders, solecisms of taste, errors of selection, to the great spiritual passion of Christianity which was still warm at the heart of the thinking world. There is, especially in early Renaissance work, an effect as of divided aims, or of methods long habituated to the old ideal and brought suddenly into the service of the new, – like Heine's "decayed gods, who, to maintain themselves after the fall of paganism, took employment under the new religion." The physical loveliness of the saints and angels of Botticelli and Fra Angelico – the last of the purely "religious" painters, in the common acceptance of the word – is hardly congruous with the loftiness of their themes, and almost belies the spiritual intensity and rapture of thought which Botticelli, in later life, drew largely from the influence of Savonarola, and infused increasingly into his own work. Giotto, the pride of the Florentine school and the dominant genius of the fourteenth century, was no less profoundly religious than these; but in the final roll of art he ranks rather as the first great *Nature*-painter than as one of a distinctly Christian lineage. Taken, like David, from the sheepfold, he brought into art a breezy, pastoral air, and painted before a wide horizon under an open sky. Fra Lippo Lippi added to that wholesome strength and sanity of sight an even clearer perception of natural beauty and grace. The glories of the physical realm, in landscape, in the power of men and in the loveliness of women, were handled now with a growing boldness which outran the delicate timidity that had restrained it in the shadow of the Church. And with the enlargement of intellectual range there came a steady increase of technical power. The skill of choice, of selectiveness in art, of composition, draughtsmanship, colouring, – in a word, the science of *expression*, was brought to bear upon the ready message waiting for the perfecting of its vehicles. The adaptation of language to thought, which was the task of the fifteenth century, was achieved by the immediate predecessors of

Raphael in a measure unequalled in the history of the modern world. And that such an adjustment should resolve itself, as it did, into a fresh conflict between the forces momentarily reconciled, proves, not that the success of the effort was spurious, but rather that the struggle between thought and language in art is but one manifestation of the eternal striving of the Spirit with the imperfect medium of the flesh.

But this rare consummation of harmony between the erstwhile conflicting principles of classicism and romance, though reaching its highest point in Leonardo and Michaelangelo, achieved in the Venetian school a technical effect which appealed even more strongly to the æsthetic passion re-born in Rossetti and his friends, as they looked back across the ages in their search for example and light. In Giorgione, the creator of idyllic *genre* painting in the fourteenth century, and in Titian, of whom Rossetti himself was in due course the natural successor, they found all the mystic sensuousness of the new Paganism in a setting which, to adapt a well-worn phrase, revealed instead of concealing the soul within. Here, at least, was the apotheosis of *colour*, which is itself a characteristic quality of all romantic revivals: wherefore painting has always been specifically the romantic medium in art, while the classic temper finds in sculpture its most congenial sphere. Classicism invariably compromises with the tints of nature; it resolves the ever-varying hues of earth and sky into the formula of the spectroscope; it tends, in its purest and noblest phases, towards marble and the statuesque. Here was the perfection of artistic language, as Ruskin would call it; the delight in strong and full utterance for its own sake, wherein lurks the perennial danger of greatness in technique. With all its glow and glory of natural life, the Venetian school was primarily decorative in character, and therefore merged the more readily into the gradual substitution of form for matter, the general deterioration of naturalism into sensuality, which overtook Italian art after the decadence of Raphael.

Together with the more robust conception of the physical life which supervened in the thirteenth and fourteenth centuries, there came a change, partial indeed, but progressive, in the ideals of womanhood. The Madonnas of Botticelli were instinct with a warmth and sensitiveness unknown before in Christian art. If they were immaculate, their perfectness was that of a God-possest humanity rather than of a humanized Godhead. Their faces shine with natural pity and awe and tenderness and love, – the love of the true *Mater Dolorosa*, sad with

> "The burden of the mystery,
> … the heavy and the weary weight
> Of all this unintelligible world."

They see the shadow of the Cross upon the holy Child, and their passionate life quivers before the Death to be. The same brooding sense of mystery, the same large and intense compassion for the "world-sorrow," yet mingled with a certain austerity of outlook upon its strife, is the dominant note of Leonardo's masterpiece of a later date, "La Gioconda" ("Our Lady of the Rocks"); often compared with that triumph of a more modern Renaissance, Albrecht Dürer's "Melancholia," with which it shares in the attainment of perfect harmony between classic and romantic art.

Yet the return of art in the fourteenth century from the angelic to the human world did not go far enough to affect the ideals of womanhood beyond this single aspect – the aspect of maternity. The early Renaissance painters did indeed humanize, in conception and presentment, the virgins and the venerable mother-saints of Christendom; but their imagination never concerned itself with what may be termed the independent humanity of womanhood. They painted always under the sway of that central and dominant *motif* of the Christian mythology, – the idea of woman as the receptive and passive vehicle of the God-man; and never presented woman as daughter, sister, lover, or wife, apart from the concurrent idea of potential motherhood. This limitation –

unfortunately for art – instead of being removed by a further broadening of thought and vision as the Renaissance proceeded, was emphasized in the fifteenth century by the influence of Raphael, who cultivated and stereotyped his own ideal of the "for-ever-motherly" until – so subtle is the influence of fixed types in pictorial art upon the current standards of truth and beauty – the maternal function came to be regarded as the sole and sufficient object of a woman's existence; and the conventional Madonna-face of Raphael became a bondage from which Christianity has taken more than three centuries to set itself free.

For the advent of Raphael into Italian art marked the beginning of the degradation of the pure and wholesome naturalism achieved in the Renaissance into a coarse materialism which in its turn degenerated into a false and shallow conventionality, and had an effect infinitely mischievous upon Italy, still more so upon France, and through France upon the England of the Stuart and Hanoverian periods. It might almost be said that the greatness of Raphael was the weakness of modern art. The immediate result of a triumph in technique – of a great success in the wedding of perfect utterance to noble thought – is sometimes to produce, in the moral atmosphere around it, a sense of finality, a relaxing of tension, in which the soul is overpowered by its own conquest of the medium, and loses itself in the facile freedom thus attained. The disciples of Raphael, counting him to have achieved the highest perfection, modelled themselves upon his manner, and thence upon his mannerisms, without question or reserve; just as, in metaphysics and philosophy, the schoolmen argued from Aristotle without any reference to the external world, and, bound in the thrall of his genius, followed implicitly the narrow trend of his reasoning, until, entangled in theoretical cobwebs of their own spinning, they lost altogether the use of the inductive method, founded upon observation and experiment, which is the only true basis of knowledge. Imitation may be the sincerest form of flattery, but it is sometimes a fatal hindrance to progress. Its maleficence in the world of mental science is not greater than the mischief wrought in art by a spirit which does as much harm to the work of the copyist as to the reputation of the model. As Ruskin says, "All that is highest in art, all that is creative and imaginative, is formed and created by every great master for himself, and cannot be repeated or imitated by others." Raphael at first-hand was always great, often sublime. Raphael second-hand, – stereotyped, formalized, degraded by three centuries of imitations, each more laboured than the last, – became vapid, artificial, meaningless. The original inspiration was destroyed. Art lost its hold on Nature; and, severed from that sole source of power, fell into inevitable decay.

History repeats itself, but with a difference. Man's struggle, as we have said, for balance, for self-adjustment to the forces around him, and to the greater forces within, recurs in every age of the world's life, but under conditions ever new. The nineteenth century supplied such new conditions for the old task. The ground that had long lain fallow was not wasted in its time of barrenness, but made ready in unfruitful autumns for fresh seed; prepared by silent and secret forces for a new harvest. Shaken by social revolution, roused by the pressure of intellectual problems on every side, Art was confronted once more with the great realities of life and death, good and evil, and turned for guidance to the witness of the past: as a soul, once quick to action but long sunk in apathy, awakes again to the mystery of the ideal, and gathering itself together for fresh strife, calls urgently upon the old wisdom and the remembered strength of yore.

In such a spirit did Dante Gabriel Rossetti and his comrades turn from the dull abstractions of academic tradition, and lift their eyes towards that golden age whose dawning answered their own cry for light. Not to the material and redundant splendours of Raphaelesque art did they look for the inspiration of the hour; not to the pseudoclassicism of the later Renaissance, but to the pristine freshness and purity of its youth: just as we now look for the true significance of the romantic revival, not to the Postlethwaite of fashionable society, or to the weak sensuality of a drawing-room æstheticism; not to the latter-day apotheosis of lust which is but a gross travesty of the vigorous naturalism of Hellenic and early Renaissance art, but to the gracious innocence and seriousness of Rossetti's "Virgin," the noble beauty and pathos of his dying "Beatrice," and the austere tenderness of Hunt's sore-tempted "Isabella," confronting Claudio's painful face with the set resolve of her impregnable womanhood. So, seeking and following all that was best in the past, and facing, with vision clarified by that high discipline, the intellectual, social, and moral strife of the nineteenth century, the young painters set themselves "to disengage," as Sainte-Beuve says, "the elements of beauty," and to put them forth in some sort of order and lucidity, even if it were but in a tentative formula, yet to be subjected to the tests of time.

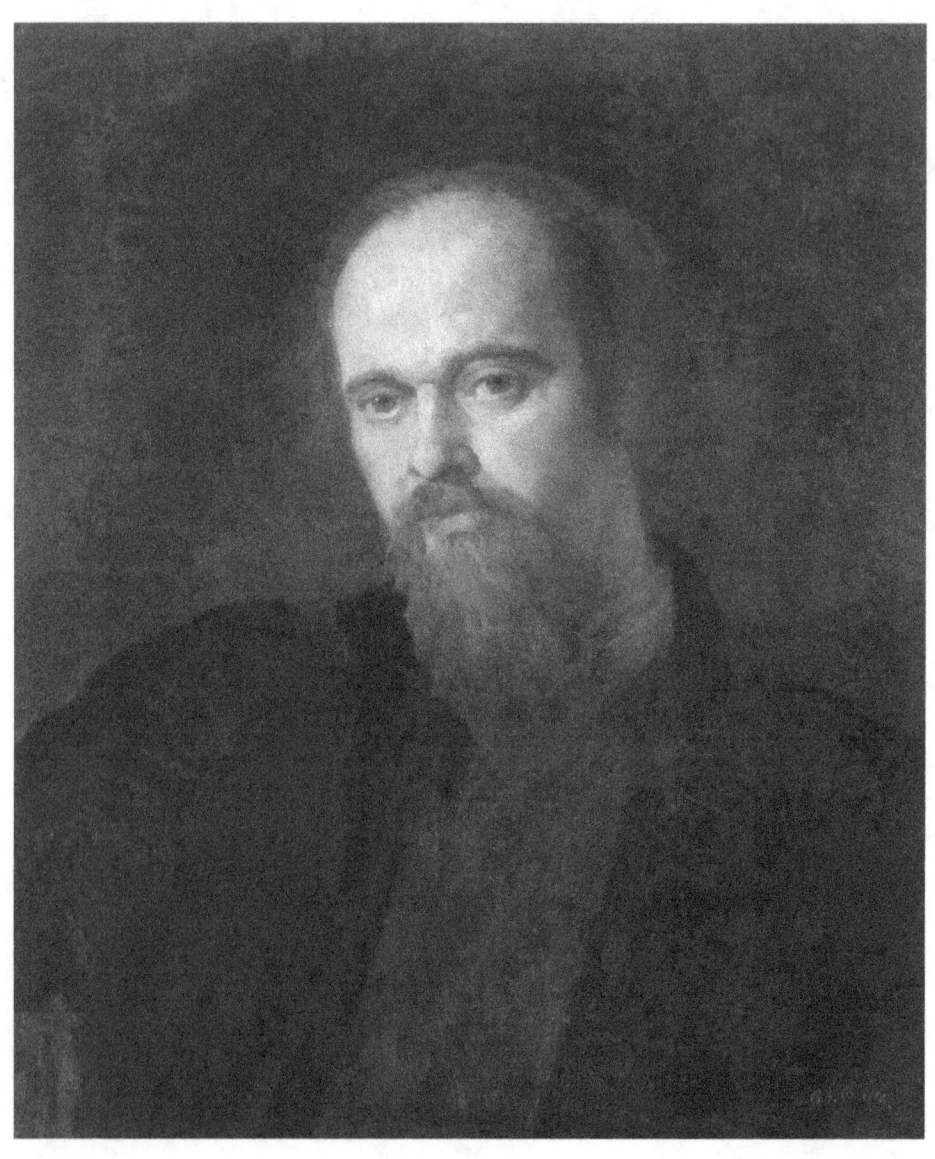

George Frederic Watts, Portrait of Dante Gabriel Rossetti

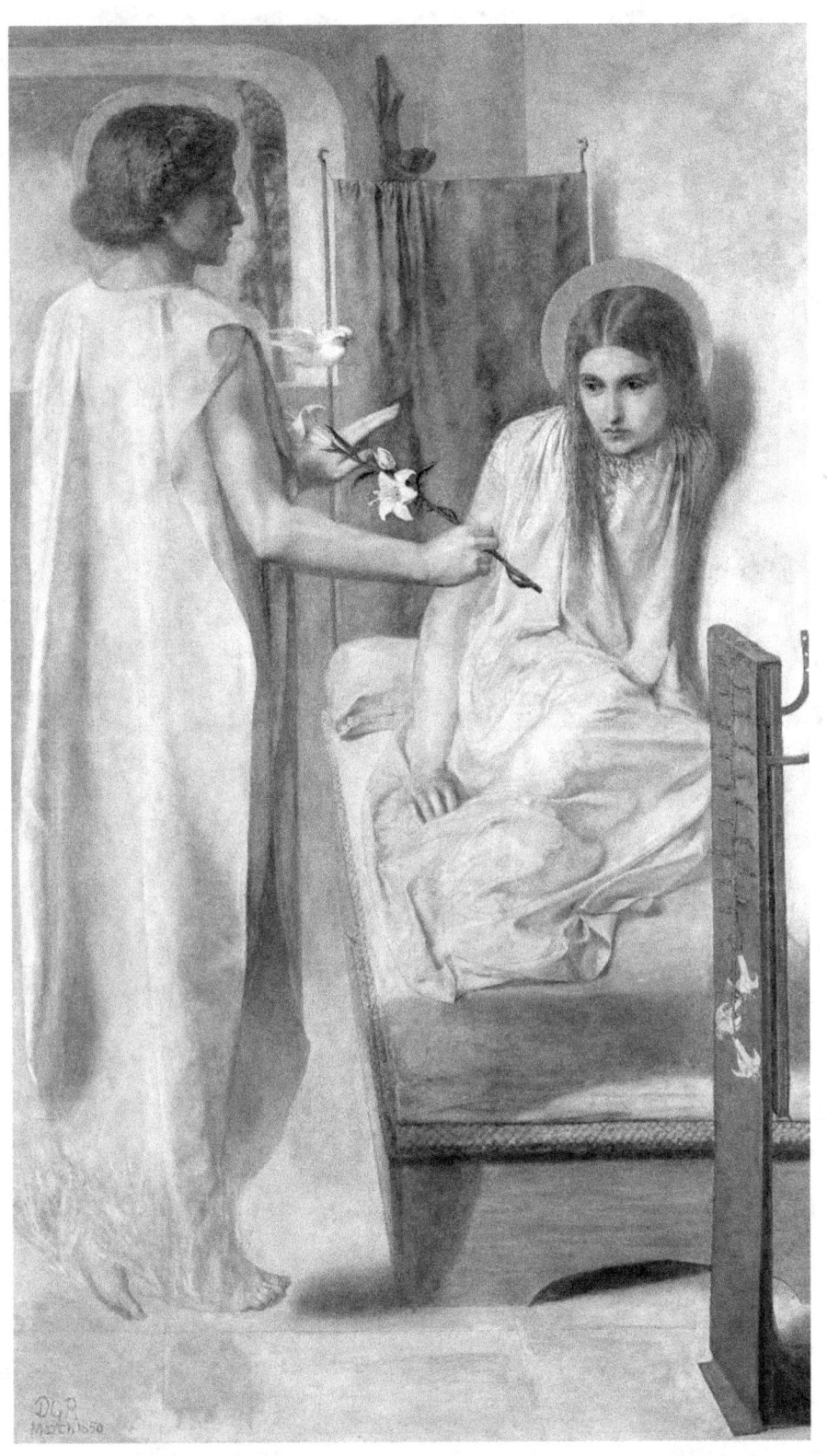

Dante Gabriel Rossetti, Ecce Ancilla Domini, 1850, Tate Britain

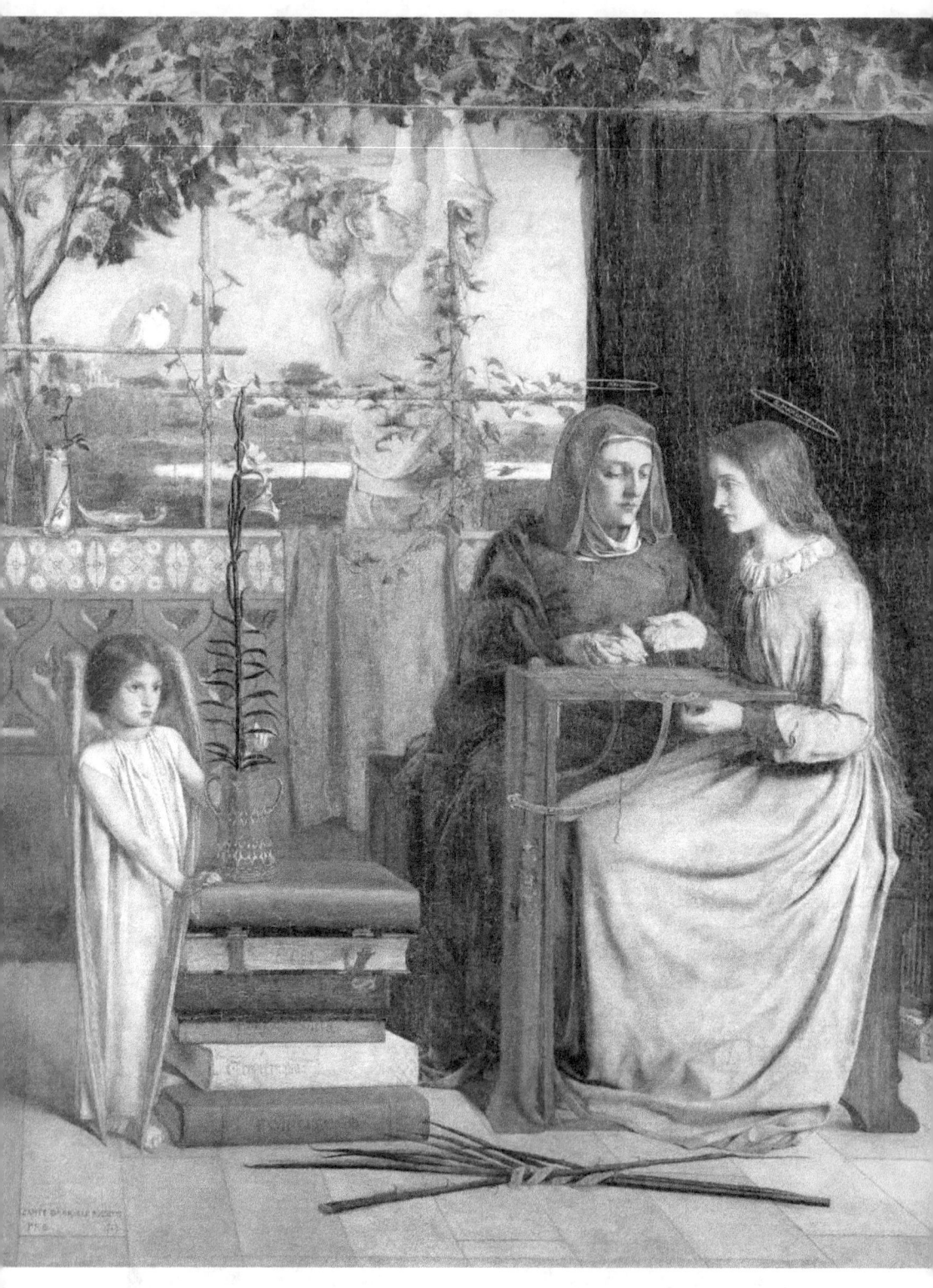

Dante Gabriel Rossetti, The Girlhood of Mary Virgin, Tate Britain

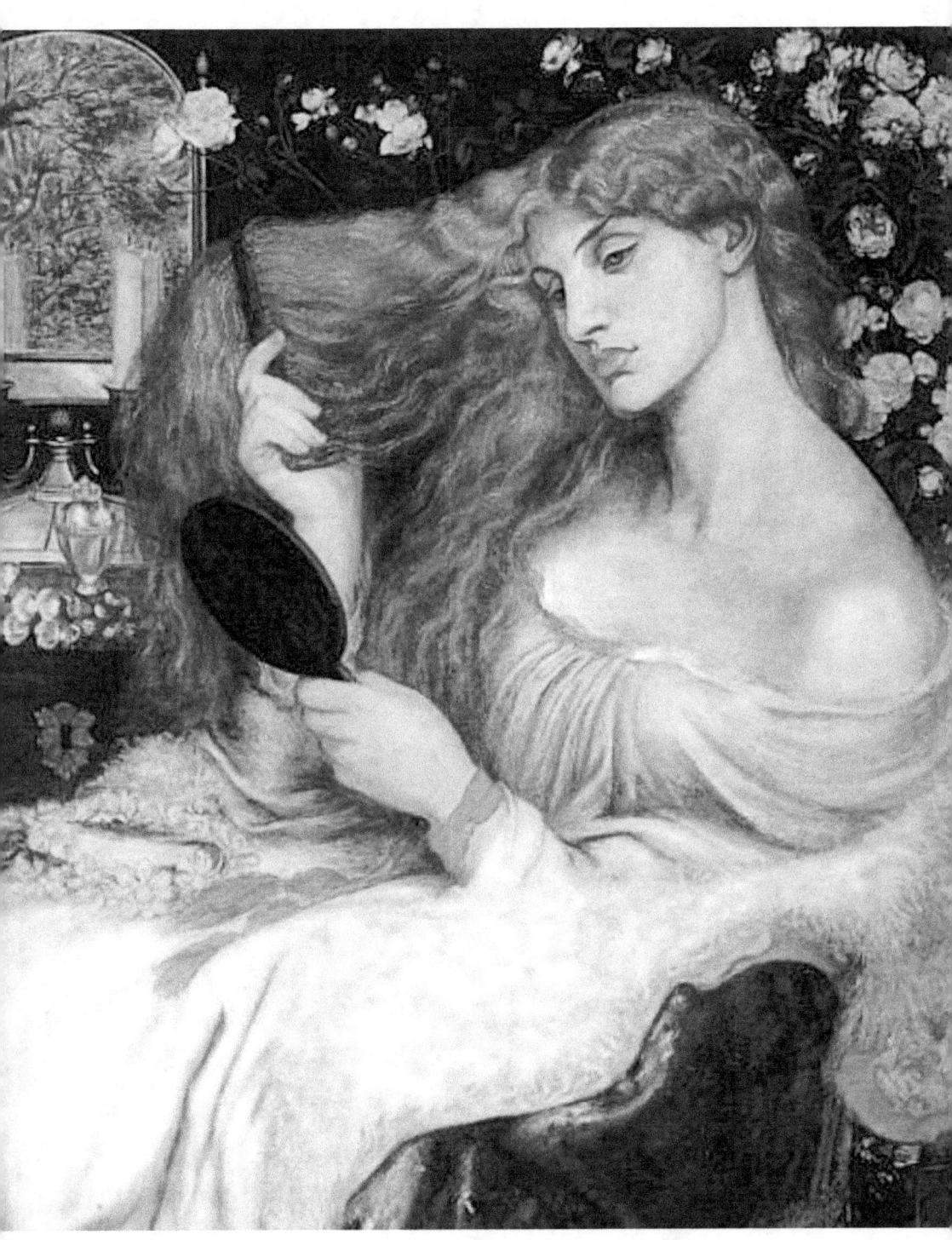

Dante Gabriel Rossetti, Lady Lilith, 1866-68, Delaware Art Museum

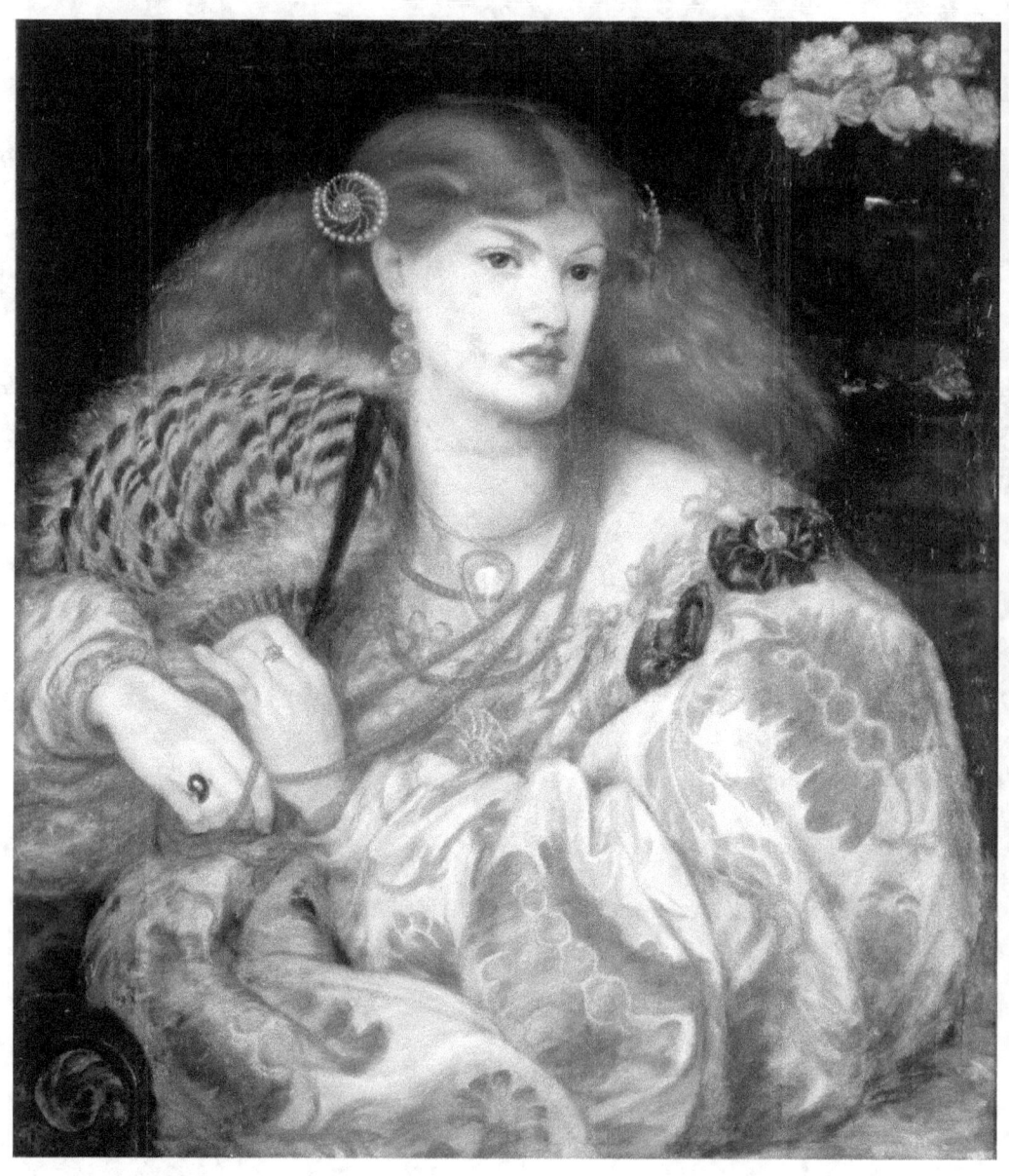

Dante Gabriel Rossetti, Monna Vanna, 1866, Tate Britain

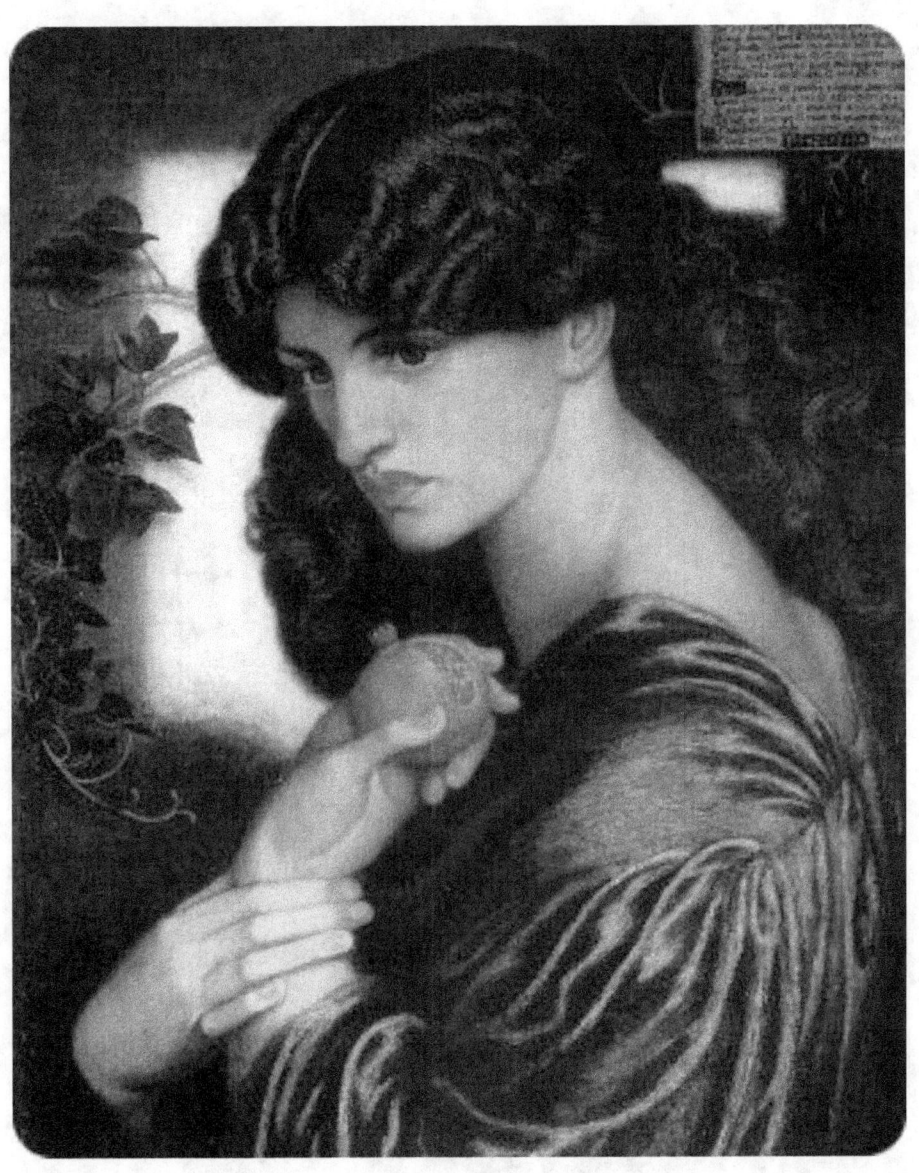

Dante Gabriel Rossetti, Prosperine, 1874, Tate Britain

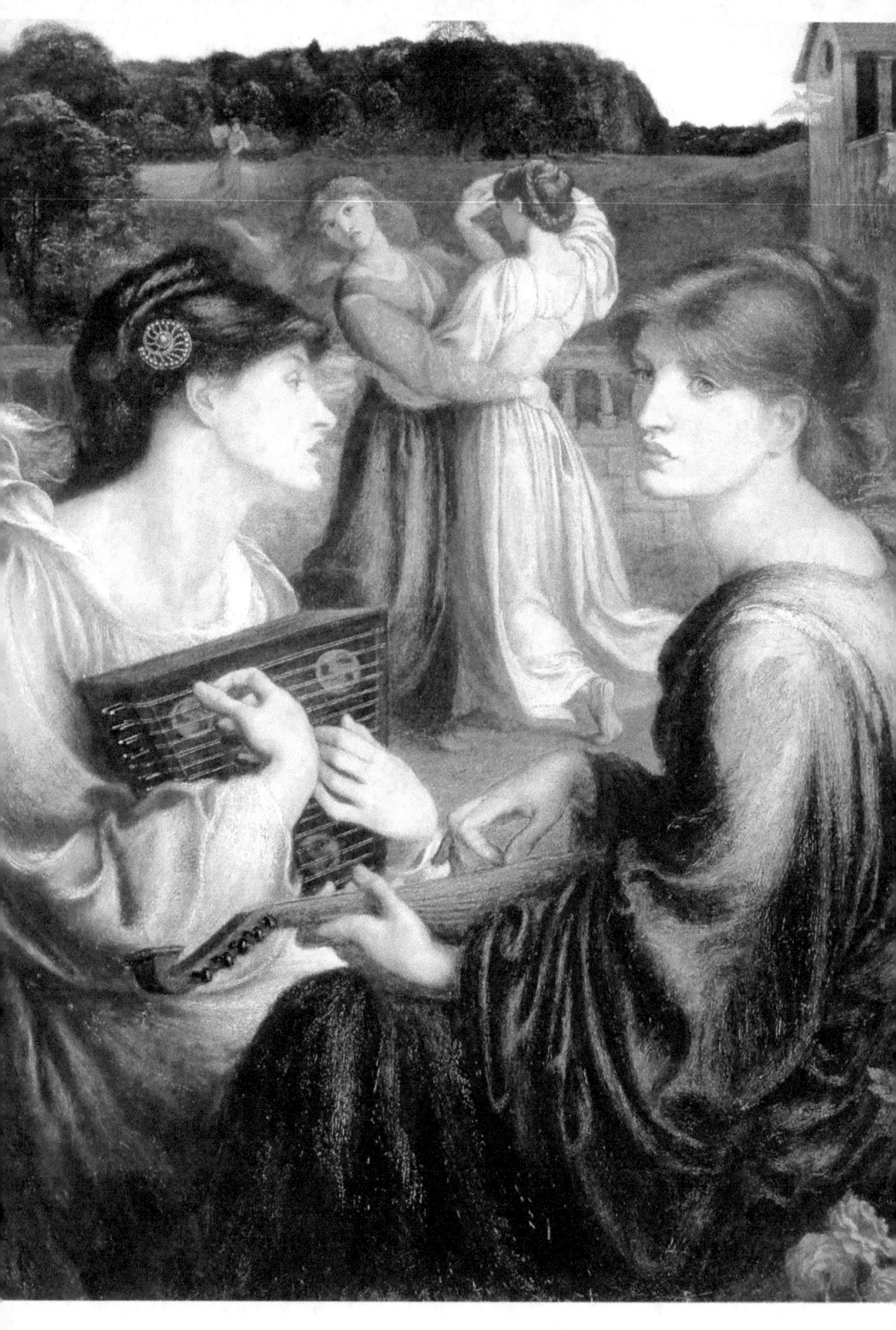

Dante Gabriel Rossetti, The Bower Meadow, 1872, Manchester

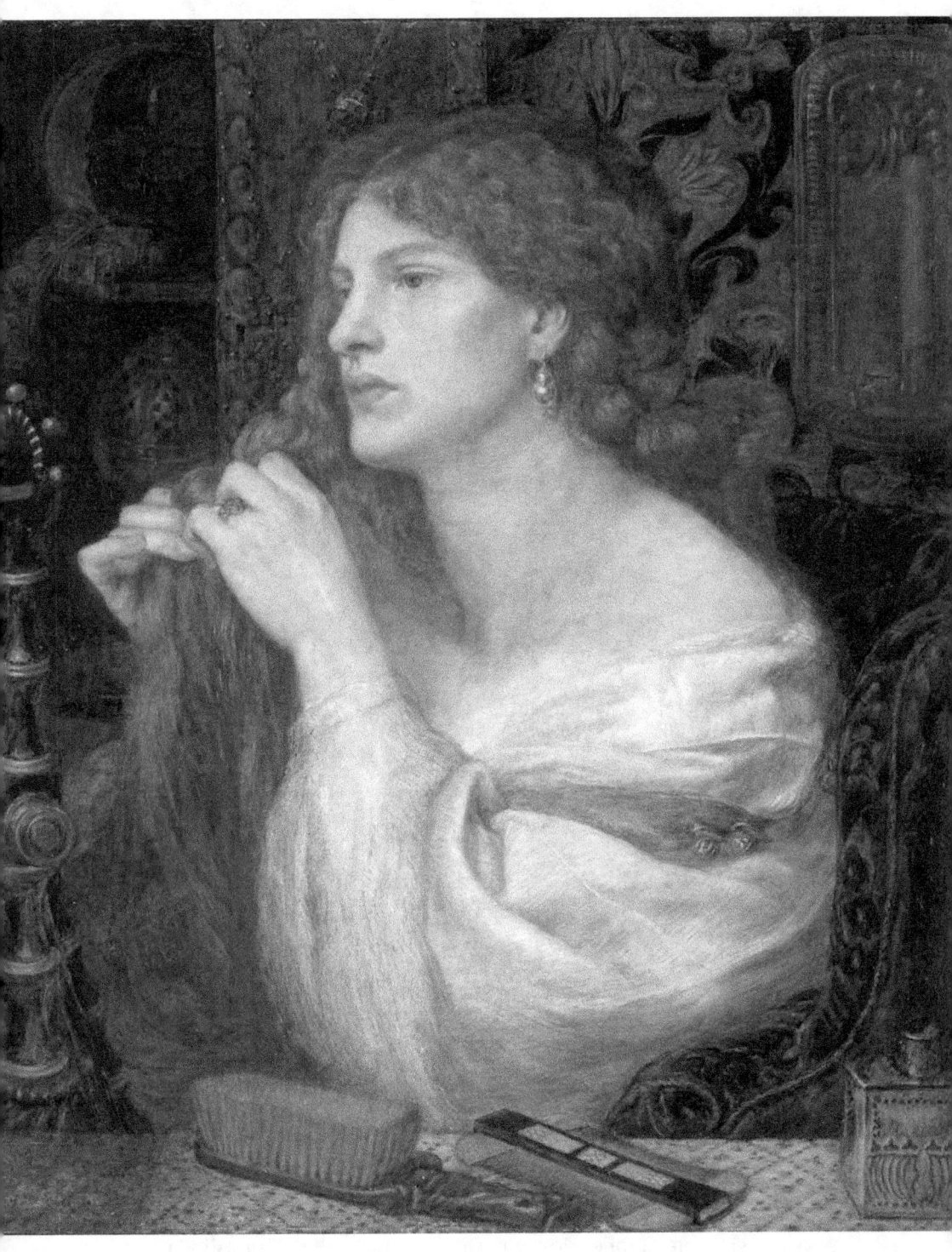

Dante Gabriel Rossetti, Aurelia (Fazio's Mistress), 1863/ 73, Tate Britain

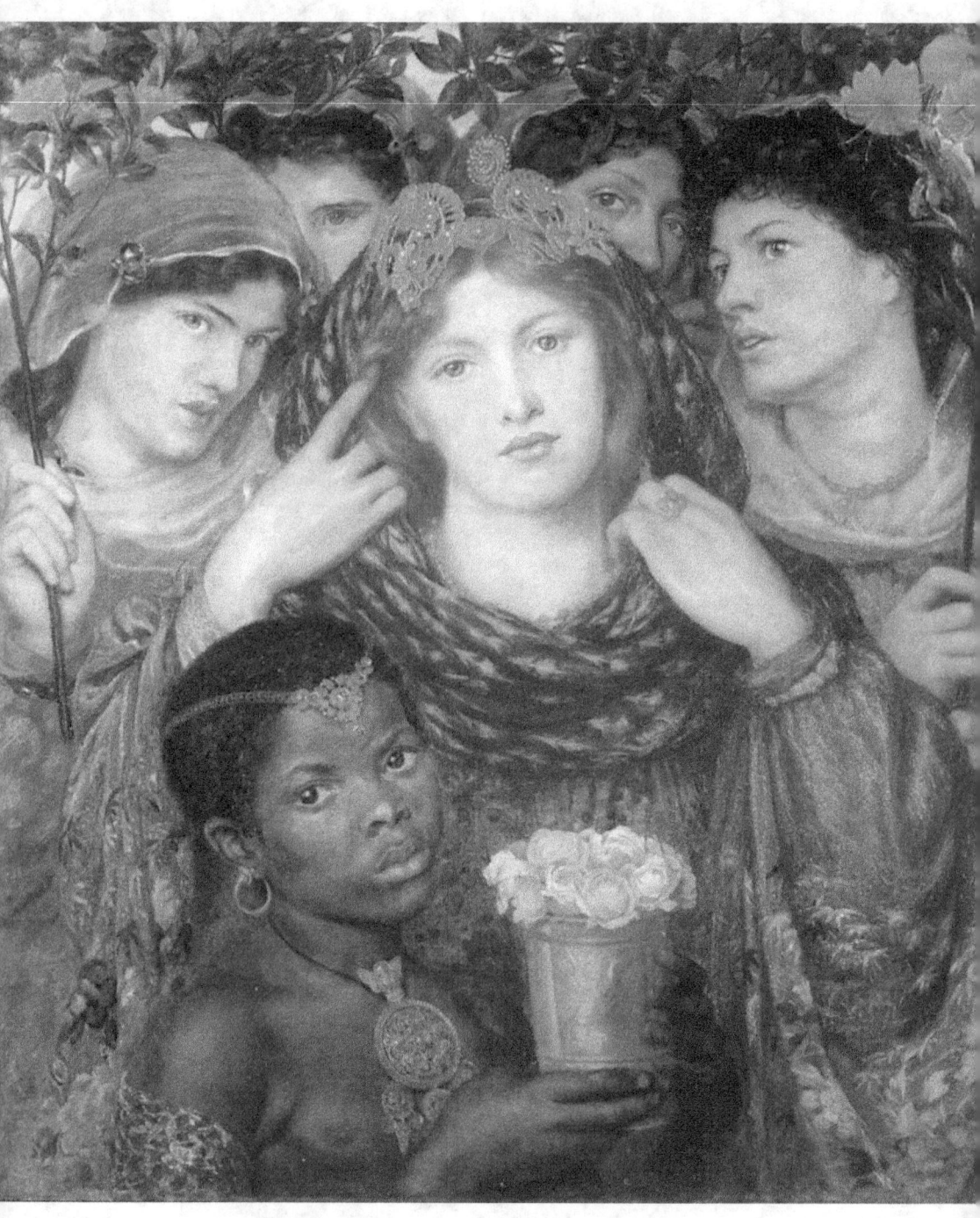

Dante Gabriel Rossetti, Die Geliebte, 1866, Tate Britain

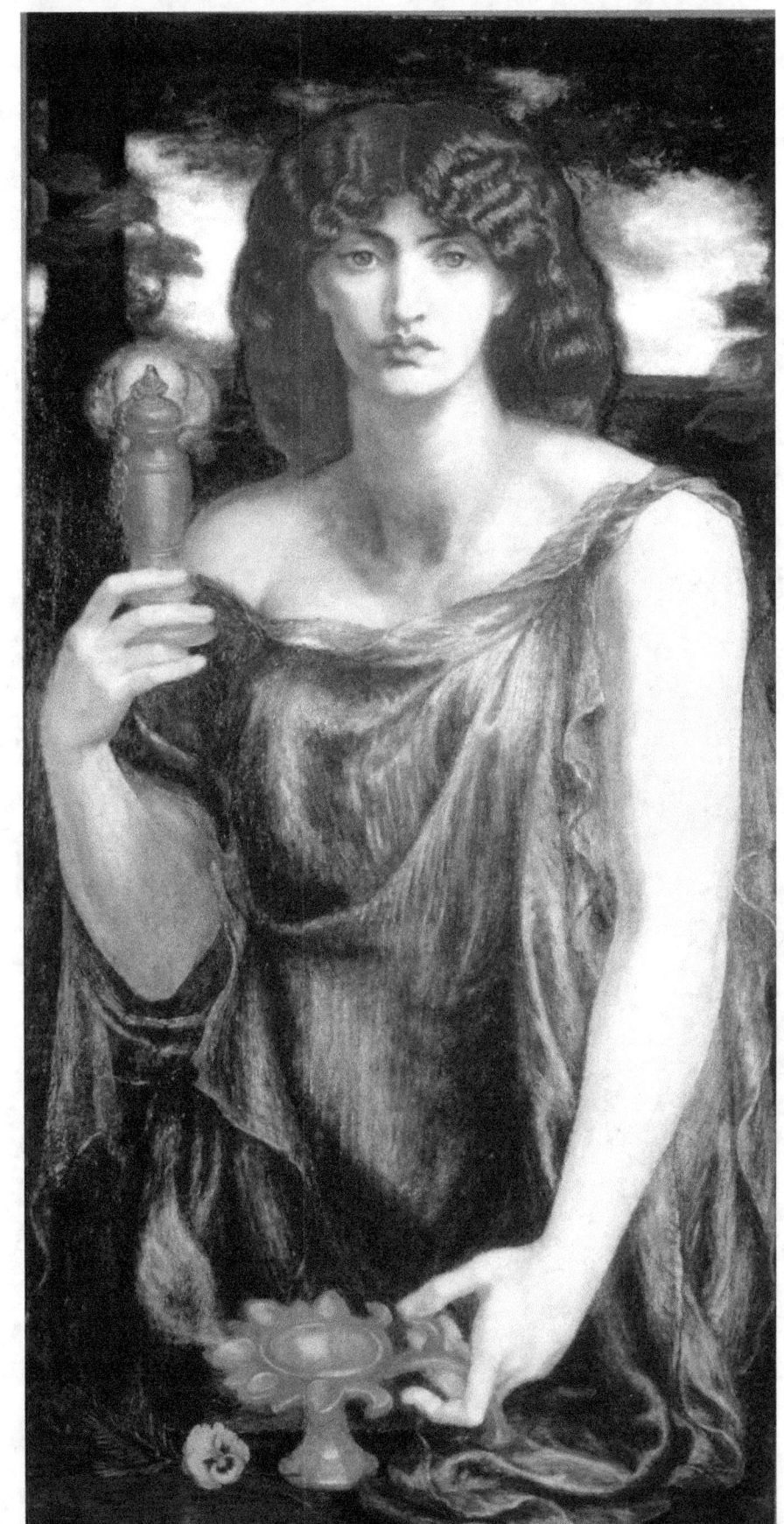

Dante Gabriel
Rossetti,
Mnemosyne,
Delaware

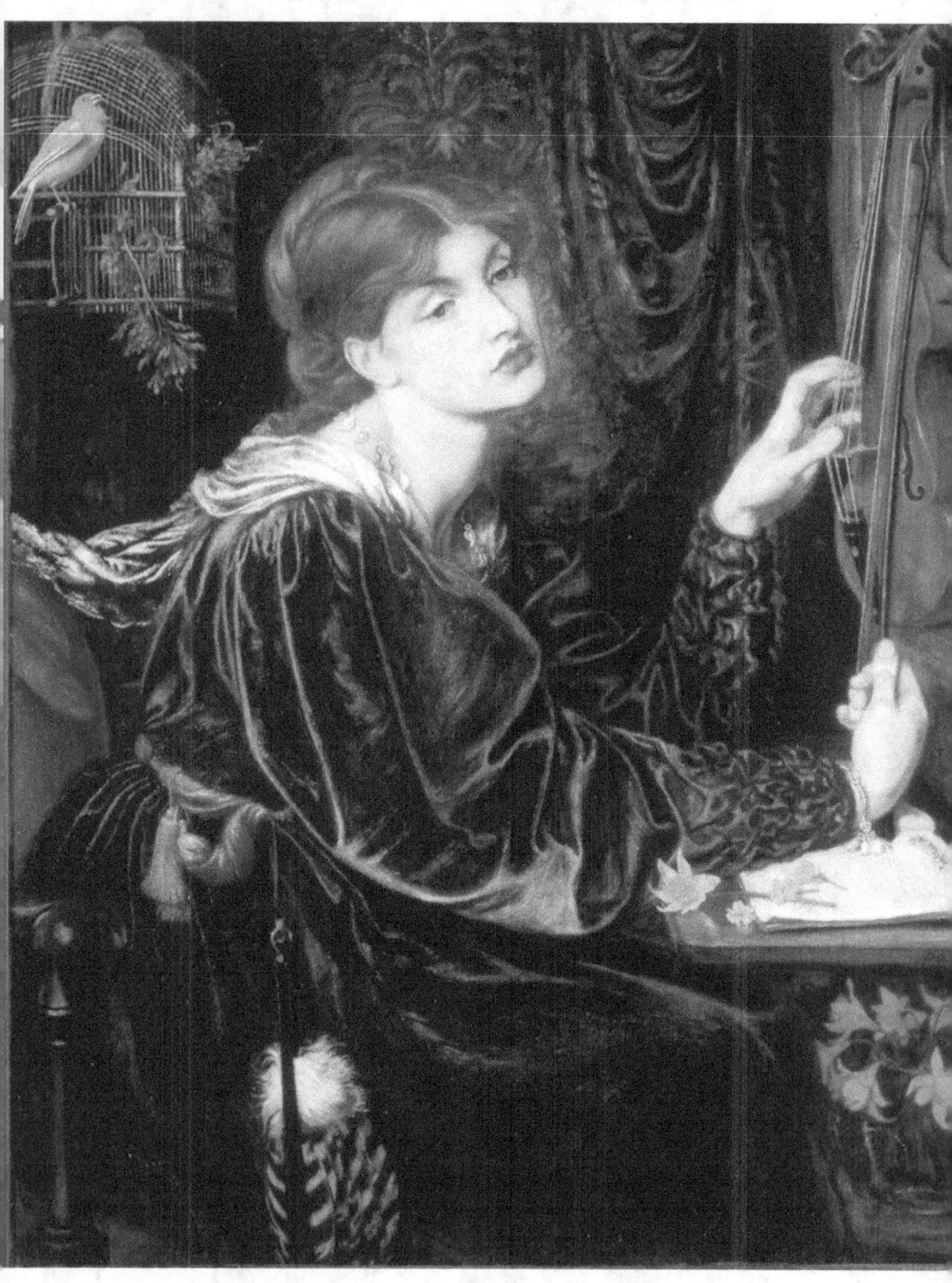

Dante Gabriel Rossetti, Veronica Veronese, 1872, Delaware

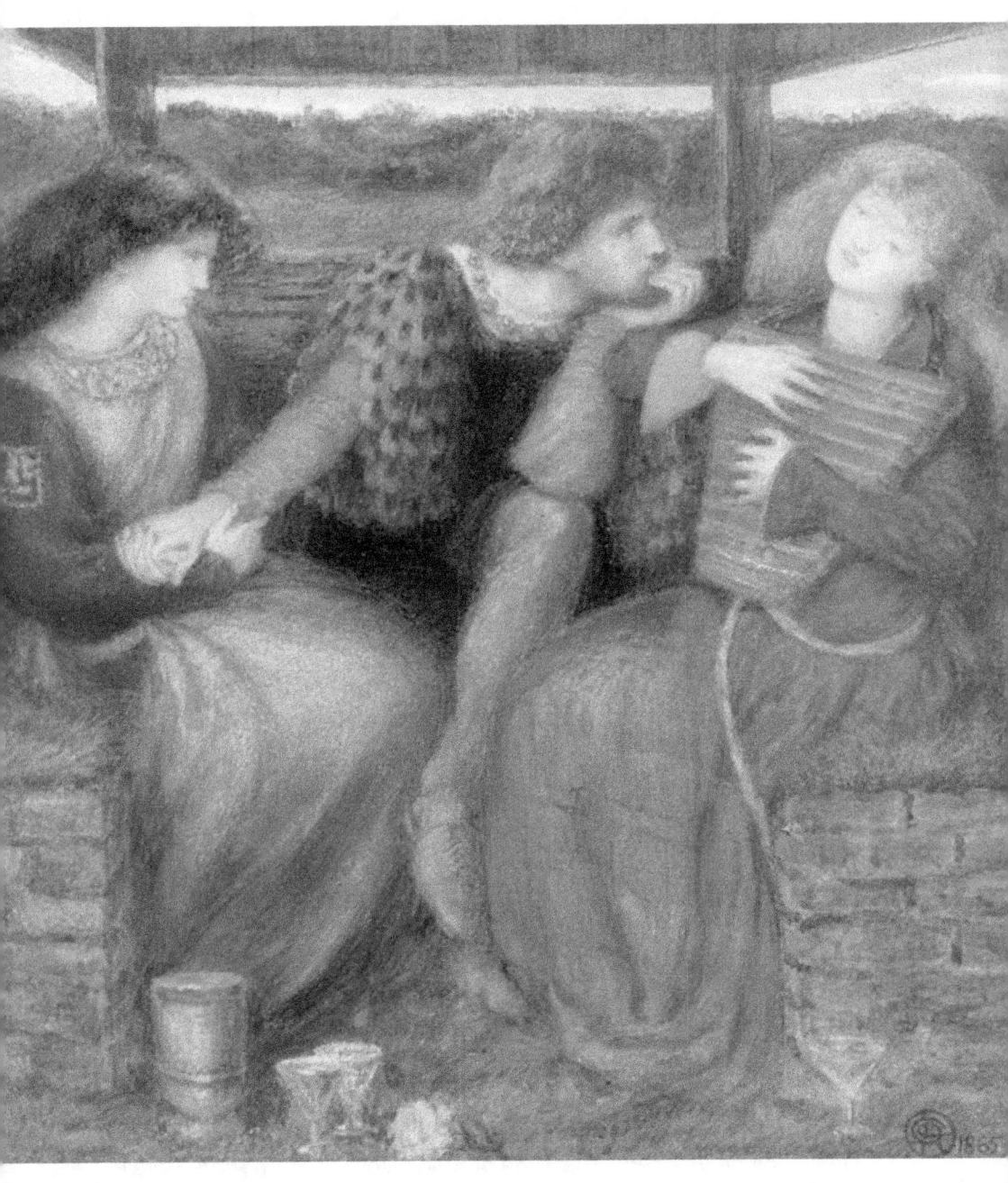

Dante Gabriel Rossetti, The Merciless Lady, 1865, private collection

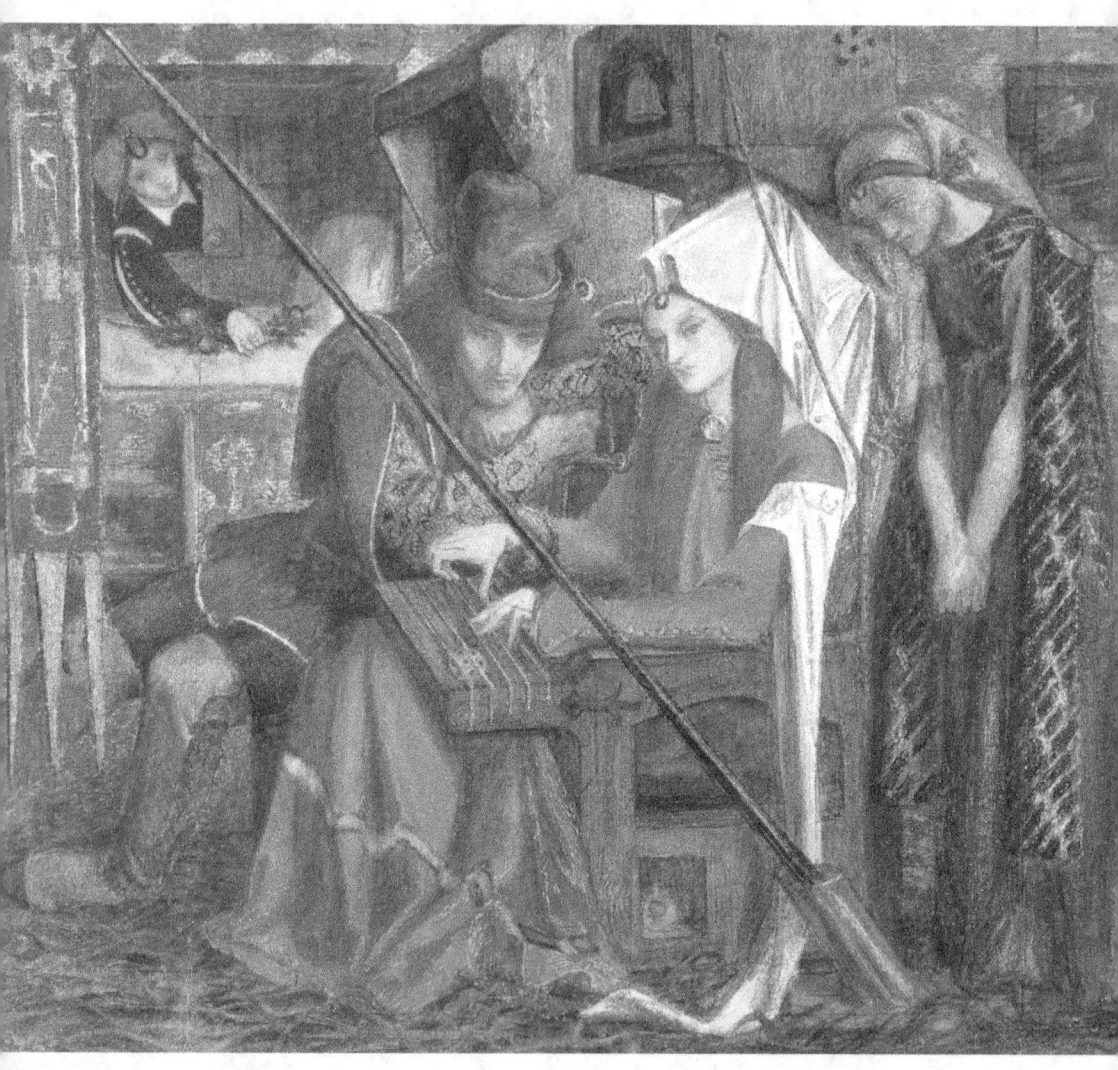

Dante Gabriel Rossetti, The Tune of Seven Towers, 1857, Tate Britain

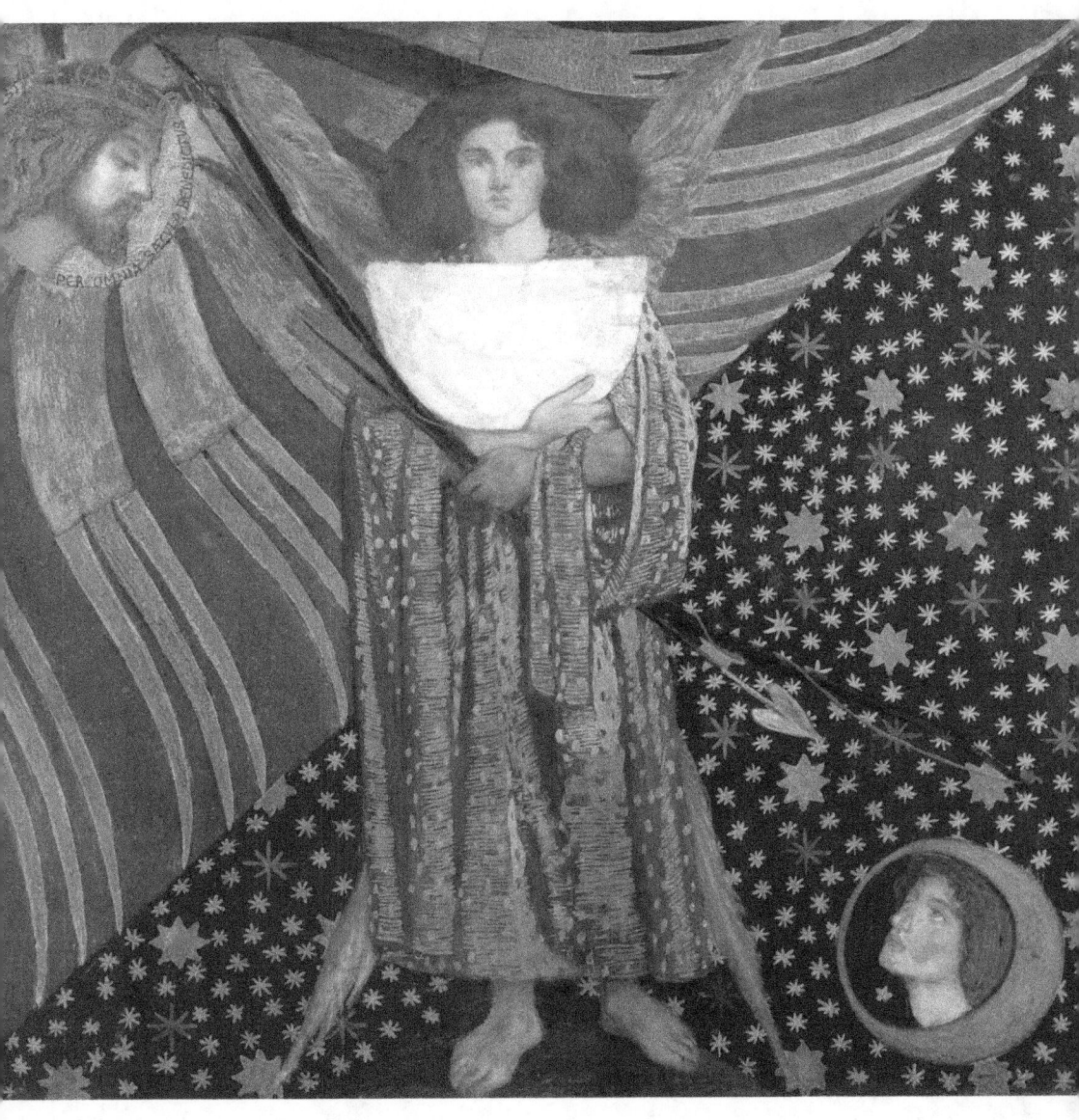

Dante Gabriel Rossetti, Dantis Amor, Tate Britain

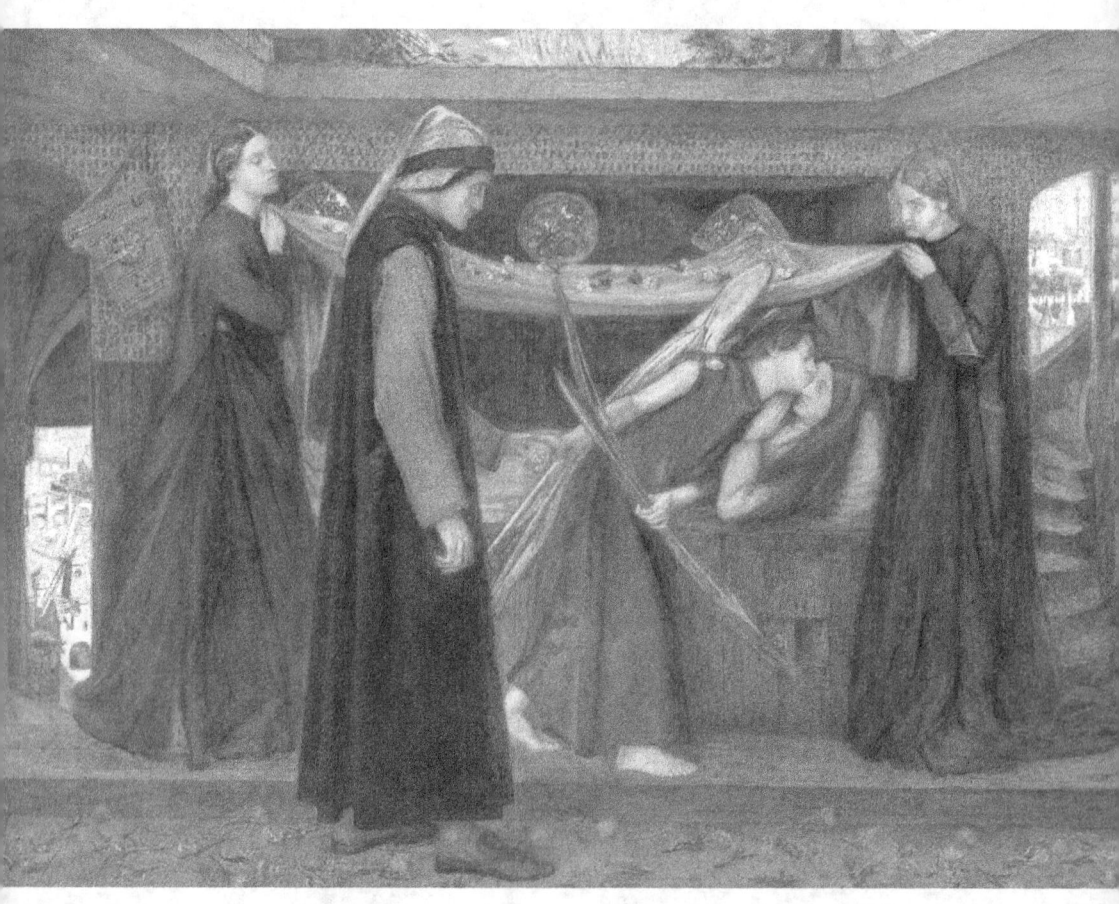

Dante Gabriel Rossetti, Dante's Dream, 1856, watercolour version, Tate Britain

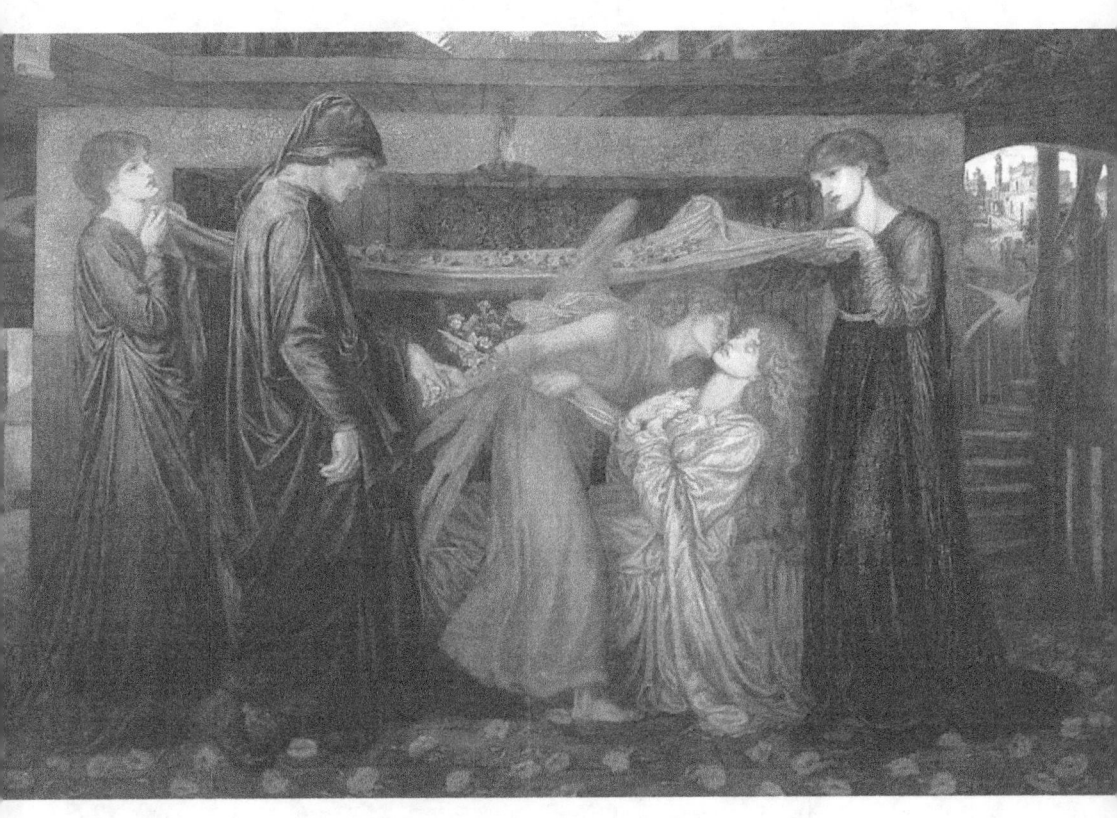

Dante Gabriel Rossetti, Dante's Dream, 1871,
Walker Art Gallery

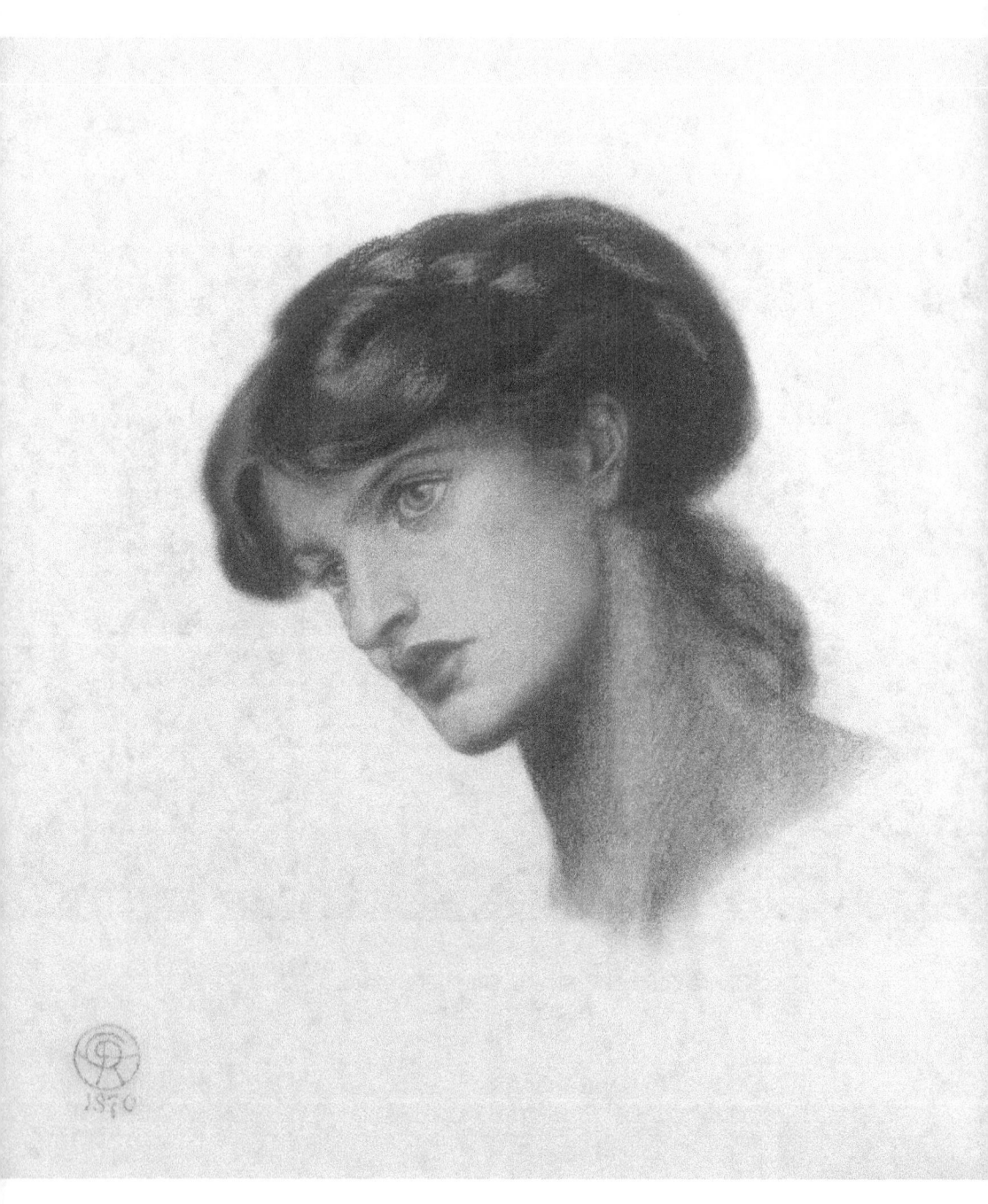

Dante Gabriel Rossetti, Study For 'Dante's Dream', Mrs. Stillman, 1870

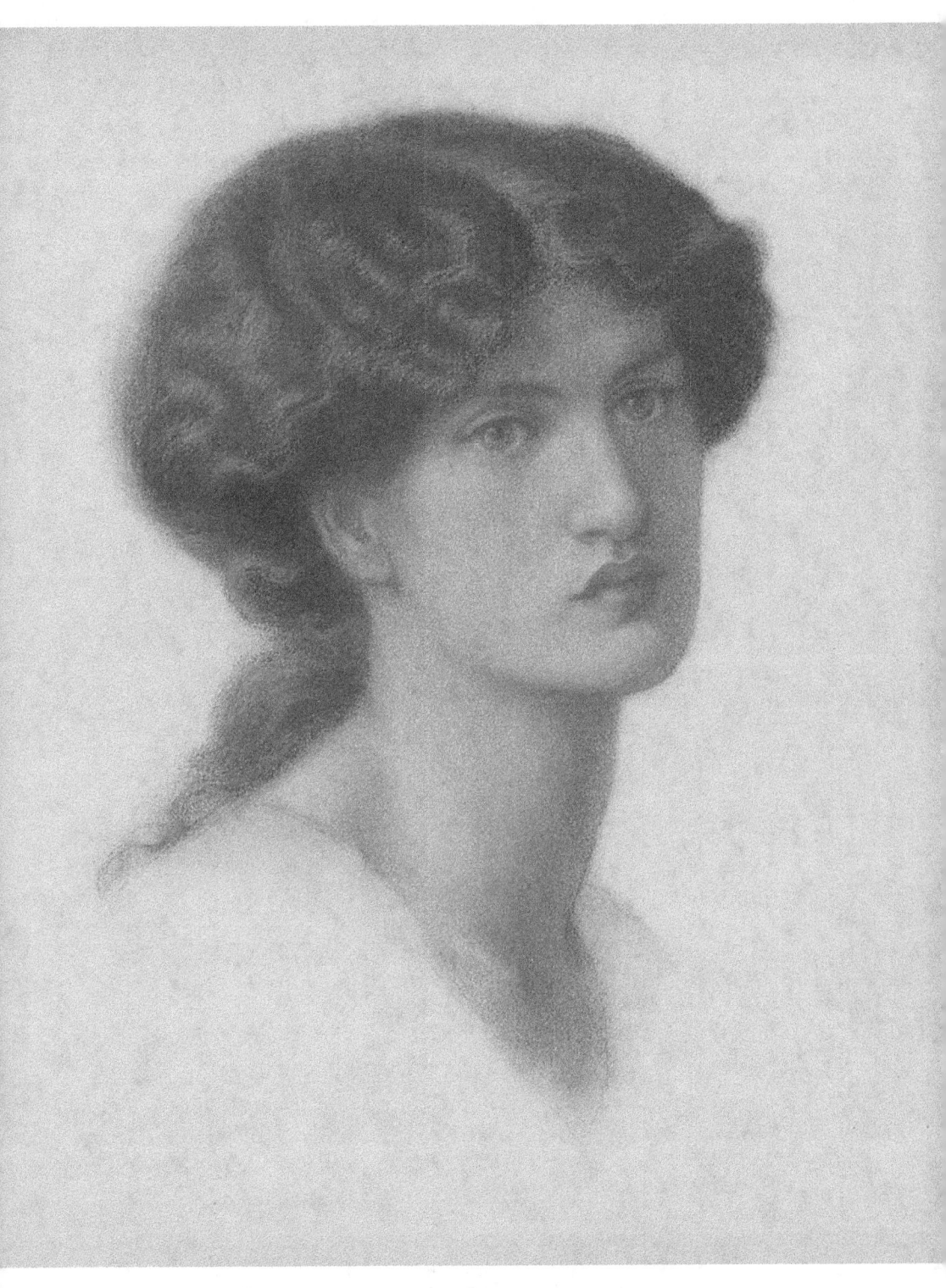

Dante Gabriel Rossetti, Portrait of Jane Morris, c. 1870

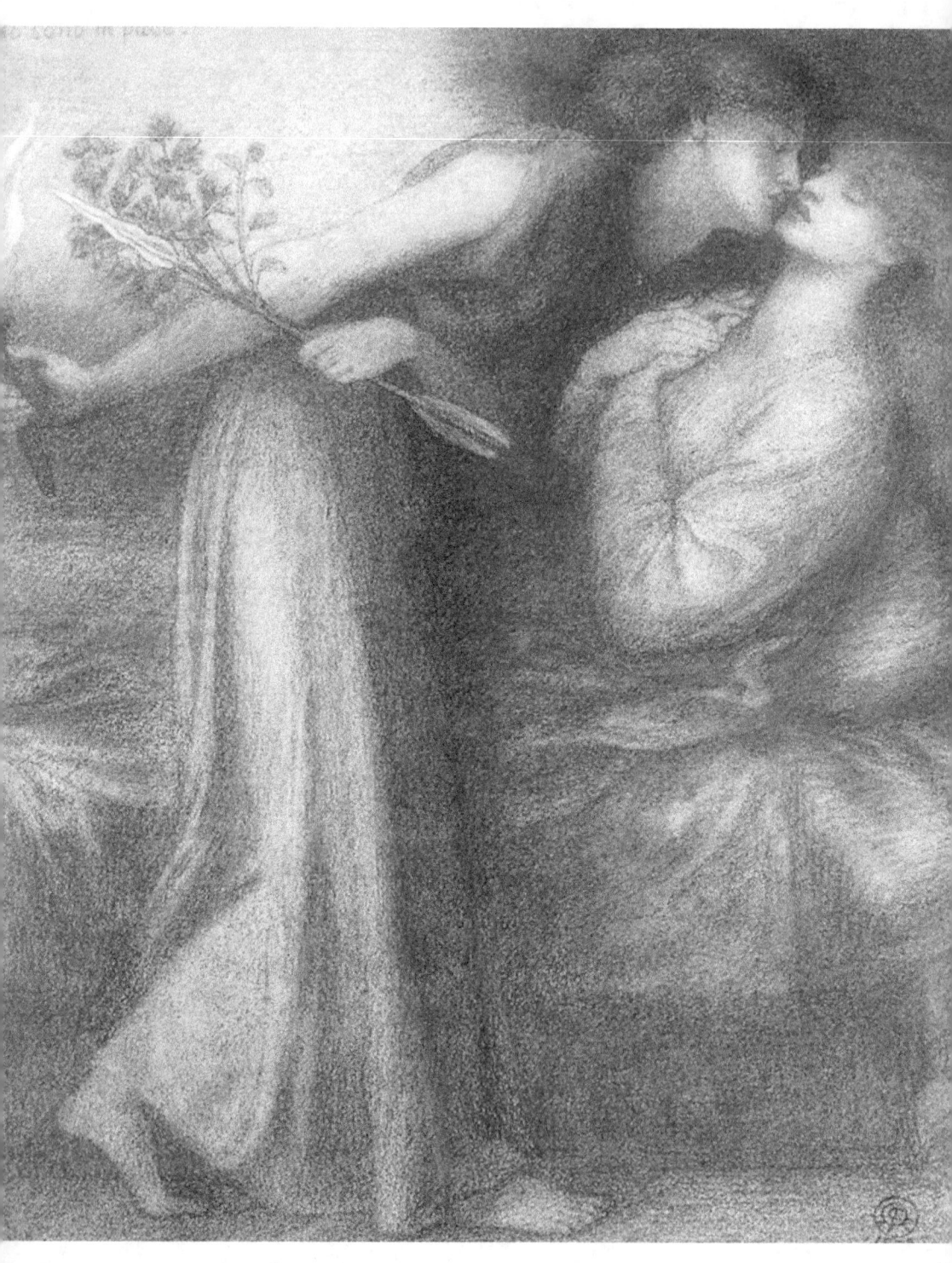

Dante Gabriel Rossetti, Io Sono In Pace, 1875, private collection

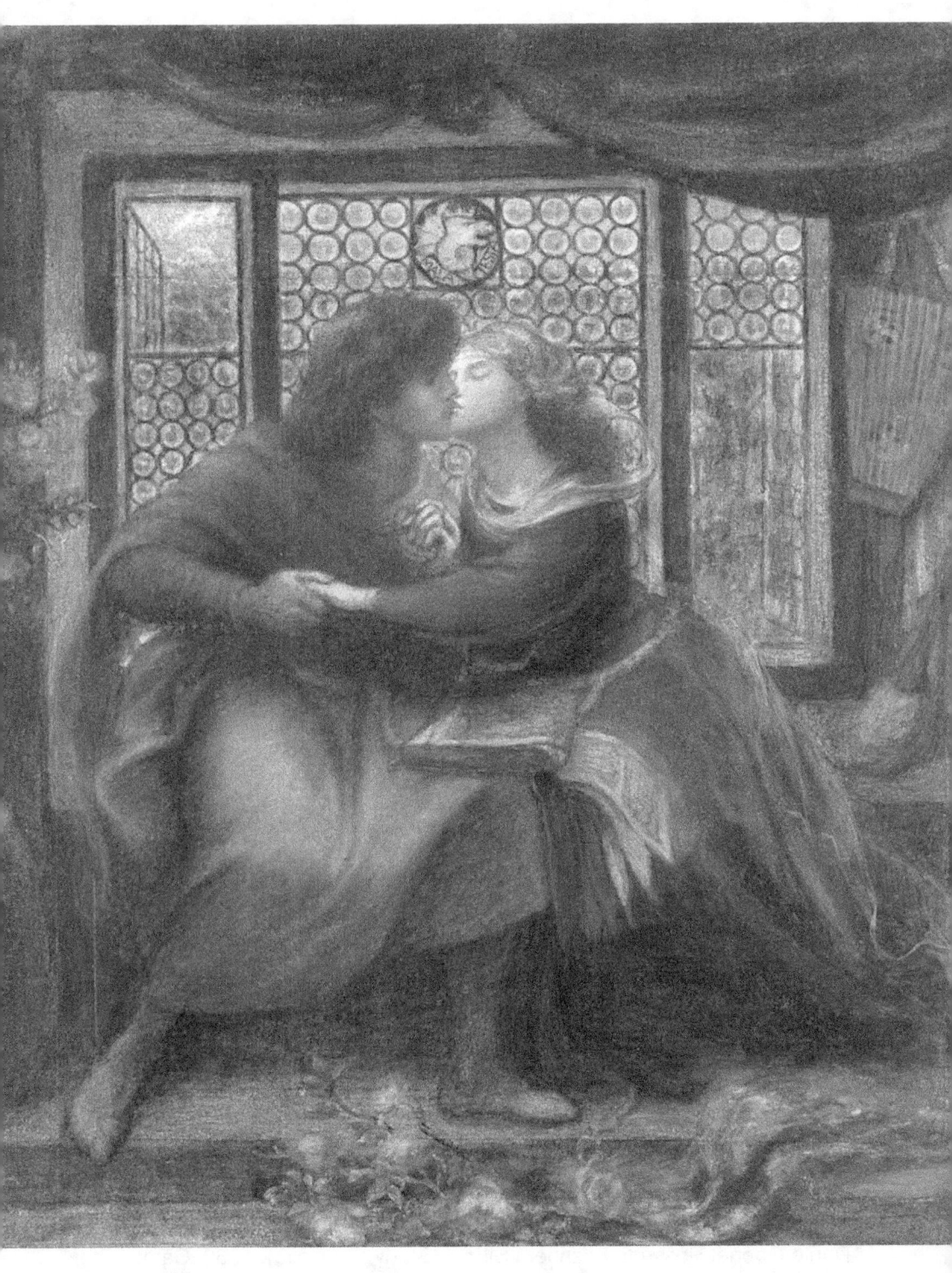

Dante Gabriel Rossetti, Paolo and Francesca da Rimini
1867, Melbourne

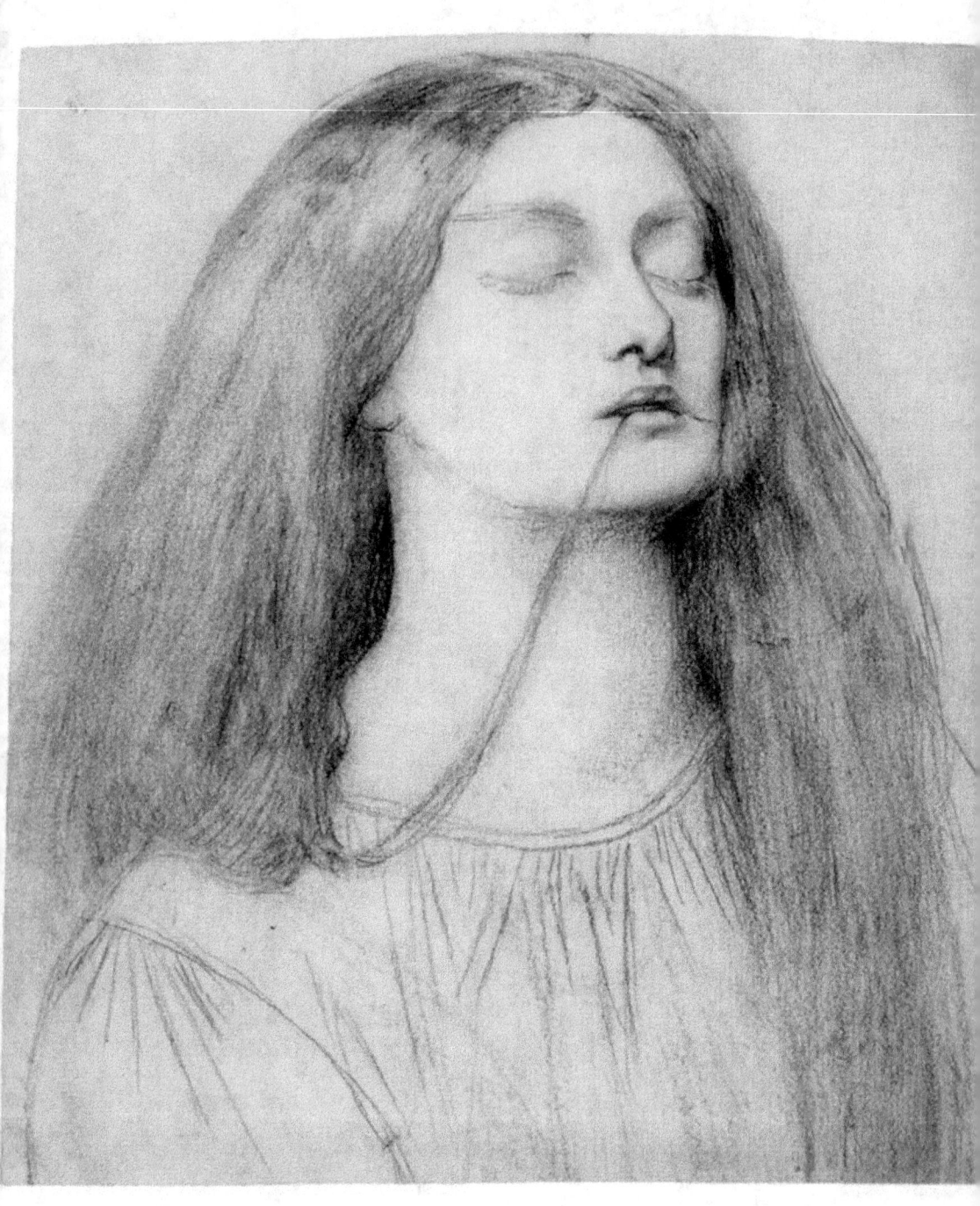

Dante Gabriel Rossetti, Elizabeth Siddal (Study For Delia), 1862, Cambridge

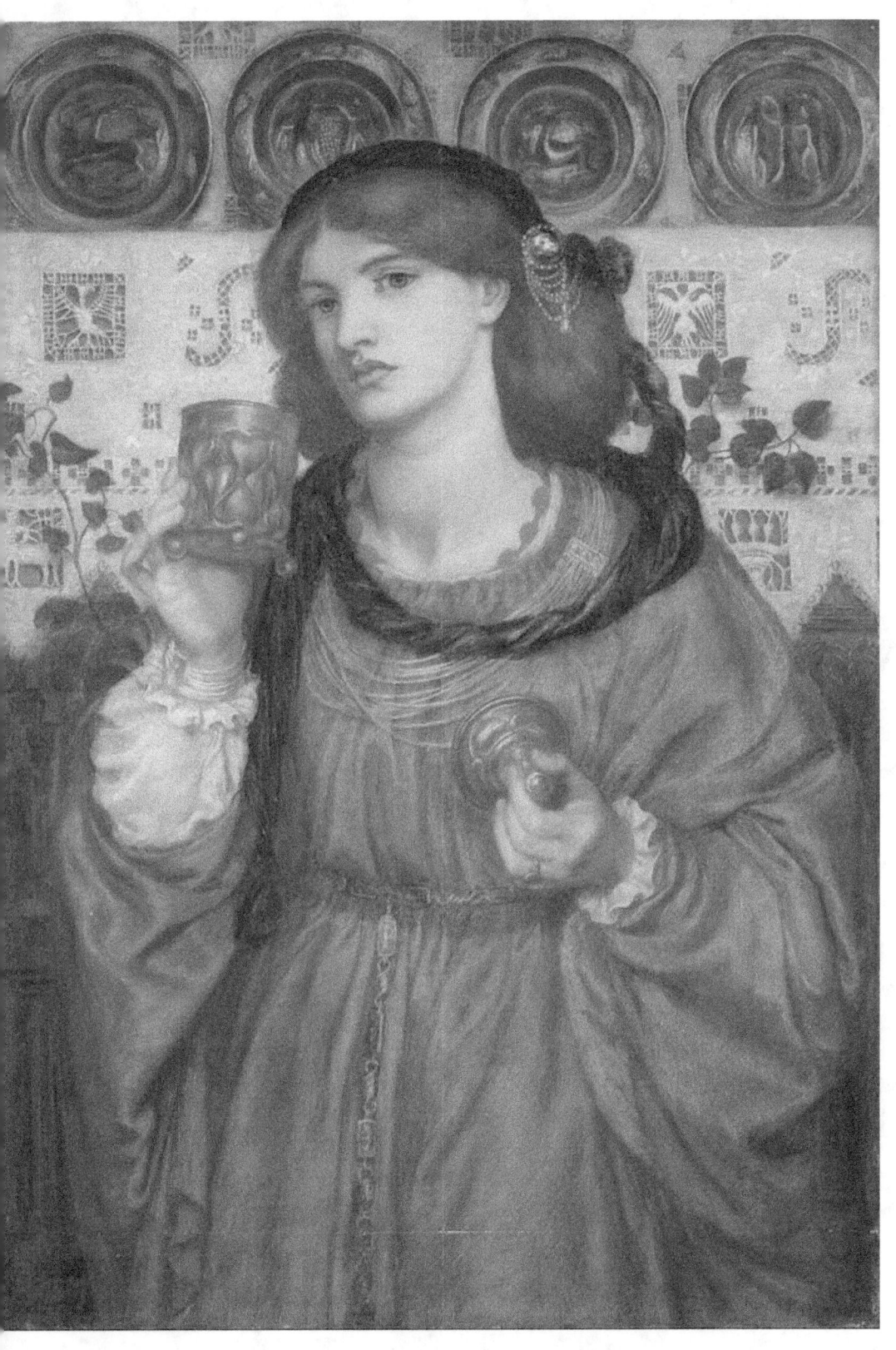

Dante Gabriel Rossetti, The Loving Cup, 1867, Tokyo

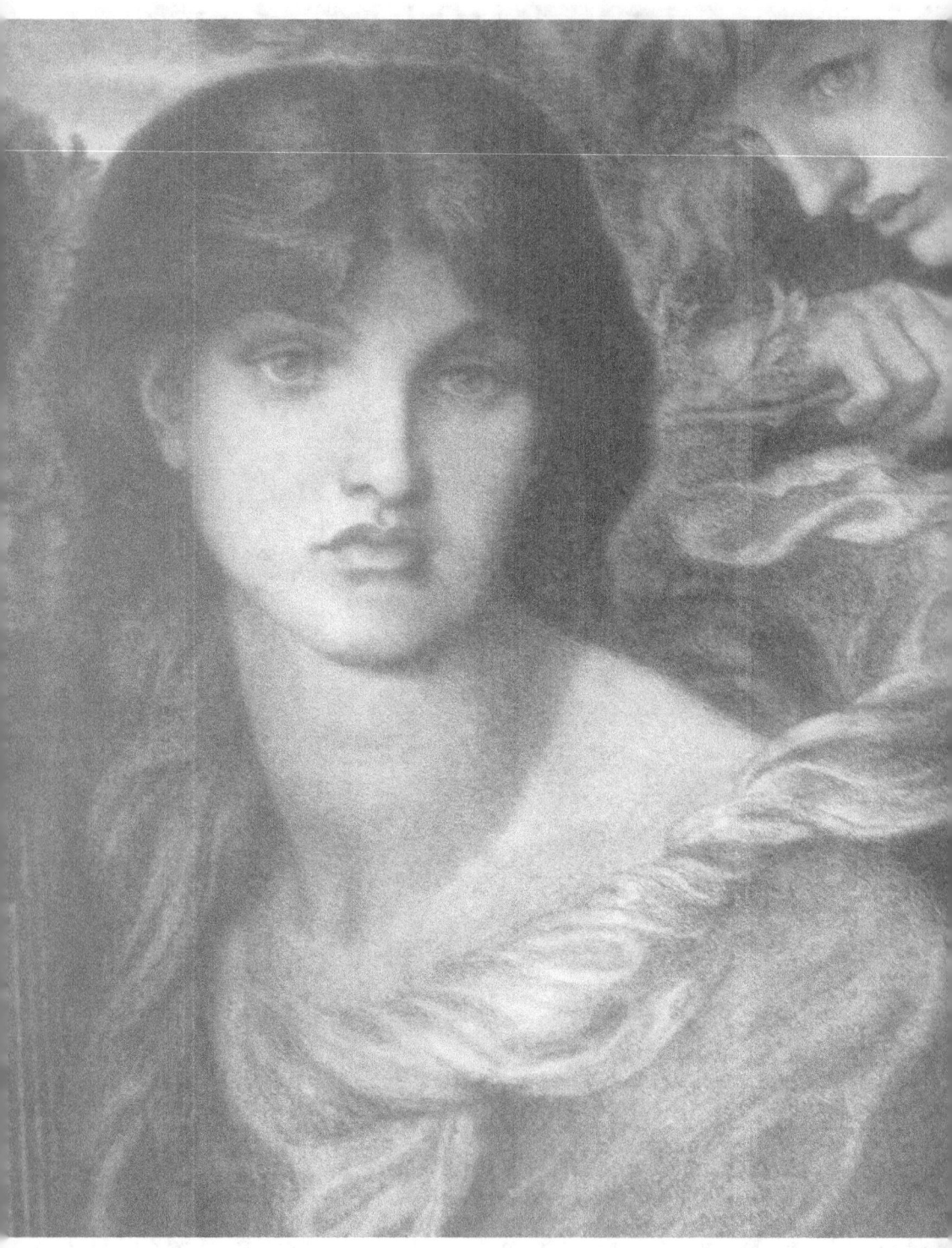

Dante Gabriel Rossetti, Ghirlandata, 1873, detail

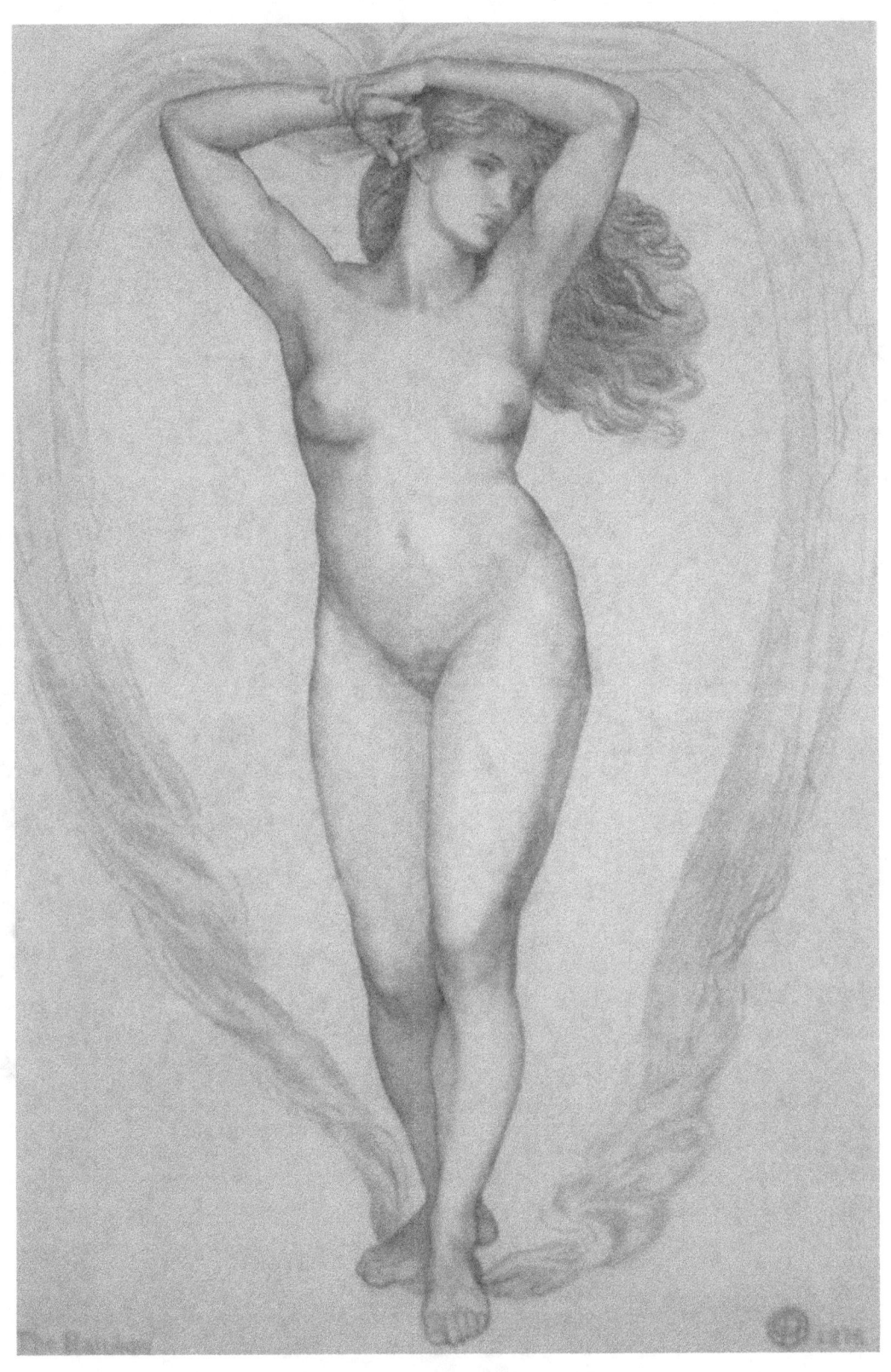

Dante Gabriel Rossetti, Spirit of the Rainbow, 1876

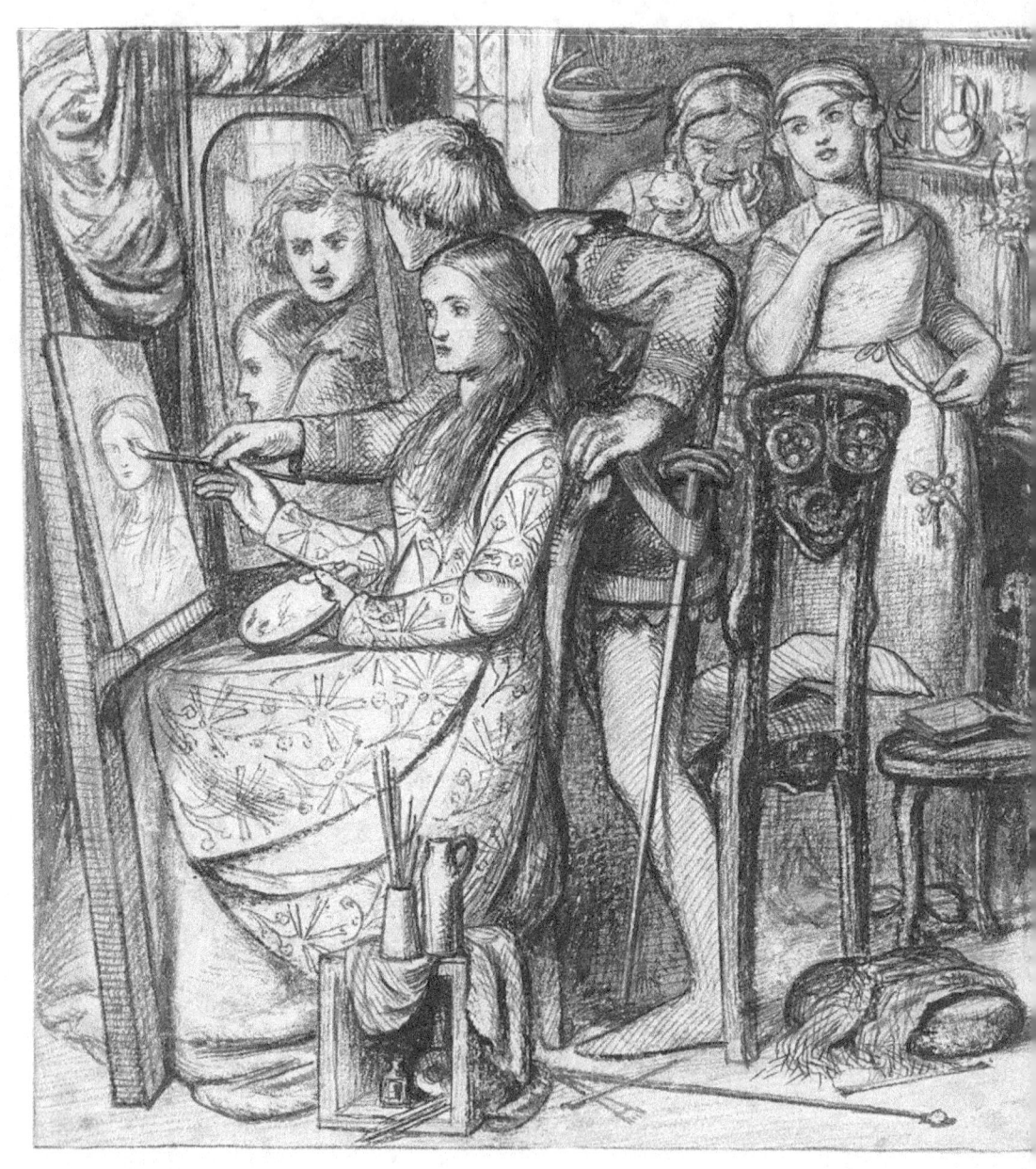

Dante Gabriel Rossetti, Love's Mirror or a Parable of Love ,
1850-52, Birmingham

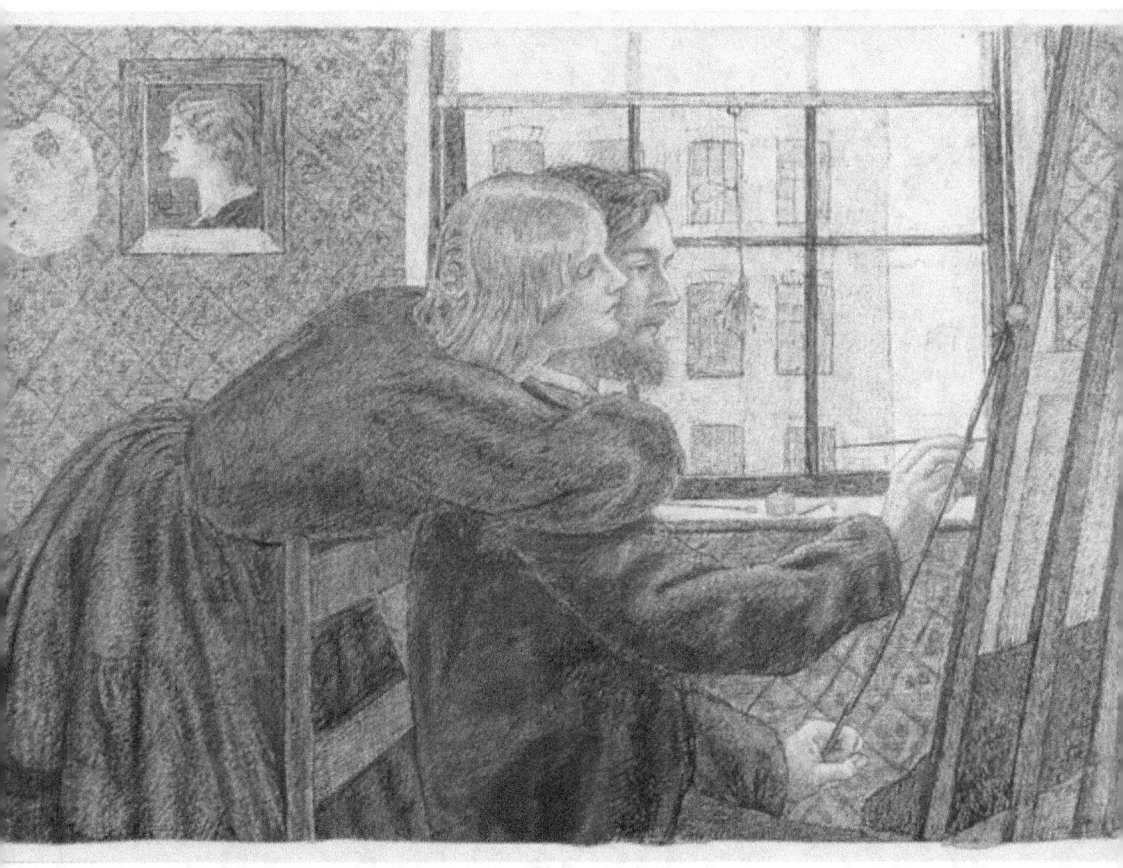

Dante Gabriel Rossetti, Fanny Cornforth and George Price Boyce, 1858

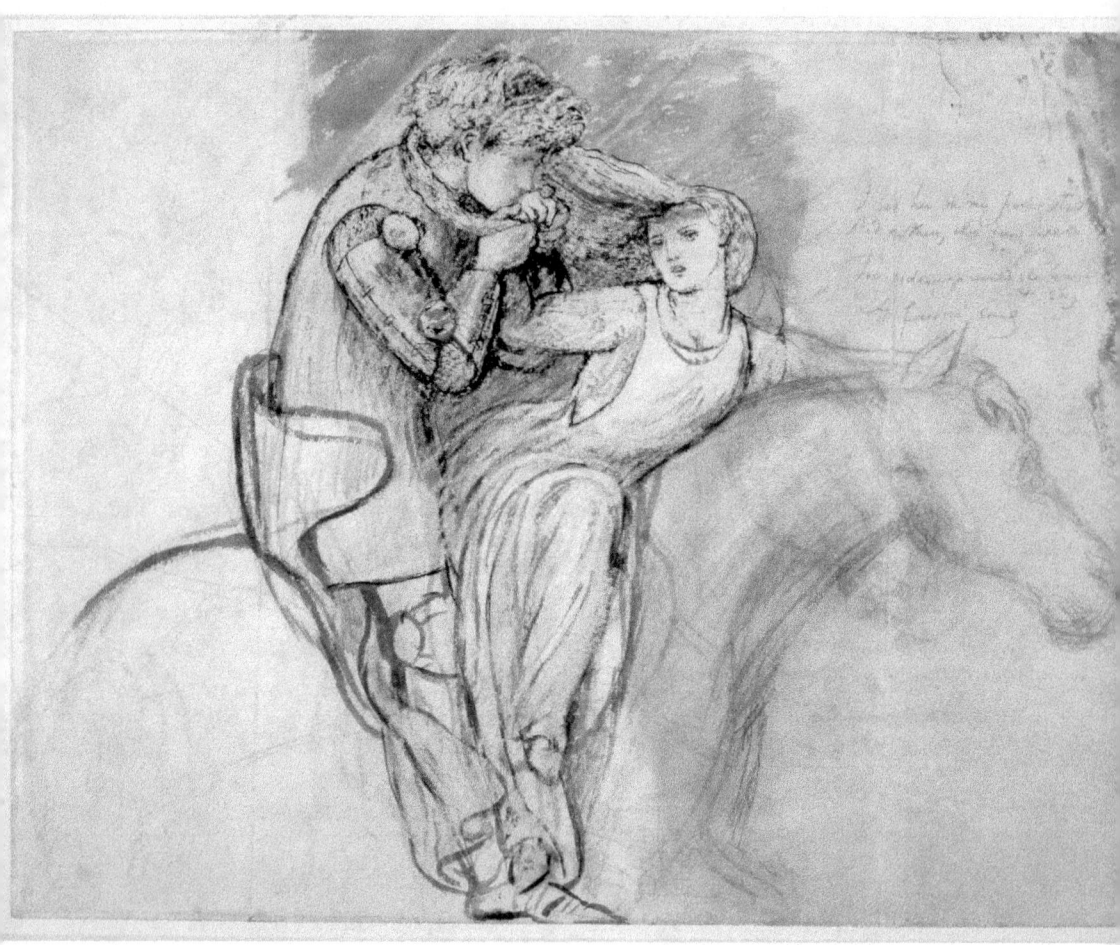

Dante Gabriel Rossetti, La Belle Dame Sans Merci, 1855

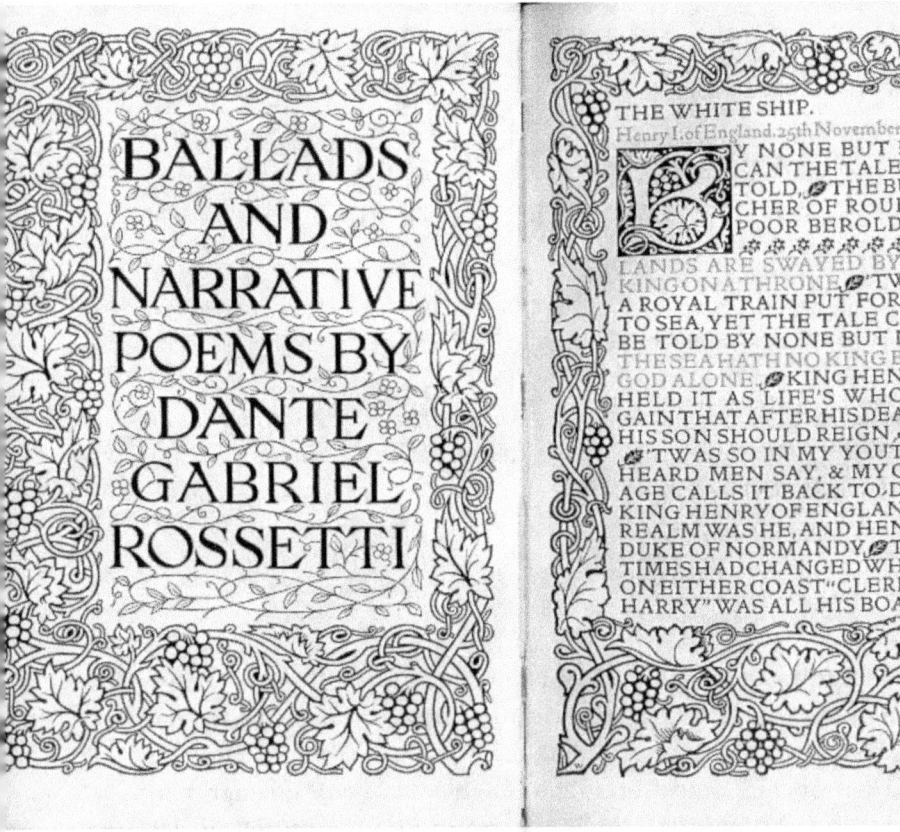

BALLADS
AND
NARRATIVE
POEMS BY
DANTE
GABRIEL
ROSSETTI

THE WHITE SHIP.
Henry I. of England. 25th November 1120

BY NONE BUT ME
CAN THE TALE BE
TOLD, THE BUT-
CHER OF ROUEN,
POOR BEROLD.
LANDS ARE SWAYED BY A
KING ON A THRONE TWAS
A ROYAL TRAIN PUT FORTH
TO SEA, YET THE TALE CAN
BE TOLD BY NONE BUT ME.
THE SEA HATH NO KING BUT
GOD ALONE. KING HENRY
HELD IT AS LIFE'S WHOLE
GAIN THAT AFTER HIS DEATH
HIS SON SHOULD REIGN.
TWAS SO IN MY YOUTH I
HEARD MEN SAY, & MY OLD
AGE CALLS IT BACK TO DAY.
KING HENRY OF ENGLAND'S
REALM WAS HE, AND HENRY
DUKE OF NORMANDY. THE
TIMES HAD CHANGED WHEN
ON EITHER COAST "CLERKLY
HARRY" WAS ALL HIS BOAST.

Dante Gabriel Rossetti, title page

CHAPTER III

THE PRE-RAPHAELITE
BROTHERHOOD

The Revolt from the Raphaelesque – Influence of Keats and the Romantic Poets – The Pre-Raphaelite Brothers and their Early Work – Travels of Rossetti with Hunt – Publication of "The Germ" – Hunt and Millais in the Royal Academy – Ruskin's Letters to the "Times" – Pre-Raphaelitism at Liverpool – The Pre-Raphaelites as Colourists.

The impulse thus given by Ruskin, in the minds of the young painters, towards the larger spiritual life and vision of the Pre-Raphaelite period, was strengthened, as Mr. Holman Hunt has told us, by the almost accidental sight of a book of engravings from the frescoes in the Campo Santo at Pisa, which fell into the hands of Rossetti and his friends while spending an evening together at Millais's house. To such aspirants as they, "crying bitterly unto the gods for a kingdom wherein to rule and create," the work of the early Italian masters here set forth, though already partially known to them in the National Gallery, opened up a new world to be conquered and explored. In the suggestive rather than successful achievements of Cimabue, Giotto, Ghiberti, and Masaccio, they discerned the wealth of *thought* to which

☆ 86

Ruskin had directed them, though the *language* was still in the course of adjustment to the meaning within. One cannot but think with a half-amused tenderness of the eager experimentalism of the young schismatics, shaking off from their feet the dust of academic propriety, and wandering back, half in jest, half in earnest, in the buoyant prowess of their youth, to the free fields wherefrom

> – "the harvest long ago
> Was reaped and garnered in the ancient barns."

It is a pleasant picture which rises in the memory, of the diverse trio, destined in after years for widely different paths of effort and success, yet welded at first in the glow of a common enthusiasm of revolt. It was impossible that they should perceive, at this early age, that the reaction in which they were united was but a preparing of the way for an artistic reconstruction which would demand from its leaders congruity of ideal as well as community of protest. The principle of non-conformity may embrace almost opposite poles of doctrine and practice, but the positive elements of a faith must possess alike the minds of its prophets if they are to pursue in permanent fellowship the goal at which they aim. As George Eliot has said, "If men are to be welded together in the glow of a transient feeling, they must be made of metal that will mix, else they will inevitably fall asunder when the heat dies out."

But there was as yet a strong practical cohesion between the grave and gentle Hunt, the brilliant, warm-hearted, and impressionable Millais, and the ardent, mercurial, and passionately imaginative Rossetti, whose personal magnetism was the immediate welding-force of the Pre-Raphaelite movement. Rossetti's proselytizing powers, and his inexhaustible enthusiasm (at least in youth) for dogmatic propaganda, were indeed a source of some embarrassment and many disappointments in the progress of artistic reform. The doctrine of Pre-Raphaelitism, however, if we may so call it – namely that in the age preceding Raphael would be found the touchstone of art, grew up too imperceptibly through mutual influences and interchange of thought to be attributed as a special tenet to Rossetti or any other of the student-band.

It was in the year 1847, before the formation of the Pre-Raphaelite Brotherhood, that the spell of Keats had come with special power upon its future leaders. Rossetti, an omnivorous reader of poetry, had already perceived both in Keats and Coleridge the essential elements of the highest romance. It is the more remarkable that Chatterton, now acclaimed as the herald of the romantic revival in poetry, as was Blake in art, had no such charm for Rossetti until quite late in life, when the tardy discovery led to an exaggerated worship. But in Keats, whose life (by Lord Houghton) Rossetti, Holman Hunt, and Millais had been reading together about this time, they found the supreme example in English poetry of that attainment of harmony between the classic and the romantic temper which was their aim in art. Eager as they now were for subject-matter whereon to exercise the artistic principles as yet but crudely formulated in their minds, they turned with new delight to the wonder-world revealed to them by the spirit of Keats, and looked with him through

> – "magic casements, opening on the foam
> Of perilous seas in faëry lands forlorn."

They saw that the reconciliation of the flesh to the spirit, which is the task of the second Renaissance as of the first, had already been achieved in poetry, and was waiting its translation into pictorial art. Keats had attained that perfect blending of the Greek spirit with the temper of romance which Rossetti was to reach in "Venus Astarte" and "Pandora."

The first organized union of workers imbued with the Pre-Raphaelite ideal, and further knit together by a common enthusiasm for the poetry of Keats, appears to have taken the form of a cyclographic society, in which the dominant spirits – Rossetti, Millais, and Holman Hunt – were soon surrounded by a group of more or less gifted companions and friends. The members were pledged to contribute original drawings in regular succession to a portfolio which was passed round for criticism by their fellows. Rossetti, who liked to rule his little kingdom with an absolute sway, seldom disputed by those who deemed submission to his imperious ways but a small price to pay for his friendship, selected from Keats's "Isabella" the following series of subjects to exercise the talents of the society: – 1. "The Lovers;" 2. "The Brothers" (of Isabella); 3."Good-bye," (the parting of Isabella and Lorenzo); 4. "The Vision" (Isabella sees in a dream the murder of her lover by her brother); 5. "The Wood" (Isabella visits the scene of the crime and secretly bears away the head of her lover); 6. "The Pot of Basil" (she buries the head in her flower-pot); 7. "The Brothers discover the Pot;" 8. "Madness of Isabella."

It does not appear that any member executed this exhaustive series of proposed sketches in its entirety. The suggestion of subjects from Shelley's "Prometheus Unbound" seems to have been no less barren of results. The only drawings from Rossetti's hand that remain to us from that portfolio are an illustration of Keats's "Belle Dame sans Merci;" a study from Coleridge's "Genevieve," over which he sat up a whole night, completing it at daybreak, and a sketch of "Gretchen in the Chapel" from Goethe's "Faust." The society included Walter Howell Deverell, an artist of rare delicacy and grace, and a man of singular personal charm, destined to play a memorable part in the life-history of Rossetti; F.G. Stephens, an intimate friend of Holman Hunt; Thomas Woolner, a young sculptor whose acquaintance Rossetti had made at the Academy Schools; J.A. Vinter, now well known as a portrait painter; and such lesser though by no means insignificant lights as J.B. Keene, F. Watkins, William Dennis, John Hancock, J.T. Clifton, and N.E. Green. It was evident that among the rising generation of painters, long before the formation of the Pre-Raphaelite Brotherhood, – even before Hunt or Rossetti had entered definitely upon such art training as they ever had – the revolt against the tyranny of the Academy was already begun, and even those least in sympathy with the Pre-Raphaelite idea found themselves drawn towards Rossetti and his friends in a common disaffection with the existing *régime*. Moreover, the success of Millais, who at the age of seventeen had gained the highest academic prize for historical painting, and was already earning well with his book-illustrations in black and white, afforded a valuable connecting-link with a larger circle of critics and sympathizers from whom were drawn some of the most faithful aides-de-camp of the Pre-Raphaelite campaign.

The poetry of Keats afforded at all events an inexhaustable treasure-house of subject-matter for the young painters, not only in their first efforts towards the romantic revival, but for many years then to come. "The Eve of St. Agnes," for example, afterwards yielded the theme of the picture regarded by some critics as Millais's greatest work, as well as of the first important painting by Holman Hunt, "The Flight of Madeline and Porphyro." This was completed at Millais's studio, at his home in Gower Street, early in 1848, and exhibited in the Royal Academy of that year; Millais having been at work meanwhile upon his "Cymon and Iphigenia."

It was not until the autumn of 1848 that a definite attempt was made to band together, in a common purpose and under a distinctive name, those of the little company of students and friends who were prepared to accept and follow openly the principle of fidelity to Nature in general and to the romantic conception of Nature in particular, – the conception, namely, of the physical world as the veil and vehicle of an immanent spirit, fateful, mysterious, and occult. An informal meeting was held at Rossetti's studio, then at 83, Newman Street, and seven members enrolled themselves under the name of "The Pre-Raphaelite Brotherhood." The union consisted of Rossetti, Millais, Holman Hunt, William Michael Rossetti, the younger brother of the painter, Thomas Woolner, F.G. Stephens, and James Collinson –

the least stable of the Brotherhood and the first seceder from its ranks. In the Academy of that year a picture by Collinson had already been exhibited, entitled "The Charity Boy's Début." He was a painter of uncertain artistic *calibre*, and of a lethargic and mystical temperament; converted to Pre-Raphaelitism by the ardour of Rossetti, but shortly forsaking his art studies and joining the Roman Catholic communion with a view of qualifying for the priesthood. This ambition also was subsequently given up, and, thus vacillating between the church and the studio, his probation ended in no particular career. The remaining members of the Brotherhood – apart from the leading painters – may be said to represent the minor literature of the movement. F.G. Stephens and W.M. Rossetti have attained permanent distinction as art-critics, while Thomas Woolner, before winning his later fame as a sculptor, gave in the form of poetry his chief contribution to the early propaganda of the Brotherhood.

The rules laid down as to method in painting, – such as, that every subject and accessory should be studied direct from nature, and from one model – do not seem to have been stringently enforced: indeed in one of Rossetti's most rigidly Pre-Raphaelite pictures, "Ecce Ancilla Domini," the face of the Virgin was avowedly painted from several models, while in that of the Angel the artist has produced a curious blending of his brother's features with those of another sitter.

It is improbable that an aversion to the one-model rule, which has been attributed to Ford Madox Brown as a reason for holding aloof from the Brotherhood, had very much to do with his decision to remain independent of it. Mr. Madox Brown was from the first in cordial sympathy with the movement, and on terms of intimate friendship with its leaders, but he foresaw the dangers of an artistic clique, and, perhaps, the impossibility of permanent consonance of method between temperaments so diverse as those of the seven members enlisted. Nor was his own strong and individualistic style of painting quite in harmony with the manner of his younger friends. He was pre-eminently an historical painter; and the critical and romantic treatment of history, though bordering very closely on Pre-Raphaelite ground, hardly came within the immediate scope of the Brotherhood. Though frequently acknowledged by his later critics as the father – or sometimes the grandfather – of the Pre-Raphaelite movement, Mr. Madox Brown consistently disclaimed any such title, and did so with no less justice than modesty. At the same time, his work was so intimately connected with that of the men whom he powerfully influenced and inspired that it may fairly be studied side by side with theirs in illustration of the dominant principles common to all.

In the autumn of 1848 it was agreed that the three chief painters should select their next subjects from Keats's "Isabella." Millais, at that time under the influence of Hunt rather than of Rossetti (who indeed was still far from adopting any definite line of *technique*), decided upon a scene depicting Lorenzo at supper with Isabella and her brothers. The pensive and earnest face of Lorenzo was painted from W.M. Rossetti. Mrs. Hodgkinson, the wife of Millais's half-brother, sat for Isabella. It would not be easy to disprove Holman Hunt's generous but weighty verdict on the finished picture, as "the most wonderful painting that any youth still under twenty years of age ever did in the world."

Hunt and Rossetti, however, were not so steadfast in their adhesion to the agreement as to the choice of subjects from Keats. Hunt indeed planned, and probably commenced about this time, his afterwards notable picture, "Isabella and the Pot of Basil;" but this, though taking rank among the best examples of his earlier style, was not finally painted until 1867. He decided to finish, for the next Academy, a picture already in hand, "Rienzi swearing revenge over the body of his brother." In this design the figure of Colonna, who endeavours to pacify the would-be avenger, was painted from W.M. Rossetti, while Dante Rossetti sat for the head of Rienzi, – and neglected, in spite of much urging from his comrades, to fulfil his own share in the "Isabella" project; but pursued work upon the most original and remarkable of his early pictures, "The Girlhood of Mary Virgin." Prior to this, he had proposed, and partly sketched, a design entitled, "Retro me, Sathana," representing a young girl walking, and earnestly reading, in a cloister, in the company of a venerable priest, while the retreating figure of Satan threatens her from the shade. This conception was never carried out; but it is probable that the now familiar sonnet bearing the same title was written about this time. The only painting of any note hitherto accomplished by Rossetti was a life-size and nearly half-length portrait of his father, finished in this same year 1848, and commissioned and bought by his godfather, Mr. Charles Lyell, of Kinnordy, Forfar, the father of the eminent geologist. This was the only male portrait Rossetti ever did in oils. In his new picture, "The Girlhood of Mary Virgin," (called at first "The Education of the Virgin") the face of the lovely child-angel was painted from a young half-sister of Woolner (though greatly modified, if not wholly re-painted, afterwards); while St. Joiachim was taken from an old family servant, and Saint Anna and St. Mary from Mrs. Rossetti and Miss Christina Rossetti respectively.

In the spring of 1849 the Pre-Raphaelite Brotherhood held their first "private view" with three important pictures, Rossetti's "Girlhood," Hunt's "Rienzi," and Millais's "Lorenzo and Isabella," duly signed and monogramed with the initials P.R.B. after the painters' names, ready for exhibition; the first appearing at the Free Gallery (formerly known as the Chinese Gallery), Hyde Park Corner, then under the management of the Association for Promoting the Free Exhibition of Modern Art, the other two at the Royal Academy, where they were favourably hung. Rossetti's picture was sold to the Marchioness of Bath on "private view" day for £80, and Hunt's "Rienzi" found a purchaser soon afterwards. "Lorenzo and Isabella," sold for £100 in 1849, was bought in 1883 by the Corporation of Liverpool for £1,120.

A tour on the Continent with Holman Hunt in September, 1849, gave Rossetti fresh inspiration from the early Italian masters and the best representatives of the Dutch school. The impressions made upon him in his twenty-first year by travel in France and Belgium are recorded for us in the wonderfully vivid and sharply-cut vignette-poems of this period. Eager as ever for emotional experience, and with the divine passion of hero-worship strong upon him, his holiday among the great painters was a delightsome pilgrimage, full of suggestion and stimulus for future work. In Paris, the sight of Giorgione's great idyll in the Louvre, "A Venetian Pastoral," drew from the young tourist a sonnet unsurpassed for sheer verbal colour and atmosphere by any of his later poems. Here, too, were written the great memorial sonnets, "Place de la Bastille," and "The Staircase of Notre Dame." On the cliffs at Boulogne Rossetti wrote "Sea-Limits." He

> – "climbed the stair in Antwerp church,
> What time the circling thews of sound
> At sunset seem to heave it round.
> Far up, the carillon did search
> The wind, and the birds came to perch
> Far under, where the gables wound."

Van Eyck and Memmeling at Bruges, Leonardo, Fra Angelico, Giorgione, and Titian in Paris, lacked no due meed of homage from Rossetti and Hunt.

It is remarkable that Rossetti never visited Italy, nor even retained, in later years, the patriotic sentiment which had so strongly pervaded the home life of his boyhood.

On the return of the travellers to London, a new development was proposed and accomplished in the public propaganda of the Pre-Raphaelite Brotherhood. It was decided to issue a monthly magazine for the promulgation of Pre-Raphaelite principles in painting and poetry. Members and sympathizers met at Rossetti's studio in Newman Street to discuss the project, and decide upon the title and contents of the manifesto. The suggestion of Mr. Cave Thomas was ultimately adopted, that it should be called "The Germ." The first number, extending to forty-eight large octavo pages, illustrated with etchings, appeared in January, 1850, published by Messrs. Aylott and Jones, of 8, Paternoster Row. The primary tenet with regard to art was thus enunciated in the preface: "The endeavour held in view throughout the writings on Art will be to encourage and enforce an entire adherence to the simplicity of nature." It would be captious, perhaps, to argue, in the face of so ingenuous an implication, that nature is not simple, but, alas! infinitely and fatefully complex without and within; presenting to the seer's eye a tangled web of visible phenomena no less intricate than the secret woof of destiny whose threads are the lives of men. To young minds, as to a young world, the vision of nature broadly outlined in generalities and clear with purpose is one of the fairest of illusions. The sternest discipline of life is to discover chaos where we imagined order and lucidity: to find interminable mazes and cross-roads for our bewilderment where in the morning mirage we had seen a plain path, an open road to the Ideal. Then we cry that Nature, and not ourself, is altered: that "there hath passed away a glory from the earth."

Happily, this disillusionment was yet far off in the future of the Pre-Raphaelite Brotherhood. In the preface to "The Germ," a special claim was made for poetry in its relation to the principles of simplicity of expression already enforced in painting; and with better reason, since painting must perforce speak exclusively by the representation of visible things, while poetry reaches directly to their inner significance. For while the painter strives so to order and depict the phenomena around him as to arrive at some sort of moral simplicity in the effect of his picture, the poet – if he be a seer – penetrates at once to the spirit of his theme, and clothes it at his own will with symbolic or dramatic expression. Hence the application of the Pre-Raphaelite principle to the writing of poetry was even more fruitful than in painting; and produced in modern English ballad and lyric verse, and even in the best prose of our own generation, a swift and incisive directness of touch, a broad and vivid clarity of impression, never so fully effected in the pictorial medium.

The first literary *débutant* in "The Germ" was Mr. Woolner, who occupied the opening pages of the January number with two short poems admirably illustrative, within their unpretentious scope and modest aim, of that naïve simplicity in the handling of complexities – the eternal childlikeness of pure romance – which is inherent in almost all great art. "My Beautiful Lady" and "Of my Lady in Death" were accompanied by an etching in two parts by Holman Hunt. Then followed an unsigned sonnet by Ford Madox Brown, and a paper by Mr. J.L. Tupper on "The Subject in Art." Mr. Coventry Patmore contributed anonymously a poem called "The Seasons," and Mr Tupper was also represented in verse. Criticism of contemporary poetry was afforded by W.M. Rossetti's paper on Arthur Hugh Clough. The remaining pages were worthily filled by the two greatest poets of the Pre-Raphaelite movement, Dante Gabriel and Christina Rossetti: the latter with "Dreamlands" and another short lyric, signed "Ellen Alleyn," the former with "My Sister's Sleep," a characteristic example of his earliest manner, written in the then uncommon metre since naturalized in our language by Tennyson's "In Memoriam," and the wonderful prose allegory "Hand and Soul." This poem – as verily it should be called, with its rich and haunting diction and its magical rhythm of imagery – is almost the sole example of Rossetti's strength in prose, only paralleled by a similar composition, entitled "St. Agnes of Intercession," of a later date. "Hand and Soul" is largely autobiographical in its narrative, being the story of a young art student of Arezzo, named Chiaro dell'Erma, possessed by new and high ideals of the painters mission, and stimulated to the better application of his own talents by the success of a younger comrade, – as we may well believe Rossetti to have been stirred and impelled by the progress of the more studious and at the same time more fortunate Millais. The speech of Chiaro in "Hand and Soul" may be taken as a declaration of Rossetti's artistic faith and principles at that period.

The second number of "The Germ," though no less

interesting and significant in subject-matter, did not increase the scant support accorded to the venture by the public at large; and since the expense of such an issue was too heavy to be borne by the little band of young and struggling aspirants responsible for its existence, the future of the magazine had to be seriously reconsidered by the Brotherhood. Mr. Tupper, however, to whose hands the printing had been entrusted, came to the rescue, and gave "The Germ" a new lease of life under the title of "Art and Poetry." The change did not serve to commend the somewhat crude propaganda to the mind of the British Philistine, and after the April number the issue was reluctantly given up; but not until its pages had glowed with the first fires, at least, of Rossetti's noblest poetic inspiration. Here first appeared "The Blessed Damozel," for which we might surely paraphrase the words of Holman Hunt on Millais, and call it "the most wonderful poem that any youth still under twenty years of age ever did in the world." Here, too, were the lyric first-fruits of his continental tour (if sonnets may, by elasticity of definition, be included in lyric poetry), "The Carillon," "From the Cliffs – Noon," afterwards called "Sea-Limits," "Pax Vobis," largely rewritten later and entitled "World's Worth," and the sonnets on "A Virgin and Child," "A Marriage of St. Katherine," "A Dance of Nymphs" (from Andrea Mantegna, in the Louvre), "A Venetian Pastoral" (from Giorgione, in the Louvre), and "Ruggiero and Angelica" (from the picture by Ingres).

Among other contents of "The Germ" and "Art and Poetry" may be mentioned Ford Madox Brown's paper on "The Structure of an Historical Picture," John Orchard's "Dialogue on Art," and Coventry Patmore's "Criticism of Macbeth." Mr. F.G. Stephens wrote under the pseudonym of "John Seward," and the publication was edited by W.M. Rossetti, then twenty years of age. Yet one more poet remains in the list of contributors, James Collinson, whose somewhat desultory but genuinely imaginative lines, "The Child Jesus: a record typical of the five sorrowful mysteries," together with an etching by the same hand, illustrate very markedly the peculiar phase of religious symbolism, combined with half-ascetic, half-æsthetic melancholy, upon which the Pre-Raphaelites were entering at this period, and which remained with one, at least, of their leaders, as a permanent and dominating element in the artistic work of a lifetime.

But while "The Germ" was speeding through its brief career, and achieving at all events some sort of *apologia* for the Pre-Raphaelite Brotherhood, the leading band of painters were further expressing and developing their principles on canvas. For the Royal Academy Exhibition of 1850, Millais had prepared two pictures destined to draw down upon himself the concentrated fury of that storm of vituperative criticism from the public press which raged unabated for five years around the work of the Brethren, and ultimately spent itself on their more or less worthy disciples and successors. It is remarkable that the chief burden of the abuse heaped upon the Pre-Raphaelites by the art censors of the period should have been borne in the first instance by one, in some respects the most brilliant of the band, who in after years departed more entirely from his early principles in painting than any other member of the Brotherhood, and gained thereby a far greater measure of general popularity than has been won, or is likely to be won at present, by any of his former comrades. Upon no example of Pre-Raphaelite work were the diatribes of the press more scathing than upon Millais's two pictures of 1850, "Christ in the House of His Parents," (often called "The Carpenter's Shop"), and "Ferdinand Lured by Ariel." "Men who knew nothing of art," says a fellow-member of the Brotherhood, Mr. F.G. Stephens, "reviled Millais because he was not of the art, artistic. Dilettanti, who could not draw a fingertip, scolded one of the most accomplished draughtsmen of the age because he delineated what he saw. Cognoscenti, who could not paint, rebuked the most brilliant Gold Medal student of the Royal Academy on account of his technical proceedings. Critics of the most rigid views belaboured and shrieked at an original genius, whose struggles and whose efforts they could not understand. Intolerant and tyrannical commentators condemned the youth of twenty because he dared to think for himself.... Intense and unflinching fidelity to nature, ardent love for colour, and a rigid resolution to paint the light of day as brightly as pigments could allow him, were among the aims of Millais, who, following the principles he championed with all his heart, found his models among his friends of English birth, and failing Eastern types, employed all his skill on British materials, relying on the really devout spirit in which he worked, and the poetic quality of his design, to produce the effect desired. He was sorely disappointed in this reliance." No less sane a journal than Charles Dickens's "Household Words," thus wrote on June 15: – "In coming before this Holy Family you must discharge from your mind all religious aspirations, all elevating thoughts, all tender, awful, sorrowful, ennobling, sacred, graceful, or beautiful associations, and prepare yourself for the lowest depth of what is mean, odious, repulsive, and revolting. You behold the interior of a carpenter's shop. In the foreground is a hideous, wry-necked, blubbering, red-headed boy in a bed-gown, and at his side a kneeling woman so horrible in her ugliness that she would stand out from the rest of the company as a monster in the vilest cabaret in France, or the lowest gin-shop in England. The two almost naked carpenters might be undressed in any hospital where dirty drunkards in a high state of varicose veins are received. Their very toes have walked out of St. Giles's." Another writer likened the figure of the boy Christ, whose hand, in the picture, has been wounded at his task, to "a miserable child scratching itself against a rusty nail in Seven Dials." To such criticism it might easily be retorted that the 77world is more deeply concerned to-day with the dark problems of Seven Dials and St. Giles's than with the life of any child in history, save in so far as the latter may illumine and interpret the mysteries of the importunate hour; and that the painter who so translates into present-day life the eternal tragedy of toil and pain as to press home to the conscience of a nation the daily re-crucifixion of the Christ in its own vast labour-houses, – whose modern reading of the ancient tale suggests the divine potentialities of all childhood and the universal pathos of human love "wounded in the house of friends," – has given us a greater picture, and a more religious picture, than if he had painted for us all the angels in Heaven.

"Ferdinand Lured by Ariel" may be taken as the first landscape produced by the Pre-Raphaelite Brotherhood. It was painted – according to the rule – directly from nature. The background was taken from a spot in a park attached to Shotover House, near Oxford, where Millais was staying as the guest of Mr. Drury. A lady who saw the young artist at work upon this subject distinctly recalls his application of a magnifying-glass to the branch of a tree he was painting, in order to study closely the veins of the leaves. This was a literal following of that patient analysis of minutiæ in nature which characterized the Italian Pre-Raphaelites, and is especially noticeable in the early landscapes of Leonardo da Vinci; though he departed in his maturity from his former love of detail, and began to conventionalize items into generalities. Even the lizards in the foreground of "Ferdinand and Ariel" were faithful portraits of certain small favourites brought by Millais from Jersey to serve their turn among his sitters. The friend who sat for Ferdinand relates that the painting of the face, though a marvel of finish, and perfect in technique, was accomplished in a single sitting. A detailed pencil drawing was already on the canvas, and the laying on of the colour occupied only five hours. The vivid colouring of the whole picture, and the use of metal instead of pigment for the gold-cloth worn by Ferdinand (after the method of the early Italian masters, followed also by Rossetti in "Ecce Ancilla Domini"), were the subject of scarcely less vehement denunciation by the critics than the painter's treatment of the Holy Family. "We do not want," they said, "to see Ariel and the Spirits of the enchanted isle in the attitudes and shapes of green goblins, or the gallant Ferdinand twisted like a posture-master by Albrecht Dürer.... A Ferdinand of most ignoble physiognomy is being lured by a pea-green monster, intended for Ariel, whilst a row of sprites, such as it takes a Millais to devise, watch the operation with turquoise eyes. It would occupy more room than the thing is worth to expose all the absurdity and impertinence of this work."

From such extravagance of hostility the efforts of Holman Hunt were spared for the present; and his contribution to the Academy of 1850, "Christian Priests Escaping from Druid Persecution" (better known as "The Christian Missionary,") though sharing in the general condemnation of the Pre-Raphaelite "heresy and schism," was not singled out for special objurgation. Rossetti's great achievement of the year was the most beautiful, and at the same time the most dramatic, of his strictly Pre-Raphaelite work, the "Ecce Ancilla Domini" ("The Annunciation,") now in the National Gallery. The first rough sketch for this picture – a small water-colour not more than six inches by four – was painted as early as 1847 in the Cleveland Street studio shared with Hunt. The completed work was rejected by the Academy, and seen only in the obscure little Portland Gallery in Regent Street.

But the following season brought a larger measure of opprobrium to Holman Hunt. In the autumn of 1850 he had spent some weeks with Rossetti at Sevenoaks, Kent, and there painted the greater portion of his picture for the next year's Academy, "Valentine rescuing Sylvia from Proteus;" a scene from Shakespeare's "Two Gentlemen of Verona." The beech-tree forest background was painted in Lord Amherst's park at Knowle, and Mr. James Lennox Hannay (who died in 1873) was the model for Valentine. The whole work was characterized by the same bold colouring and exuberance of highly wrought detail, the same rugged unconventionality of pose and gesture in the composition of the figures, that had so incensed the organs of Academic tradition in the previous year. Its appearance in the Academy of 1851 evoked a fresh outburst of official contumely, in which the painter of "Valentine and Sylvia" (as it was ultimately called), was no less severely dealt with than his comrade Millais, who exhibited at the same time "The Return of the Dove to the Ark,"

"Mariana of the Moated Grange," and "The Woodman's Daughter" – one of the finest combinations of Pre-Raphaelite landscape with the peculiar intensity of figure-drawing and character-study which was a dominant motive with the Brotherhood at this period. The assailant critics again sought to cover insinuations of gracelessness and deformity of conception beneath the looser charge of defective technique.

It was at this juncture that Mr. Ruskin, then personally unknown to the Pre-Raphaelites, and hearing privately of their aims and endeavours through Mr. Coventry Patmore, took upon himself to espouse their cause, perhaps with more ardour than discrimination, and wrote, in the spring of 1851, the now famous Letters to the "Times" which constituted the first public and authoritative vindication of the Pre-Raphaelite movement.

That Mr. Ruskin may have taken the early achievement and promise of the young painters a little too seriously, and attributed to them a more exalted conception of their mission as prophets and reformers than they actually cherished, and that he did undoubtedly misinterpret certain aspects of their religious paintings, is now widely acknowledged; nor need we hesitate to say that his influence upon the movement from first to last has been considerably exaggerated. Yet it is unquestionable that the first inspiration of Pre-Raphaelitism was largely due to his writings, and that his open championship of Hunt and Millais at a crisis of popular feeling rendered immense service to their crusade against the blind Philistinism of the British *bourgeoisie*. Replying at once to the technical indictments, Mr. Ruskin said: – "There was not a single error in perspective in three out of the four pictures in question ['The Woodman's Daughter,' 'Mariana of the Moated Grange,' 'The Return of the Dove to the Ark,' and 'Valentine and Sylvia'].… I doubt if, with the exception of the pictures of David Roberts, there were one architectural drawing in perspective on the walls of the Academy; I never met with but two men in my life who knew enough of perspective to draw a Gothic arch in a retiring plane, so that its lateral dimensions and curvatures might be calculated to scale from the drawing. Our architects certainly do not, and it was but the other day that, talking to one of the most distinguished among them, I found he actually did not know how to draw a circle in perspective.... There is not a single study of drapery in the whole Academy, be it in large works or small, which for perfect truth, power, and finish, could be compared with the black sleeve of Julia, or with the velvet on the breast and the chain mail of Valentine, of Mr. Hunt's picture; or with the white draperies on the table of Mr. Millais's 'Mariana.' And further: that as studies both of drapery and of every minor detail, there has been nothing in art so earnest or so complete as these pictures since the days of Albrecht Dürer. This I assert generally and fearlessly." "Let us only look around at our exhibitions," – continued the writer, proceeding to compare the work of the Pre-Raphaelites with the current standard of academic art – "and behold the cattle-pieces, and sea-pieces, and fruit-pieces, and family-pieces, the eternal brown cows in ditches, and white sails in squalls, and sliced lemons in saucers, and foolish faces in simpers, and try and feel what we are, and what we might have been."

Mr. Ruskin's letters to the "Times" were revised and republished a few years later in pamphlet form, introduced by the following statement in the preface: – "Eight years ago, in the close of the first volume of 'Modern Painters,' I ventured to give this advice to the young artists of England: That they should go to Nature in all singleness of heart, and walk with her, laboriously and trustingly, having no other thought but how best to penetrate her meaning; rejecting nothing, selecting nothing, and scorning nothing: advice which, whether bad or good, involved infinite labour and humiliation in the following it; and was therefore, for the most part, rejected. It has, however, at last been carried out, to the very letter, by a group of men who, for their reward, have been assailed with the most scurrilous abuse which I ever recollect seeing issue from the public press."

Upon this endorsement of the Pre-Raphaelite aim there

followed an indictment of the Raphaelesque tradition still surviving in the training-schools of British art, in a passage which, through much quotation, has now become a familiar example of the controversial literature of the Pre-Raphaelite movement. "We begin," said Mr. Ruskin, "in all probability, by telling the youth of fifteen or sixteen that Nature is full of faults, and that he is to improve her; but that Raphael is perfection, and that the more he copies Raphael the better; that after much copying of Raphael he is to try what he can do himself in a Raphaelesque but yet original manner; that is to say, he is to try to do something very clever, all out of his own head, but yet this clever something is to be properly subjected to Raphaelesque rules, is to have a principal light, occupying one-seventh of its space, and a principal shadow, occupying one-third of the same; that no two people's heads in the picture are to be turned the same way, and that all the personages represented are to possess ideal beauty of the highest order, which ideal beauty consists partly in a Greek outline of nose, partly in proportions expressible in decimal fractions between the lips and the chin; but partly also in that degree of improvement which the youth of sixteen is to bestow upon God's work in general."

It is not difficult to trace, in the light of those utterances, the point of departure between Mr. Ruskin and the Pre-Raphaelites in their conception of that universe of Nature which they had studied with the like faithful care. Revolting from the quasi-perfection of Raphaelesque art, Ruskin had thrown himself upon Nature with the confidence of finding in her the absolute perfection vainly sought in the work of man. He had embraced without question the monistic theory of Nature as essentially beneficent and beautiful, and had never faced the principal of dualism which has been and must yet remain the crux of modern philosophy. Hence he failed to grasp the more romantic and subtle conception of the physical world as the scene, and not the drama, of life, which was immanent in the beginnings and revealed with the maturity of the Pre-Raphaelite movement. It has been remarked by an astute critic that three of the greatest writers of the Victorian age – Ruskin, Carlyle, and Browning – have been ruined as thinkers by their ignorance of the law of Evolution, with all that it implies of waste and suffering, of sacrifice and conflict and loss. Ruskin's philosophy of nature was founded upon an old and discredited cosmogony; and however remote may have been the thought of the Pre-Raphaelite painters from the purely intellectual conclusions of physical and mental science in the nineteenth century, however apart they may have lived from theological and ethical controversy, it can safely be said that no contemporary artist save Tennyson, in poetry or painting, has imbibed more completely that spirit of mystical and irresponsible conflict with Nature which they drew from the atmosphere of mediæval romance. They understood that he who returns to Nature, returns, as another writer has bluntly expressed it, to a great many ugly things. "We need," says Mr. Frederic Harrison, "as little think the natural world all beauty as think it all horror. It is made up of loveliness and ghastliness, of harmony and chaos, of agony, joy, life, death. The nature-worshippers are blind and deaf to the waste and the shrieks which meet the seeker after truth. What a mass there is in Nature which is appalling – almost maddening to man, if we coolly resolve to look at all the facts, as facts!"[*3] It was well that the Pre-Raphaelite painters should return, as they did, to the reverent and unbiassed portrayal of the natural world as it presented itself to their eyes. That they should follow with absolute fidelity the phenomena around them, "rejecting nothing, selecting nothing, and scorning nothing," was the essential preparation for artistic reform. But that they should advance from such a discipline to something of the selectiveness of fine art, was a step from the analytic method to a constructive effort based on that analysis and not – as in the Raphaelesque convention – independent of it. In all the highest Pre-Raphaelite work we feel instinctively that Nature is not the subject, but only the accessory, of the painting. Undoubtedly the new note struck in 1849 was, as Ruskin says, a note of resistance and defiance. But the revolutionary impulse had yet to be developed on reconstructive lines; and this development, though powerfully stimulated by the independent genius of Millais in the first four years of the Brotherhood, passed ultimately into the hands of Rossetti and Holman Hunt.

But Ruskin's championship of Hunt and Millais when the powers of orthodoxy were against them and their friends were few, and his no less generous patronage of Rossetti in the succeeding years, did much to turn the current of critical favour in the direction of the Pre-Raphaelite ideal. Hunt's picture, "Valentine and Sylvia," after its merciless ordeal of ridicule and abuse in London, was rewarded by a £50 prize at the Academy of Liverpool, – the first English city to give public recognition and support to the rising school. The story of the steadfast encouragement accorded to the Pre-Raphaelites by the Liverpool Academy during the next six years, in which the annual prize of £50 was granted in every instance to pictures either by Millais, Holman Hunt, Ford Madox Brown, or a painter of kindred aims – Mark Anthony, – and of the dissensions which arose in and round the Academic Council when in 1857 the prize was once more won by Millais, affords an interesting side light upon the artistic controversy of the period. A leading literary newspaper attacked the Liverpool Academy in the bitterest terms for what it called "the Pre-Raphaelite heresy," and Mr. Ruskin again came forward in the press to the defence of the painters. In the following year another nomination of Madox Brown by the Council for the award in question brought the strife to a crisis; the Town Council withdrew its financial support from the Academy, and rival exhibitions were opened, resulting in failure on both sides. Time, however, worked a significant revenge. Not long after the press attack upon the Academy Council, one of the original members of the Pre-Raphaelite Brotherhood, Mr. F.G. Stephens, was appointed art-critic of the very journal that had so violently forsworn "the Pre-Raphaelite heresy." Twenty years later, the finest English art gallery outside London was erected in Liverpool through the munificence of Mr. (afterwards Sir) A.B. Walker, recently deceased; and yielded some of the most important spaces on its walls to pictures of the highest level of the English Pre-Raphaelite school.

The history of the last two decades has indeed wrought a sufficient vindication of the general methods of these young painters, and supremely of their practice as colourists; and it is in the sphere of the colourist that their influence upon contemporary art has made itself felt more deeply, perhaps, than in any other branch of technique. But to the vindication of history has been added in recent years, by the painter most bitterly attacked at the time for his innovations in colour – Sir John Millais – a defence which has now become almost an aphorism in English studios. "*Time* and *Varnish* are two of the greatest Old Masters," says the artist, writing in 1888 under the title "Some Thoughts on our Art of To-day"; "and their merits are too often attributed by critics to the painters of the pictures they have toned and mellowed. The great artists all painted in *bright* colours, such as it is the fashion now-a-days for men to decry as crude and vulgar, never suspecting that what they applaud in those works is merely the result of what they condemn in their contemporaries. The only way to judge of the treasures which the old masters of whatever age have left us, is to look at the work and ask oneself 'What was that like when it was new?' Take the 'Bacchus and Ariadne' in the National Gallery, with its splendid red robe and its rich brown grass. You may rest assured that the painter of that red robe never painted the grass brown. He saw the colour as it was and painted it as it was – distinctly green; only it has faded with time to its present beautiful mellow colour. Yet many men now-a-days will not have a picture with green in it; some even going so far, in giving a commission, as to stipulate that the canvas shall contain none of it. But God Almighty has given us green, and you may depend upon it, it's a fine colour."[*4]

The writer then describes the gradual fall of Sir Joshua Reynolds before the short-sighted demand for "subdued colour" which had become current among the art *connoisseurs* of his day, and which at last induced him, against his better judgment, to create immediate "tone," at the sacrifice of durability, by the use of that pernicious medium, asphaltum; with the result that all his extant work so accomplished is now in a deplorable state of decomposition and ruin.

With such examples before them of the evil of yielding to the demands of ignorance, and lowering in any way one's standard of practice before a popular cry, the Pre-Raphaelite Brothers, whose first word in art sounded, as Ruskin said, the note of resistance and defiance, did not scruple to make merry over the weaknesses of a school of painting founded on Sir Joshua Reynold's "Discourses." Mr. Madox Brown tells us how Rossetti loved to quote from the diary of B.R. Haydon: – "Locked my door and dashed at my picture with a brush dripping with asphaltum." But of Rossetti's cordial admiration for Haydon's genius a contrasting anecdote is evidence: – A friend, discussing with him the relative merits of Haydon and Wilkie, contended that the head of Lazarus was the only fine thing Haydon ever produced. "Ah!" burst out Rossetti, "but that one head is worth all the puny Wilkie ever produced in his life!"

Rossetti's practice, it may here be said, differed from that of his Pre-Raphaelite comrades in the matter of varnish. The strong impulse towards the fresco-method, which was initiated in him, in his student days, by Madox Brown and the Westminster Cartoon competitions, resulted in his avoidance, throughout the best years of his work, of glaze and sheen in painting. From the first, Rossetti hated varnish: hence were developed the fresco-like, pure, and lustreless depths of colour which mark his finest technical level. But his entire confidence in the "Old Master," Time, to enhance and vindicate his rich green glories in drapery and background is sufficiently attested by his unhesitating and masterly use of green in nearly all his greatest pictures. Not even the verdant gorgeousness of "Ferdinand and Ariel" can compare with the deep, chastened splendour of the green in "Beata

Beatrix" and "Mnemosyne," or in "The Beloved," "Veronica Veronese," "La Ghirlandata," "The Blue Bower," or, more daring still, in the wonderful series of water-colours which occupy the transition period of Rossetti's Pre-Raphaelite work.

CHAPTER IV

PERIOD OF TRANSITION

Influence of Browning and Tennyson – Comparison of Rossetti and Browning – Influence of Dante – Introduction to Miss Siddal – Rossetti's Water-colours – Madox Brown and Romantic Realism – The Dispersal of the Brotherhood – Departure of Woolner – Ideals of Portraiture – Rossetti and Public Exhibitions – Death of Deverell – Rossetti's Friendship with Ruskin – Apostasy of Millais – The Rank and File of the Movement – Relation to Foreign Schools.

While Millais and Holman Hunt were outwardly dominant in the region of reform, and, in the exhibitions of 1850–51, were leading the Brotherhood Militant boldly into the enemy's camp, Rossetti was entering upon a phase of doubt and perplexity, of self-distrust and hesitation, which resolved itself into an important crisis in his artistic development. A variety of circumstances diverted him in 1850 from the special line of religious painting, exemplified in "The Girlhood of Mary Virgin" and "Ecce Ancilla Domini," which had been the chief outlet of his early enthusiasms in art, – if indeed so inadequate a phrase be permissible in regard to pictures which must rank with the purest products of his genius in its pristine robustness and simplicity. An incident in the studio-annals of the Brotherhood now turned him aside from the mediævo-religious manner adopted directly and literally from the early Italian masters. Rossetti's convert and disciple, James Collinson, striving to imitate afar off the sincere habit of his leader, set to work upon a congruous subject, "The Renunciation of St. Elizabeth," and produced a picture so mystical in conception and so hysterical in sentiment, albeit not without a certain grace and beauty of its own, that the sound and practical good sense which tempered the mysticism of Rossetti revolted at once from the extravagance of such a style. He now perceived the danger of pursuing too exclusively a path bordering on the metaphysical and occult, and quickly sought to brace and strengthen both his own imagination and that of his comrade, by departing for a time from the field of what is commonly called "sacred" art, and seeking fresh inspirations in a less rarefied air.

Other influences, chiefly of a personal kind, began to play around Rossetti at this time. He had moved, early in the year 1850, to a suite of rooms at 14, Chatham Place, Blackfriars; a block of houses since demolished, but then hospitable enough in a sober charm of environment; within view of the river and the historic horizon of its shores, and of certain grim but not wholly unromantic vistas of the great metropolis. In this home was spent the happiest decade of Rossetti's life. Here began, soon after his settlement in the new abode, his friendship with the greatest poet of the Victorian age, and with another conspicuous in the second rank of its singers, – Tennyson and Browning, – both destined to exercise a strong influence on Rossetti's art, though (singularly as it happened) not on his poetry; which remained, through years of intellectual intercourse and the reading together of each other's verse, absolutely unaffected by either of the widely different poetic styles of the then Laureate and his great contemporary.

It is not easy for a succeeding generation to understand with what enthusiasm, with what delight and invigoration, the little company of painter-poets plunged into the writings of Browning when, following Rossetti, who was first on the track of the new fount of refreshment, they discovered therein the tonic which they needed. No better antidote to the sensuous mysticism into which some of the Pre-Raphaelites were threatening to lapse could have been found than the wholesome modernity and salutary brusquerie of the author of "Pauline" and "Bells and Pomegranates." It was probably because they stood most in need of his gospel that the influence of Browning was at first more strong upon the readers than that of Tennyson, who affected them in the direction of pure romance, and distilled for them all that was sanest and noblest in the mediæval world.

In the autumn of 1850 Rossetti began, during his stay with Hunt and F.G. Stephens at Sevenoaks, a number of sketches with a view to a large and elaborate picture of "Kate the Queen," from Browning's well-known lyric. But he could never satisfy himself with the design, and after much toil, disheartenment, and perplexity, the subject was abandoned, like many more promising themes which from time to time inspired Rossetti. The entire year, save for the success of "Ecce Ancilla Domini," had been one of disappointment to him, and of disconsolate struggles for a new departure. He had made many futile attempts at designs for "The Germ," but none pleased him, and now he was casting about for new matter and media. For, as his standard of excellence rose higher, he began to feel more acutely his technical shortcomings, – the results partly of his incomplete training and desultory study in youth, partly of singular ill-luck in his figure-models, and partly also of a curious constitutional deficiency – not of industry *per se*, but of the faculty to direct and apply his industry along right lines. No modern artist has disproved more completely than Rossetti the barren platitude which defines genius as "the capacity for taking infinite pains." Comparison between Rossetti and Browning in their struggle with mental tendencies unfavourable to lucid and well-ordered art is too obvious to demand pursuit in detail. Both took the prescribed "infinite pains," but neither in the most profitable directions. Browning was over-charged with thought; Rossetti with imagination; and both were cumbered with the difficulties of artistic speech. The art of Browning has frequently been pronounced crude, raw, and "undigested." One would hesitate to apply such terms to any work of Rossetti's; for his, even at its most elemental stages, generally erred in the direction of strained and laboured purism, being over-wrought rather than unripe in conception or performance. In both artists, an exuberant activity of output was combined with a curious inability to undergo the full discipline of just and coherent expression. Browning's prolific and incorrigible chaos of diction and metre, and Rossetti's want of balance and sobriety in draughtsmanship, are but instances of the too frequent impediments of genius in the process of transmission. Rossetti, when he attained perfection in technique – and that he did so absolutely and repeatedly can no longer be questioned – seemed to stumble on it, as we have already suggested, by a sort of exquisite chance, a divine surprise, rather than a logical issue. And, manfully as he strove to recover in technical science, and did indeed recover to a marvellous degree, the lost ground of early days in a splendid maturity, his sense of perfect drawing was too fine for him not to suffer keenly – so long as that sense remained unimpaired – from that inability to realize at will his own ideals of perfection, which to every true worker is the only thing to be called failure.

Distracted as Rossetti was throughout his life by the very richness and fertility of his own genius, torn ever between divided aims and conflicting purposes, the more mutually obstructive because of the restless and hyper-sensitive nature which was the field and victim of their strife, the difficulty of concentrating that genius upon the highest aim and purpose within its proper sphere was never more stubborn than at this period. So largely did the poetic impulse, in his youth, predominate over the pictorial method, that, as he himself declares in a letter written in retrospect, it was not until 1853, when he was twenty-five years of age, that he definitely adopted painting as his life-study and profession, and relegated his literary efforts to a subordinate place. Subordinate they were in name and for a time only: to be put forth with fresh ardour and greater mastery at intervals of his painting, and to surpass it in some respects in the essentials of fine art. Rossetti had yet to learn that he, even more than Hunt and Millais, was primarily and supremely a colourist in the broadest sense of the word.

But a still deeper and more abiding influence from the literature of the past was by this time ascendant in Rossetti's mind. The love of Dante, already inherent in him, was nurtured by many tender associations of youth: it now increased and swayed him as a direct and urgent spiritual power. In 1845 the vague spell of the old name upon the young namesake had changed, for the latter, into an eager study of his great poetic inheritance. The magic and majestic visions of the "Purgatorio" and "Paradiso," and still more, the unforgettable life-tragedy of their seer, had sunk deeply into Rossetti's thought, until, from his own recreative alembic of fantasy, he began, about 1850, to bring them forth again on paper and canvas, in a rich and profuse miscellany of rough sketches and brilliant vignettes and colour-studies, too often left unfinished at a point of high promise and alluring suggestions of success.

It is not difficult to trace, through the strange parallels of circumstance and destiny, the sombre charm that bound the exiled poet of the fourteenth to him of the nineteenth century. It has been said that no ascendancy of a great poetic personality over one born in a later age has been more potent and fruitful in art than that of Dante Alighieri over Dante Gabriel Rossetti. In 1849–50 we find the latter sketching, first in ink and then in colours, the historic or legendary meeting of Dante and Beatrice Portinari at a marriage feast, when Beatrice is said to have laughed with her companions at the shyness and confusion of the young patriot-guest. The second of these sketches was severely criticised when exhibited in 1851–52, on account of a daring juxtaposition of bright light green and bright light blue in the colour scheme. This bold experiment was afterwards defended by

Ruskin by analogy with the natural disposition of green grass, etc., against a summer sky.

It was at this time also that another new and important personal influence came upon Rossetti's life. James Collinson had now separated from the Brotherhood, and was succeeded, at all events probationally, by Walter Howell Deverell, through whom, by one of those strange chances which sometimes modify in a moment the destinies of a lifetime, Rossetti made the acquaintance of Miss Elizabeth Eleanor Siddal; a young girl of such remarkable beauty that Deverell at once asked her to sit to him as a model, and introduced her to Rossetti for the same purpose. The story runs to the effect that Deverell, who was himself of singularly handsome and winning presence, accidentally caught sight of Miss Siddal's face, with its regular, delicate features and profusion of rich, dark auburn hair, in the background of a shop-window where she – the daughter of a Sheffield cutler – was engaged as a milliner's assistant. To Deverell, being at that time in search of a model for his new picture, "Viola," from Shakespeare's "Twelfth Night," the sight of such a face was doubly welcome. He quickly made such frank and honourable advances as his graces of person and character facilitated, and Miss Siddal's *début* in the studios of the Brotherhood brought not only to Deverell a perfect Viola, but to Rossetti an ideal and actual Beatrice. For the young artists soon found their model to be – in the old fairy-tale phrase – "as good as she was beautiful." Of that goodness and beauty, that incomparable charm of talent and of character, of manner and temperament, which soon made her the centre of the warmest admiration and affection, enough has long since been written, by those who knew her, to render the tardy praise of less qualified historians alike needless and impertinent. The members of the Brotherhood vied with each other in the endeavour to immortalize her in their paintings. Rossetti, Hunt, and Millais did so with unqualified success. Rossetti, in his turn, discovered that she herself possessed extraordinary aptitude for art. He gave her lessons in drawing and painting, and the two worked together upon kindred ideals. Her presence in the studios was soon upon the footing of equal friendship and pleasant *cameraderie*. The vigour of her imagination is best seen in a water-colour drawing, "Sir Patrick Spens," in Mr. Theodore Watts's collection. It represents the wives of the men on the doomed ship waiting in agonized expectancy upon the shore.

Soon a different and deeper attachment sprang up between teacher and pupil. Her exquisite spirit, her gracious ways, appealed as deeply to Rossetti's sensitive and passionate nature as did her beauty to his æsthetic judgment. His love for her was as the gathering up of all the scattered forces of his being into one consecrated worship. It may well be that the progress of courtship was not invariably favourable to the progress of art, but several rough portraits by Rossetti of himself and Miss Siddal, and of Rossetti by his fair companion, remain as pleasant witnesses of idle hours, and are at the same time drawn with singular vividness and force.

Early in 1851, or perhaps at the close of the previous year, Miss Siddal appears to have given sittings to Holman Hunt for the face of Sylvia in his picture of "Valentine and Sylvia," already referred to. Rossetti sat with her as the Jester in Walter Deverell's "Viola" – his most successful picture; taken from the scene in which the Duke asks the Jester to "sing again that antique song he sang last night." The artist served as his own model for the Duke.

It appears probable that Rossetti and Miss Siddal were engaged as early as 1853, though the relationship was not openly avowed for a considerable period, and did not terminate in marriage until 1860. Rossetti's pecuniary position, at the outset of his career, was naturally uncertain; nor did it materially improve with subsequent prosperity and fame; for his tastes and habits, according to the traditions of artistic Bohemia, were as luxurious and improvident as his earnings were precarious. Miss Siddal, too, was delicate in health. An early sketch of her, from Rossetti's hand, and now in the South Kensington Museum, representing her as she stands by a window, in a gown of quaint simplicity and soberness, gives perhaps the truest impression of her personality that could be selected from the portraits of that period. The artless and yet somewhat austere pose, the fragile grace and slightly languid sweetness of aspect, afford a key to the criticism once passed to the effect that "she would have been a Puritan if she had not been an invalid." The latter she never was in the sense of chronic inactivity, but of such delicacy as to give a peculiar tenderness to her service as a model, and unhappily both to delay and abbreviate the short period of married life.

To some critics it has been a source of regret that Rossetti should have come in youth so unreservedly under the spell of a type of beauty as exclusive as that of this well-beloved model. The rare blending of spiritual with sensuous charm which she presented in feature and expression so fully satisfied his own ideal of that harmony as to make him dwell upon, and perhaps specialize it, in a way which constituted a danger to his art; inducing him to read into other feminine types the individual characteristics of the one. Fortunate as he was in after life in obtaining for his models some of the most beautiful and cultured women in the artistic and literary circles of London, his tendency was almost always to look at them, as it were, in the light of that established ideal, and to conceive them as versions merely of that elemental loveliness which so dominated his thought. But it was inevitable that a temperament like Rossetti's should specialize, through their very intensity, the dominant characteristics most familiar to his pencil and his brush. The case of Miss Herbert, an accomplished actress who gave him a number of sittings in the next decade, is perhaps the most striking exception to the rule; but her style of beauty was in too complete a contrast to that of Miss Siddal (being of a severe, robust, and Hellenic type) to allow of any compromise between the features of the two.

The combined influence of Browning and Tennyson among contemporary poets, and the increasing sway of Dante over the young painter, inclining him the more strongly in the direction of historic romance, produced, as we have seen, a somewhat desultory course of pen-and-ink sketches and water-colour studies during the next few years. The interval from 1850 to 1858 may be reckoned as Rossetti's second period. After the completion of "Ecce Ancilla Domini," he painted no important oil picture until the Llandaff "Triptych" of 1859, and the contemporary "Bocca Baciata," which stands first in point of time, and high in point of merit, among the masterpieces of his maturity.

Yet the water-colours of the second period, capricious and experimental in treatment as many of them are, include some of the most valuable, because the most characteristic and significant, of Rossetti's work in the realm of pure romance. In these rough and often hasty sketches, sometimes less than twelve by twenty inches in size, his imagination seems to have been exercising itself upon the poetic subjects that haunted him by turns with the vividness of actual life, more vital and urgent than the realities of every day. Several, indeed, of the finest of these water-colours are now dated, on good authority, as early as 1848–49; such as the lovely little sepia sketch, "The Sun may Shine and we be cold," given to his friend, Alexander Monro, a young Scottish sculptor of high promise, whose early death from consumption removed an artist who could ill be spared from the small and never very strong sculpture-branch of the Pre-Raphaelite movement. To this period also belong some of the most important of the Dante subjects. From 1849 is dated "A Parable of Love," one of the best of Rossetti's early drawings in pen and ink. The lady is seated at an easel on which she has been painting her own portrait from a mirror at her side. Her lover, bending over her from behind, lays his hand upon hers to guide the brush anew. Mr. Woolner served as the model for the lover. A pen-drawing from Browning's "Sordello," entitled "Taurello's First Sight of Fortune," also belongs to 1849, together with the powerful little sketch, "The Laboratory," from the same poet, showing a strange, brilliant, witch-like or almost serpent-like woman in an alchemist's shop, procuring from him some fateful elixir wherewith to play upon her rival and avenge herself upon the lover, once her own.

One of the most beautiful water-colours of 1850 is the "Morning Music;" a dainty little half-length figure of a white-clad girl seated at her toilet, another maiden brushing her long bright hair, while her lover stands, making music from some archaic instrument, at her side. At this time also Rossetti made the first sketch of a subject which fascinated him with peculiar force almost throughout his artistic career, and to which he returned again and again in several media, even within a short time of his death, but without ever achieving a finished picture – "Michael Scott's Wooing."

In 1851 were made the best of several water-colour drawings from the subject of "Lucretia Borgia," and the first pen and pencil sketches of a subject suggested by the famous Döppelgänger legends of northern Europe. The design for "How they met themselves" remains among the very highest of Rossetti's conceptions in pure romance. The final pen-and-ink version was not done till 1860, nor the water-colour till 1864. The subject demands further study in a separate chapter, together with the principal Dante sketches in this group. Several drawings from Shakespearean subjects, including "Benedick and Beatrice" ("Much Ado about Nothing") and "Orlando and Adam in the Forest" ("As You Like It"), were also executed about this time.

Mr. F.G. Stephens traces some interesting modifications of Rossetti's technique between the years 1850 and 1853 to the influence of his comrades in the course of associated work. From Millais he seems to have gained something of the easy grace and suavity of style which was lacking in his first too strenuous work; from Holman Hunt, the scrupulous and laboured detail which readily became as exhaustively (and sometimes exhaustingly) symbolic as Hunt's own; and from Ford Madox Brown a certain robust breadth and dramatic mastery which was needed to lift his subjective creations into a large and quickening atmosphere. Probably it was the influence of Madox Brown that led him to the field of stern and practical social problems, of everyday romance;

to deal with the eternally crucial relationship of frail womanhood to passionate manhood, and all its sweet and bitter and profound significance upon the life of humanity, as he dealt with it in the wonderful "Hesterna Rosa" ("Yesterday's Rose") of 1851, in "The Gate of Memory" six years later, and in the great realistic picture, "Found," which was begun in 1852, but which, after many vicissitudes of neglect, spasmodic effort, and frequent despair, remained still unfinished at the painter's death. It may be wished that Rossetti had pursued more thoroughly the *motif* which thus yielded some of the most remarkable and suggestive of his designs. This group, however, again affords a subject for consideration on a future page.

But the year 1853 saw also the first outward signs of the breaking-up of the Pre-Raphaelite Brotherhood. Thomas Woolner, the oldest member of the Brotherhood, at this time twenty-eight years of age, being still unable to earn a living in London by his art, now determined to emigrate to Australia, where some friends of his family were already established at Melbourne, and to try his luck at the gold-diggings, which were at that time a source of much excitement and speculation in English circles. Woolner had already achieved some unpretentious but exceedingly thoughtful and conscientious work in sculpture, but he had not met with much academic recognition, nor with any substantial favour from the art-patronising public. For many years a pupil of Behnes, he entered the Academy Schools in 1842, and contributed a large composition of life-size figures representing "The Death of Boadicea" to the Westminster Cartoon Competition of 1844. His contributions to the Royal Academy exhibitions in Trafalgar Square had included "Eleanor Sucking the Poison from the Wound of Prince Edward" (1843), "Alastor" (from Shelley, 1846), "Feeding the Hungry" (bas-relief, 1847), "Eros and Euphrosyne" and "The Rainbow" (1848), and portraits of Carlyle and Tennyson. At the British Institution he had also exhibited a statuette of "Puck" (1847) and "Titania Caressing the Indian Boy" (1848). He sailed for Australia in the spring of 1853, accompanied by a promising young sculptor named Bernhard Smith (who died somewhat prematurely in 1885), and followed shortly afterwards by E.L. Bateman, another close sympathizer with Pre-Raphaelite aims. Woolner returned to England early in 1857, and then executed the fine bust of Tennyson recently placed in Poets' Corner, Westminster Abbey. His later work, however, can hardly be classed with that of the Pre-Raphaelite band. He died on the 7th of October, 1892.

In the summer of the same year the Brethren agreed to paint together a group of their own portraits, in order to send them over as a gift to their distant comrade on the gold-fields of the Antipodes. Accordingly, they met one day at Millais's studio in Gower Street. There were present Dante and W.M. Rossetti, F.G. Stephens, Millais, and Holman Hunt. Mr. W.M. Rossetti, ranks the results in the following order of merit: – The portrait of Stephens by Millais, of Millais by Hunt, of W.M. Rossetti by Millais, of Dante Rossetti by Hunt, and of Hunt by Dante Rossetti.

Rossetti himself, as we have already seen, produced but very few male portraits. The large oil-painting of his godfather, Mr. Charles Lyell, and the pencil drawings of his father and grandfather; the water-colour sketches of Browning and Swinburne, and the admirable life-size chalks of Mr. Ruskin, Mr. Theodore Watts (said by Mr. Swinburne to be his masterpiece in portraiture), Mr. F.R. Leyland, Dr. Gordon Hake, Mr. George Hake, and Mr. W.J. Stillman, two or three pencil drawings of Madox Brown, and the painting of Holman Hunt, as above recorded, seem to exhaust the list of his efforts in that field, if we exclude the consideration of many excellent likenesses which occur among his *genre*-pictures. W.M. Rossetti, for instance, sat more than once to his brother for the head of Dante, and many other important figures; in fact, there was a general practice of mutual accommodation among the Brothers in serving as models one to another.

Yet the immense influence of the Pre-Raphaelite movement upon English portraiture in the latter half of the nineteenth century would be difficult to over-estimate. It must be remembered that the first principle of Pre-Raphaelitism – namely, that nature, including human nature, is to be painted truthfully and unflinchingly as it presents itself to the painter's eye – strikes directly at the root of the conventional habit, which aimed at "idealizing" the subject into something far superior to the present reality. Still, as "the eye sees what it brings the power to see," so the rightly-trained artist sees infinitely more than the casual observer, and his purest realism becomes the highest ideality. For in order to represent nature truly, something more is demanded than imitation. Diderot tells a story of a painter well known to him and to fame, who, on beginning work upon a new subject, always went down upon his knees and prayed to be delivered from the model. There was a grain of truth in his notion. To be delivered from the letter in order to apprehend the spirit, yet to follow faithfully the visible in order to attain the invisible, is the task of the portrait-painter. The mistake of the pseudo-classic idealists, as of the impractical folk in other walks of life, is to suppose that by aiming at the spirit they are absolved from the letter altogether; not perceiving that to gain the spirit they must reach *through* the letter, and *beyond* it. Every true portrait-painter is an idealist in this highest sense, that he perceives and reproduces the inmost and essential Self of his sitter, and in supreme moments resolves, as Spinoza would have it, the "potential human" into the "actual divine." He portrays scrupulously the outward aspect, but interprets the whole by that pervading spirit from within to which the outward aspect has given him – as a seer – the key. The face he paints is not transfigured by his own imagination, his own conceit, however fair, of what that face might or ought to be; but it is revealed in its own distinct and actual being by a witness which, if truthful, must be as generous as stern. It is the immortal and inevitable "Thou Thyself" of which Rossetti sings:

"I am Thyself – what hast thou done to me?

– And Thou Thyself to all eternity!"

Yet if we may risk a paradox, it is precisely in the *reality* that there lies the *potentiality* of the life within; behind the physical *is* abides the spiritual *may be*; the "everlasting no" of the uncompromising realist, sifting, limiting, and analyzing down the human unit into bare and rigid matter, often conceals the hidden hope and promise of the idealist's "everlasting yea." Hence a great portrait is charged to the full with latent possibilities of character and destiny. It suggests forces as well as phenomena, causes as well as effects, inherent tendencies as well as facts. Someone has said that a human face should be either a promise or a history. The definition is too narrow. Every face, save perhaps in childhood, and not always with that exception, contains both promise and history inextricably blended each with each. A great portrait must be passionately personal, intensely individual; presenting one single, complete, and separate identity to the eye and mind, and yet in a very real sense *im*personal, having a certain universal, humanitarian significance. For the artist's hand sets the human unit in its place in the great Family; lifts it on to the broad planes of the world's common life. As his eye sees all things, like Spinoza, *sub specie eternitatis* – sees Time in the light of Eternity – so it sees one Man in the light of Humanity. He knows no isolations of being, conceives no man as "living to himself;" but is concerned ever with relationships and imperative sympathies between the subject of his portrait and the rest of mankind; so that the personality that looks forth from his canvas, faithfully and profoundly interpreted by his own, has in it the elements of appeal and challenge, and sends out a radiance of vitality to its spiritual kin.

In this ideal of portraiture the young Pre-Raphaelites had been confirmed by Ruskin long ago; and he had pointed them to the incomparable portraits of Dante by Giotto, of Petrarch by Simon Memmi, and of Savonarola by Fra Bartolomeo, as examples among the Italian Pre-Raphaelites of the attainment of such success. Rossetti and his comrades in their turn, more especially some of the younger and more independent spirits not actually or permanently connected with the Brotherhood, developed and perfected the ideal to a degree incalculably fruitful in contemporary art. It will hardly be disputed that in Mr. G.F. Watts, one of the truest Pre-Raphaelites in aspiration and temper, though utterly distinct from them in original genius and intellectual range, England has found at last her greatest portrait painter, while to Millais, one of the original members of the Brotherhood, the judgment of posterity will attribute a scarcely less exalted place. They found the art of portraiture degraded, almost without exception, to the lowest level of trivial prettiness as regards women, and vulgar affectation in dealing with men. "The system to be overthrown," as Ruskin said, "was one of which the main characteristic was the pursuit of beauty at the expense of truth." And such pursuit leads in all ages to the same inexorable fatality, – the beauty so gained is always of a false and spurious kind. The ancient allegory of Pandemos and Urania is for ever true in art. The seeker for ideal beauty seeks it only in visible forms, pursues it through the physical world alone, awaits it at the doors of sense merely, and is straightway ensnared by the earthly Pandemos, the Venus of the flesh. But let him steadfastly set his soul to the higher worship, let him seek reverently the moral and spiritual loveliness of human character in the great *is* and the greater *may be* of the throbbing, actual life around him, and surely he will be brought into the near presence of the heavenly Urania; surely he will pass, with Rossetti, through "Body's Beauty" to "Soul's Beauty," and worship with him

> – "that Lady Beauty in whose praise
> Thy voice and hand shake still, – long known to thee
>   By flying hair and fluttering hem, – the beat
>   Following her daily of thy heart and feet,
> How passionately and irretrievably,
> In what fond flight, how many ways and days!"

The attention of Mr. Ruskin had meanwhile been diverted to some extent from the work of Millais and Hunt by his entrance in 1854 upon a close personal friendship with Rossetti, which lasted in cordial fidelity for some ten or twelve years. At the time of his first public championship of the Pre-Raphaelite Brotherhood, Mr. Ruskin had known nothing of Rossetti's work, inasmuch as it had never yet appeared on the walls of the Academy or in any of the popular exhibitions of the period. But, for such unintentional and unconscious neglect of the real leader of the movement which he so warmly endorsed, the great critic now made ample reparation. He became a constant and generous patron of Rossetti's pictures until the painter passed, about the year 1865, into his third artistic period, and developed methods less in accordance with Ruskin's especial tenets. That the gradual severance of intimacy between artist and buyer should have been brought about by the former's independence of spirit and resolute adherence to his own inspirations and aims, in the face of some, perhaps, over-officious criticism and counsel from his patron, is certainly no discredit to Rossetti. At the same time, the art-world owes a debt of gratitude to Mr. Ruskin for having so long encouraged, by his support and sympathy, the production of those exquisite water-colours which Rossetti, unsettled as he then was in habits of painting, might not otherwise have accomplished in such splendour and cogency during his transition period.

And to these years of intimacy with Ruskin belong nearly all the finest drawings of his "Morte D'Arthur" series, such as "King Arthur's Tomb" (called sometimes "The Last Meeting of Launcelot and Guinevere," though the design by no means gives the impression of a meeting in the flesh), "The Damozel of the Sanct Grael," "The Chapel before the Lists," "The Meeting of Sir Tristram and Iseult," "Sir Galahad in the Ruined Chapel," "Sir Galahad and Sir Bors," "Launcelot Escaping from Guinevere's Chamber," and "The Death of Breuse sans Pitié;" together with a fresh and important group of Biblical subjects treated in a more daringly romantic manner than before, including "The Passover in the Holy Family," "Bethlehem Gate," "Ruth and Boaz," "The Crucifixion," "Mary in the House of John," and the first sketch for "Mary Magdalene at the Door of Simon the Pharisee;" also the "Triptych" for the altar-piece of Llandaff Cathedral, "The Infant Christ Adored by a Shepherd and a King." The Dante subjects again appear in 1854–55, with "Francesca di Rimini," "Paolo and Francesca," "Matilda Gathering Flowers" (from the "Purgatorio"), "Dante's Vision of Rachel and Leah," "Dante at Verona," and the first version of the picture afterwards among Rossetti's masterpieces, "Dante's Dream." The little drawings of "The Tune of the Seven Towers" in 1850, "Carlisle Tower," "Fra Angelico Painting," and "Giorgione Painting" in 1853, "The Queen's Page" (from Heine) in 1854, "Fra Pace" and "Monna Rosa" in 1856, "The Blue Closet," "The Blue Bower," "The Bower Garden," and the first design for a favourite subject variously known as "Aurelia" and "Bonifazio's" or "Fazio's Mistress" in 1857; these, together with some further sketches for "La Belle Dame sans Merci," a number of portraits of Miss Siddal, Browning, Tennyson, and Swinburne, whom he knew in 1857, are but a selection from the almost countless studies, in pencil, pen and ink, neutral tint, water-colour, and occasional oil, scattered over Rossetti's transition period.

"St. Luke the Painter," in 1857, is notable as being Rossetti's first success in coloured chalk; a medium which he affected more freely in after years, and with extraordinary power and felicity; the medium, in fact, in which some of the noblest of his later half-length symbolic figures were executed.

After the year 1850 Rossetti almost ceased to exhibit in picture galleries. A very few of his pictures, including the "Bocca Baciata" and a version of "Lucretia Borgia," were thenceforth seen in the Hogarth Club, a small society of artists and amateurs to which he belonged, and others afterwards in the Arundel Club, which he joined in 1865. An important exception, however, was made to this rule of seclusion in 1856, when a small but highly representative Pre-Raphaelite Exhibition was opened at 4, Russell

Place, Fitzroy Square. Among Rossetti's contributions were the first water-colour draft of "Dante's Dream," already alluded to, and its pendant, "The Anniversary of the Death of Beatrice," "Hesterna Rosa," "The Blue Closet," and "Mary Magdalene." The other exhibitors were Millais, Holman Hunt, Madox Brown, Arthur Hughes, Charles Collins, William Davis, W.L. Windus, Inchbold, Seddon and Brett. The "Dante's Dream" re-appeared at the Liverpool Academy in 1858, together with "A Christmas Carol," and "The Wedding of St. George"; "Fair Rosamund," and "The Farmer's Daughter" (study for "Found") went to the Royal Scottish Academy in 1862; and "Mary in the House of John" appeared at the Fine Art Society's Galleries in 1879. A version of "Pandora," in 1877 or 1878, and a lovely little water-colour, "Spring," in 1879, were lent by their purchasers to the Glasgow Institute of Fine Arts; "Tibullus's Return to Delia" was similarly lent to the Albert Gallery Exhibition at Edinburgh in 1877; and in 1881 the Loan Exhibition at the Royal Manchester Institution included four important water-colours – "Proserpine," a "Lucretia Borgia," "Hesterna Rosa," and "Washing Hands;" and five oils – "Proserpine," "Two Mothers," "Joli Cœur," "A Vision of Fiametta," and "Water-Willow." These instances complete the brief list of Rossetti's pictures exhibited in public galleries during the lifetime of the artist.

In the year 1854, the Pre-Raphaelite Brotherhood, already practically broken up by divergence of method in the leading painters, and changes of aim and sphere among the lesser lights of the revolutionary dawn, may be said to have been finally dispersed by the lamented death of Walter Deverell, and the departure of Holman Hunt for a lengthy sojourn in the East, there to paint directly from nature – according to the much boasted but oft-broken rule – the backgrounds and appurtenances of those Biblical subjects to which he was now strongly drawn. The death of Deverell at an early age was a heavy personal bereavement to Rossetti, and an occasion of genuine grief to all the Brotherhood, with whom he was exceedingly popular. Nor was the loss to art easily reparable, or the work of his surviving comrades unaffected by the removal of a painter of such singular purity and grace. He was a son of the Secretary of the Schools of Design, which were the precursor of the South Kensington Science and Art Department.

Rossetti and Millais were thus, in 1854, left alone as practical painters; W.M. Rossetti having been from the first exclusively a *littérateur*, while F.G. Stephens, after having produced in youth some work of high quality on strictly Pre-Raphaelite lines, had by this time adopted the same sphere of energy, especially in the realm of the art-critic.

But the phase of doubt and hesitation, of compromise (in no invidious sense) between the first inflexible attitude of revolt and the further impulse of re-construction, which had overtaken the Brotherhood in 1851, was by no means the special ordeal of Rossetti. It came soon afterwards upon Millais with an equal import and significance; as though each must pass, in individual experience, through the several stages of destructive and re-creative energy, first of protest, then of reform, and afterwards of reconciliation and progress, which they had recognized in the history of the past, and which their own work as a whole afforded to the history of the nineteenth century. They had to exemplify, each for himself, the resolute overthrow of partial and degenerate principles, and the pursuit, more or less successful, of a further and perhaps undefined ideal, or the reaction towards that very order against which their own strenuous protest had been set. And it is remarkable that, in the case both of Rossetti and of Millais, the painter should have reached his highest level of excellence in art precisely at the moment when his methods were the most unsettled and his principles the least assured. The most discerning critics now agree in placing the high-water mark of Rossetti's genius in the midst of this transition period, ranging from 1850 to 1860, or, if the decade may be stretched by a license of etymology, covering the "Beata Beatrix" of 1863. And it is scarcely disputable that the supreme achievements of Millais lie within a narrower space, comprising chiefly the "Hugenot" and "Ophelia" of 1852, "The Order of Release" of 1853, "Autumn Leaves" and "The Blind Girl" of 1856, and "The Eve of St. Agnes" in 1863, which really belongs in conception and spirit to the Keats epoch, if we may so call it, which gave birth to the Pre-Raphaelite Brotherhood. Just as in the dawn of the Italian Renaissance the point of absolute greatness in art was gained at the momentary coalition of the old forces with the new, when the classic spirit was conquered and absorbed by the spirit of romance, and the romantic spirit still beat tremulously about the new world's doors, so in the struggle of the modern Pre-Raphaelites to reconcile the new impulse with the heritage of the past, the triumph came in the midst of the conflict rather than after the victory. Just as Leonardo and Michaelangelo gathered up and combined the discordant elements of the strife around them into a noble harmony of art, so did the Pre-Raphaelites attune and interpret the diverse forces of their own revolution when they felt its import most acutely, and least knew whither it would lead them. And to almost opposite poles of thought and sentiment were Millais and Rossetti led.

The extraordinary change which gradually came over the work of Millais after his election to the Associateship of the Royal Academy in 1854 – the youngest painter, with the exception of Lawrence, ever admitted to that rank – has been the subject of much criticism and controversy. It has been contended by several writers that Millais lacked original imagination, and could not sustain his early level without the constant inspiration and stimulus of Rossetti and Hunt, both of whom were by this time absorbed in fresh developments of their own. More ardent apologists have claimed that his Pre-Raphaelite period was but a curious episode in Millais's career; a mere incident in the growth of a genius too brilliant to submit for long to bias from without; and that his impressionable nature was only temporarily swayed by the proselytizing enthusiasm of his comrades. It is hard to attribute the qualities of his finest work – qualities of a high imaginative order, as in "The Eve of St. Agnes," or "The Enemy Sowing Tares," to any genius but his own, or to believe that the painter of "Ophelia" and the "Blind Girl" was not himself profoundly moved by the pathos and tragedy which he therein conceived. Nor can it be urged that the exigencies of ill-fortune, the stress of poverty, or any of those dire necessities of fate which have driven many a true artist on the downward road, drove Millais to paint as unblushingly for the Philistine market as he had formerly done for an obscure and despised coterie of artistic revolutionists. Free as he always was of pecuniary care, and favoured by destiny with all the pleasures of domestic and social prosperity, if he was spoilt, it was by success, not failure; if corrupted, it was by popularity, not neglect: though it must be remembered that none of the Pre-Raphaelites can justly pose as martyrs in the matter of a livelihood.

Nor is it permissible to urge that fame, at first well earned and richly justified, entitles any great painter to repudiate the convictions and ideals on which that fame was built, or to play with a reputation won at a heavy cost to himself and others. It can only be assumed that Millais, in forsaking the high and steep paths which he had once chosen, sincerely followed what he felt to be a more excellent way, and honestly believed his decadence to be an advance upon his maturity. To doubt this would be to pass the sternest moral condemnation on an artist of incomparable endowments, and to brand him as the wanton betrayer of a sacred trust, the deliberate concealer of a divine talent, for which, at the ultimate judgment-seat of art, the inevitable account must at last be given.

Speaking of this turning-point in Millais's career, Mr. Ruskin said in 1857: – "The change in his manner from the years of 'Ophelia' and 'Mariana' to 1857 is not merely Fall; it is Catastrophe; not merely a loss of power, but a reversal of principle; his excellence has been effaced 'as a man wipeth a dish – wiping it and turning it upside down.'"

But the Pre-Raphaelite movement, so far from being at an

end, was now only emerging from the first tentative phase of its activity. It had yet to be absorbed in a larger reformation, and to act thereby even more potently than if it had remained the specific crusade of a clique or faction. The difficulty which the historian finds at this crisis in the artistic career of Rossetti and his friends, and still more so in their subsequent developments, – the difficulty of defining strictly Pre-Raphaelite work, and of deciding as to who of the now rapidly expanding circle of painters may justly be claimed as Pre-Raphaelites, is itself evidence of the permeating force of the initial movement, and of the ready soil which was prepared for the dissemination of its dominant ideas. For the circle of literary and artistic aspirants, patrons, students, amateurs, and connoisseurs of many grades and varied gifts who now surrounded Dante Rossetti, included men whose names afterwards became honoured in fields of art quite untouched by Pre-Raphaelitism in its distinctive form, but imbued through their influence with fresh and quickening impulses of revival.

One of the most poetic of the painters intimately associated with the Brotherhood was Arthur Hughes, who, though only eighteen at the time of its formation, took an active share in its practical work, and painted, according to its main tenets, with a rare facility and tender charm. He was born in London in 1832, passed through the Academy Schools without much recognition, but won cordial admiration among the limited company who could then appreciate his work, by his beautiful "April Love" in the Academy of 1854. He was also singularly successful at a later date in a subject from Keats's "Eve of St. Agnes" – the source of inspiration for some of the finest work of the Pre-Raphaelite leaders at various times. Like Millais and several others of the band, he attained considerable popularity as an illustrator of books. His religious paintings, moreover, will demand attention among those of his more illustrious friends. "The Cottager's Return" and "The Reaper and the Flowers" may be remembered, among others of his always graceful pictures, by those who recall the first decade of Pre-Raphaelite propaganda in public exhibitions. He sat as the model for the hero in Millais's "Proscribed Royalist" of 1853.

Charles Allston Collins, a son of William Collins, R.A., and brother of Wilkie Collins, painted for some time in the manner of the Pre-Raphaelites, but subsequently devoted himself to literature. His first exhibited picture, "Convent Thoughts," in the Academy of 1850, shared with Millais's "Christ in the House of His Parents," the torrent of opprobrium showered on the innovators in that eventful year. Yet three of his works were accepted by the Academy the following season, – "Lyra Innocentium," on a verse from Keble; representing a young girl in a white gown against a background of blue; "May in the Regent's Park," a wonderfully minute study of foliage, as if seen through a window opening close upon the trees; and "The Devout Childhood of Saint Elizabeth of Hungary," calling to mind the treatment by James Collinson of the familiar renunciation-legend anent the same much-maligned saint. The Elizabeth of the "Childhood" is depicted as a homely-looking little girl of thirteen, kneeling at the iron-barred oaken door of a chapel in the Palace grounds. Her missal is laid on the doorstep beside her, and she is imagined, according to the account of her early piety, to be at prayer on the inhospitable threshold of the shrine to which she cannot for the moment gain access. Charles Collins acted as Millais's model for "The Hugenot" and "The Black Brunswicker." He married a daughter of Charles Dickens, who posed with him as the lady in the "Hugenot."

William L. Windus, a Liverpool artist and member of the Academy of that city, made his modest but genuine fame chiefly through his powerful romantic picture of "Burd Helen," the "burd" or sweetheart of the Scottish border ballad, who swam the Clyde in order to avenge herself upon a faithless lover. The work was pronounced by Ruskin to rank second only in order of merit to Millais's "Autumn Leaves" in the Royal Academy of 1856. He painted altogether some eight or ten pictures of a very earnest and imaginative kind, of which one of the finest was entitled "Too

Late," and represented a dying girl whose lover had forsaken her and returned too late for reparation. "The Surgeon's Daughter" is also remembered as a composition of much chastened and subdued power. Windus ceased painting at an early age, and was lost sight of by the Brotherhood.

Robert B. Martineau was a pupil of Holman Hunt, but painted, among some three or four pictures which constitute the brief total of his achievements, only one of striking merit, – "The Last Day in the Old Home," which for sincerity and depth of feeling won considerable appreciation in 1865. His career was cut short by untimely death soon afterwards.

Cave Thomas, who so infelicitously christened "The Germ," had gained a prize in the Westminster Cartoon competition, and was the painter of one very beautiful picture, "The Protestant Lady," exhibited in the Academy, and greatly admired by the Brotherhood. He published in 1860 a monograph entitled "Pre-Raphaelitism Tested by the Principles of Christianity;" and subsequently became art professor to the Princess of Wales.

Mr. Frederick Sandys was not personally known to the leading Pre-Raphaelites until 1857, and was by that time too original and accomplished an artist to be claimed by them as a disciple, but his work was for some time intimately associated with theirs. He was to the last a valued friend of Rossetti, who always affirmed that while in draughtsmanship he had no superior in English art, his imaginative endowment was of the richest and rarest kind.

Mr. Henry Wallis is justly remembered by his one great picture, "The Death of Chatterton," which touched popular feeling as its true pathos and dignity deserved to do, and won universal praise.

Mark Anthony is rightly regarded by the Pre-Raphaelites as the most poetic of their landscape painters. His grandly simple and reposeful "Old Churchyard" will compare even with Millais's "Vale of Rest," and his "Nature's Mirror" with Mr. Burne-Jones's "Mirror of Venus" in later years. Mr. John Brett, now famous in seascape, was for some time intimate with the Brotherhood; and among friends and sympathizers on a similar footing may be mentioned Val Prinsep, Thomas Seddon, J.D. Watson, J.F. Lewes, W.S. Burton, Spencer Stanhope, M.F. Halliday, James Campbell, J.M. Carrick, Thomas Morten, Edward Lear, William Davis, W.P. Boyce, J.W. Inchbold, and, by no means least, John Hancock, a young sculptor who won an Art Union prize in 1848 with a bas-relief of "Christ's Entry into Jerusalem." He was a friend and fellow-worker with Woolner, and fell so far (with Rossetti) under the fascination of the Dante legends as to accomplish a very fine statue of "Beatrice" in or about 1852. One other artist of the first rank in his generation remains to be named, – Frederick Shields, an intimate and warmly-loved friend of Rossetti, cherished by him in close and unbroken companionship even to the hour of death; and in point of critical estimate pronounced by him to be one of the greatest of living draughtsmen, taking rank with Sir Frederick Leighton, Sir Noel Paton, and Mr. Sandys.

Such were a few of the personalities that gathered between 1848 and 1858 around the three prime movers in the Pre-Raphaelite revolt. To claim them as merely, or chiefly, satellites drawn into the orbit of genius, or as forming a distinct and coherent school, would be both foolish and unjust. To attempt an estimate of their relative merit independent of, or in proportion to, the artistic work of the Brotherhood, would be no less invidious than unprofitable. The glory of Pre-Raphaelitism was that it gave the utmost play to individual methods, and even idiosyncrasies, – nay, that its very first principle was "each for himself" – painting his own impressions, his own ideals – and no imitation of one artist by another. Its primary insistence lay on the watchword of all Protestantism – the authority of the individual conscience as against that of a class or a system, and the immediate access for every soul to the source of its highest inspiration. Therefore the "diversities of gifts" which flourished and increased under the sway of the Pre-Raphaelite spirit were the best evidence of that spirit's quickening power. "A man will always emphasize," says

Mr. P.G. Hamerton, writing on the ultimate effects of the movement, "those truths about art which most strongly recommend themselves to his own peculiar personal temperament. This comes from the vastness of art and the variety of human organizations. For art is so immense a study that no one man ever knew the whole truth about it." In other words, all the Pre-Raphaelite painters in any sense worthy of the name are intensely individual in quality, and cannot be classed, arranged, or compared together in the order of a system or a school. Each artist must make his original and distinctive contribution to the sum-total of artistic truth; must paint the single aspect, or the most familiar aspect, of the life around him which presents itself to his mind. The more honest he is, and the more true to his own observations and convictions, the more inevitably will he see the world through his own spectacles – well for his superficial happiness, at all events, if they be rose-coloured, and not of a more sombre hue. "We all," says another art-critic,[*5] "have a sense of some particular colour, and because we can paint this colour best we do so at all times and in all places. This may be unconscious on our part – this predilection for a particular colour; but we all unconsciously blab the fact to others; we talk in our dream of art, and tell all our secrets. Old David Cox, when out sketching with his pupils, would go behind them while at work and say to one, 'Ah, you see green;' to another, 'You see purple,' 'You see red,' 'You see yellow.' So it is with the colour vision of many who are called Masters. We can identify almost any landscape of our more prominent painters by their special idiosyncrasy of colouring, such as Cuyp with his evening yellows, Linnell with his autumnal browns, or Danby with his sanguinary sunsets. These colours, which are exceptional with external nature, are the rule with them. Not only is this so with regard to colour, but, more or less, we put ourselves, form and feature, into our work, and paint our own character, physical as well as mental, in all we do. Raphael, on being asked where he obtained the type of his Madonna, replied, 'out of his own head,' which really meant that he had unconsciously painted his own fair features: and this ideal was what he eternally repeated. So was it with Michaelangelo, Leonardo, Murillo, Rubens, Vandyke – they all portrayed themselves recognizably. There is a picture of Jesus and the twelve Apostles in which the whole thirteen faces are all alike, and every one an identifiable copy of the painter's own. Of course where the face and form are noble we have the less to object to."

This indeed is the crux of the whole matter. As the man is, so will his work be. To portray one's very self – and first to have such a self as can dignify the portrayal; to paint faithfully what one sees – and first to see the true and the beautiful in the familiar and the commonplace; to depict the world in which one lives – living in a world apart, noble and fair, full of opportunities, if also of mysteries, with bright horizons, however low the sun; and yet to be ever conscious of wider worlds than the imagination can compass though the heart may yearn over them like the heart of him who said *Homo sum; nihil humana mihi alienum puto*: this is fine art; this is "the vision and the faculty divine." "Produce great Persons!" cries Browning, – "the rest follows." Therefore it is safe for those who in any real sense know Rossetti to prophesy, with Mr. Harry Quilter, that "the day will surely come when it will be seen that the essence of what is now known as Pre-Raphaelitism was not the influence of a school or a principle, but simply the influence of one man, and that man Dante Gabriel Rossetti." Personal ascendency, says Emerson, is the only force much worth reckoning with. And if that ascendency, over many who never saw Rossetti on earth, has become an intimate and precious inspiration, a motive-impulse abidingly sacred and high, what must it have been to those who knew him in the flesh?

Mr. W.M. Rossetti thus succinctly sums up the immediate issue of the movement which his brother inspired: – "As it turned out, the early phases of the movement did not repeat themselves on a more extended scale. Partly, no doubt, through the modification of style of the most popular Pre-Raphaelite, Mr. Millais, and partly through the influx of new determining conditions, especially the effect of foreign schools and of Mr. Leighton's style (this was written in 1865), Pre-Raphaelitism flagged in its influence towards the production of what are distinctively termed Pre-Raphaelite pictures just at the time when it had virtually won the day. But the movement had broken up the pre-existing state of things, and the principles and practices which it introduced took strong root, and germinated in forms not altogether expected. Pre-Raphaelitism aimed at suppressing such styles of painting as were exemplified by Messrs. Elmore, Goodall, and Stone at the time of its starting; *and it did suppress them.*" [*6]

The relation of Pre-Raphaelitism to the "foreign schools" here referred to is as much a matter of historical controversy as the relation of Rossetti to Italy is of biographical criticism; nor is it easy to determine how far the Pre-Raphaelite movement in England was the effect or the cause of similar waves of experiment in France and Germany, and how far all such impulses were but the symptoms of a great social and ethical development in European life. But while the Barbizon School must be seriously recognized as working side by side with the Pre-Raphaelites upon kindred ideals, and even surpassing them at some points in a certain largeness of outlook on humanitarian themes, the influence of Cornelius and Overbeck in Germany, with the very crude and sickly mediævalism which they affected, has no doubt been greatly overrated, and may be dismissed as having very little to do with the main current of the romantic revival. In France, Corot and Millet, Daubigny and Rousseau, had taken their stand against the old Heroic School in art, just as Théophile Gautier and Victor Hugo had taken it against the Academies of literature. In England, it was the task of Rossetti and his comrades "to force," as it has been aptly expressed, "an artificial art backed upon nature's reality; and they did it amid neglect, misunderstanding, and even coarse vituperation."

CHAPTER V.

LATER DEVELOPMENTS
OF THE MOVEMENT.

*The Pre-Raphaelites as Book-Illustrators – Moxon's "Tennyson" –
The "Oxford and Cambridge Magazine" – The Oxford Frescoes –
Oxford Patrons of Millais and Hunt – Departure of Hunt for Palestine
– The Pictures of Madox Brown – Further Developments of Rossetti's
Painting – Marriage and Bereavement – "Beata Beatrix" – Replicas –
Life at Chelsea – Later Models – Designs for Stained Glass – Visit to
Penkill – "Dante's Dream" – Publication and Reception of the "Poems"
– Paintings of Rossetti's Last Decade – Death at Birchington.*

The first and most fruitful decade of Pre-Raphaelitism in painting
and poetry saw also the excursion of several of its leaders into the
realm of book-illustration. In 1855 Rossetti, Millais, and Arthur
Hughes combined to make a series of drawings for the second
edition of a little volume of verse entitled "Day and Night Songs,"
by William Allingham, a young poet well known to the
Brotherhood since 1849. The efforts were not of an ambitious
character. The weird little group of fairies dancing in the
moonlight, by Arthur Hughes, reflected vividly the influence of
Blake. Rossetti's "Maids of Elfinmere" were of his most angelic-

mediæval type, ascetically beautiful, and yet, if the phrase may be permitted, with a certain sensuous severity of look, a delicate and half-mystic passion, as of pure spirits newly wakened to the tenderness of the flesh.

A more important experiment in the same direction was made in 1857, when Rossetti, Millais, and Holman Hunt appeared among the illustrators of Moxon's edition of "Tennyson." Intimately charmed as they had all been with the "Idylls of the King," and with such entirely "Pre-Raphaelite" poetry as "The Lady of Shalott," the draughtsmen could hardly have found a more congenial sphere for design. The volume affords one of the most interesting records of the transitional work of the three painters. Woolner's fine medallion of the young laureate formed the frontispiece. Then followed Millais's "Mariana" – a composition wholly distinct from, and far inferior to, his "Mariana in the Moated Grange," which had been shown in the Academy of 1851. The face of this Mariana is hidden in her hands as she turns with bowed head from the window, and from the sunset that mocks her grief with its imperturbable glory heedless and afar. Much less conventional in spirit is the passionate, strained figure of Rossetti's "Mariana in the South," crouching on her unrestful bed, and kissing the feet of the crucifix above her as she draws from her bosom the "old letters breathing of her worth."

In the design for "The Lady of Shalott" Holman Hunt exhibits traces – very unusual for him – of the influence of Rossetti upon his own work. For pathetic dignity and sensuous grace, the entangled lady, girt about with the web of dreams, might well stand among Rossetti's children, and not be detected as of other birth. Rossetti's own "Lady of Shalott" is much less fair a type, and belongs to the earliest and most archaic manner of his Arthurian period. Much more characteristic of the painter's individuality is Holman Hunt's "Oriana," a grave, strong woman like his later Madonnas, whose mien belies the conventional sex-theory which ascribes to man alone the "wisdom-principle," and assigns to womanhood the principle of "love."

☆ 139

Rossetti, again, seems to have been largely influenced by Madox Brown in his illustration to "The Palace of Art," save for the highly characteristic drawing of the girl at the organ, whose pose is almost identical with that of the dead Beatrice in "Dante's Dream," of a much later date. "Sir Galahad" is, however, entirely original in manner, and represents the best level of Rossetti's Arthurian designs. It shows the knight halting, weary but not dispirited, at a wayside shrine, and bending with worn and yet resolute face over the holy water that awaits the pilgrim-worshippers. His horse, bearing the white banner marked with the red cross of sacred chivalry, stands at the gate, and a group of nuns are seen within, ringing the chapel bell.

The facile simplicity and grace of Millais, who was more accustomed to the task of book-illustration than his collaborateurs, found favourable scope in "Edward Grey" and "The Day-dream," in which the figure of the half-awakened girl in the Sleeping Palace is drawn with exquisitely tender charm.

The edition, on the whole, probably tended to increase the reputation of the Pre-Raphaelites as draughtsmen, and to dispel some hard-dying illusions as to their distinguishing qualities in design, though its independent merits were not of exceptional mark.

Only once again does Rossetti appear in the field of book illustration. In 1862 he executed two designs for the first volume of poems published by his sister, Miss Christina Rossetti, under the title of "Goblin Market." These drawings ("Buy from us with a golden curl" and "Golden head by Golden head") were followed in 1866 by two more of a similar character ("The long hours go and come and go," and "You should have wept her yesterday"), to illustrate the second volume of poetry from the same pen, entitled, "The Prince's Progress."

But the fame of the Pre-Raphaelites as poets was already enhanced, within an increasing circle of appreciators, by the publication, in 1856, of a journal which may, to some extent, be regarded as a successor to the "The Germ." "The Oxford and

Cambridge Magazine," edited by Mr. Godfrey Lushington, had the better fortune to survive for a year, in monthly numbers; though all its contents were anonymous, and its issue involved no less labour and anxiety on the part of its sponsors, if not so much pecuniary onus as in the case of the more luxuriously printed and illustrated "Germ." The new publication contained several of Rossetti's finest poems, such as "The Staff and Scrip," and "Nineveh," and a series of mediæval romances and poems by two young artists destined henceforth to be intimately associated with the Pre-Raphaelite movement, and to exert important influence on its later developments – William Morris and Edward Burne-Jones. Both were Oxford men, and had been close friends at Exeter College, whence in 1856 came Burne-Jones to London with the express desire of meeting and knowing Dante Rossetti, his senior by five years; he having been born in Birmingham on the 28th of August, 1833, and educated at King Edward's School in that city, proceeding to Oxford in 1853.

It was at the Working Men's College in Great Ormond Street that Burne-Jones first saw Rossetti, and, through the introduction of Mr. Vernon Lushington, entered upon the friendship which was to save him (as his friend William Morris was similarly saved) from adopting, as had been intended, the Church as his profession, and thus depriving, the world of a service no less religious in the highest sense, and no less potent a factor in the ethical awakening of to-day.

The Working Men's College, now rich in annals of some of the most significant intellectual movements of the mid-century, was at that time a centre of enthusiastic work in art and literature. Rossetti and his friends took a considerable share in the lecturing and class-teaching of which Charles Kingsley and F.D. Maurice were the popular and indefatigable leaders. Hither also came Ruskin, of whom Rossetti records with loyal admiration how one night, being asked in an emergency to address the drawing-class, he made, without any preparation, "the finest speech I ever heard."

Rossetti's growing intimacy with Oxford collegians, and the ties of sympathy already formed in Oxford round the Pre-Raphaelite painters by the *clientèle* of Millais and Hunt, now led him into an enterprise which has been the subject of much Philistine mirth, and of some laboured apologetics on the part of the too-serious historian. There is no doubt that Rossetti and his collaborateurs made quite as merry as any of their critics over the ludicrous failure of their *début* as fresco-painters in 1857. But it was very natural that Rossetti, with his early enthusiasm for the fresco style yet awaiting an outlet, should have seized eagerly at the chance of trying his 'prentice hand on so engagingly favourable an area as the new hall of the Oxford Union Debating Society. Visiting the city in company with William Morris during the summer months, Rossetti was shown over the freshly completed building by his friend Mr. Woodward; and observing the blank spaces of the gallery window-bays, impulsively offered to paint on them a series of the "Morte D'Arthur" subjects which had so much engrossed his fancy during the past three years. The suggestion was readily agreed to, and Rossetti began to collect recruits for the campaign, which he perceived would afford ample scope for other labour than his own. Accordingly, at the commencement of the long vacation, a company of six young enthusiasts, embarrassingly ignorant of the first technical elements of mural painting, but unabashed by any such details in the path of success, fell confidently upon their fascinating task. The party consisted of Rossetti, Burne-Jones, William Morris, Arthur Hughes, Val Prinsep, Spencer Stanhope, Alexander Monro, and J. Hungerford Pollen, then Proctor at the University, who had already won some distinction by his painting of the beautiful roof in Merton College Chapel. The roof of the Debating Hall was now successfully painted, in a grotesque design, by William Morris, who also undertook one of the window-bays, and proposed as his subject "Sir Palomides' Jealousy of Sir Tristram and Iseult." Alexander Monro, the sculptor of the party, executed the stone shield over the porch. Burne-Jones selected for his fresco

"Nimuë brings Sir Peleus to Ettarde after their Quarrel;" Arthur Hughes proposed "Arthur Conveyed by the Weeping Queens to Avalon after his Death;" Val Prinsep, "Merlin Lured into the Pit by the Lady of the Lake," and J. Hungerford Pollen, "King Arthur Receiving the Sword Excalibur from the Lady of the Lake." Rossetti's subjects were "Sir Galahad Receiving the Sangrael" and "Sir Launcelot before the Shrine of the Sangrael." The knight, in this last design, has just attained the sacred goal of his pilgrimage, and in his weariness has sunk down in sleep upon the threshold; but his sleep, even in that hour, is haunted by the face of Guinevere. So powerful was this composition in romantic force and imaginative fervour, especially in the haunting, passionate face of the Queen, as to make the speedy obliteration of this and its companion frescoes the more deplorable, in spite of the obvious crudities and incompetencies that blemish the whole series of designs. Obliterated they became, however, and hopelessly beyond restoration, within a very short time of their commencement; – finished they never were. Incredible as it seems, in these days of superior wisdom in the Young Person anent matters of Art, these brilliant young painters of 1857 – three at least of them now in the first rank of fame in their several spheres – had not even attempted to prepare the raw brick surface for the reception of their pigments, but had cast their ordinary oil-colours direct upon the inhospitable wall. Time and the atmosphere made short work of such artless challenges of decay; and before any of the frescoes had attained completion the ardent little band were obliged to confess themselves defeated, and to retire somewhat ignomin-iously from the field. The enterprise had its pathetic, its humorous, and its entirely delightful side. The financial arrangement with the Oxford Union Council was that they should defray all necessary expenses incurred by the artists; and of this advantage the young Bohemians appear to have availed themselves to the full. Anecdotes abound to tell of the hilarious but very harmless festivities which mitigated the discouragements of their task. A contemporary undergraduate well recalls the mirth and chatter which he heard day by day as he sat in the adjacent library. Such a group of congenial spirits could not fail to enjoy the conditions of their companionship as much as the audacity of their task. They were favoured, further, with a new acquaintanceship of a very welcome kind; for it was here that another young poet, Algernon Charles Swinburne, was now introduced, as an undergraduate at the university, to the artists at their work, and added an important link to the chain of memorable friendships woven in these early years among the galaxy of genius which has illumined the England of to-day. It was in Oxford also, at the theatre one evening, that Rossetti saw, and succeeded in getting introduced to, the beautiful lady who afterwards became William Morris's wife, and Rossetti's most cherished friend through all his troubles. She was the model for his "Day-dream" and several others of the finest of his maturer works.

The hapless frescoes are now hardly recognizable upon the Oxford walls, but their dim ghosts linger, like the kindly witnesses of days fruitful, at least, in loves and friendships of sacred import on the lives of the young sojourners in that "home of lost causes, and forsaken beliefs, and unpopular names, and impossible loyalties," as Matthew Arnold called it.

Moreover, it was at Oxford that the Pre-Raphaelite movement, five or six years earlier, had found some of its first and most generous patrons; such as Mr. James Wyatt, the well-known picture-dealer, who was among Millais's readiest buyers, but died in 1853, and Mr. Thomas Combe, the University printer, who, through Millais's influence, purchased Holman Hunt's youthful and little-known picture, "Christian Priests Escaping from Druid Persecution," in 1850. About three years later, Holman Hunt was on a visit to Mr. and Mrs. Combe while his greater work, "The Light of the World," was in process; and at their house he became acquainted with the young curate of St. Paul's, Oxford; Venables by name. He was a man saintly in face and character; afterwards Bishop of the Bahamas, and long since dead. Whether he actually gave sittings to Hunt, or was avowedly the model for the Christ of the picture, does not appear, but those who knew Venables at the time insist upon the absolute faithfulness of the portraiture. This face it was which certain critics, unable to dissociate their conception of the Saviour from the conventional Raphaelesque type, condemned instantly as "the face of a Judas." The picture was purchased by Mr. Combe, and subsequently presented by his widow to Keble College, Oxford, where it hangs to-day. Of the difficulties which attended the painting, and of the extraordinary labour bestowed upon it as it slowly grew beneath his hand in the little studio then at Chelsea, Mr. Hunt has given us his own significant record, – how, night after night, when the moon was in a favourable quarter, he would so dispose his curtains and draperies, easels and lamps, as to yield him the peculiar light for which he was striving, and at the same time to afford for curious observers an endless speculation as to the mysterious proceedings of the eccentric young artist within. "The Light of the World" is now perhaps the most familiar, to English eyes, of any Pre-Raphaelite pictures, unless we except the less esoteric "Hugenot" of Millais.

The "Hugenot," indeed, would undoubtedly be taken by general estimate to point the high-water mark of Millais's fame and genius, in spite of the splendour of the "ninth wave" – if one may push the metaphor so far – which issued ten years later in "The Eve of St. Agnes" and "The Enemy Sowing Tares." The "Hugenot" appeared with "Ophelia" in 1852; Hunt's "Light of the World" in 1854. And the "Hugenot" it was that first took unmistakable hold upon the public taste, and created a higher taste than it appealed to, carrying the emotion awakened with it on to higher planes than had yet been reached in English criticism. "The Order of Release," in the following year, consummated the triumph of the young painter, and was enhanced in fame by Kingsley's allusion to it in "Two Years Ago." "The Proscribed Royalist" and the "Portrait of Ruskin" may be regarded as the last products of Millais's rigidly Pre-Raphaelite period, which terminated, with Rossetti's, about 1853. "The Rescue" and "The Random Shot," or "L'Enfant du Regiment," in 1855, "Sir Isumbras at the Ford: A Dream of the Past," or "Knight Crossing a Ford," in 1857, and "The Vale of Rest," in 1858, are purely transitional works, while, with the notable exception of the two later masterpieces specified above, "The Black Brunswicker" of 1860, may be said to mark the final merging of the Pre-Raphaelite heretic into the popular Royal Academician. His formal election as R.A. took place in 1863. He was made, in 1883, a member of the Institute of France, and was, in 1885, the first English artist to be offered and to accept a baronetcy of the United Kingdom. He has also become a member of the Academies of Edinburgh, Antwerp, Rome and Madrid, and has been honoured at Oxford with the complimentary degree of D.C.L. His marriage in early life with Miss Euphemia Chalmers Gray was anticipated in one of the most pleasing of his female portraits in 1853.

Meanwhile the companion of his student days had entered upon a path of more obscure and arduous toil, in the pursuit of an ideal too exalted to endure compromise with any standards of the merely picturesque, or to lend itself readily to fluent and attractive expression. The work of Holman Hunt, among all the Pre-Raphaelite painters, has remained the most consistent and exclusive in its aims and methods, and the least affected by surrounding influences, either from his comrades or from the critical world. His artistic development has been the most faithful to its origins, and has presented the most unbroken continuity of thought and sentiment in its progress from the first "note of resistance and defiance" to the larger harmony of maturer years. The boundaries of his transition-period are more difficult to define than in the case of Millais and Rossetti; but, at the same time, the pictures that issued from his studio while Rossetti was dabbling in experimental water-colours, and Millais compromising brilliantly between original genius and the sweet laxities of fame, were of a passion and mastery which he never exceeded. Before the completion of "The Light of the World," in 1854, Hunt had already painted "The Awakening Conscience" (1853), "Claudio and Isabella" (1851), "The Hireling Shepherd" (1852), and "The Strayed Sheep," called also "Our English Coasts" (1853). He now departed to commence those long, solitary, and most fruitful sojourns in Jerusalem, Bethlehem, and less frequented parts of Palestine, which gave us, at the cost of years of intense and continuous labour, such great imaginative creations as "The Scapegoat" in 1855, "Christ in the Temple" in 1860, "The Shadow of Death" in 1874, and "The Triumph of the Innocents" in 1885. "The Shadow of Death" was purchased for £10,500; a price unparalleled for the work of any other living painter. The picture now hangs in the Manchester Corporation Gallery. Seven years were spent over "The Triumph of the Innocents," pronounced by Ruskin to be "the greatest religious picture of the age." The final version, completed in 1885, has recently been acquired by the Walker Art Gallery in Liverpool, where it completes, with Millais's "Lorenzo and Isabella" and Rossetti's "Dante's Dream," a noble trio of the best Pre-Raphaelite type. Reverting, as he did but once, to more purely romantic subjects, and to that haunting theme of Keats which first inspired the young Brotherhood, Mr. Holman Hunt produced in 1867 the finest of his work in that direction, in the brilliant "Isabella and the Pot of Basil," which was the outcome of a visit to Florence in that year. His only important picture of later years has been the "May Morning on Magdalen Tower," a fascinating reminiscence of Oxford life, exhibited in 1889.

Even more obscure and remote from the general routine of the modern studio, more independent of criticism or of patronage, was the earnest and thoughtful work of Madox Brown. In his case the early discipline of art study, and the isolation of unconventional ideals, had been courageously survived before he knew Rossetti, and his path already chosen on the heights of original thought. "He was," says Mr. W.M. Rossetti, "distinctly an intellectual painter; intellectual on the side chiefly of human character. The predominant quality in all his works is a vigorous thinking out of the subject, especially as a matter of character, and of dramatic incident and expression thus resulting. This is the sort of intellect peculiarly demanded by pictorial art."

It is noticeable also that the two senior members, if they may be so claimed, of the Pre-Raphaelite circle, though not of the actual Brotherhood – Ford Madox Brown and George Frederick Watts – were the only painters who brought into the movement any direct training from the continental schools. The latter, one year older than Madox Brown, was born in London in 1820, and succeeded in getting a picture into the Royal Academy as early as 1837. The prize of £300 gained in 1843 in the Westminster Hall Competitions enabled him to spend three years in Italy, after which, on his return, he won a prize of £500 in the same contest, with two more colossal frescoes of a similar kind.

Madox Brown, meanwhile, was entering upon the more uncompromising phase of reform. It was during his studies in Rome and Paris, when the Gothic traditions of Belgium had been strongly tempered by the Latin heritage of the south, that the Pre-Raphaelite idea began to shape itself in his mind, and to develop in him an original art which should create its own conditions and methods, yield a rich harvest of artistic if not of professional success, and exercise an immense power for good over the movement which his own single-handed battle with convention largely stimulated and inspired.

"Wicliff Reading his Translation of the Bible to John of Gaunt" was afterwards acknowledged by Madox Brown as his first distinctly Pre-Raphaelite picture; begun in 1845, and shortly followed by "Pretty Baa-Lambs" – the only other work which the artist claimed as being painted implicitly in the early Italian style. The latter was subjected to much derisive criticism in the press. Yet the later work of this unquestionably great painter, maintained as it was on his own rigidly independent lines, and never merging into the fervid neo-Romanticism of Rossetti, Millais, and Hunt, may justly be accepted, like theirs at its best, as a consistent and superb development, in a modern atmosphere and in the face of modern problems, of the principles followed by the Italian Pre-Raphaelites, and which *as principles* are adaptible in infinite variety to the fresh needs and new perplexities of successive generations of men.

In 1849 the work of Madox Brown appeared for the first time beside that of Rossetti. "Cordelia's Portion," a highly imaginative and nobly dramatic composition, was hung in the Free Exhibition at Hyde Park Corner, in company with Rossetti's "Girlhood of Mary Virgin." His next important picture, "Chaucer at the Court of Edward III.," occupied the painter for several years, and was produced at the Royal Academy of 1851 – the memorable season of Hunt's "Valentine and Sylvia," and Millais's "Woodman's Daughter." The "Chaucer," now in Australia, received the Liverpool Academy's annual prize of £50 in 1852, and was selected by Government for the Paris Exhibition Loan Collection of English paintings in 1855.

The departure of his young friend Woolner for Australia in 1854 suggested to Madox Brown the subject of his most popular and in some respects his most successful picture, "The Last of England," finished in 1855, and now exhibited in the Art Gallery of the Corporation of Birmingham. It was his visit to Gravesend, to bid farewell to Woolner as he embarked for the Antipodes, at the time when the emigration movement was at its height, that inspired the elder painter with that homely idyll of emigrant life – that masterpiece in the dramatic and emotional presentment of modern and familiar romance. In 1857 he painted his great symbolic picture "Work," which has been pronounced "the finest Pre-Raphaelite picture in the world;" a verdict not without justification, but bordering on those facile abstractions of criticism wherein the sense of comparative excellence is apt to lose itself in the confusion of diverse methods in art. The picture now hangs with the masterpieces of Rossetti, Millais, and Holman Hunt, in the Walker Art Gallery at Liverpool. Among the many friends of that period who gave sittings to the artist for the principal figures were Frederick Denison Maurice and Thomas Carlyle.

Of the achievements of Madox Brown in the more obviously romantic and naturalistic fields, perhaps the best known is the intensely passionate and brilliant "Romeo and Juliet" parting at daybreak in the loggia to Juliet's chamber. In the same category, though of various range and style, may be briefly mentioned "Waiting" (1855), a fine study of firelight and lamplight, which appeared in the Russell Place Pre-Raphaelite Exhibition of 1856, "The Death of Sir Tristram," "King René's Honeymoon," the much earlier "Parisina and Manfred on Jungfrau," and "The Dream of Sardanapalus," a work of recent years. The romantic treatment of historical subjects is represented by the cartoons before mentioned, executed prior to 1848, and by such later compositions as "Cromwell Dictating to his Secretaries," "Milton and Marvel," and "Cromwell on his farm at St. Ives," completed in 1873. Of his religious pictures perhaps the most familiar is the austerely beautiful "Entombment;" but it is not easy to excuse the discreditable oblivion permitted in this country to such paintings as "Jesus Washes Peter's Feet," "The Transfiguration," "Our Lady of Good Children," or "Elijah and the Widow's Son;" – oblivion only too explicable by a single trait of national character: that the average Briton will accept any innovation of taste or doctrine that will allow him to take his pleasure with the least amount of intellectual disturbance, but he will never forgive the artist who calls upon him to *think*. Happily some worthier, though very far from adequate, recognition has been accorded to the almost colossal task of the painter's later years – the great series of historical frescoes on the walls of the Town Hall, Manchester, commencing with the building of Manchester by the Romans, and bringing the history of the city pictorially down to the present day. Outliving many younger leaders of the Pre-Raphaelite movement, Madox Brown died on the 6th of October, 1893.

The artistic development of Madox Brown does not, then, offer any abrupt or marked transition from the first crude workings to the perfected application of the Pre-Raphaelite idea. This he pursued steadfastly, and with an unhasting diligence and quiet independence of spirit which indicates his kinship of temperament to Holman Hunt rather than to his impulsive and volatile pupil Rossetti, or to the impressionable Millais of early days. The complete outward divergence between the art of Madox Brown and that of Rossetti after, let us say, the "Triptych" for Llandaff Cathedral, painted by the latter in 1859–1860, illustrates not only the consistent progress of the former in his own distinctive line, but also the extraordinary fertility and cumulative splendour of Rossetti's genius, which could create for itself during the next fifteen years so much more original and versatile a habit wherewith to clothe the noble and exquisite visions that thronged his imagination, each with the urgency of "a presence that is not to be put by."

For the last twenty years of Rossetti's artistic life he was known, and should be judged, supremely as a colourist; and from 1862 to 1874 his technical power reached its highest level. After completing in oils the "Triptych" for the Llandaff altar-piece, "The Infant Christ Adored by a Shepherd and a King," Rossetti began to pursue more carefully, and with increasing success both from the æsthetic and the professional point of view, the system of half-length or three-quarter length female figure-studies, chiefly symbolic in motive, which he had already attempted brilliantly in the "Bocca Baciata" ("The Kissed Mouth") of 1859, and which afterwards yielded such imaginative and technical triumphs as "Beata Beatrix" (1863), "The Blue Bower," one of the most brilliant and sensuous of his paintings (1864); "Lady Lilith," the type of purely physical loveliness, described in his sonnet "Body's Beauty" (1864); "Il Ramoscello" ("The Branchlet"), or "Bellbuona" ("Fair and Good"), a gem of pearl-white colouring (1865); "Monna Vanna," a superb study in white and gold (1866); "Venus Verticordia," personifying again the earthly Pandemos, with the apple of temptation in her hand (1864–1877); "The Beloved, or the Bride of the Canticles;" and "Sibylla Palmifera" ("Beauty the Palm-giver"), both typifying intellectual and spiritual beauty (1866–1873); "The Loving Cup" (1867); "Aurelia," or "Fazio's

Mistress" (Angiola of Verona, loved by Fazio degli Uberti, mentioned by Dante), another somewhat sensuous model (1863–1873); "La Pia," the unhappy and captive wife of Nello della Pietra (from Dante's "Purgatorio"), seen in her prison overlooking the Maremma (1868–1881); "Mariana," from Shakespeare's "Measure for Measure" (1869–1871); "Pandora opening her fatal casket" (1869–1875); "Proserpine," empress of Hades, enchained to the nether world (1872); and "La Ghirlandata" – "The Garland Girl" – (1873). Into these splendid and highly finished studies of the mystic beauty of womanhood, Rossetti poured the full soul of his gospel of romantic love – the love of absolute Beauty absolutely worshipped to the utmost reaches of a consecrated sense, – "Soul's Beauty" and "Body's Beauty" now analyzed and set in contrast each with each, now reconciled and made at one in the last harmony of perfect life. And in these great creations – revelations rather, and perceptions of the inmost verities of things, Rossetti attains the consummation of imaginative art – the crowning of romanticism with the purged inheritance of the classic ideal. It has been claimed that romance treats of characters rather than types; prefers, as we have said, the particular to the universal; and that Rossetti's women are but splendid models, lovely sitters brought by a happy chance into his path, and used by him as the illustrations of that individual beauty which appealed most strongly to his taste. But in these rich harvests of his technical maturity the very realism has discovered the ideal, and as in pure portraiture, the sincere essence of classicism is regained.

A peculiar pathos must for ever be associated with one of the first, and, in the judgment of many, the most beautiful, of these half-length oils, the exquisite "Beata Beatrix," now in the National Gallery. It is the supreme pictorial record of that central tragedy of Rossetti's life, even more intimately revealed to us in his verse, which set him at the side of Dante among mourning poets. On the 23rd of May, 1860, Rossetti married, at Hastings, the beautiful and gifted woman of whom his courtship had lasted nearly ten years.

The wedding had been delayed again and again through the uncertain health of Miss Siddal and the precarious circumstances of the brilliant but wayward young painter's life. It was now accomplished with every augury of long-anticipated joy. The honeymoon was spent in a brief tour through Belgium, concluding with a few days in Paris, where Rossetti made his little impromptu sketch – so entirely out of his wonted trend of themes – "Dr. Johnson and the Methodist Ladies at the Mitre;" a pen-and-ink drawing which he afterwards repeated in water-colours.

Thence to the old rooms in Chatham Place, Blackfriars, partially rebuilt and redecorated for the happy event, Rossetti brought home his bride. The face of the long-desired wife now haunts the painter's easel more continually than before, and recurs with ever-varying charm in nearly all his sketches and the very few finished pictures of the next two years. To this period belong "Lucretia Borgia" (entirely distinct from the "Borgia" of 1851); "The Heart of the Night" (from Tennyson's "Mariana in the South"); the beautiful "Regina Cordium" – "Queen of Hearts" (a title also used for other portraits at different dates); "Bethlehem Gate," and the best of several subjects dealing with the legend of "St. George and the Princess Sabra," together with "Monna Pomona" and "The Rose Garden" of 1864, "Sir Tristram and Iseult Drinking the Love Potion" (1867), "Washing Hands" (1865), and many replicas of the Dante pictures of the previous decade. And in the numerous rough and half-finished portrait sketches, nameless but unmistakable, of Rossetti's "Queen of Hearts" during those two brief years, the shadow of the coming bereavement can be traced in the gradually sharpened features, the more and more fragile hands, the look of increasing pallor and weariness in the earnest face which rests, in one of the latest drawings, on the pillow all too suggestive of its habitual place. On the 2nd of May, 1861, Mrs. Rossetti gave birth to a still-born son. From the consequent illness she rallied considerably during the autumn of that year, and the immediate cause of her death in February, 1862, was, unhappily, an overdose of laudanum, self-administered after a day of fatigue, during the brief absence of her husband from the house. Of the circumstances of the fatal mischance, in so far as they can ever be gleaned from that calamitous hour, of the utterly unexpected shock awaiting Rossetti's return, and of the grief-stricken apparition which aroused the household of Mr. Madox Brown on Highgate Hill at dead of night with incoherent news of the fatality, enough has already been written by those whose sad privilege it was to share in some measure with the overwhelmed sufferer the long pain of that supreme bereavement. The pathetic incident that added to the sadness of the burial, when the young widower hastily gathered up all his poetic manuscripts of the past ten years and laid them beside the fair face in the coffin, a symbol of that best part of himself which he felt must go also to that untimely grave, has become an oft-told tale; and may now be laid in the reverent silence of affection and regret. Nor can the agony and prostration of the succeeding months be fitly recorded save in his own chronicles of song – the great elegiac "Confessio Amantis" of the "House of Life" sonnets.

Recruiting at last in slow degrees his powers upon brush and canvas, he dedicated their first-fruits to the painting of that most beautiful and faithful memorial of the beloved dead – "Beata Beatrix," the Blessed Beatrice – Dante's Beatrice; for the immortal story loved in youth had now redoubled its hold upon his heart. The picture was commissioned by Lord Mount Temple, who was from this time one of Rossetti's most generous patrons and intimate friends. It was begun at Mr. Madox Brown's house, "The Hermitage," on Highgate Hill, but finished at Stobhall, in Scotland, whither Mr. Brown and an equally devoted friend, Dr. John Marshall, had taken the painter in the hope of restoring his now shattered health and assuaging the sorrow that had occasioned its collapse. Rossetti afterwards said of the "Beata Beatrix" that no picture had ever cost him so much to paint, but that in no other task had he been conscious of so perfect a mastery of his instruments.

It should be remembered that of this picture, and indeed of several of Rossetti's finest and best-known works, certain indifferent replicas exist which have been frequently mistaken for their originals. The "Beata Beatrix" in the Birmingham Art Gallery was only half painted by Rossetti, and finished by Madox Brown. Again in the case of "The Blessed Damozel" of a much later date, the more familiar version is the inferior one. There was also a smaller replica of "Dante's Dream," shown in London at the Guildhall Loan Exhibition of 1892. Moreover, it was Rossetti's habit to execute most of his pictures in more than one medium; thus many of his early pen-and-ink drawings were presently reproduced in water-colour; the water-colour designs of 1852–1862 were afterwards transferred to oils; and most of the important oil-paintings of his maturity were duplicated in coloured chalk; some even passing through the pencil, ink, and water-colour stages also. Not infrequently it happened that the chalk version surpassed all the others, as, for instance, in the grand "Pandora" of 1878–79, the most powerful of all his drawings in that medium, and perhaps the greatest of his symbolic figures. Very often, too, he would begin a picture on a very small scale, and gradually enlarge it through successive stages to its final size, as in the case of "Monna Rosa," concerning which he writes on the 18th of June, 1867, to his patron, Mr. F.R. Leyland, one of the most constant and sympathetic of his buyers and friends, – "The picture is much advanced and in every way much altered, as I have again had it considerably enlarged! To begin a fresco as a pocket-miniature seems to be my rule in Art."

The domestic calamity of 1862 rendered a change of residence imperative to the young widower, left desolate amid surroundings charged to the utmost with poignant memories of the past. The old rooms in Chatham Place became unbearable to Rossetti, full as they were of associations of courtship as well as of married life. He sojourned for a time in chambers in Lincoln's Inn Fields, and in the autumn of the same year he moved to No. 16, Cheyne Walk, Chelsea, where he lived intermittently up to the time of his death. It was a fine old house, well suited to be an artist's abode; and especially fortunate in a large garden, which became a valuable resource to Rossetti in those sad days in store for him when any emergence from the seclusion of home grew more and more distasteful to his mind.

By the end of October Rossetti seems to have been established in his new dwelling, which thenceforth it was his pleasure to adorn with all the quaint old curios he could lay his hands on. In the natural revulsion of overwrought feeling, he threw himself upon decorative hobbies of many kinds; developed a passion for blue china and antique pottery; cultivated oriental textures and old oak; and haunted second-hand furniture warehouses with the pertinacious enthusiasm of the devout lover of a bargain. His shelves groaned under their picturesque load of reliquary wares and studio-properties gathered from every age and clime. Here, too, flourished a whole colony of curious animals, such as he delighted to indulge with unbridled license in his domains, – to the produce of countless anecdotes of their pranks, and of the embarrassment of their victims.

The house was shared for some time with three brother-poets, – Swinburne, George Meredith, and W.M. Rossetti. The last-named was for a considerable period a constant inmate; the others, less domesticated, and of strong peculiarities (as is the way of genius) of habit and of taste, presently departed, and their places knew them only as visitors to the brilliant haunt of many other literary celebrities of the day. It has been observed that the most intimate friends of Rossetti's later years were drawn from the ranks of literature rather than art, – a circumstance which need not, however, be too closely paralleled with his own frequent and increasingly successful reversions to the poetic field. It must be remembered that the Pre-Raphaelite movement presents a combination of the highest poetry with the highest pictorial and decorative art incomparable with anything since the days of Michaelangelo. It was natural that the poetic wing of Pre-Raphaelitism, so to speak, should attach itself more and more firmly to the great group of independent and specialistic poets of the age, of whom no counterparts in original genius are to be found outside Pre-Raphaelitism in modern English art. As early as 1855 we find Rossetti well acquainted with Tennyson and in close friendship with Browning and Mrs. Browning; afterwards with William Morris, several of whose poems were inspired by Rossetti's pictures; whose first volume, "The Defense of Guenevere," was dedicated "To my Friend Dante Gabriel Rossetti, Painter," in 1858; and whom Rossetti pronounced to be "the greatest literary identity of our time;" then with Swinburne, whom he placed "highest in inexhaustible splendour of execution," and whose first-fruits in the tragic drama, "The Queen Mother," in 1860, were similarly inscribed; and later still with Philip Bourke Marston, the blind poet; with George Meredith, Edmund Gosse, John Payne, and many others of the choicest if not the most popular qualities of song. From among the earliest of those memorable friendships there is preserved to us a fascinating record of one autumn evening, typical of many more, when the Rossettis and the Brownings assembled together to listen to Tennyson as he read from manuscript his latest poem; – it is the now familiar pen-and-ink sketch of "Tennyson Reading Maud;" one of those marvellously vigorous and convincing thumb-nail drawings which it was Rossetti's wont to evolve, in his inimitable method, from the initial focus of a single blot.

In 1865 we find Rossetti writing to the "Athenæum" to correct a statement which seems to have been made to the effect that he, known chiefly as a water-colour painter, was now attempting a return to oils. The artist protested that he was then, and always had been, an oil-painter; and indeed, as we have seen, he was just now at his zenith of power in that medium, though the contrary impression made on the public is easily explicable in the light of his water-colour work of the previous decade, and of the Russell Place Exhibition of 1856.

By this time the irreparable loss of the one loved model of his early prime was in some degree mitigated, from the artistic side, by the good fortune which secured for him henceforward some of the most beautiful sitters known to the artistic world of the day; women of high culture and distinction, who added to their willing service in the studio the grace of personal friendship and, in several instances, of patronage of the most sympathetic kind. The austere and robust beauty of Miss Herbert, the accomplished actress to whom he was introduced in 1859, lay, as has been already said, entirely apart from his most cherished ideals, and seldom appears in his symbolic paintings. But Mrs. Aldham Heaton, a frequent and valued purchaser, and a lady of presence more congruous with his favourite type, sat for what appears to have been a second "Regina Cordium" in 1861; while in 1864 was commenced his long and most artistically fruitful acquaintance with Miss Wilding, the beautiful girl who served as the model for "Sybilla Palmifera," "La Ghirlandata," "Dis Manibus," "Veronica Veronese," "The Sea-Spell," and several others of his most delicate and spiritual faces, including a third "Regina Cordium" in 1866. Miss Spartali, afterwards Mrs. Stillman, was also a favourite model for some years, and sat for "Fiametta" (distinct from "A Vision of Fiametta" in 1878), and for the lady on the right of the funeral couch in "Dante's Dream," – a work which remained on hand throughout this period.

Apart from the models of his principal pictures, Rossetti painted at different times a goodly number of female portraits, commencing the list of sitters with his mother and younger sister (the elder died at a somewhat early age), and including Lady Mount Temple, who became, with her husband, one of the few intimate friends of his seclusion in later years, Miss Alice Boyd, the kindly hostess of some of his happiest visits to Scotland, yet to be recorded, Mrs. William Morris and her daughters – among them Miss May Morris, now Mrs. Halliday Sparling, who also appears in the "Rosa Triplex" of 1869 and 1874, Mrs. Burne-Jones, Mrs. Dalrymple, Mrs. H.T. Wells, Mrs. Leathart, Mrs. Lushington, Mrs. Virtue Tebbs, Mrs. C. A. Howell, Mrs. Coronio, Miss Heaton, Miss Williams, Miss Kingdon, the Misses Cassavetti, Miss Baring, and Mrs. Banks.

Twice during these years of the gradual maturing of his technical power in oils did Rossetti make excursions into a distinctive branch of decorative art, the practice of designing for stained-glass. As early as 1860, William Morris, Burne-Jones, and a few others interested in this much-neglected craft established a firm which was known for some time under the name of Morris and Co., and for which in 1861 Rossetti executed a series of seven effective cartoons for church windows illustrating the "Parable of the Vineyard," or the "Wicked Husbandmen." Both designs are of extraordinary vigour and dramatic intensity; strongly mediæval in directness and simplicity, but with a large coherence and fulness of conception, and a harmonious richness of workmanship breathing a more modern spirit into the ancient tale. The dignity and earnestness of the drawing places it on a level with the best work of his purely romantic period, but its technical finish shows the more perfect balance between conception and execution which he was rapidly attaining in his maturity. The designs are now to be seen in the church of St. Martin on the Hill, Scarborough.

A similar work was undertaken by Rossetti six years later, when it was proposed to dedicate a memorial window to his aunt, Miss Margaret Polidori, in Christchurch, Albany Street, Regent's Park, where she had long been a regular attendant until her death in 1867. Rossetti chose for his subject "The Sermon on the Plain." This design also was executed in stained-glass by the firm of Morris and Co., and placed in the church in 1869.

By this time Rossetti's commissions for pictures had happily become so numerous as to justify his seeking competent assistance in his studio. His friend Mr. Knewstub, at first a pupil, filled for some time the office of assistant. Then Mr. Henry Treffry Dunn was engaged in 1867, and remained with Rossetti almost up to the date of his death. It seems to have been in the years 1867–68 that his health, never fully re-established after the physical and mental prostration of 1862, began to give way beneath that most terrible and relentless of nervous maladies, the special curse of the artistic temperament – insomnia. To that slow and baffling torment, by which Nature sometimes seems to be avenging herself in a sort of frenzied jealousy upon her own handiwork, Rossetti's highly wrought sensibilities and overwhelming imagination made him the more easy prey. His whole being was constitutionally endowed with that fatal faculty of visualizing the invisible, of suffering more acutely under imagined than under realized pains (though both were laid upon him) which, like an all-consuming fire, burns itself out only with the life that feeds it. Of such sleepless nights as thus become the terror of their victims, haunted with all memories and all fears, Rossetti has left us many a painfully vivid word-picture in his poetry; supremely, perhaps, in that most tragic sonnet, "Sleepless Dreams" –

"Girt in dark growths, yet glimmering with one star,"

ending with the despairing cry upon the deaf goddess of repose –

"O Night, Night, Night! art thou not known to me,
A thicket hung with masks of mockery,
    And watered with the wasteful warmth of tears?"

Many such nights Rossetti bore, we may well believe, before he fled at last, when rational means seemed of no avail against his malady, to that most dangerous source of ease, the too free use of chloral. Several times he partially shook off the habit, and intervals of comparative comfort and cheerfulness were frequent until 1872, when other phases of illness, independent of it though still of nervous origin, further undermined the constitution already weakened by years of abnormal strain. A respite of a very pleasant kind was afforded him in the successive autumns of 1868–69 by his visits to Miss Boyd at Penkill, in Perthshire, where, in company with other congenial spirits, he spent some weeks of comparative happiness and ease. Here he was induced to resume his poetry, which, save for a few significant sonnets, had lain in abeyance since that sad day on which he had buried his manuscripts in the grave of his early love. Now, yielding with much reluctance and conflict of heart to the persuasion of friends who knew the value of the poems thus lost to literature, he gave permission for the coffin to be exhumed, and the manuscripts removed. The story of this delicate task, and of its judicious and successful fulfilment under the personal superintendence of two or three intimate friends of the widower, has already been related in detail by one of the eye-witnesses aforesaid. The poems, after seven years' concealment in the quiet grave in Highgate Cemetery, were duly restored to their author's hand. This having been done, he set to work arranging, re-writing, and adding some of the finest work of his poetic maturity to a collection of poems which should be an immortal record and perpetuation of his love.

Towards the close of 1869 Rossetti began to share with his friend William Morris the romantic and picturesque old manor house of Kelmscott, near Lechdale, in Gloucestershire; a district full of interesting landscape, and haunted by the inspiring shade of Shelley, who there wrote his characteristic fragment, "A Summer Evening in Lechdale Churchyard." The scenery of the surrounding country is brought in vivid glimpses here and there into Rossetti's poetry, as, for instance, in "Down Stream" ("Between Holmscote and Hurstcote") and other lyrics of his later life. Here he painted "The Bower Maiden" – a pretty country lass with marigolds. But a great part of his time was still spent at home in Chelsea, where in 1871 he at last completed the finest oil version of "Dante's Dream." Save for the incomparable "Beata Beatrix," it is the summing-up of all his highest interpretations of the Dante spirit; the consummation of his gospel of romantic love. His friend Mr. Val Prinsep quotes Rossetti as writing in a letter about this time: – "I should like of all things to show you my big picture 'Dante's Dream' now, if you are ever in town. Indeed, I should probably have written to you before this of the picture being in a state to see, on the chance of its accelerating your movements townwards, but was deterred from doing so by the fact that every special appointment I have made to show it has been met by the clerk of the weather with such a careful provision of absolute darkness for that day and hour, that I tempt my fate no more in that way, as the picture cannot absolutely be seen except in a fair light, and one's nerves do not hold out for ever under such onslaughts.... Everyone who has seen the 'Dante's Dream' (not yet quite finished, but close upon), has seemed so thoroughly pleased with it that I think I may hope without vanity some progress has been made, and this I feel sure I shall carry on in my next work. Of course I have only shown the 'Dante' to a few, as otherwise I might spend my time in nothing else, the picture blocking up the whole studio when displayed."

Ten years later, in 1881, the "Dante's Dream" gained for the painter one of the very few popular triumphs of his lifetime. It was exhibited at Liverpool, bought by the Corporation of that city for £1,500, hung in the Walker Art Gallery, where it now remains; and instantly took rank among the greatest masterpieces of modern art. "Fifty years hence," said Sir Noel Paton, "it will be counted among the half-dozen supreme pictures of the world."

The story of the last ten years of Rossetti's private life, clouded by frequent ill-health, and disturbed by that most intolerable of a poet's trials, a literary controversy, remains yet to be told by him who shared most intimately the seclusion and the affliction of that troublous period, Mr. Theodore Watts; whose oft-quoted sonnet to his friend, as Mr. Coulson Kernahan has said, gives a fuller picture of Rossetti than volumes of prose could do, and therefore commands insertion here:

"I told thee of an island, far and lone,
    Whose shores are as a harp, where billows break
    In spray of music, and the breezes shake
O'er spicy seas a woof of colour and tone,
While that sweet music echoes like a moan
    In the island's heart, and sighs around the lake,
    Where, watching fearfully a watchful snake,
A damsel weeps upon her emerald throne.

Life's ocean, breaking round thy senses' shore
    Struck golden song, as from the strand of day:
    For us the joy, for thee the fell foe lay –
Pain's blinking snake around the fair isle's core,
    Turning to sighs the enchanted sounds that play
Around thy lonely island evermore."

The mingled pain and privilege of Mr. Watts's ministry was shared to a great degree by Lord and Lady Mount Temple, Mrs. Sumner, Dr. Gordon Hake and his son, Mr. George Hake, Mr. Madox Brown, Mr. Frederick Shields, and Mr. Sandys. Mr. Leyland also saw him frequently, and added generous and unremitting friendship to his patronage of the wayward painter's work. He was the purchaser of some of the most important pictures of Rossetti's last decade, including the beautiful "Dis Manibus," or "The Roman Widow," (1874), which remains unsurpassed for delicate purity and depth of colour by any of the masterpieces of his prime; "Mnemosyne," or "La Ricordanza," or "The Lamp of Memory" (1876–78), one of his most noble and impressive symbolic figures; "The Sea-Spell," (1875–77), and a replica of "The Blessed Damozel" (1873–77), which he painted for Mr. William Graham in illustration of his own poem:

"The Blessed Damozel leaned out
    From the gold bar of heaven;
Her eyes were deeper than the depths
    Of water stilled at even:
She had three lilies in her hand
    And the stars in her hair were seven."

The publication, in 1870, of Rossetti's volume of "Poems," containing, together with some of his loveliest short lyrics, "The Blessed Damozel," and the "House of Life" sonnets, led the way for that unfortunate attack upon him in the critical press which undoubtedly contributed to the shortening of his days, however regrettable may have been the hyper-sensitive manner in which the poet met his arraignment. In 1871 an article signed "Thomas

Maitland" was published in the "Contemporary Review," entitled "The Fleshly School of Poetry," in which Rossetti's poems were attacked, from an avowedly moral point of view, on the ground of sensuality. Ignoring the essential principles of all Rossetti's work – the sacredness of the senses as the instruments of the soul – the meaning of all physical beauty as the witness of an immanent God – the writer deliberately charged him with pandering to the lowest instincts of his readers, and being, in short, the prophet of that later and grossly materialistic phase of European art of which the very name *Pre*-Raphaelite was a repudiation. It is not surprising that to a deeply (if undefinedly) religious nature like Rossetti's this should have seemed the hardest blow that could have been dealt at his art and at him. The publication of the magazine article, however, seriously disconcerted him at the moment. It was not until the offensive and wholly unfair indictment was re-issued in the following year in pamphlet form that it began to assume a more serious aspect in the victim's eyes. Criticism of his poetic methods he could have borne with equanimity. Indifference and neglect seldom troubled him. He cared little for popularity, and was no seeker after fame, although he naturally desired the appreciation of those whose judgment was of real account in literature. But he did care for his general reputation as a clean-lived and pure-minded man. This charge assailed the ethical foundations of all his work. He had seen in the loveliest things of earth the vessels and channels of the loveliness of heaven. And that this should be counted to him for sensuality – that the love which had been to him "a worship and a regeneration" should be held up to scorn as a gross and carnal passion – that was the intolerable thing!

Not that he lacked defenders. His own answer, under the title of "The Stealthy School of Criticism," in the columns of the "Athenæum," was more than supported by Mr. Swinburne's indignant challenge, "Under the Microscope;" and other loyal friends contributed to a sufficient vindication. Save in the too morbid imagination of the poet, the attack soon lapsed, for the most part, into the oblivion it deserved; more especially since the writer, a few years later, had the manliness to retract his charge, and to make a candid apology, though a tardy one,for having uttered it. But not so easily could the pain given to Rossetti be overcome. He now began to shrink intensely from society, fearing at all points to encounter that suspicion of his artistic work. Suffering acutely from nervous prostration and insomnia, he yielded himself the more fully to the fatal chloral habit which only aggravated his condition. In the autumn of 1872 he spent some weeks at the house of Dr. Gordon Hake at Roehampton, and proceeded thence with Mr. Madox Brown, Mr. George Hake, and Mr. Bell Scott to Stobhall in Perthshire, on the Tay. Returning to the south in improved health, Rossetti and Mr. George Hake proceeded at once to Kelmscott Manor, where they settled for a considerable time. Rossetti indeed remained for nearly two years, gradually resuming his artistic work, and regaining at times something of his old vivacity and high spirits: only a few friends went to and fro in visits full of mutual delight and inspiration. The beautiful old house, and the quaint, romantic chamber that served for studio, became the resort of poets and artists, critics and connoisseurs, disciples and aspirants, in companies small indeed, but brilliant and memorable as any that gathered round the young Pre-Raphaelites in Newman Street or the maturer masters of art and song that assembled in Cheyne Walk, Chelsea. Mr. William Morris and his family were there frequently; Dr. Gordon Hake made a visit, and afterwards embodied his memories in his sequence of sonnets addressed to Mr.Theodore Watts, "The New Day," one of which deserves quotation:

"O happy days with him who once so loved us!
    We loved as brothers, with a single heart,
The man whose iris-woven pictures moved us
    From Nature to her blazoned shadow – Art.
How often did we trace the nestling Thames
    From humblest waters on his course of might,
Down where the weir the bursting current stems –
    There sat till evening grew to balmy night,

Veiling the weir whose roar recalled the strand
    Where we had listened to the wave-lipped sea,
That seemed to utter plaudits while we planned
    Triumphal labours of the day to be.
The words were his: 'Such love can never die;'
The grief was ours when he no more was nigh."

And as his health continued to improve, Rossetti's poetry and painting rose again to their highest level. The former, indeed, is thought by some sound critics to reach at this juncture a superb merit unattained before; for it was here that he wrote the first of the three great romantic ballads which mark the zenith of his poetic power. "Rose Mary" stands supreme in this incomparable category. Nor did he ever far surpass, if at all, his pictures of this period, – "The Bower Maiden" (1873) for frank and vigorous natural beauty in the pretty child with the fresh-blowing marigolds, "Dis Manibus" or "The Roman Widow" (1874) for delicate and simple pathos in the treatment of the classic world; and "Proserpine" (1874) for the sombre moral tragedy symbolized in the classic story, seldom, if ever, so interpreted on canvas before.

In these years also he painted the beautiful "Garland Girl," "La Ghirlandata" (1873), and "Veronica Veronese" (1872), called at first "The Day-dream," but wholly distinct from the later work of that date; reverted, or endeavoured to revert in sketches, to his old fantasy of "Michael Scott's Wooing," and resumed a subject begun in 1864, but never quite fully worked out, "The Boat of Love," suggested by Dante's second Sonnet, – "Guido, vorrei che tu e Lapo ed io," and representing Dante and Beatrice embarking in a boat with his friend and brother-poet Guido Calvacanti, and his lady Giovanna, and Lapo degli Uberti and his love.

In the autumn of 1874 Rossetti returned to Chelsea, and again made his headquarters at 16, Cheyne Walk, where he remained, save for two visits to the seaside, until 1880. Here he worked from time to time at the picture illustrative of his own early poem, "The Blessed Damozel," – the sole instance, by the way, of Rossetti's completion of a subject in verse before attempting it on canvas; and began what promised to be among the most profound of his mystical creations, "The Sphinx" or "The Question," and also the last subject he ever took from the "Vita Nuova" of Dante, "La Donna della Finestra," or "Our Lady of Pity." These two, as well as "The Boat of Love," remained unfinished in his studio. To this fruitful decade belong an excellent replica of an early water-colour, "The Damozel of the Sanct Grael" (1874); the exquisite crayon drawing "The Spirit of the Rainbow" (1877); and four splendid oils, "The Sea Spell" (1876), "A Vision of Fiametta" (1878), "The Day-dream" and "Mnemosyne" or "The Lamp of Memory" (1880). To 1875 is due "La Bello Mano" ("The Beautiful Hand"). In 1879 he made a crayon drawing, which he called "Sancta Lilias," for an Annunciation; depicting a girl unfolding a white scarf from a tall lily which she carries in her hand; but the sketch was never finished, nor advanced beyond the crayon stage.

In 1875 Rossetti took for a time a pleasant and secluded house near Bognor, – Aldwick Lodge, standing in its own grounds, wellnigh buried in shrubbery, in a lane west of the town, and near (as Dr. Hake tells us in some delightful reminiscences of a visit there) "to the roughest bit of beach on the Sussex coast." Here, gathering together his mother, sister, and aunts, and such intimate friends as Dr. Hake and Mr. Theodore Watts, he enjoyed at the close of this year a Christmas week to which he afterwards looked back as to one of the happiest he ever spent.

It was at Bognor that Rossetti, influenced, no doubt, by his companionship, woke for the first time to the magic of the sea. It is extraordinary that so passionately romantic a spirit as his should have remained, until the eve of his fiftieth year, absolutely unaffected by that profound and intimate sway which the sea holds over the poetic nature once brought, however distantly, within even the rumour and echo of its majestic voice. Now the spell he had so long eluded was cast upon him with irresistible force. He began to haunt the shore with a child's eagerness for the grandeur and the urgent mystery of tides. Day after day he paced the beach for miles together, pursuing the new vision, the new rapture of the stimulated sense. The surf, tumultuous and loud on that wild coast, enthralled him like a charm; the waves drove his fancy to new spheres; his poetry was turned to fresh scenes and subjects; he began to write "The White Ship," the first, though perhaps not the greatest, of his historic ballads. For the time, he was absorbed almost wholly in that revelation of splendour and power, – in the primal glories of sea and sky; "two symbols of the infinite," as the captive Mazzini called them.

But when we wonder at the lateness of this æsthetic development on Rossetti's part, we must remember that he was naturally without that love of terrestrial and cosmical Nature for her own sake that is the commonly-accepted attribute of poets. There was in his whole being no trace of Pantheism, no worship of external loveliness apart from conscious life. To him the sole joy of life was in the human; the supreme tragedy of life was in the sexual. The conception of the two elemental principles – the man-principle and the woman-principle – striving, uniting, prevailing, against all the forces of destiny, sufficed him for his conception of the universe. He was utterly alien to the Wordsworth spirit; its serene monism was abhorrent to him. Apart as he lived from intellectual speculation, he was, in his unformulated and unconscious philosophy, dualistic to the core; as all true Romance must ever be. For the essence of Romance is in its recognition of the conflict between matter and spirit, between Nature and Man. Even its joy and exultation in the physical life as the channel of the Higher Spirit takes its glory from the sense of conquest over the Lower Spirit which threatens it from the same unknown world behind all. Therefore there lies always beneath the awe and wonder of romance towards the natural and the supernatural world a deep instinct of rebellion, of antagonism, which debars it from the Wordsworth spirit, at peace with earth and heaven. Resignation there may be in romance; acquiescence, never. There may come, indeed, a passionate and whole-hearted love of natural scenery, a frank delight, as in the Celtic temper, in every external object that can minister to man's æsthetic enjoyment of beauty as a revelation of the divine. But the limits of the divine grow more perceptible as man emerges from the childhood of the world. "There hath passed away a glory from the earth." Rossetti knew this – "knew" it, not in the intellectual sense of the word; and therefore he could never turn to Nature for that regenerating rest and peace which in some moods – not quite the highest – she can give. He never gained that next stage of spiritual emancipation and enrichment at which the sense of conflict is its own reward; as when the soldier, with "his soul well-knit" and every nerve schooled and chastened on the eve of a great battle, feels a profound repose, a diviner calm than that of the acclaimed victor. "The man who, though his fights be all defeats, still fights" – as Coventry Patmore sang while Rossetti was yet young – has verily seen "the beginnings of peace."

It was at Bognor, too, that he began work upon the most ambitious of all his great symbolic figures, the "Venus Astarte," or "Astarte Syriaca," in which he strove – vainly perhaps, but with a superb effort towards a superhuman task – to combine and express all the mystic sensuousness and occult magic of Orientalism with the clear and scientific wisdom of the Western world. The Syrian Venus stands "between the sun and moon a mystery," attended by winged and torch-bearing choristers; eloquent of the painter's long and last struggle to reconcile sense, emotion, and intellect in the highest consummation of pictorial art.

In the following summer (1876) Rossetti paid a pleasant visit, at the invitation of Lord and Lady Mount Temple, to their house at Broadlands, in Hampshire, where he made some progress with the best version of "The Blessed Damozel." The predella to this work, in which the lover left on earth is seen waiting beside a river for the vision of the Beloved, was painted from the beechwoods of the neighbourhood.

In 1876 Rossetti went with Madox Brown, Mr. George Hake, Mr. Theodore Watts, and his mother and sister to Herne Bay. Ill health had now settled permanently upon him, and painting became more difficult and intermittent, yet his technical power remained for the most part singularly unimpaired. In 1878 he completed "A Vision of Fiametta," – an admirable and wholly new version of the subject from Boccaccio which he had treated some years back. Fiametta is in the painter's thought an angel of immortality:

"Gloom-girt 'mid Spring-flushed apple-growths she stands"

– his bright Easter-maiden, with the crimson bird on the bough beside her, the symbol of warm, full-blooded life, as is the soft red robe she wears, – of life so rich and sweet as to yield the guarantee of victory; the spirit that can defy death and be its own assurance of resurrection. The apple-blossoms fall in scattered petals to the ground as she pushes the boughs apart with her lifted hand. Behind her is a stormy April sky, but around her head there plays a light, as of hope beyond the grave. She is the covenant of eternal spring, for she

– "with re-assuring eyes most fair,
A presage and a promise stands; as 'twere
    On Death's dark storm the rainbow of the soul."

But now the time was nigh when "Death's dark storm" must break upon Rossetti. The last great and sane strength of his genius was spent upon poetry, – in the crowning of his romantic ballads with the masterpiece of their class, "The King's Tragedy." This was published, in a volume entitled "Ballads and Sonnets," in 1881. The previous year had seen the completion of the last important picture that ever came fully finished from his hand, – an oil version of the almost full-length figure replicated several times, under the name of "The Day-dream," and consisting of the most beautiful and perfect of his portraits of Mrs. William Morris.

Of the laborious conscientiousness of Rossetti's practice in painting it may here be said that it has been greatly underestimated by those who only saw the less serious side of his complex and self-contradictory nature. That "the capacity for taking infinite pains" developed with the genius which gave it scope is abundantly attested by those who witnessed not only his restless roving from one task to another, but also the ungrudging concentration of toil which he bestowed in turns upon them all. Mr. Shields, who for years was a constant companion in Rossetti's studio, says in his too-brief record of that intimacy: – "One evening when the fine full-length figure, holding an open book and honeysuckle, called 'The Day-dream,' was nearly completed, I found him standing far off from it in the dusky light and searching it critically. 'It seems to me, that the lower limbs are too short: what do you think?' An examination compelled me to endorse his fears. It was enough. Condemnation to the effacement of half the picture was instantly passed. Long sprays of young sycamore, rich with the ruddy buds of early spring, crossed before the lady's green skirt. That sacrificed, it was not possible to save the foliage, and the season was too far advanced for fresh reference to nature. The first necessary step therefore was to copy these on to a clean canvas; that done, he determinately scraped out the large erring surface, corrected the proportions of the figure, and then calmly re-painted all, striking lastly the sycamore boughs into their new places from the rescued studies." An even more laborious re-painting, says the same authority, was effected in the final oil version of "Dante's Dream," completed in 1871. The figure of one of the ladies attendant at the bedside of the dead Beatrice failed to satisfy him in the disposition of her drapery. At the last moment he set to work to make entirely new studies for the robe in question, and almost wholly re-painted the figure that wore it.

In the autumn of 1881, which witnessed the publication of his second volume of original poetry, Rossetti went with his friend Mr. Hall Caine, the eminent novelist, to spend some weeks at a little farmhouse in the Vale of St. John, near Keswick, Cumberland. The surrounding scenery was of a wildly beautiful kind, well calculated to soothe and inspire the city-pent poets; but Rossetti was by this time too ill to find relief from nervous strain in the long walks which he had enjoyed at Bognor. He paced instead, for hours together, the quaint little sitting-room where, night after night, he would read aloud from the treasures of modern fiction. Of Rossetti's acute critical faculty, and his sound literary judgment alike in poetry and prose romance, abundant testimony has been given by the many privileged to enjoy from year to year, especially in the period of his prime, the inestimable help and delight of his enthusiastic counsel and his frank, outspoken, but never ungenerous criticism. Such witness is fully endorsed by Mr. Caine's records even of this last autumn of his life, when, through shattered health and failing hopes for his own future, he retained in a great measure the mental vision and acumen of happier days, as well as his own creative power in design and poetry. Rossetti never tired of these nightly discussions of the inexhaustible topics of literary art: he loved to prolong them far into the morning hours; and often, as his friend has told us, they saw the sunrise break over the great hills as they went at last to rest.

Nor was the year without fruit in painting. The pathetic picture of "La Pia," a new design in oils, though with a title used for a sketch in 1867, ranks high among his later performances. The subject, briefly broached in Dante's "Purgatorio," deals with the imprisonment of the young wife of Nello dell' Pietra of Siena in a fortress in the Maremma, in the midst of a noxious swamp. Rossetti was still at work, too, upon the great symbolic picture in which he was endeavouring to sum up all that he had implied in his maturer treatment of womanly beauty, – the mystic and solemn "Venus Astarte" or "Astarte Syriaca" (the Syrian Venus). The "Cassandra" proposed by him somewhile previously was never far advanced, but he had painted in 1880 a somewhat inferior oil version of a subject which had been the favourite of his youth, "The Salutation of Beatrice."

One of the very few public triumphs which came to Rossetti

in his lifetime stands in the annals of 1881. His great picture, "Dante's Dream," painted ten years earlier, was purchased by the Corporation of Liverpool for £1,500, and hung in the Walker Art Gallery, where it was at once hailed with general and almost unalloyed praise.

Early in February, 1882, prostrated by an attack of a semi-paralytic character, Rossetti was removed to Birchington-on-Sea, near Margate, where his old friend, Mr. John P. Seddon, had generously placed a house known as West Cliff Bungalow at his disposal. Mr. Hall Caine went with him, and they were soon joined by the artist's mother, sister, and brother, and visited frequently by Mr. Watts, and by the young poet Mr. William Sharp, Mr. Shields, and Mr. Leyland, who brought with him Rossetti's long-trusted medical adviser, Dr. John Marshall, to add his counsels to the unremitting care of the local physician, Dr. Harris.

Even within sight of the fast-approaching end, his earnest spirit did not falter in its aspirations, nor was the grasp of the busy hand upon its loved work relaxed altogether. He now executed a beautiful little oil sketch of a subject which he had attempted many years before – "Joan of Arc Kissing the Sword of Deliverance;" a striking and pathetic allegory of his own soul's attitude, as he stood ready to greet with glad and fearless reverence the long-impending sword of the last Deliverer. He was one of those to whom, as George Eliot once said, early death takes the aspect of salvation.

At Birchington he reverted also to his picture of ten years back, "Proserpine." His last poetry was written less than a week before his death, in two sonnets illustrative of his yet unfinished picture, "The Question," or "The Sphinx," in which the figures of Youth, Manhood, and Age appear before the Mother of Mystery. Early in youth Rossetti had made a resolution that no day should pass without some piece of work, however imperfect, issuing from his hands, and amid much pain and weakness, sorrow and discouragement, he kept that resolution almost till his dying day.

On Good Friday, the 7th of April, he became rapidly worse, but remained cheerful and composed. On Easter Day the shadow of death hung over the little household. In the evening the group of watchers gathered with increasing apprehension round the bed. "I think I shall die to-night," said Rossetti quietly, some hours before the end. Soon after nine o'clock a momentary struggle gave warning of the approaching rest. His mother, sister, and brother, Mr. Theodore Watts, Mr. Shields, Mr. Hall Caine, Dr. Harris and the nurse were with him, when, twenty minutes later, he passed away, meeting the Deliverer in perfect calm; seeing, as he himself expressed it, "on Death's dark storm the rainbow of the soul."

On Easter Monday Mr. Shields, at the request of the bereaved family, made a careful and accurate pencil drawing of the head of his late friend as he lay ready for the last sad rites. A plaster cast of the head, by Brucciani, was also made, but was not considered satisfactory.

It was decided that the funeral should take place at Birchington; and there, in the quiet little graveyard on the cliffs, Rossetti was laid to rest. Mr. William Sharp and Philip Bourke Marston (who died five years later) were among the mourners, besides those already gathered in the house of grief.

The quiet hamlet of Birchington-on-Sea is now a well-loved place of pilgrimage. The quaint, un-English-looking house in which the poet-painter died is honoured as "Rossetti Bungalow." In the old, shingle-towered, ivy-grown church, a stained-glass memorial window, his mother's gift, shows, in the one light, his own design, "The Passover in the Holy Family," and, in the other, Christ giving sight to a blind minstrel, – the work of his old friend, Mr. Shields. In the churchyard, opposite the south-west porch, the old verger shows, with touching pride and enthusiasm, a beautiful Runic cross, on the face of which is this inscription:

HERE SLEEPS
GABRIEL CHARLES DANTE ROSSETTI,

HONOURED UNDER THE NAME OF
DANTE GABRIEL ROSSETTI,
AMONG PAINTERS AS A PAINTER,
AND AMONG POETS AS A POET.
BORN IN LONDON,
OF PARENTAGE MAINLY ITALIAN, 12 MAY, 1828.
DIED AT BIRCHINGTON, 9 APRIL, 1882.
And at the back the following:
THIS CRUCIFORM MONUMENT,
BESPOKEN BY DANTE ROSSETTI'S MOTHER,
WAS DESIGNED BY HIS LIFELONG FRIEND,
FORD MADOX BROWN,
Executed by J. & H. Patteson,
And erected by his brother William and sister Christina Rossetti.

Another interesting memorial has since been established in the form of a drinking fountain, designed by Mr. Seddon, with a bronze bust modelled by Mr. Madox Brown, erected by subscription in 1887 in front of the old house, 16, Cheyne Walk, Chelsea, which was Rossetti's home for twenty years.

An estimate of the disposition and character of such a man as Rossetti will not be lightly attempted by those who can only honour his memory from afar; having never added to the deep enjoyment of his art the privilege of personal intercourse with the artist. His tender and passionate affection, his chivalrous loyalty, his gracious *bonhomie*, his winning dignity, are matters so familiar to all who really knew him, as to render eulogy alike superfluous and impertinent. Of the other side of that magnetic personality, – of his hyper-sensitive pride, his morbid isolation of his suffering self from those healthy breezes of broad intellectual life which it is so easy to prescribe, so bitterly hard for a nature such as his to stand against, – of these things it may be said with all sympathy and reverence that they were the price of his greatness. There are some temperaments so finely organized, so delicately strung, that even joy is painful to them. They cannot lose in the sense of delight the consciousness of what that delight has cost them. They perceive so acutely the realities, the conditions, of life, that an hour of rapture makes them more quick to the pain behind and before. Such was Shelley, such were Keats and Byron; such was Dante Gabriel Rossetti. It is the curse of the artistic temperament: it is the blessing of Art.

"There are some of us," said Shelley, "who have loved an Antigone before we visited this earth, and must pursue through life that unregainable ideal." "I think," he added, in words that might well be applied to Rossetti, "one is always in love with something or other; the error consists in seeking in a mortal image the likeness of what is, perhaps, eternal." In other words, Rossetti was an idealist, and for the idealist there is no primrose path to heaven. His soul was too open to the ideal to be proof against the actual. His whole nature was like an Æolian harp, responsive through the whole gamut of thought and sense to every breath of circumstance or destiny that played about the world around it. For him there was no life without emotion. He craved sensation, as one craves a narcotic, to destroy its own results. *Ennui* was his bane. Nothing in his history is more pathetic than his need, in later years, of the perpetual ministry of close friends. The delicate instrument that could never be silent was hard to keep in tune. It demanded a firm and tender hand laid upon all those quivering strings of being to merge the discords into some sort of harmony, even if it were always in a minor key. Such a hand he found more than once among those that knew and loved him, but he found it supremely in the friendship of Mr. Theodore Watts, to whom his last poems were dedicated.

On the following pages: works by the Pre-Raphaelite artists, followed by other 19th century artists.

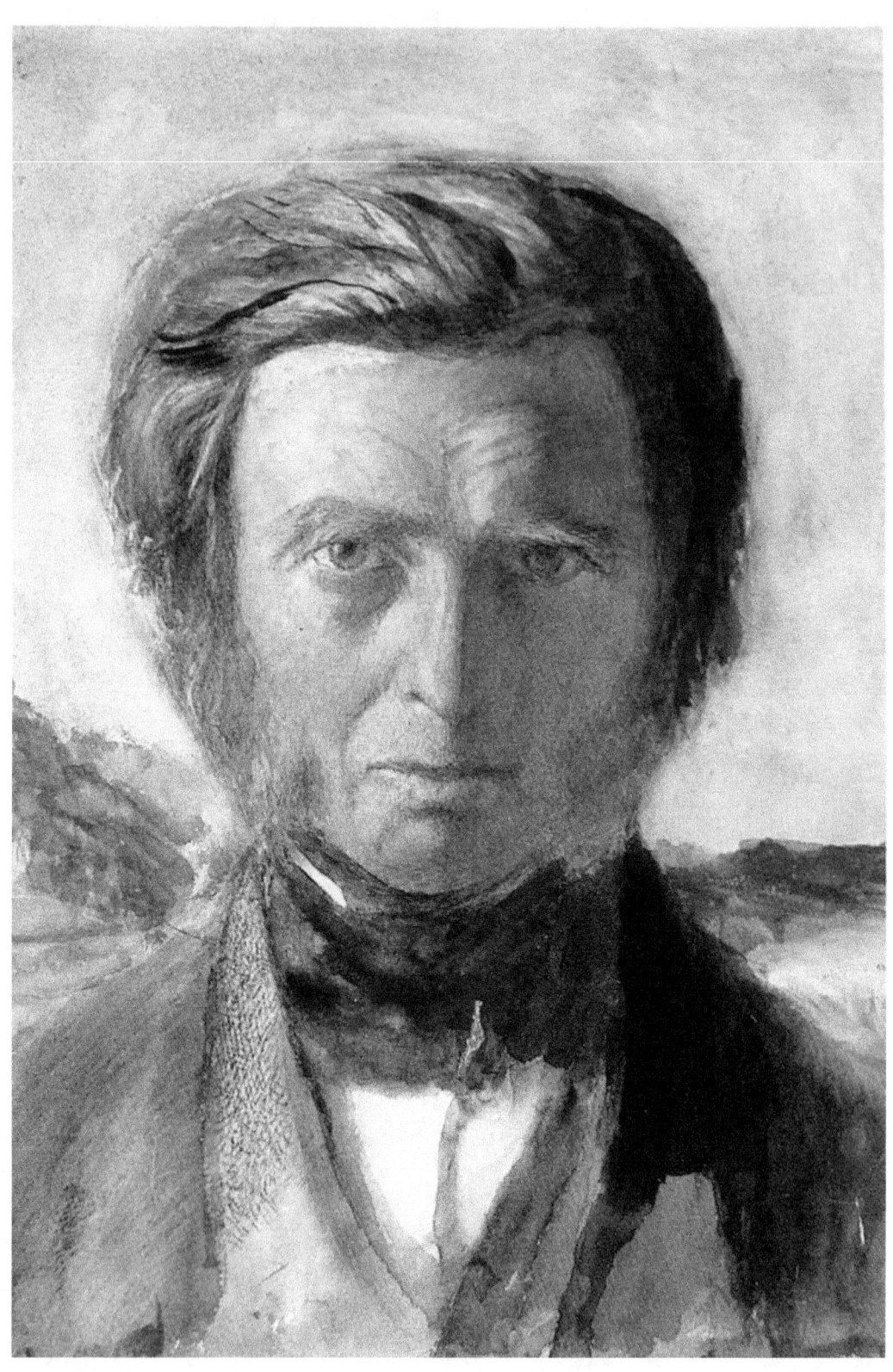

John Ruskin, Self-Portrait, 1875

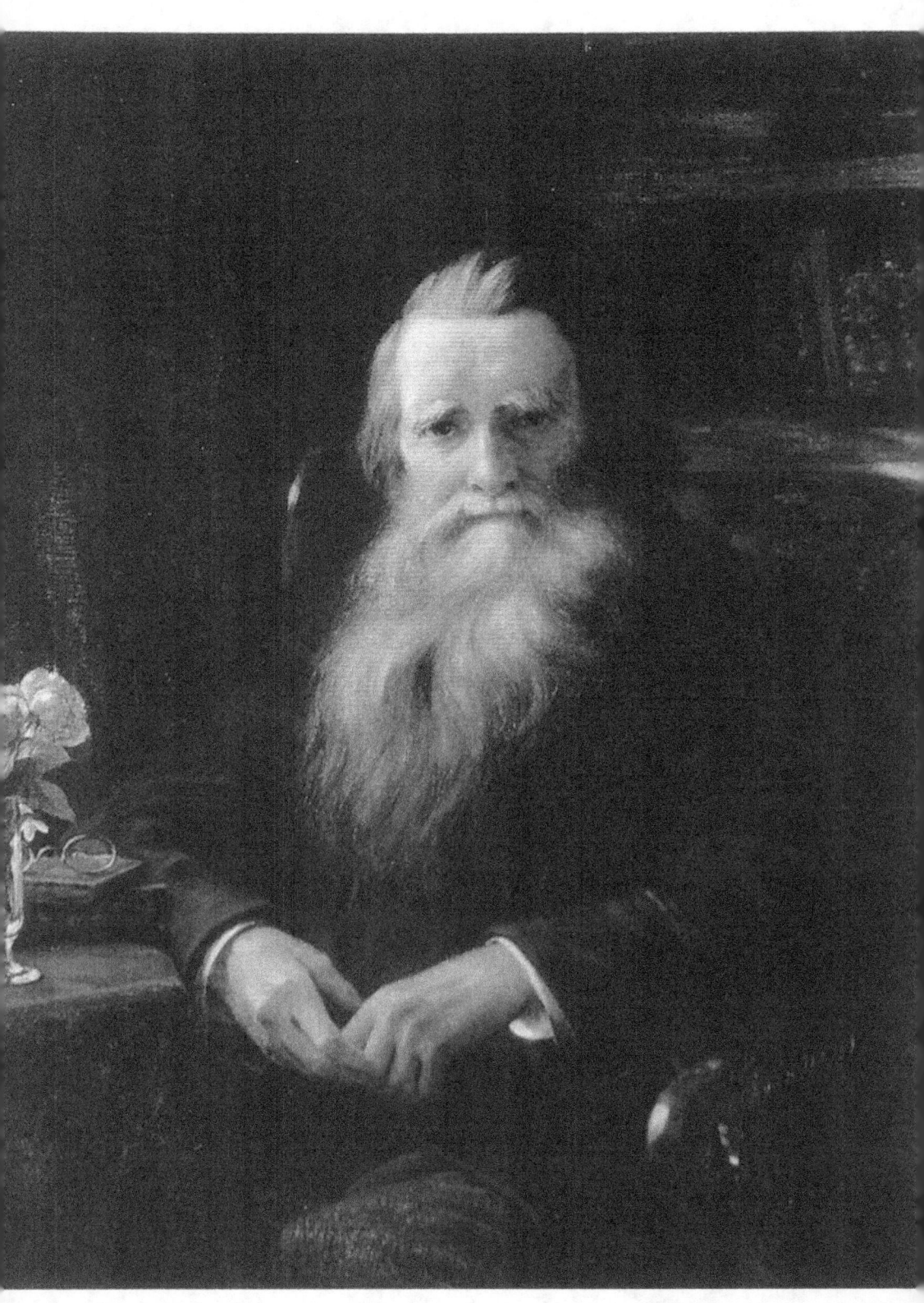

W.G. Collingwood, John Ruskin, 1897

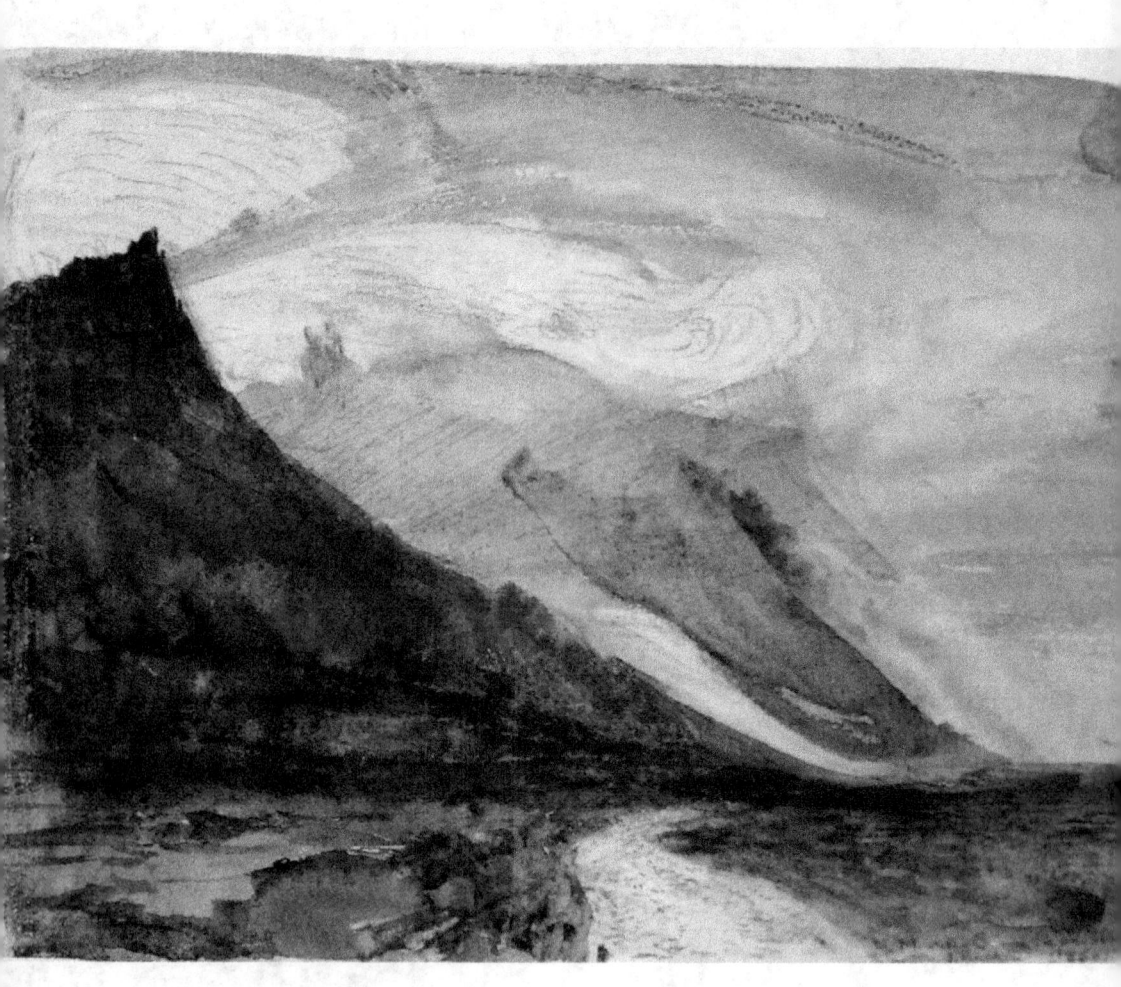

John Ruskin, Moonlight, Chamonix, 1888

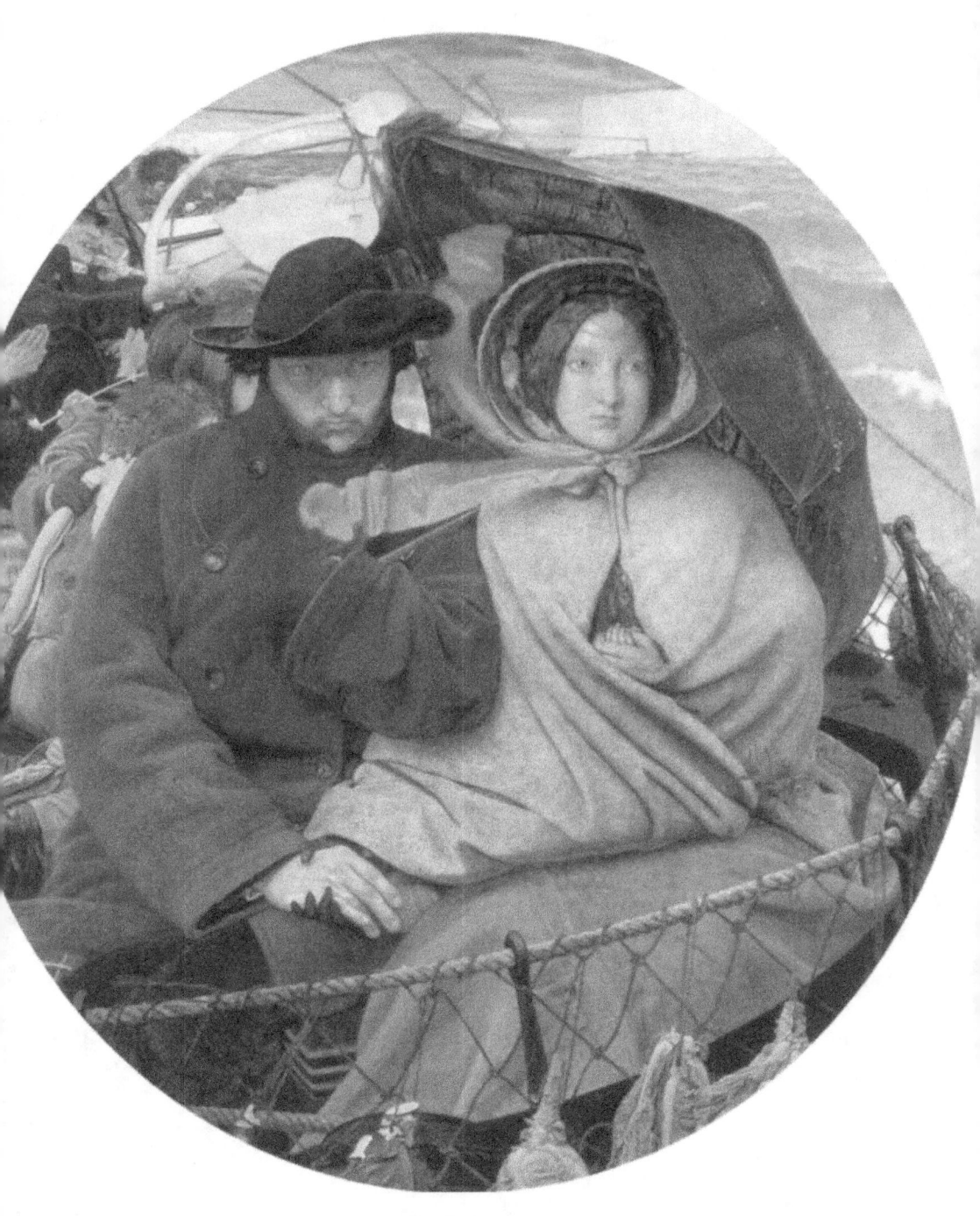

Ford Madox Brown, The Last of England, 1855,
Birmingham

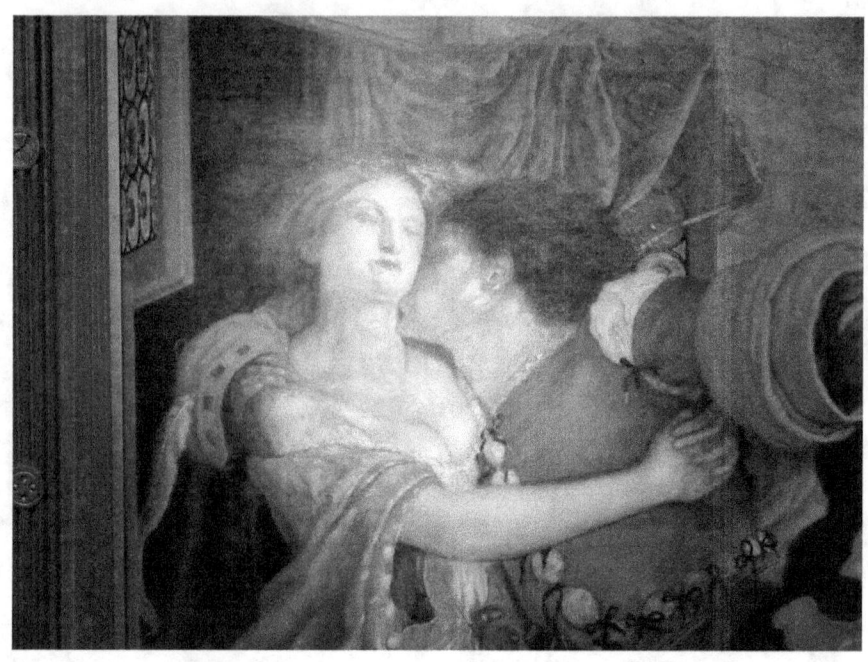

Ford Madox Brown, Romeo and Juliet, 1869-70, Delaware

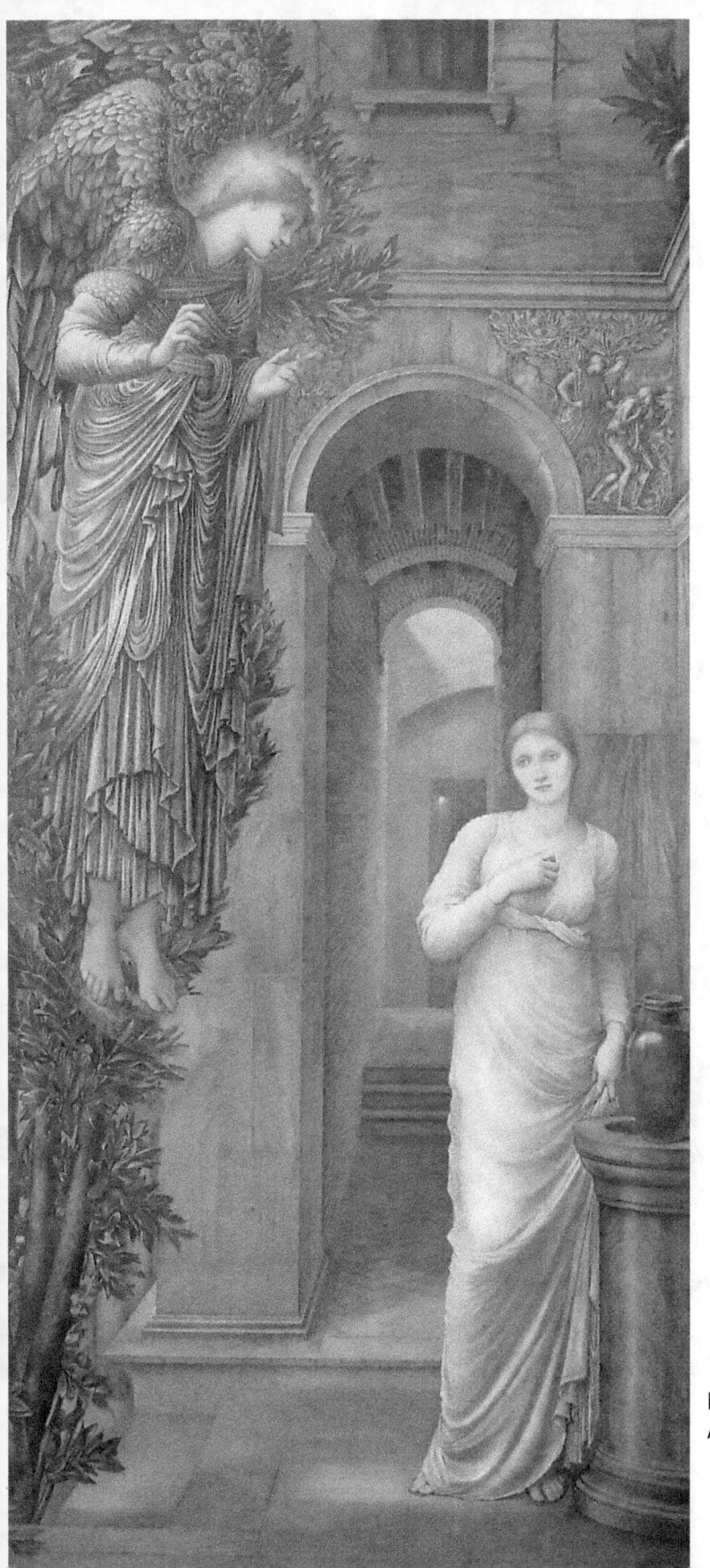

Edward Burne-Jones,
Annunciation, 1879

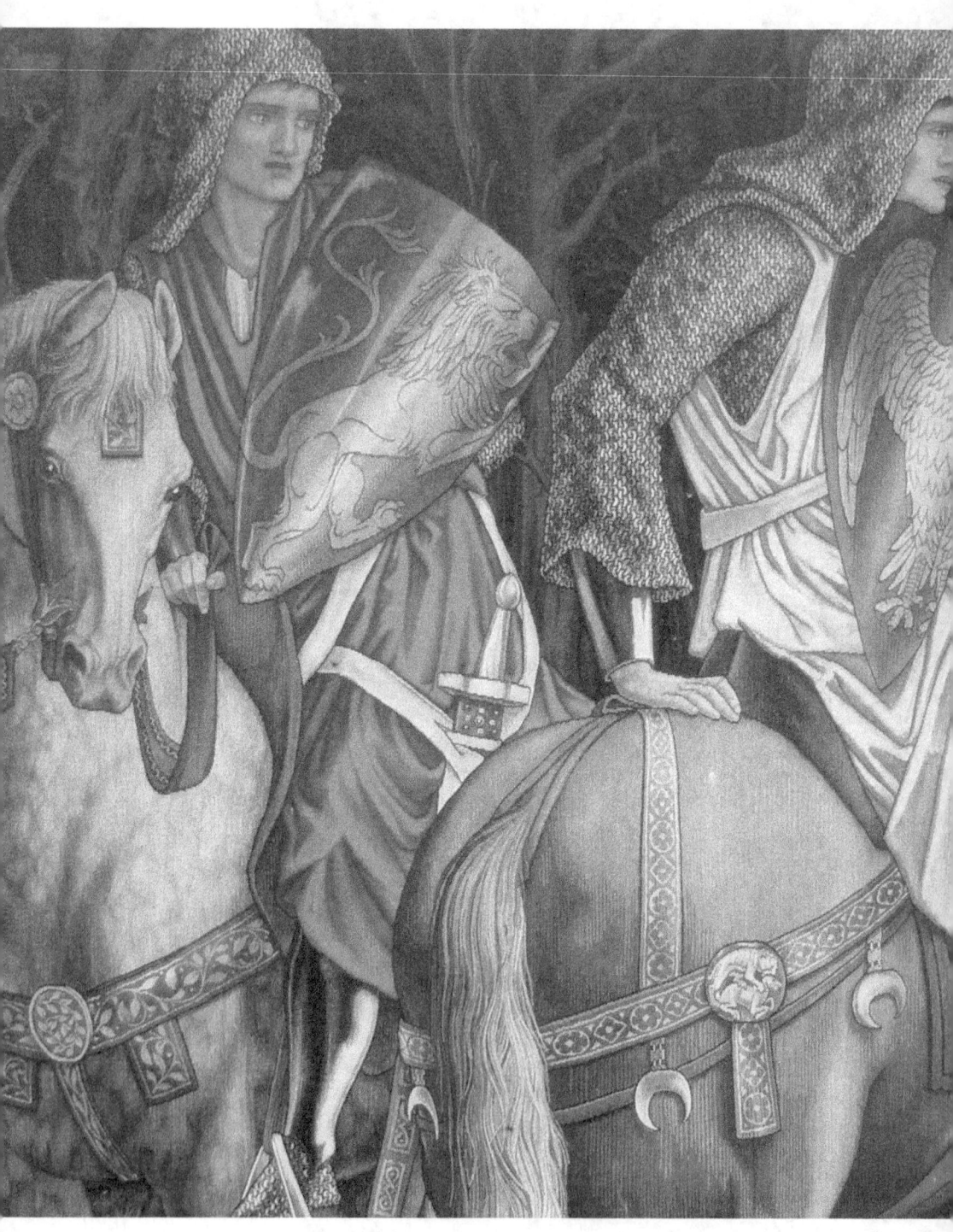

Edward Burne-Jones, The Fall of Lucifer, 1894, detail

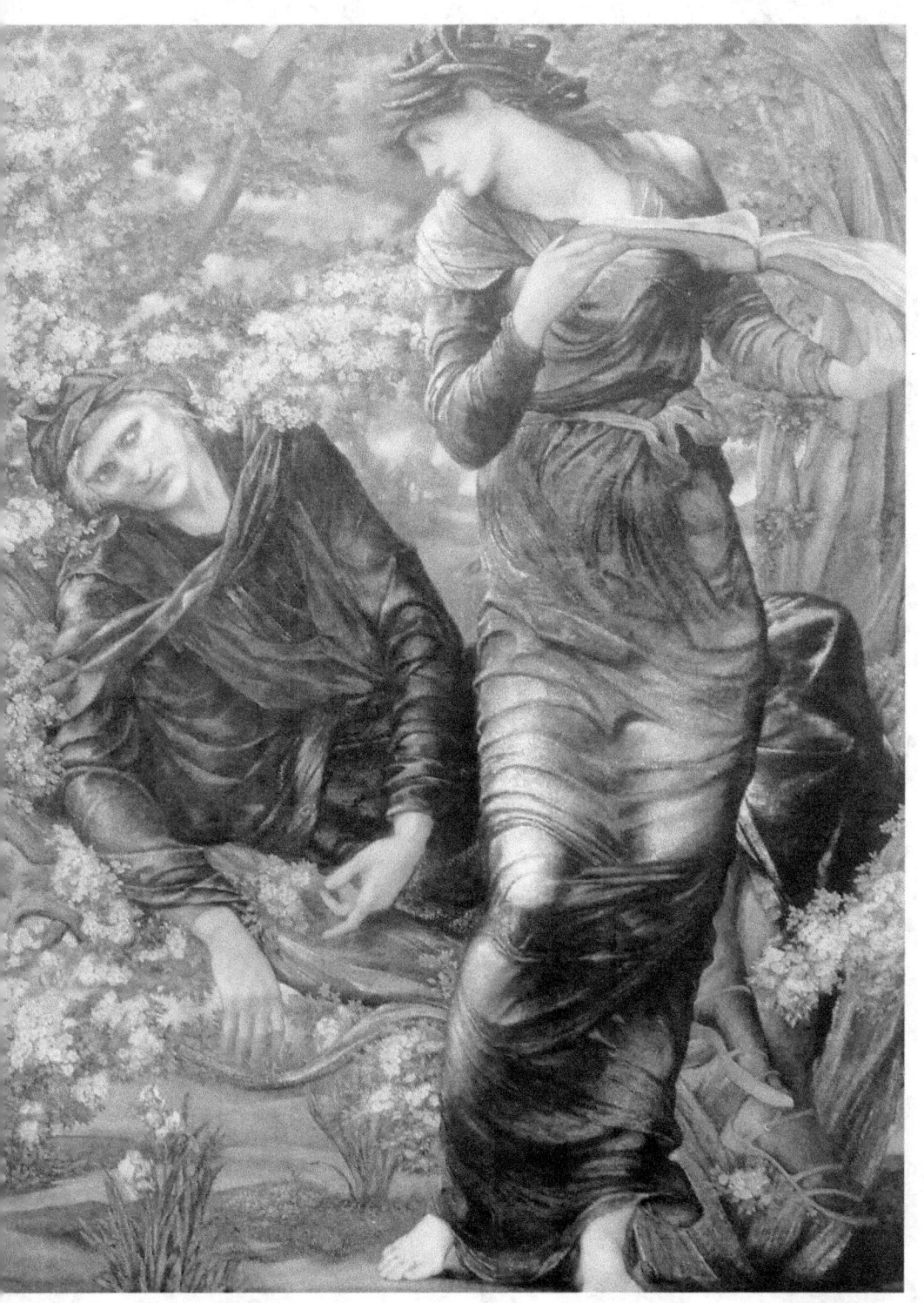

Edward Burne-Jones, The Beguiling of Merlin, 1874

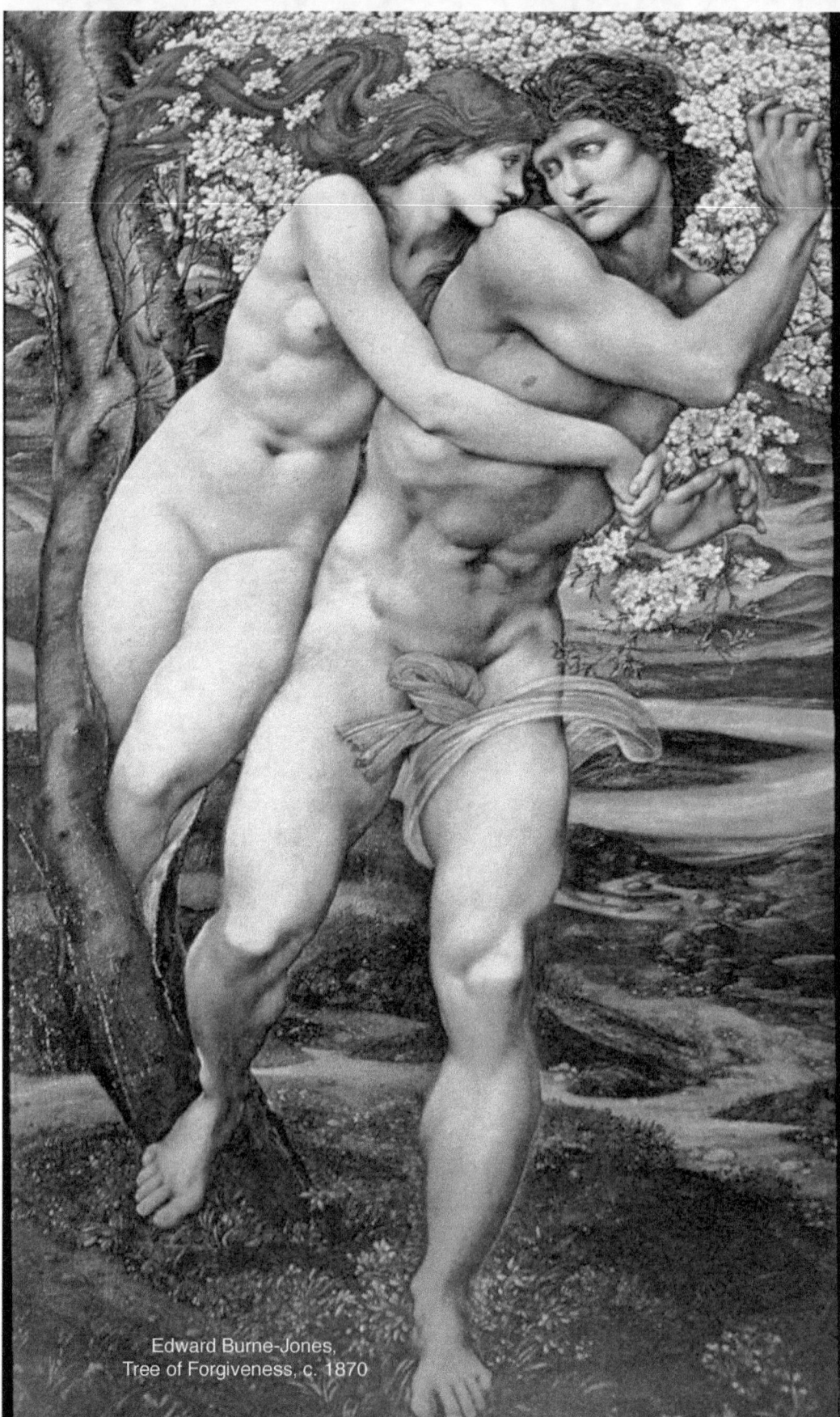

Edward Burne-Jones,
Tree of Forgiveness, c. 1870

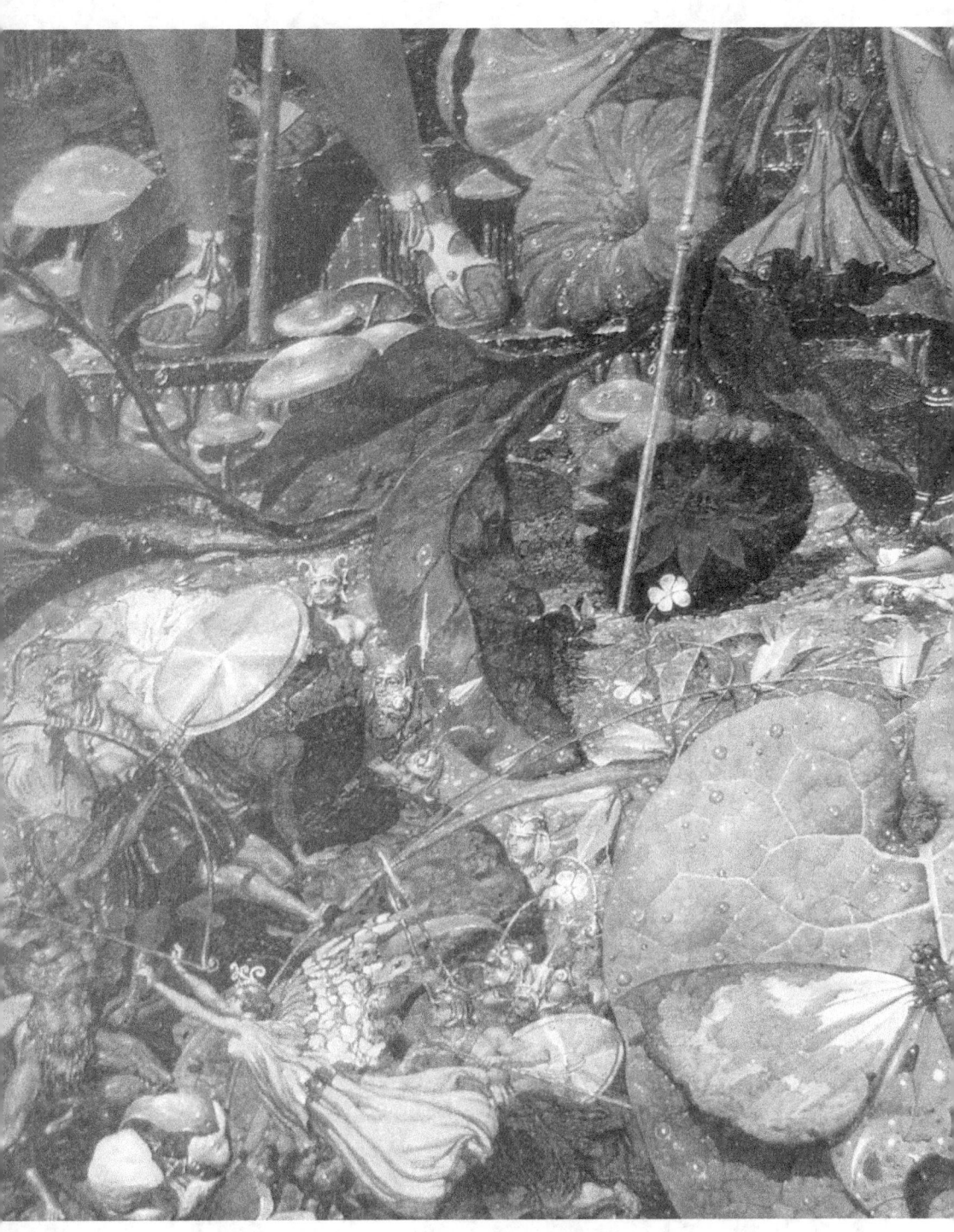

Richard Dadd, Contradiction: Oberon and Titania, 1854/ 58, detail

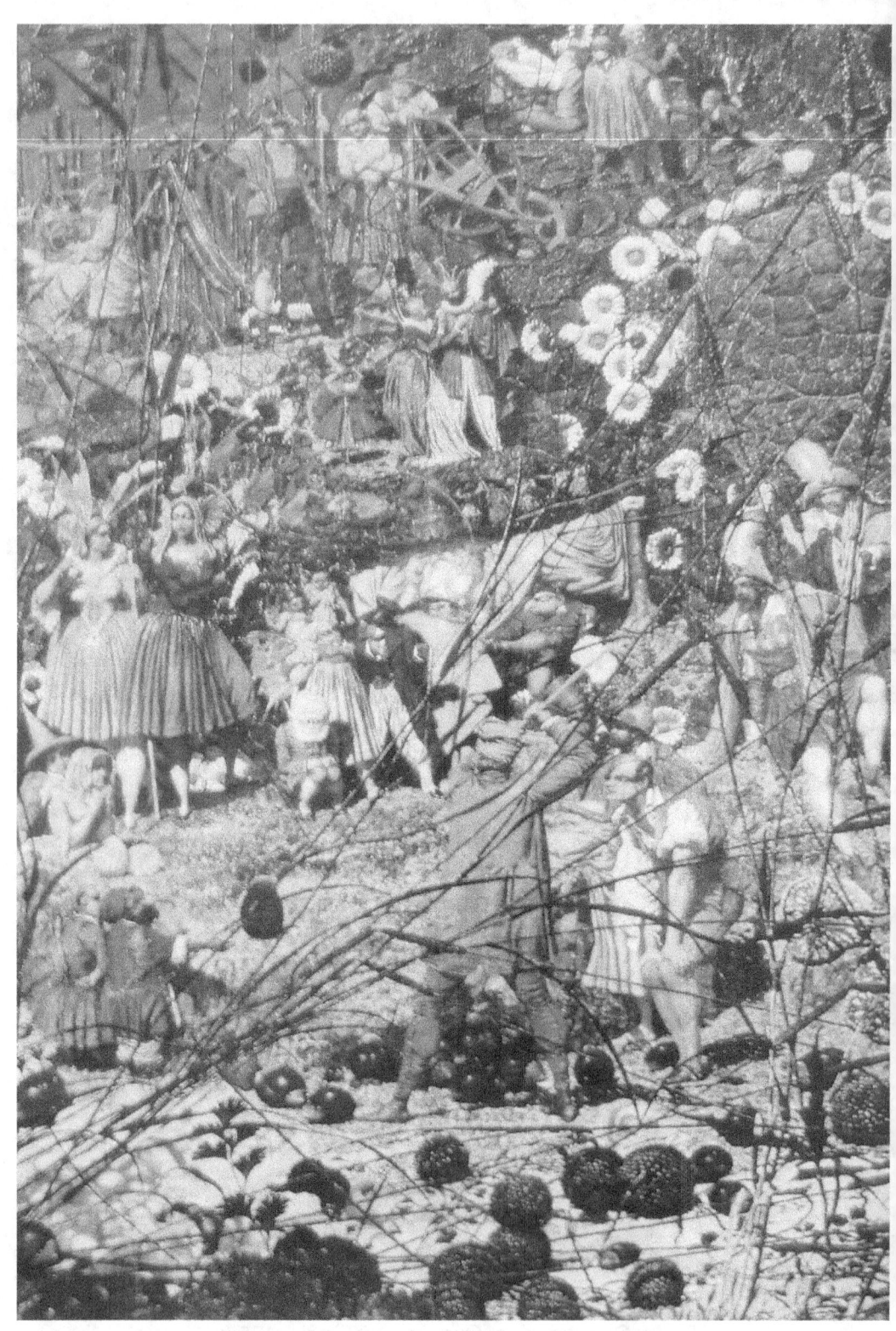

Richard Dadd, The Fairy-Feller's Master-Stroke, Tate, London

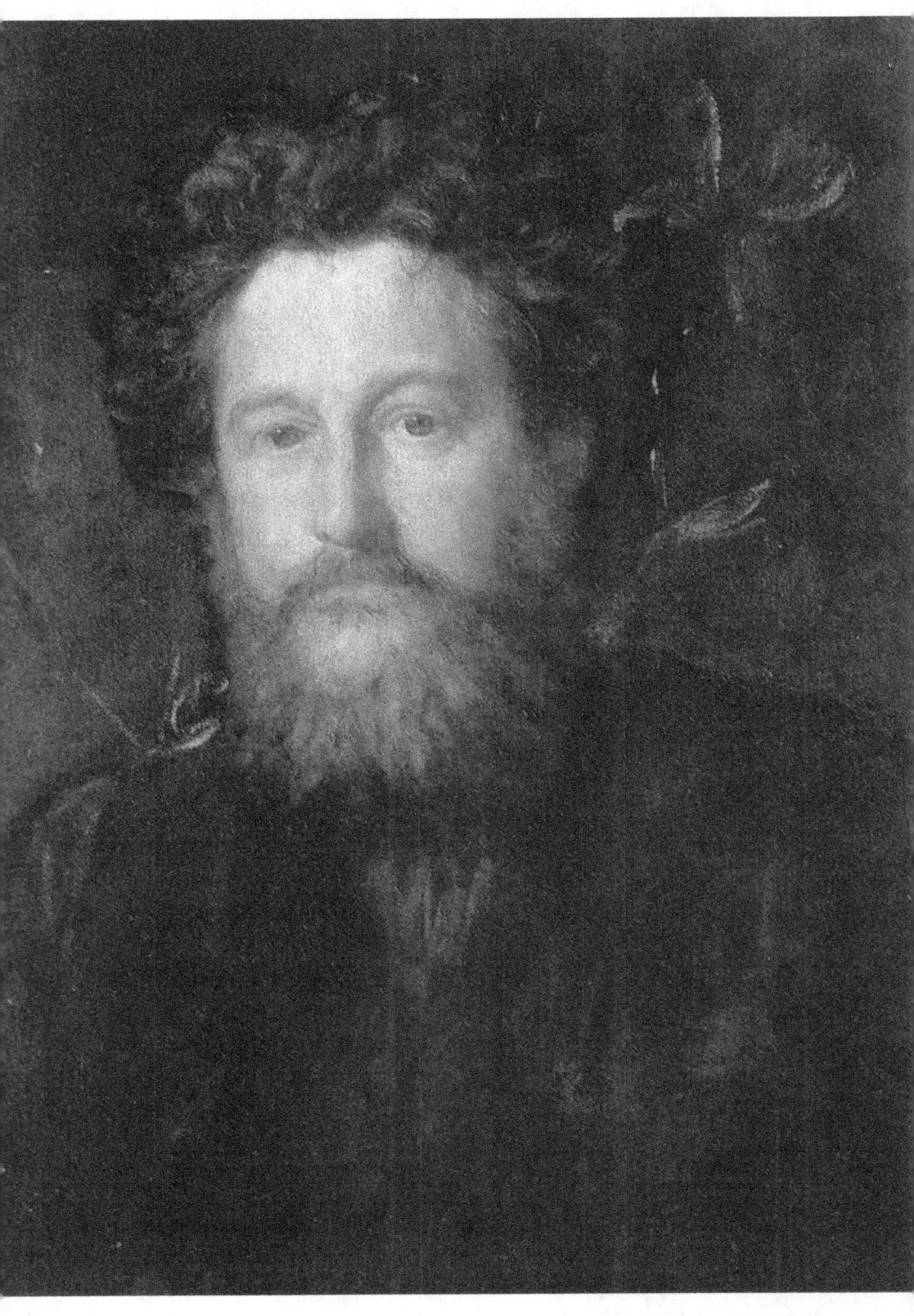

George Frederic Watts, Portrait of William Morris, 1870

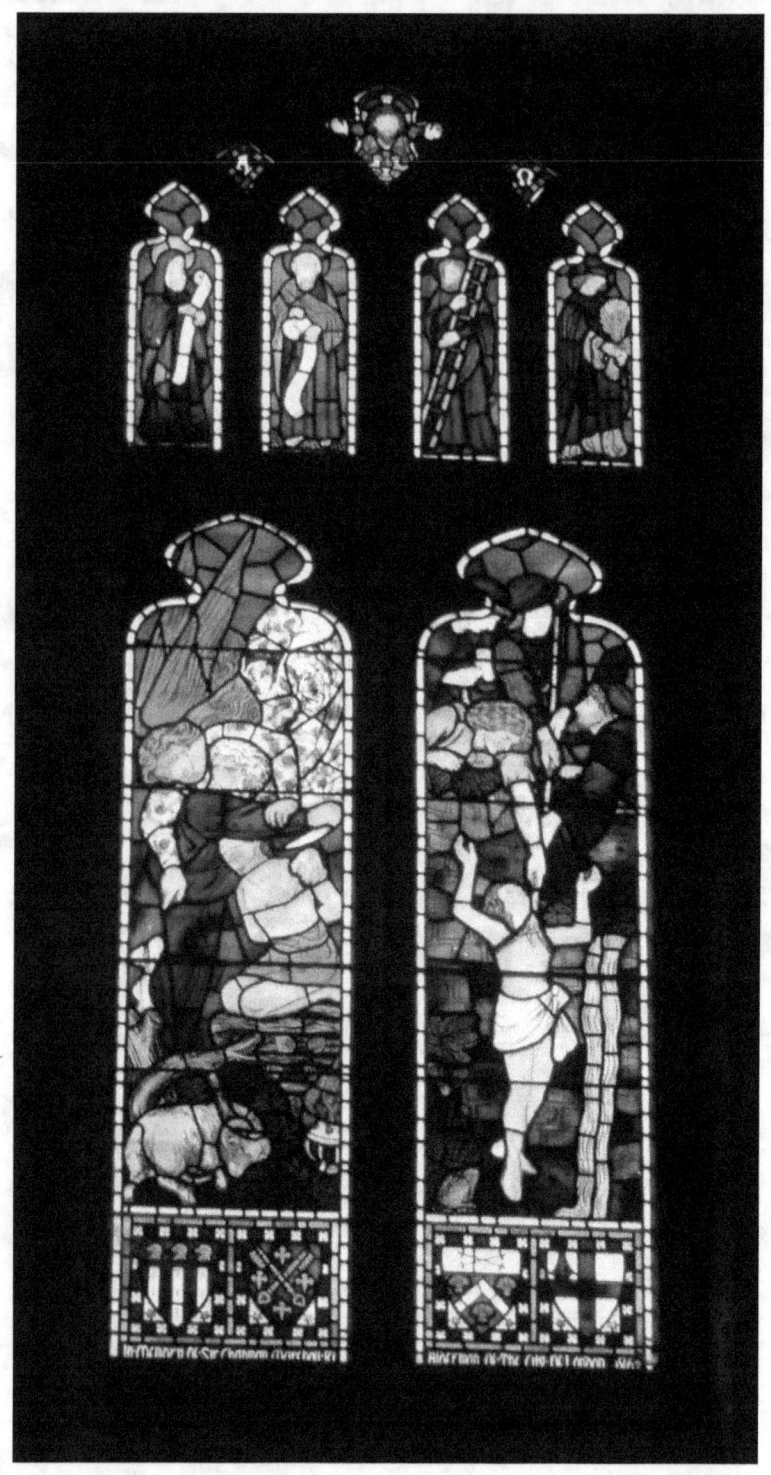

William Morris, Glass, Peterborough Cathedral, 1870

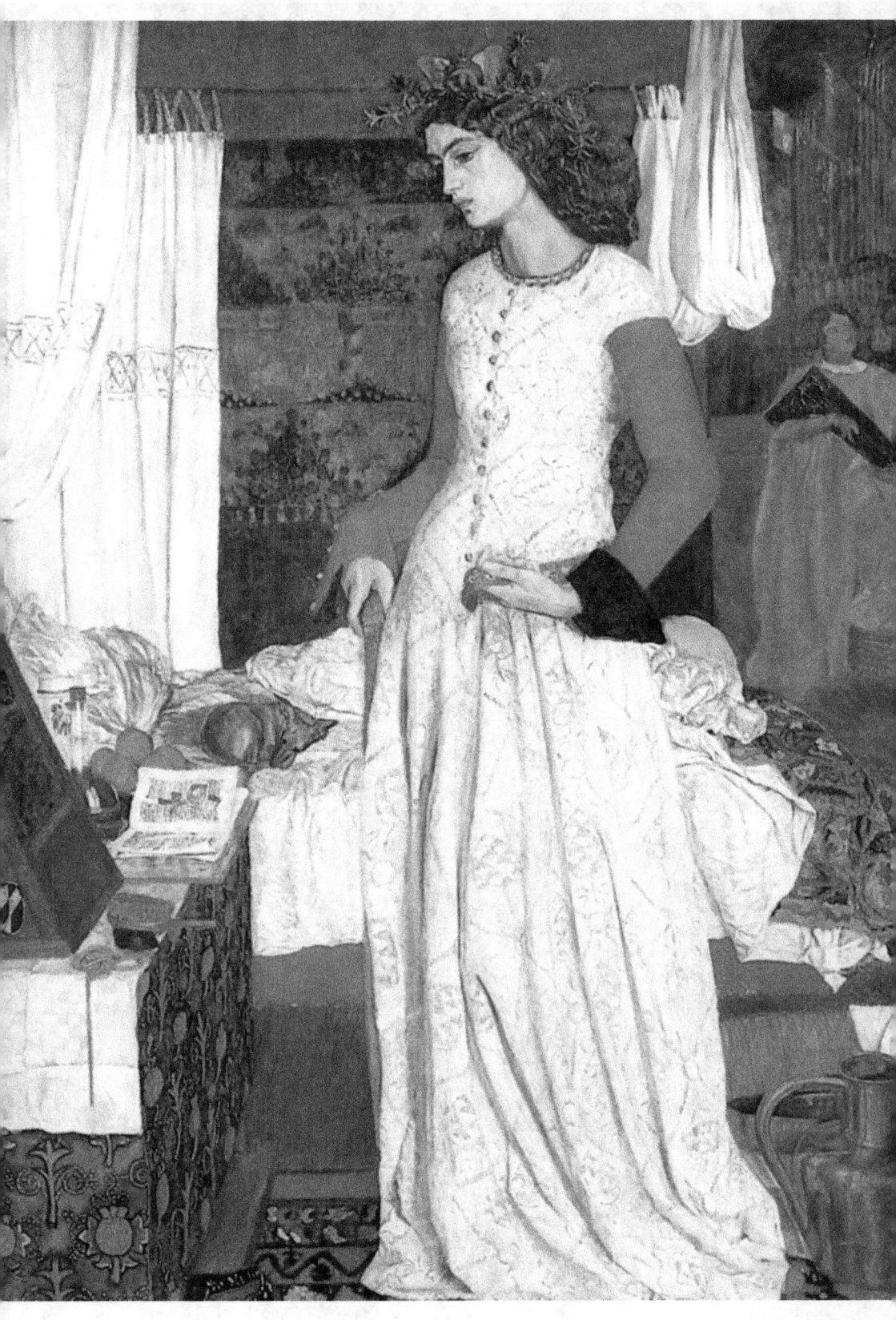

William Morris, La Belle Iseult, 1858, Tate Gallery

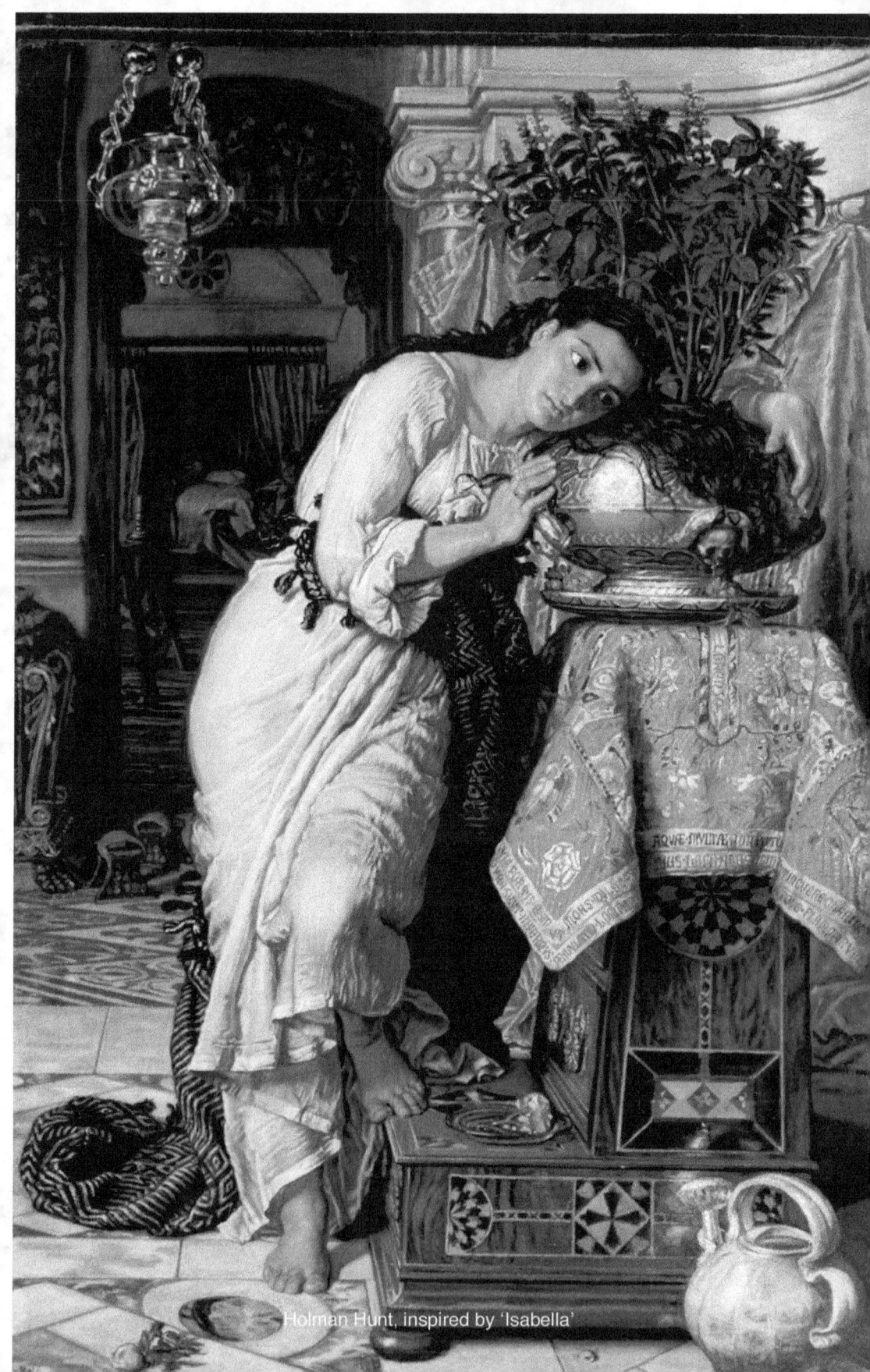

Holman Hunt, inspired by 'Isabella'

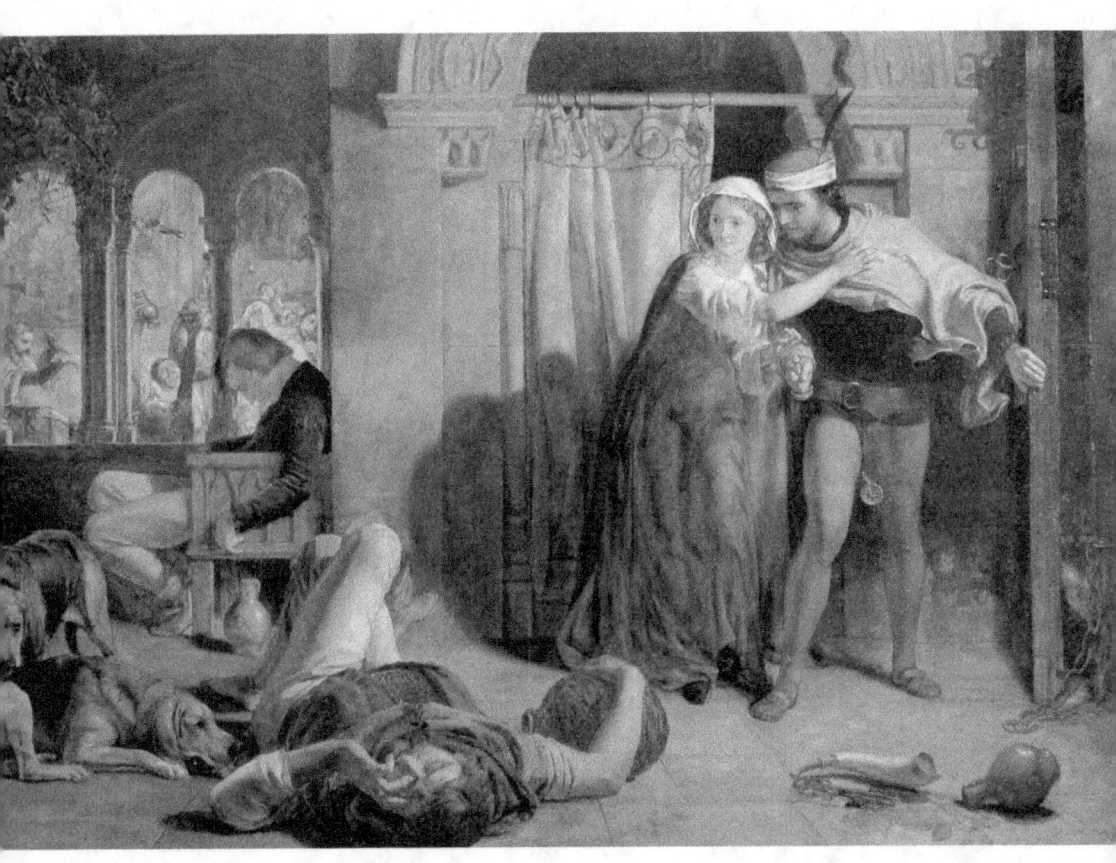

John William Holman Hunt, The Flight of Madeline and Porphyro

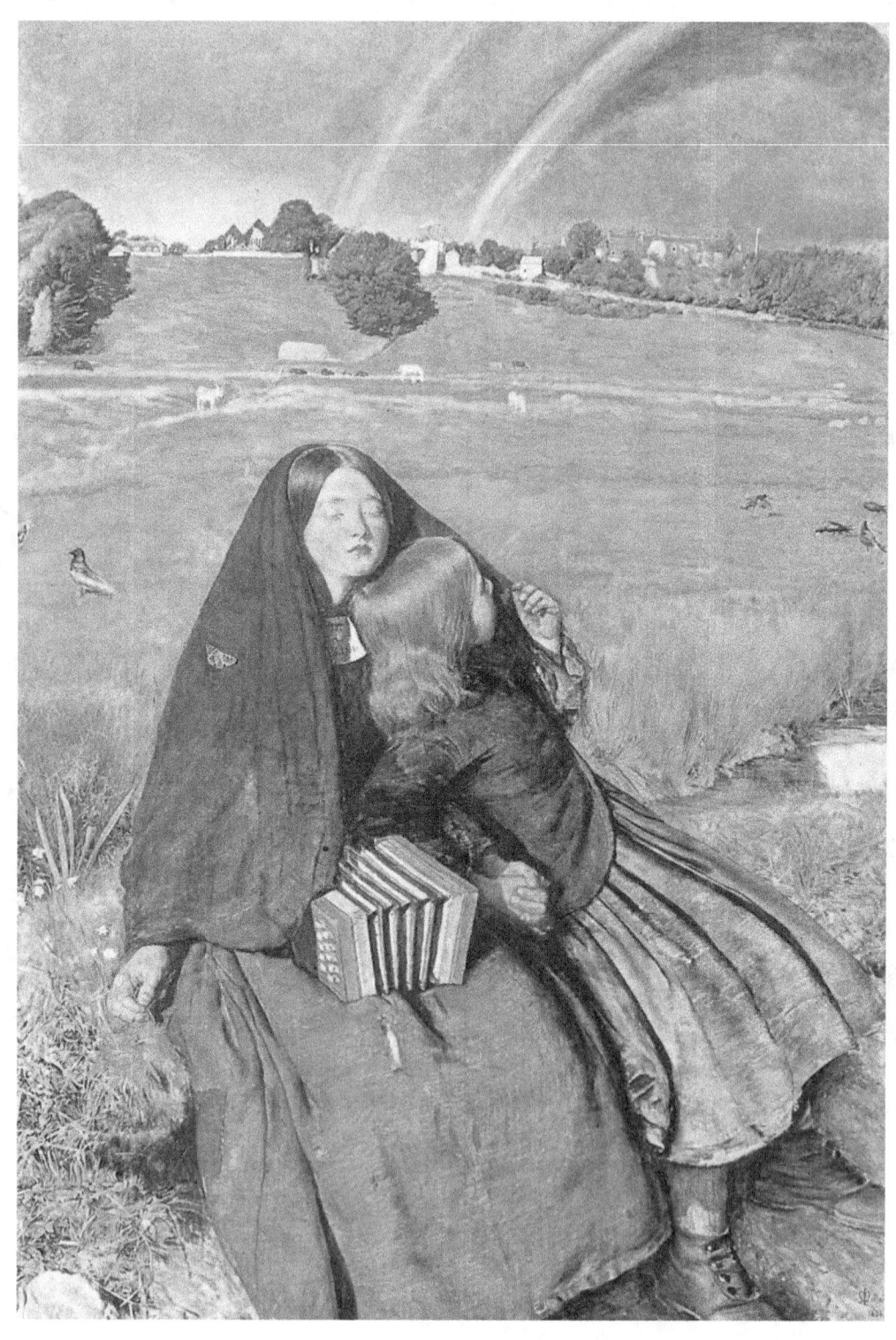

John Everett Millais, Blind Girl, 1885, Birmingham

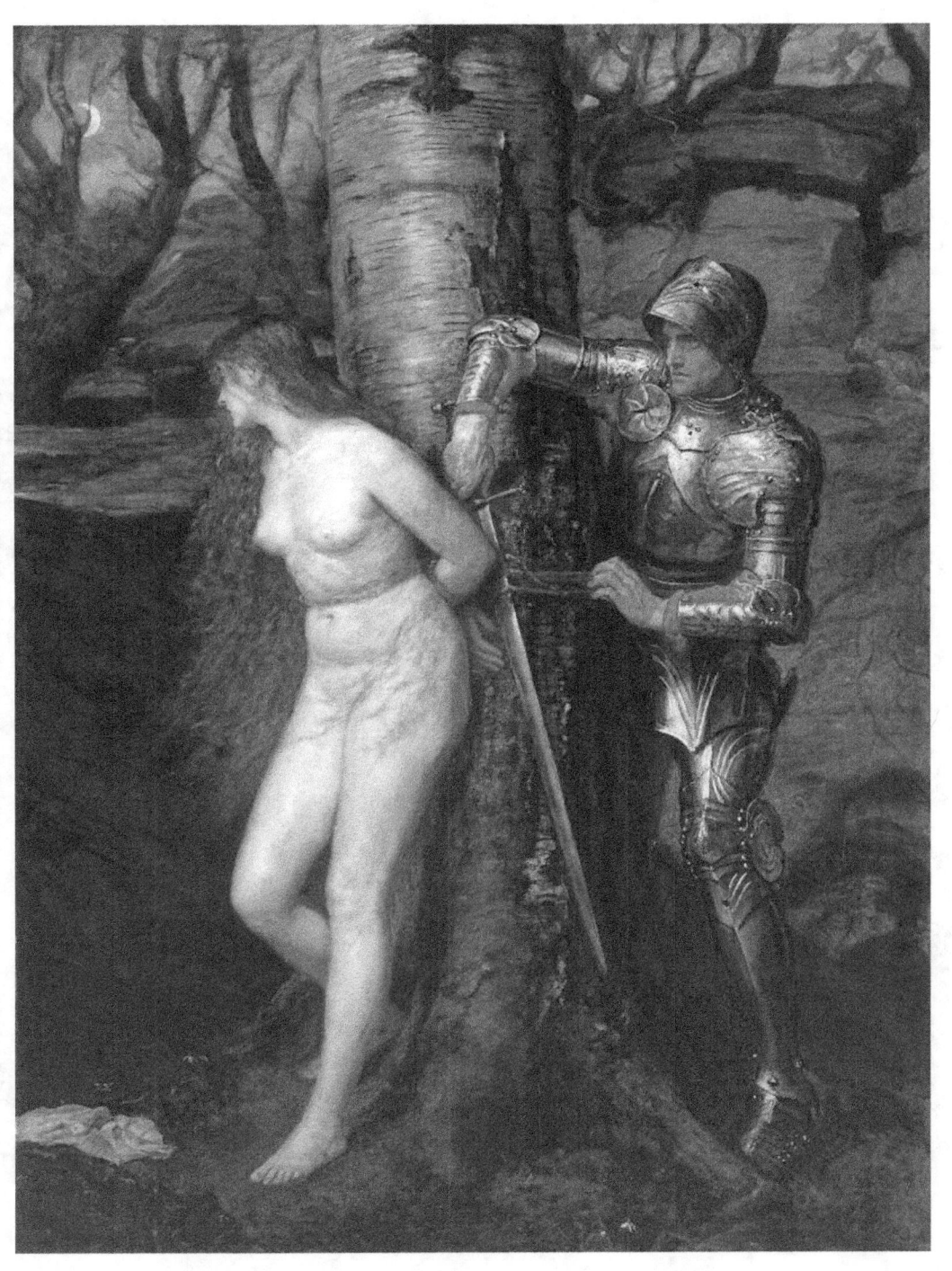

John Everett Millais, The Knight Errant, 1870, Tate, London

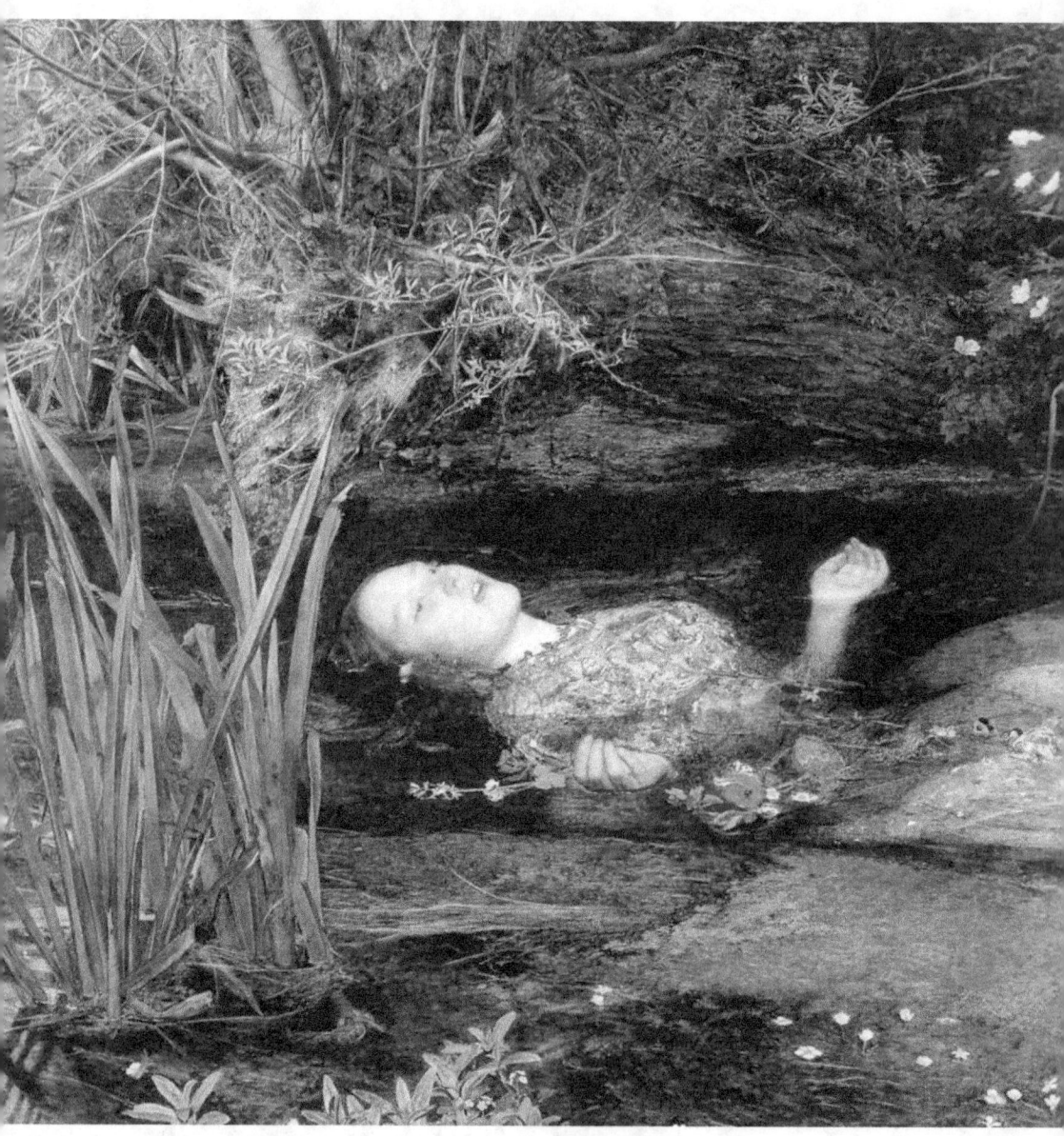

John Everett Millais, Ophelia.

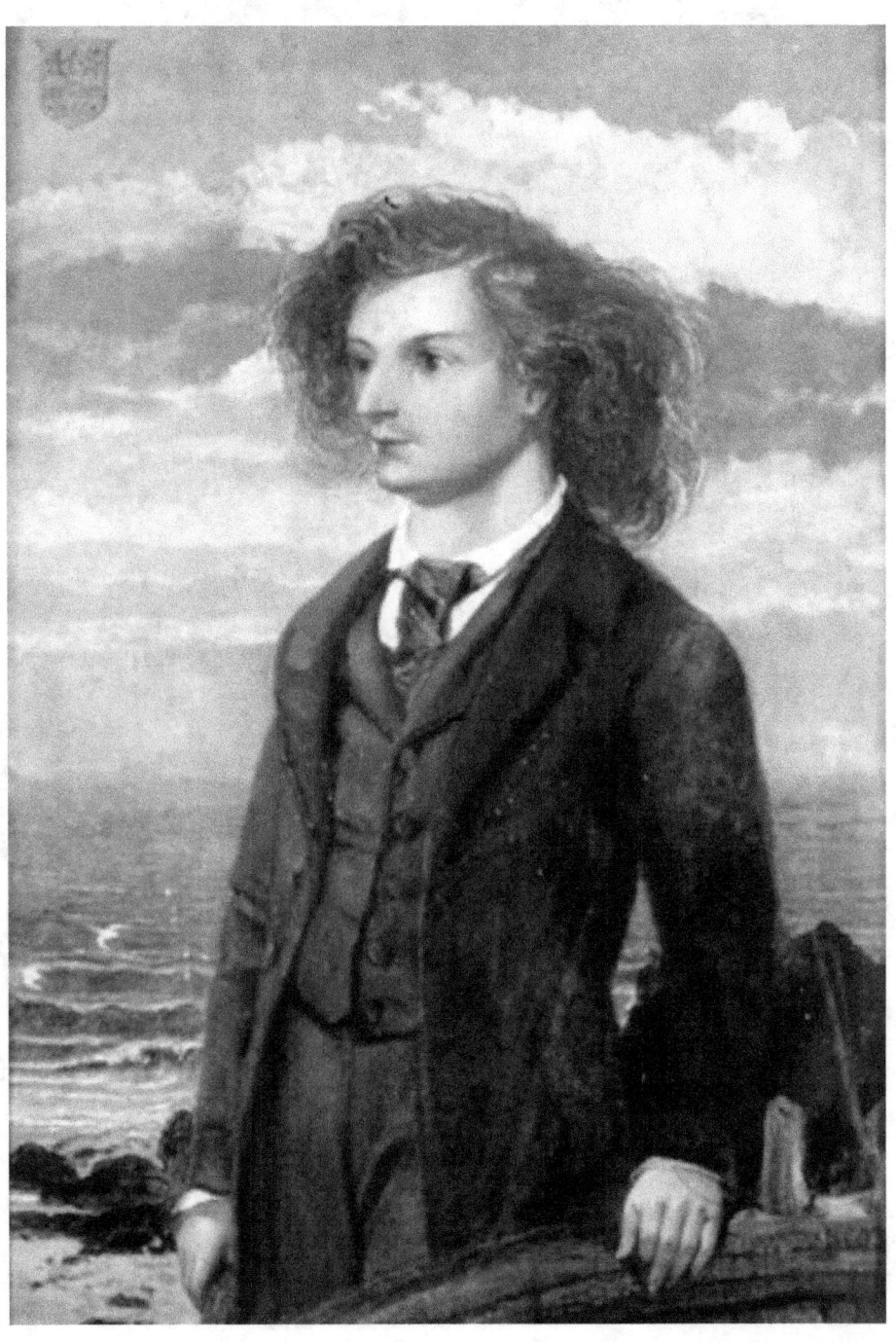

William Bell Scott, Algernon Charles Swinburne, Baillol College

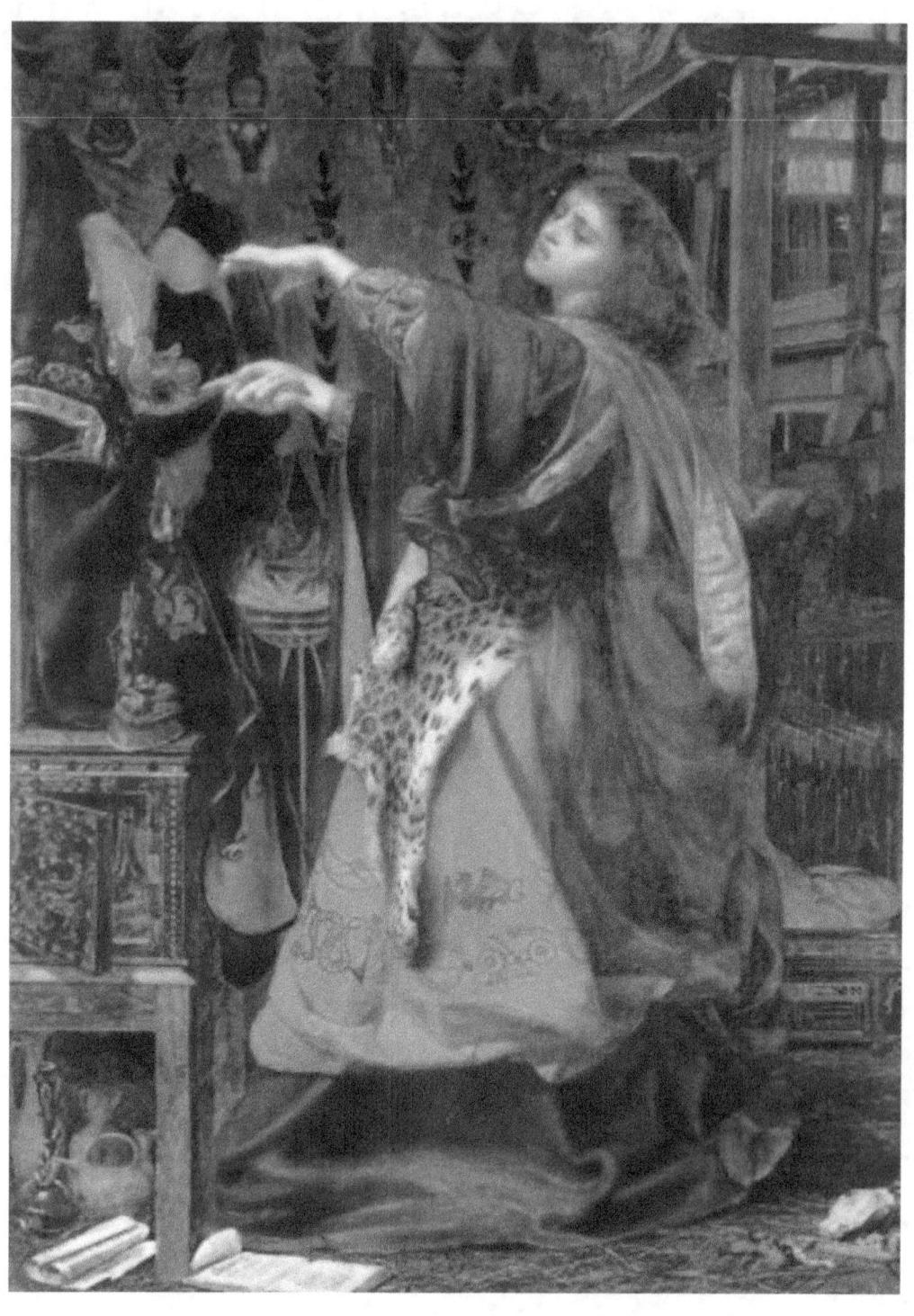

Frederick Sandys, Morgan le Fay, 1863-34, Birmingham

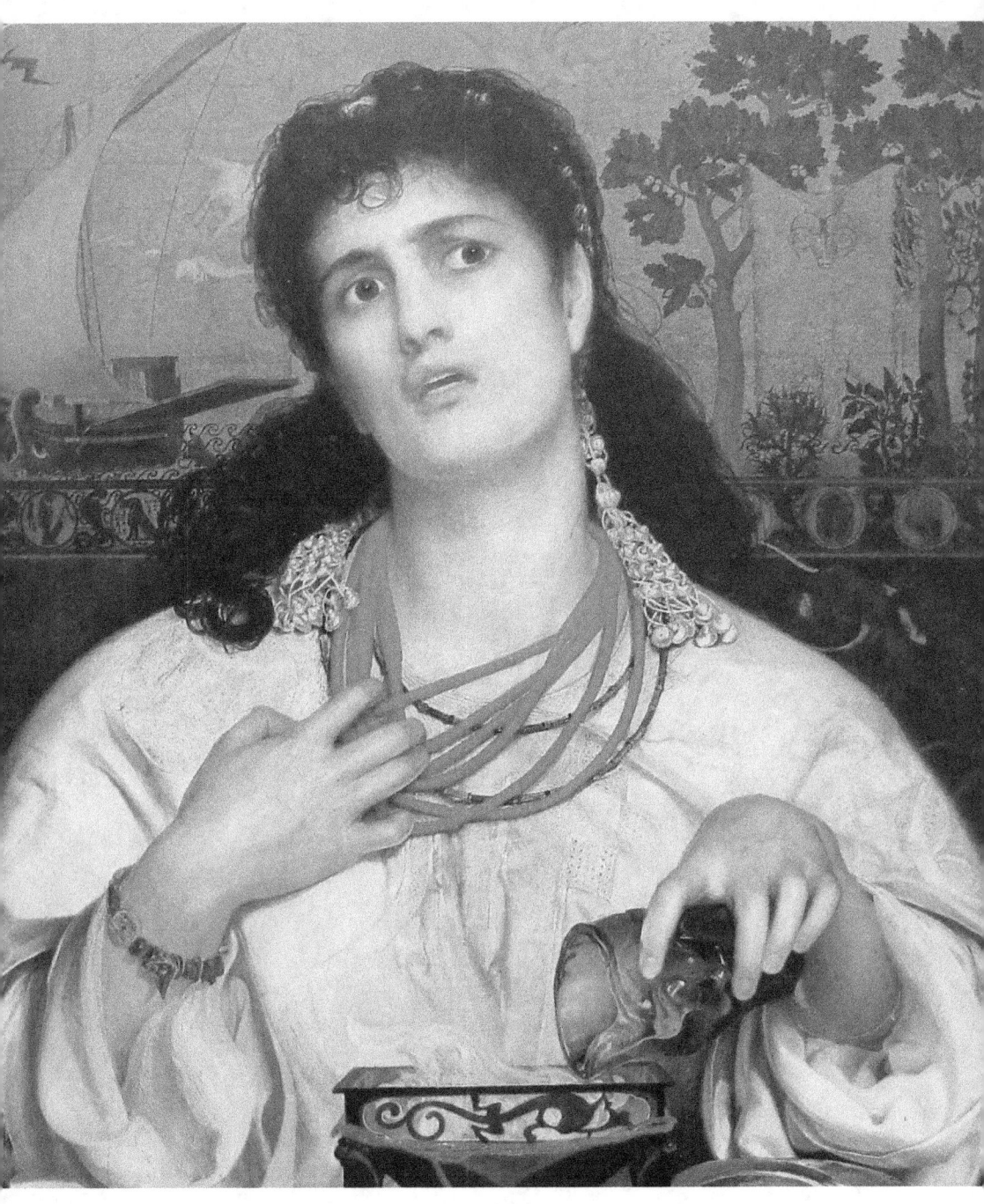

Frederick Sandys, Medea, 1868

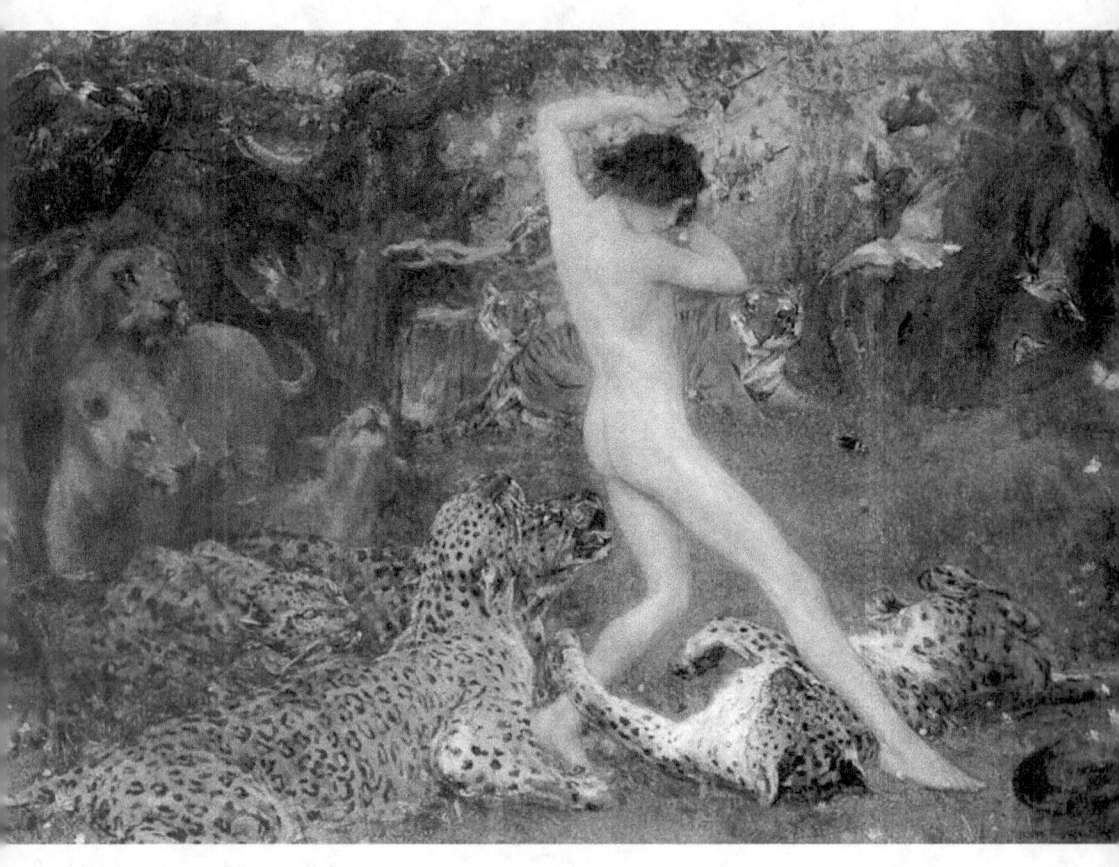

John Macallan Swan, Orpheus, 1896

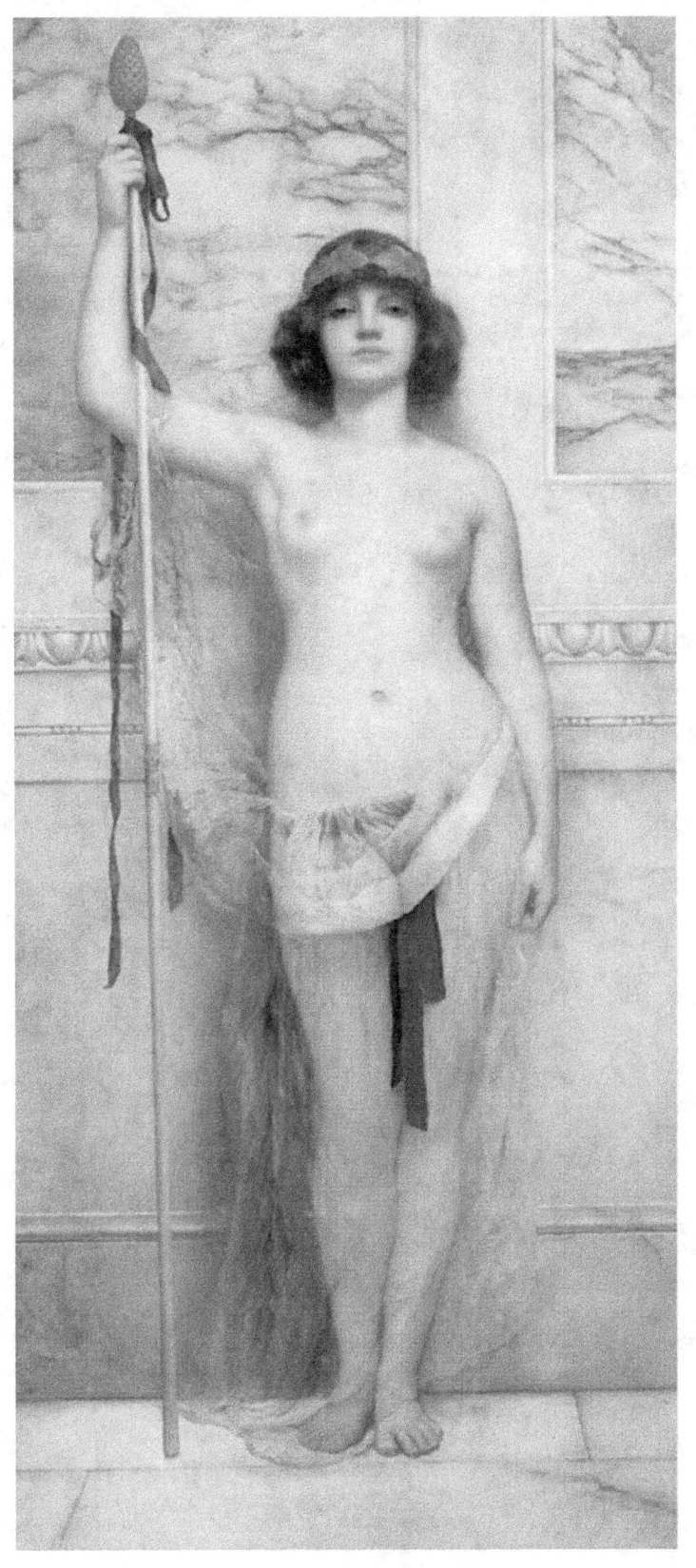

John Godward, A Priestess, 1893

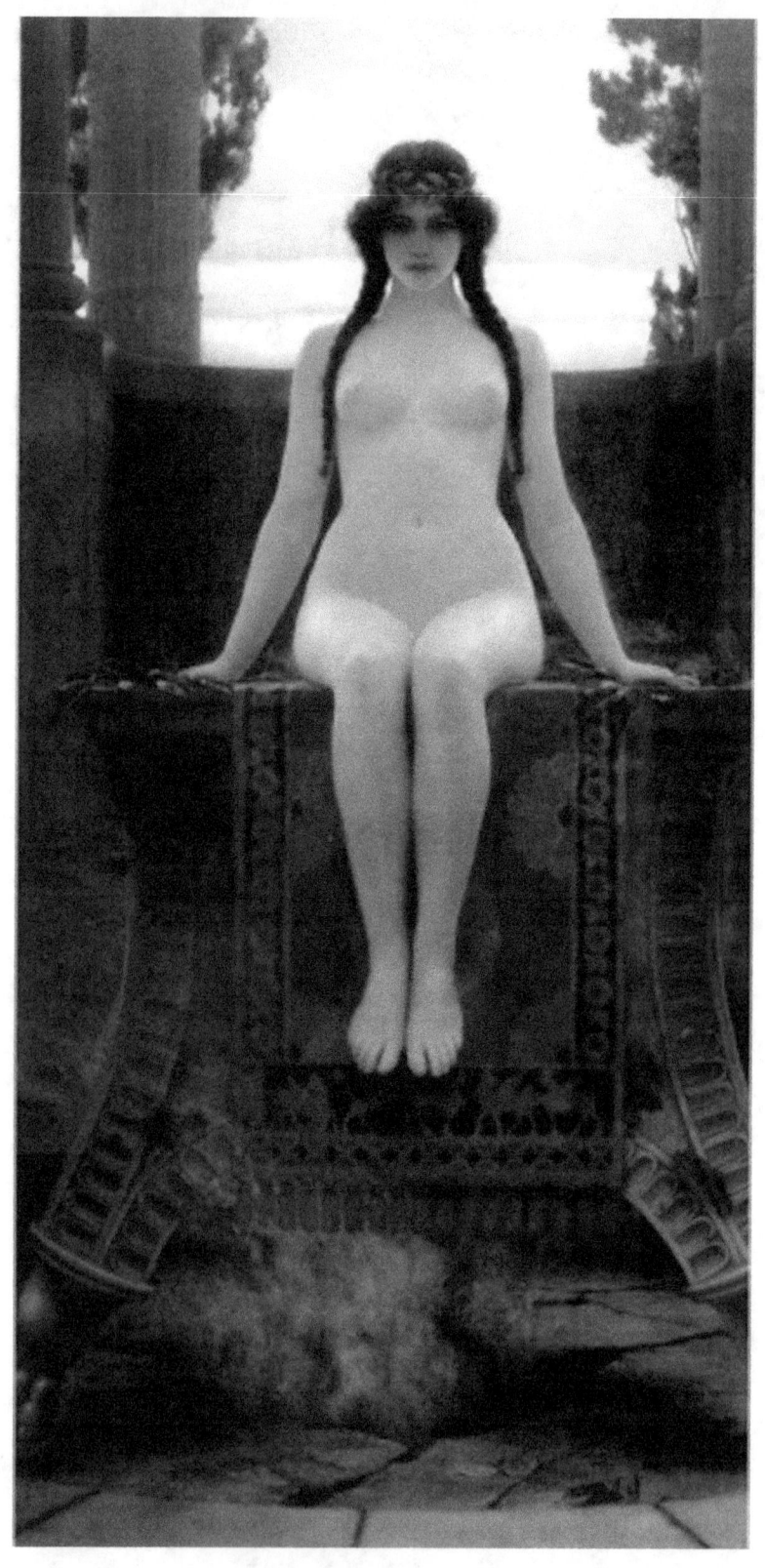

John Godward, The Delphic Oracle, 1899

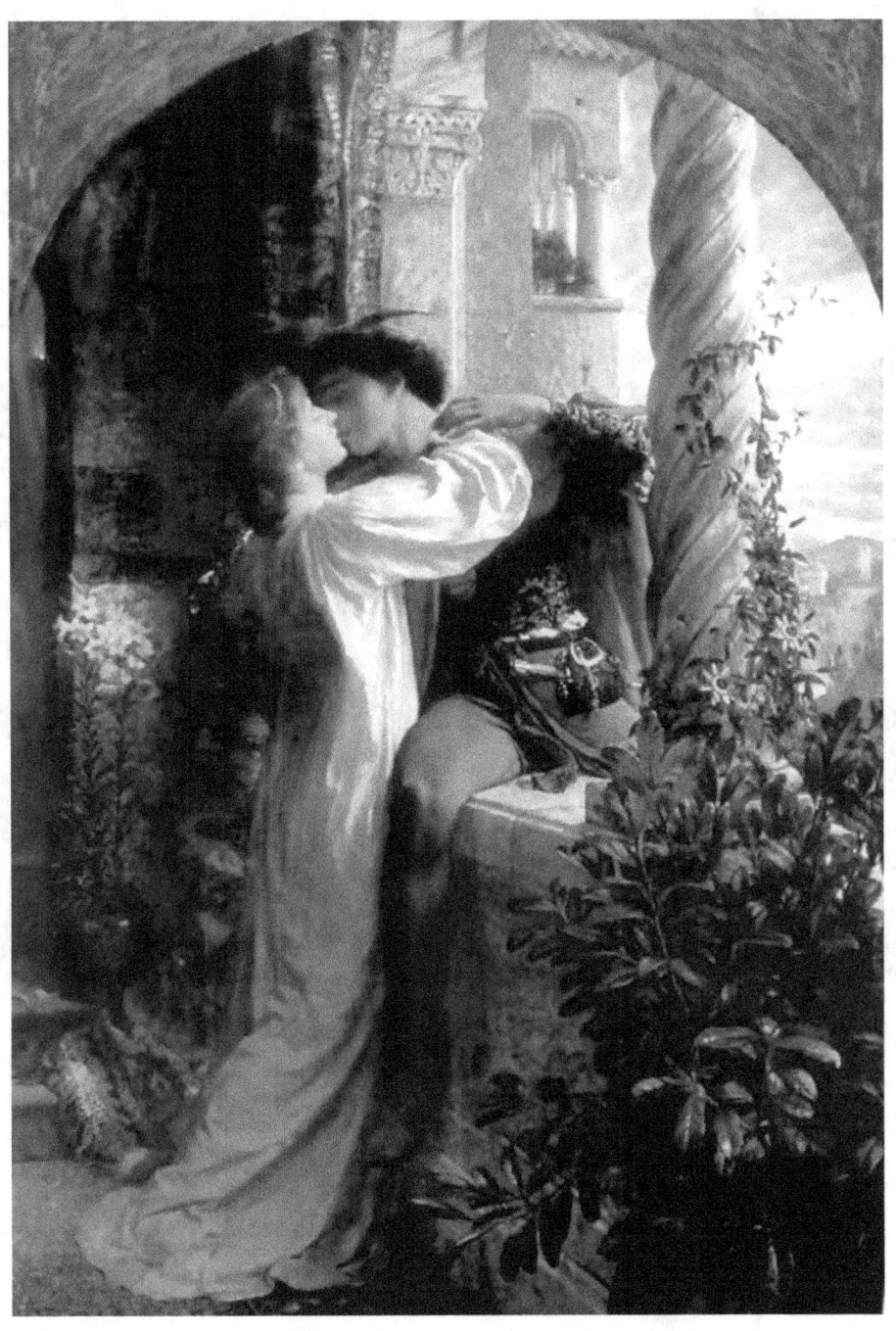

Francis Dicksee, Romeo & Juliet, 1884, Southampton

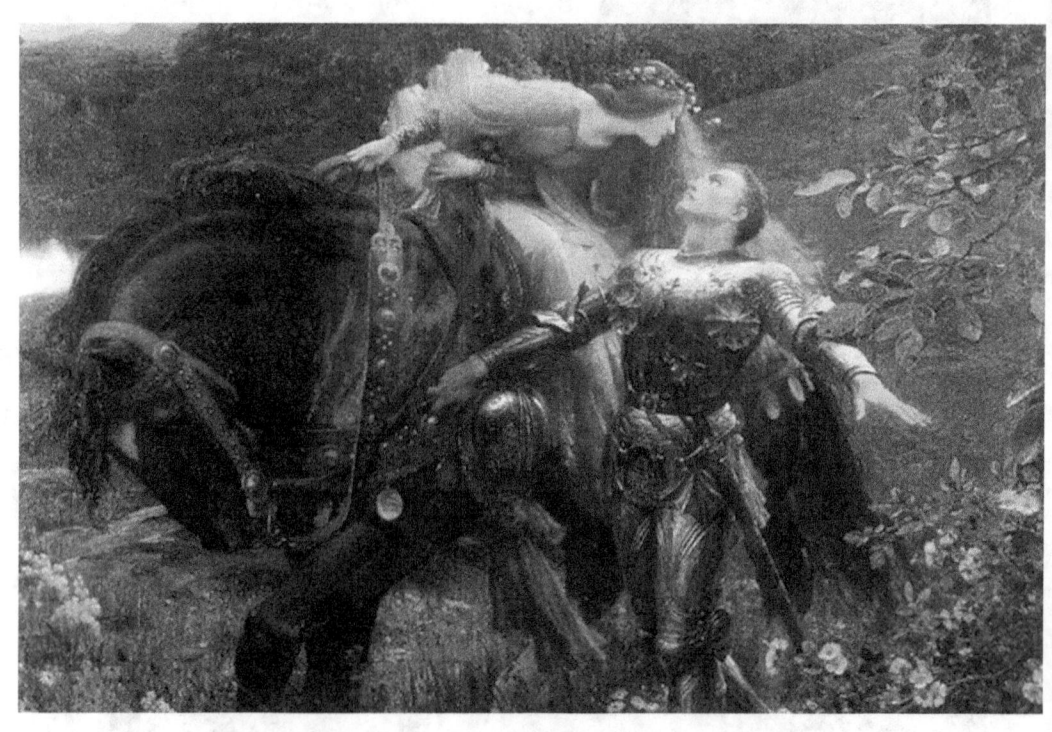

Sir Francis Dicksee, 'La Belle Dame Sans Merci'

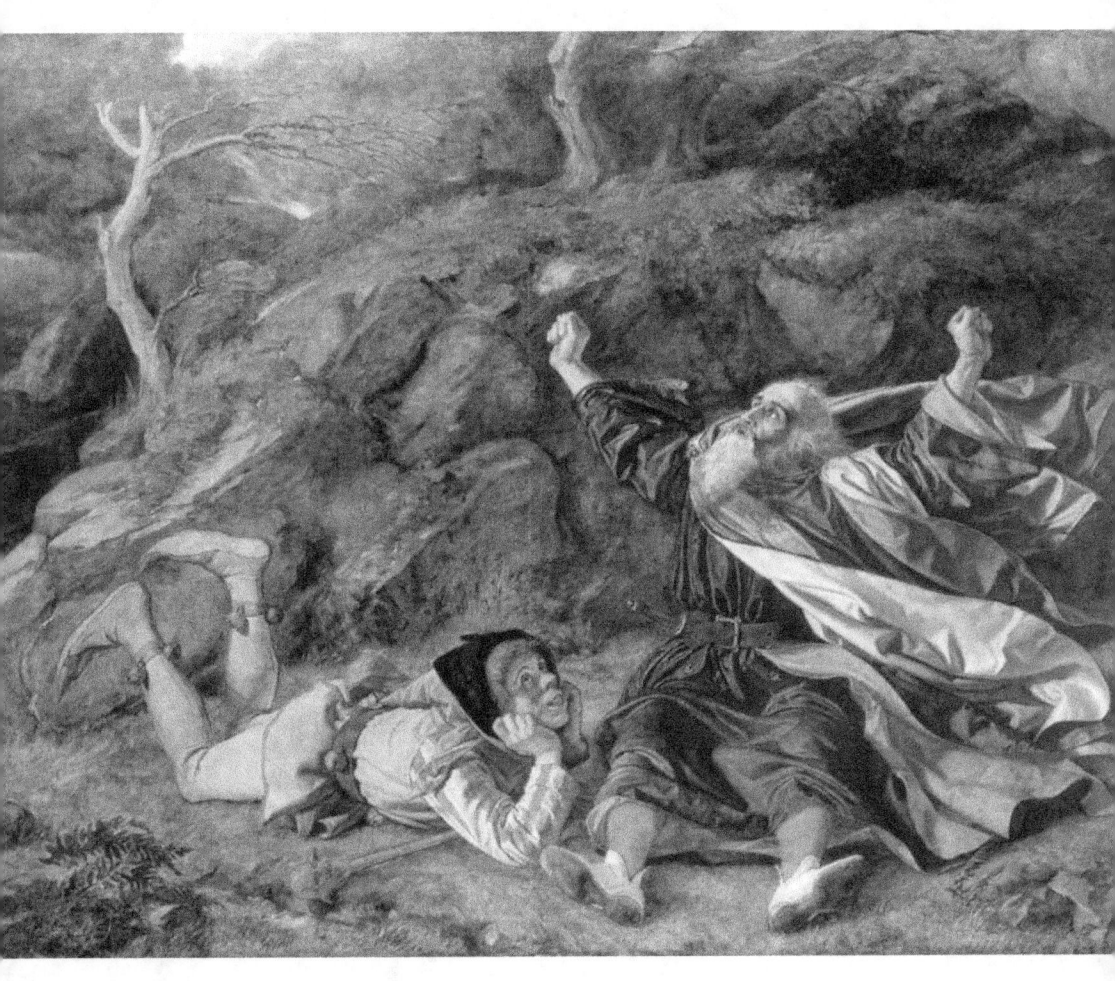

William Dyce, King Lear and the Fool In the Storm, 1851, Edinburgh

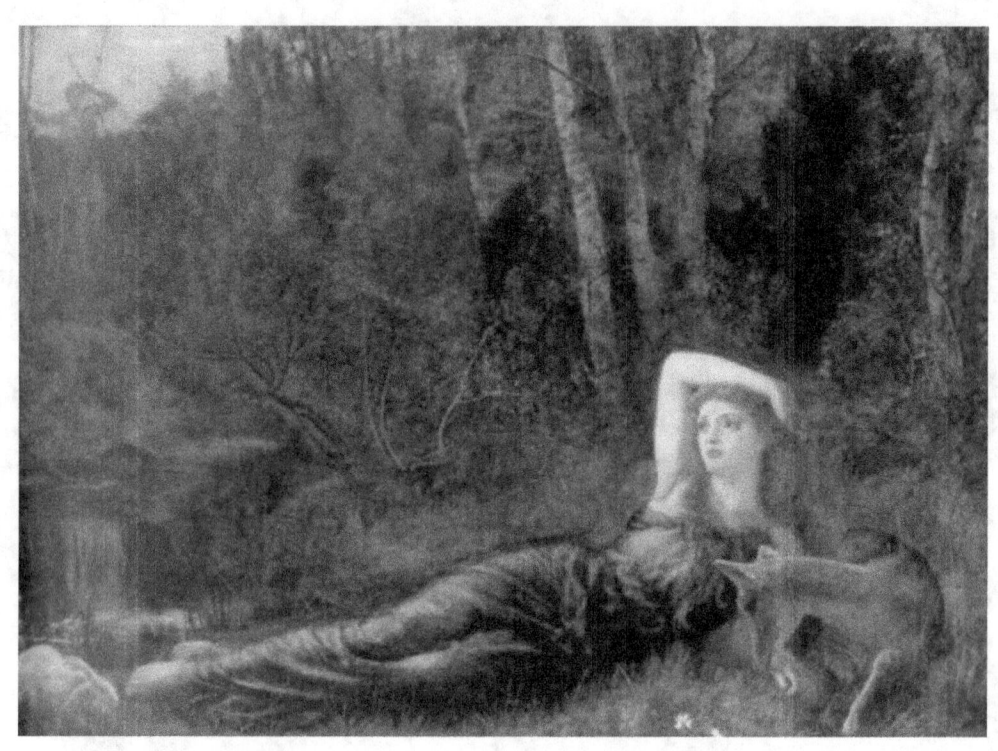

Arthur Hughes, Endymion

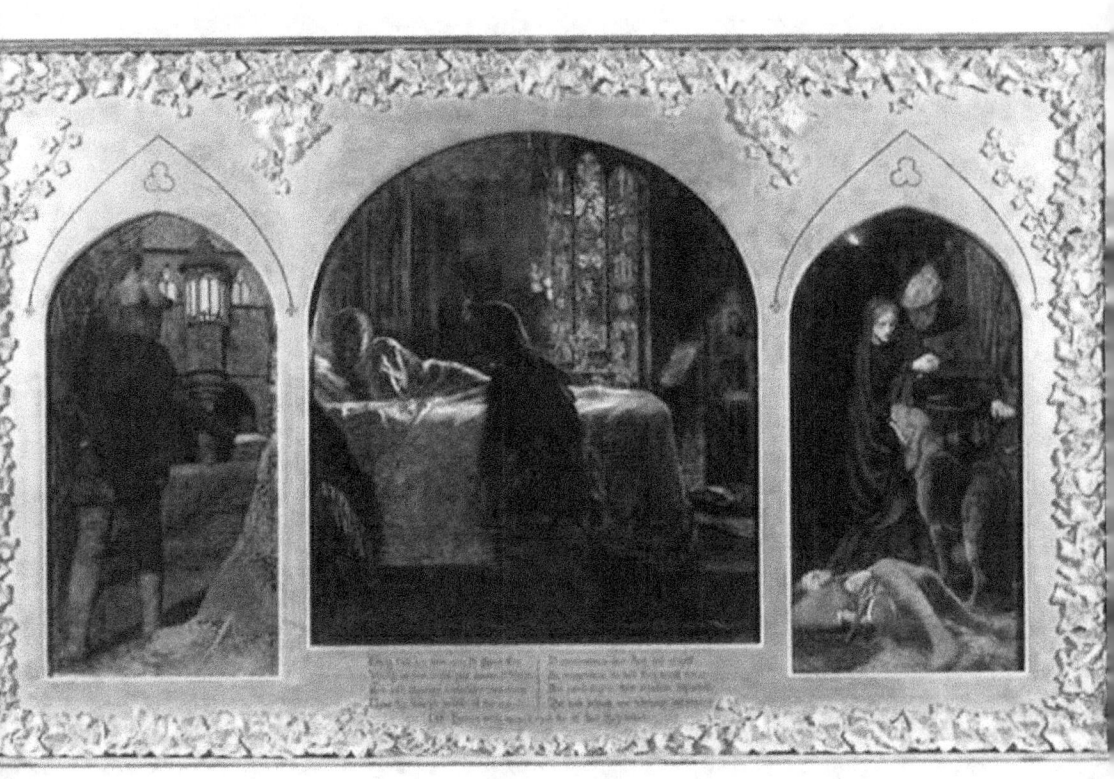

Arthur Hughes, The Eve of St Agnes

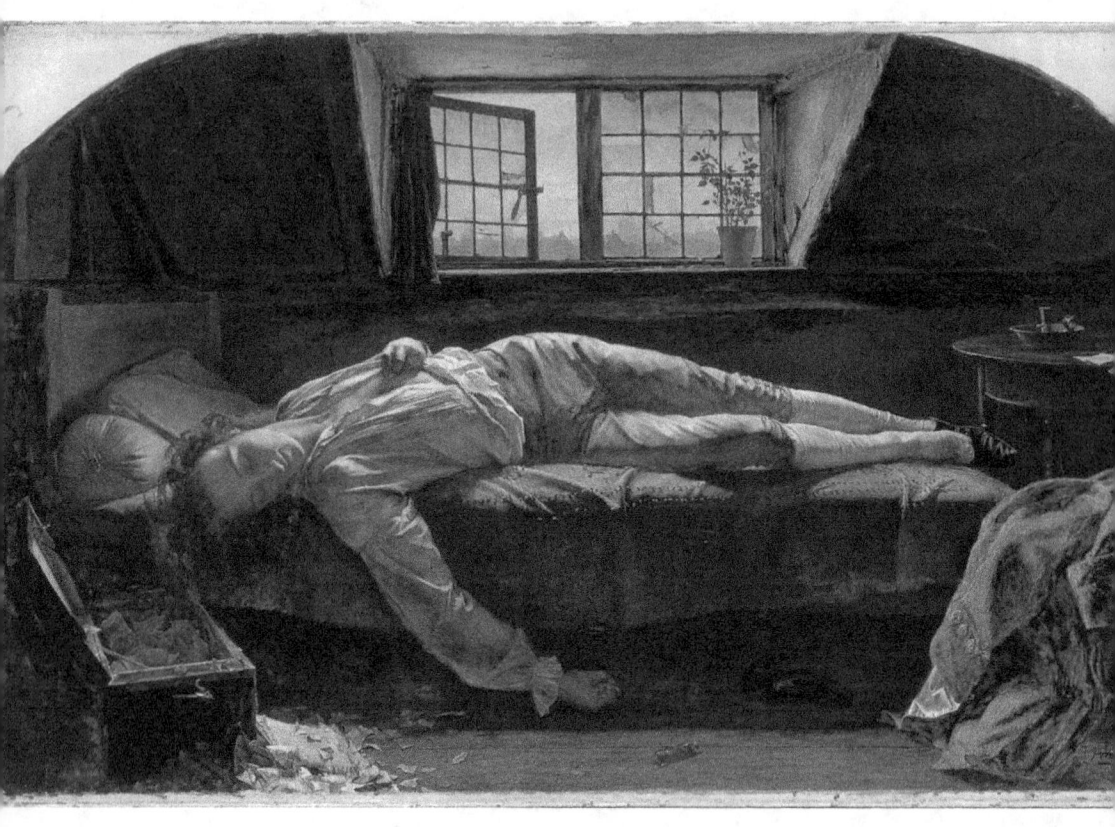

Henry Wallis, Chatterton, 1856, Tate Britain

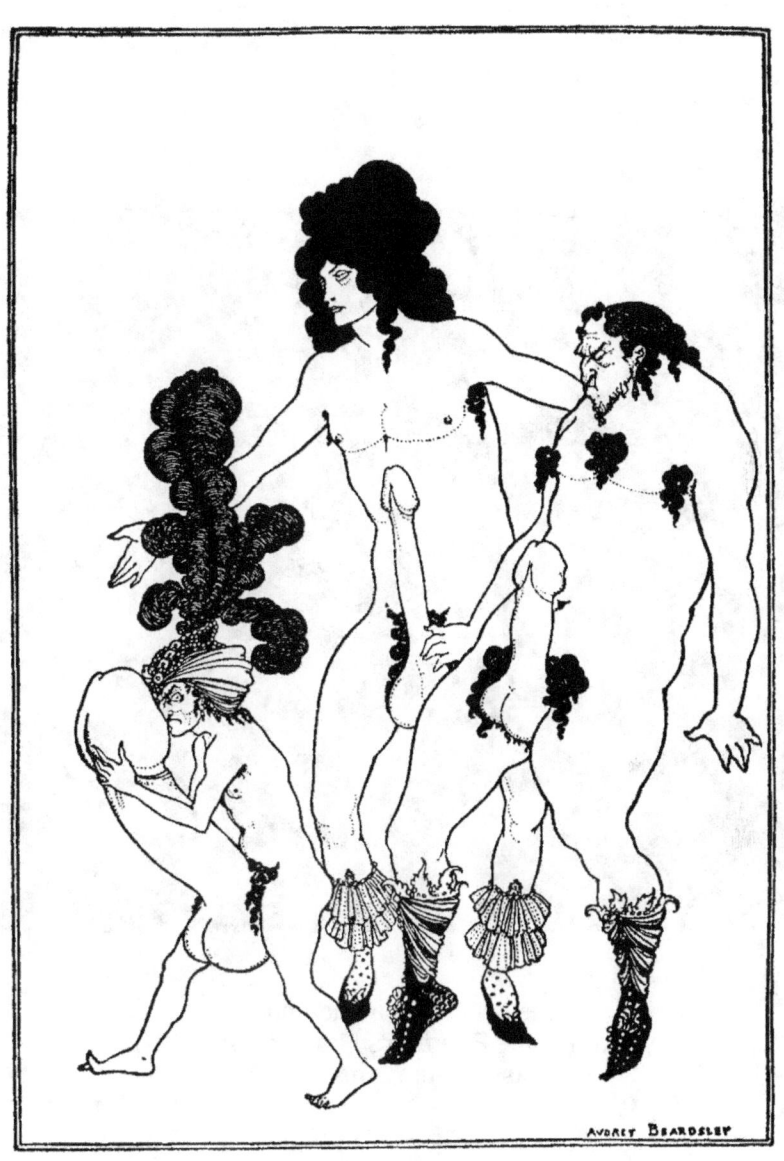

Aubrey Beardsley, Aristophanes, Lysistrata, 1896

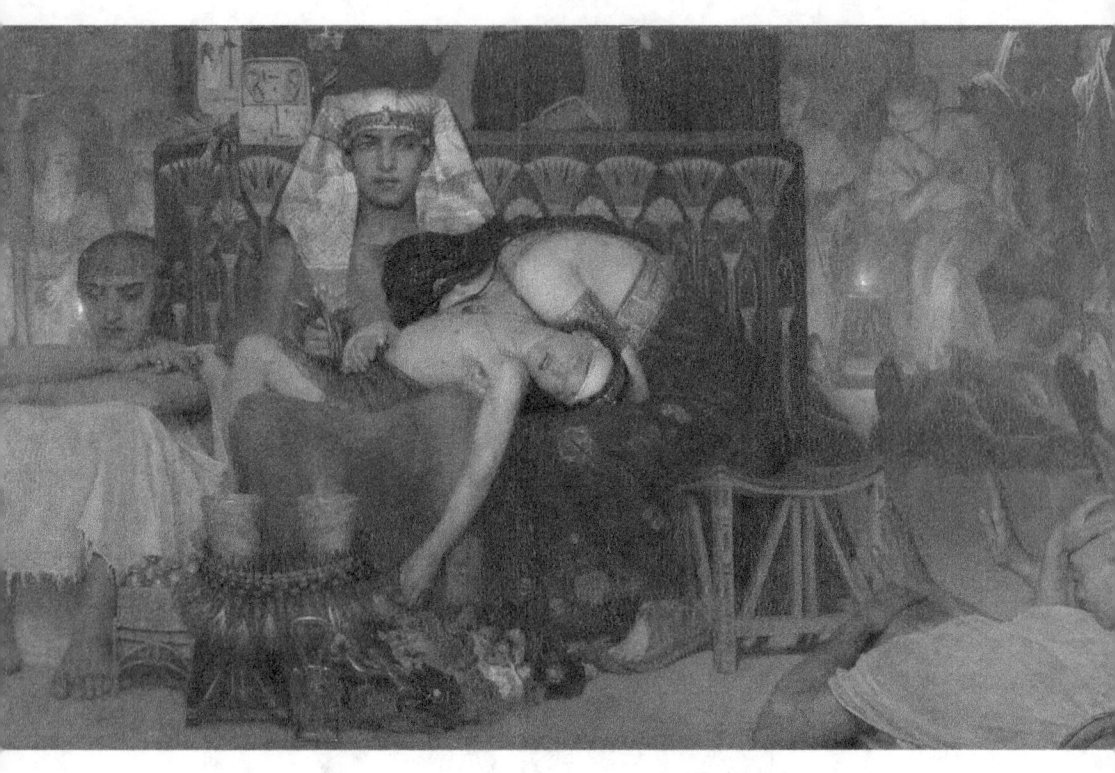

Lawrence Alma-Tadema,
The Death of the Pharaoh's Firstborn Son, 1872,
Rijksmuseum, Amsterdam

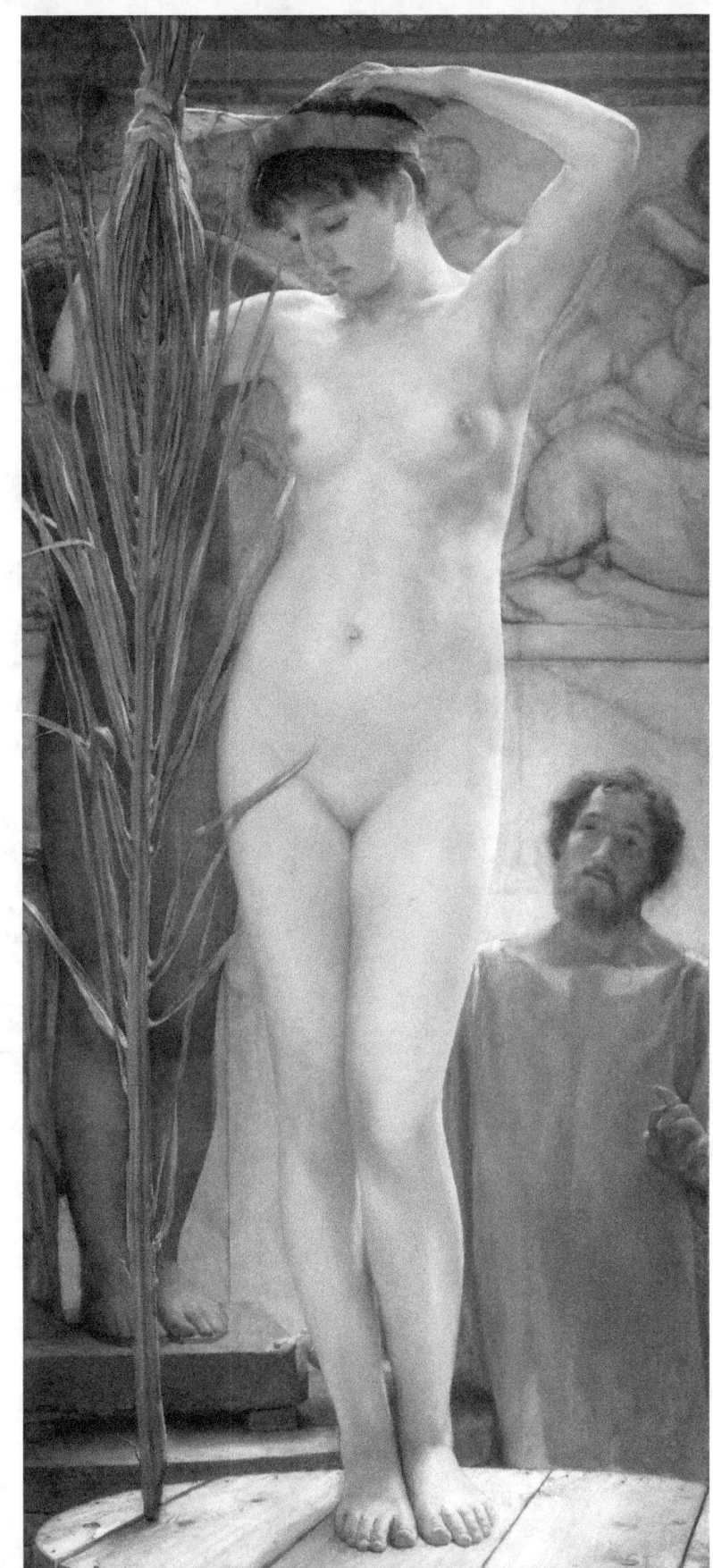

Lawrence
Alma-Tadema,
A Sculptor's Model,
1877, private
collection

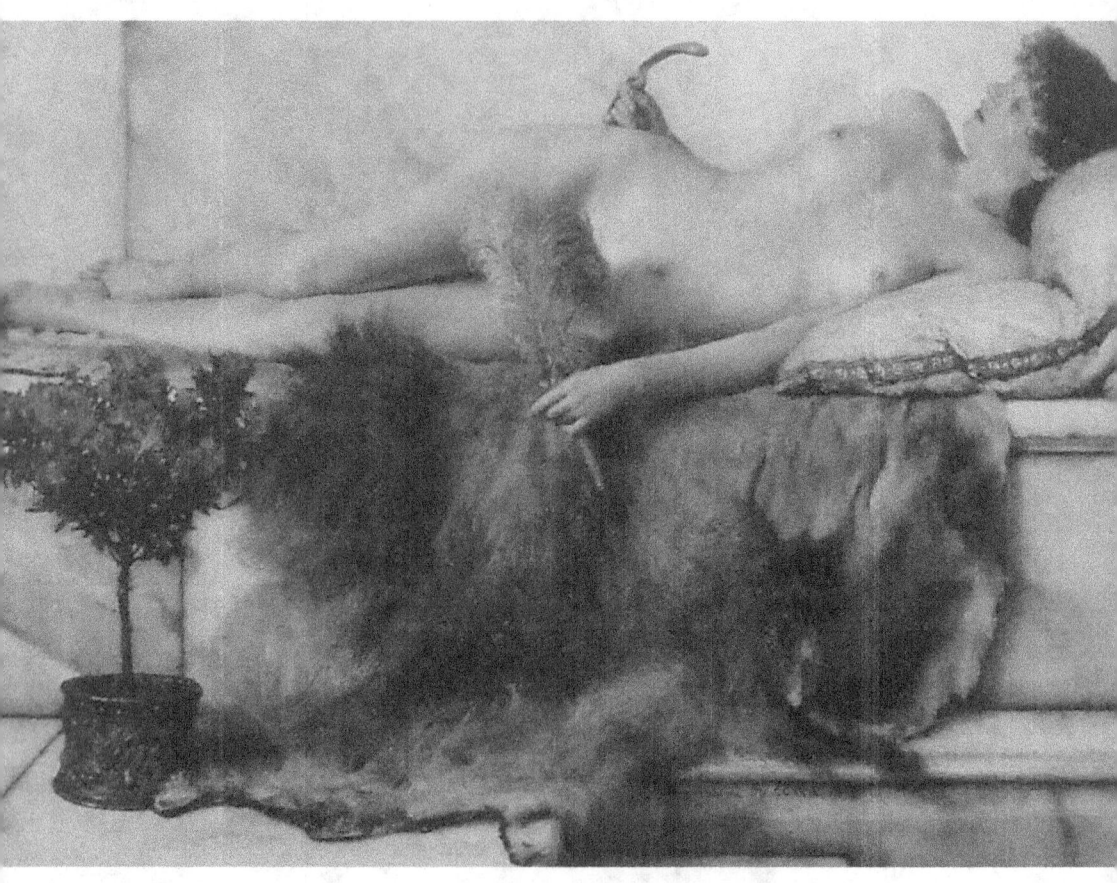

Lawrence Alma-Tadema, In the Tepidarium, 1881,
Lady Lever Art Gallery, Liverpool

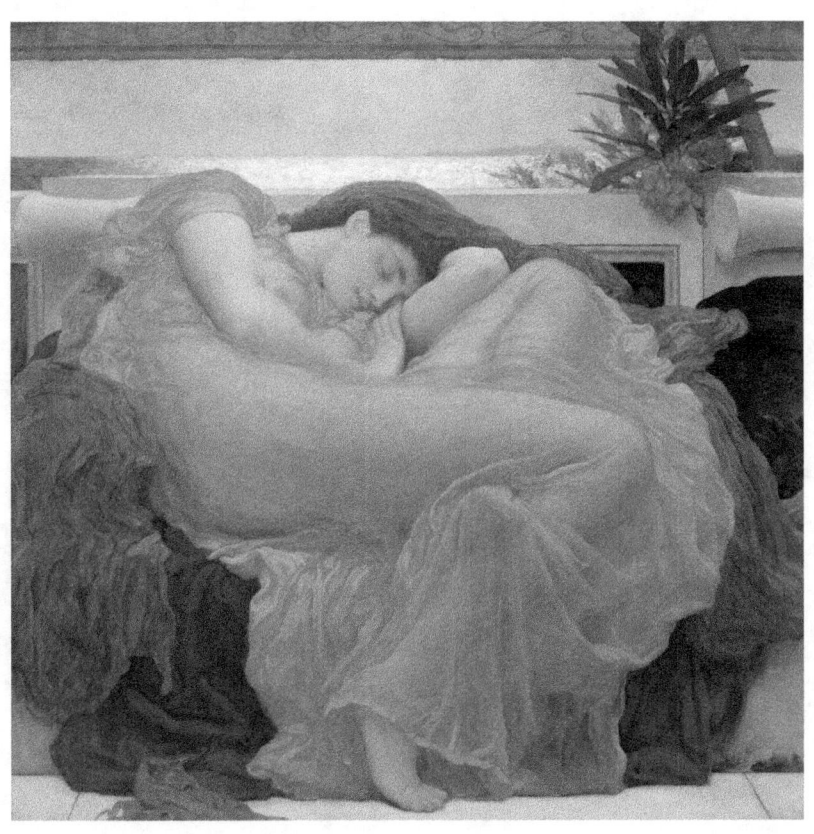

Lord Leighton, Flaming June, 1895, Puerto Rico

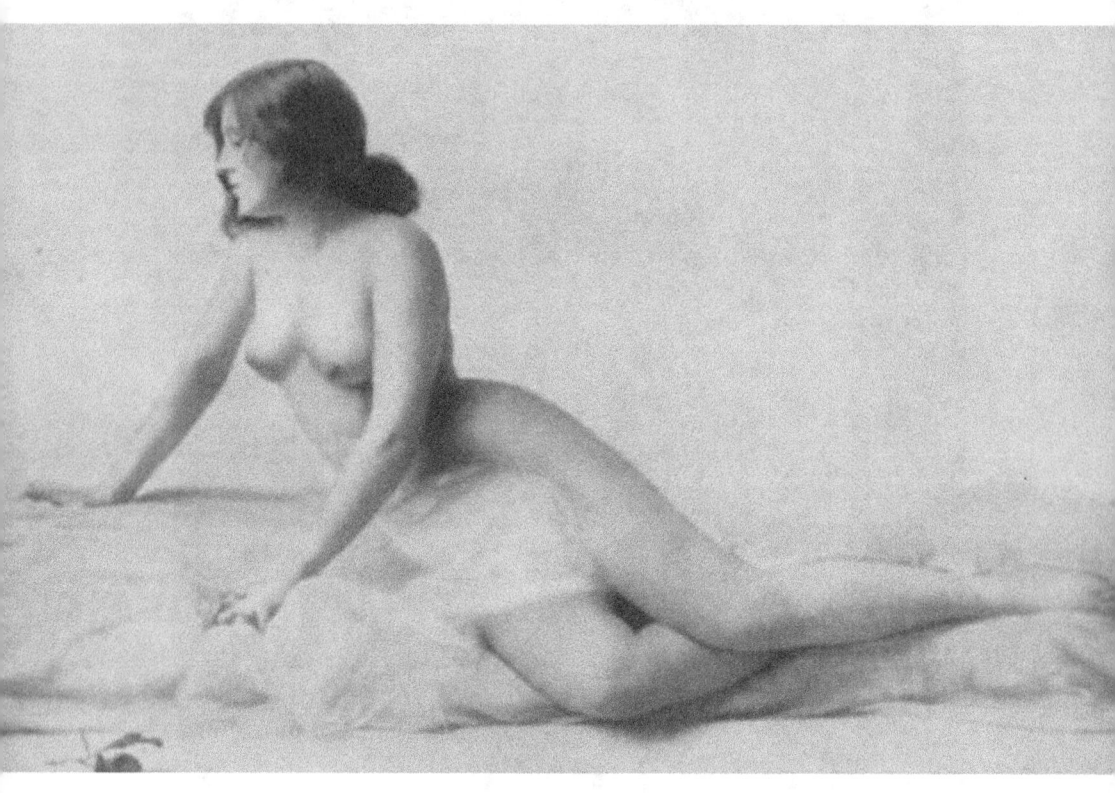

Frederick Armstrong, Greek Slave,
1909, drawn from Lord Leighton

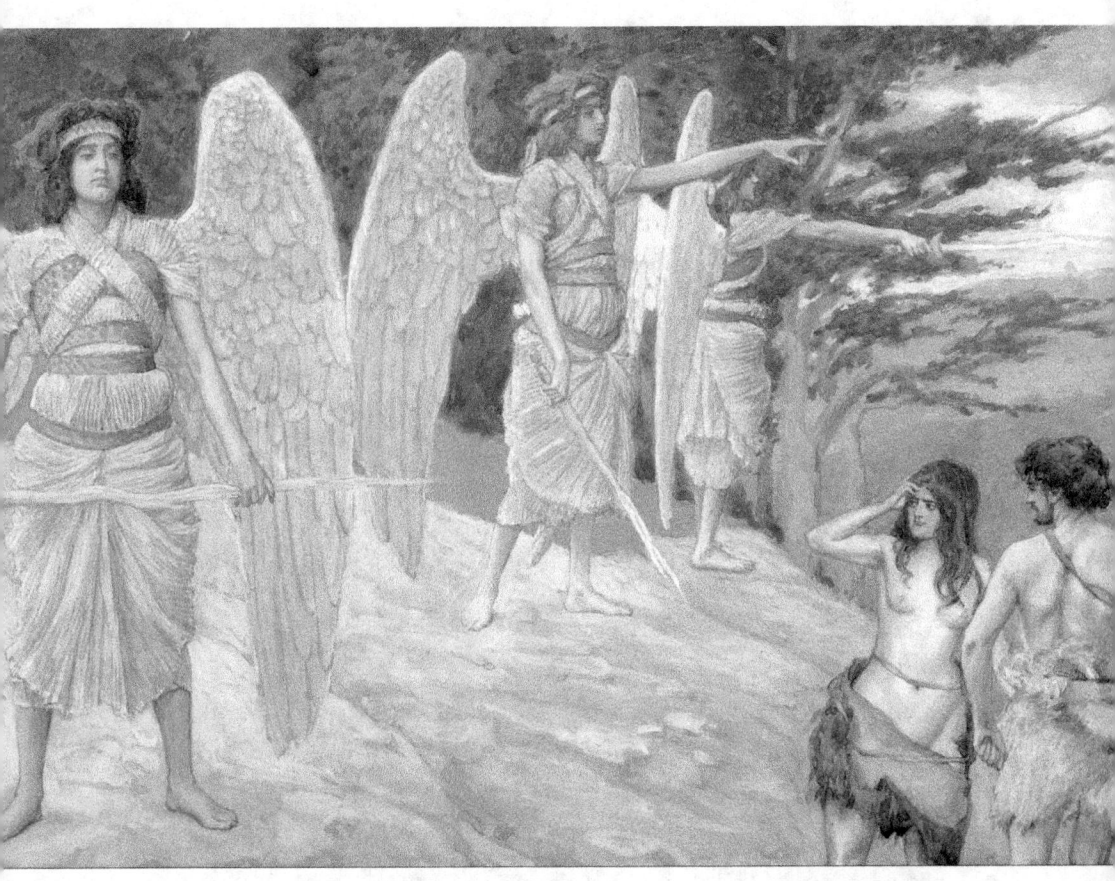

James Tissot, Adam and Eve Driven From Paradise, Jewish Museum, NYC

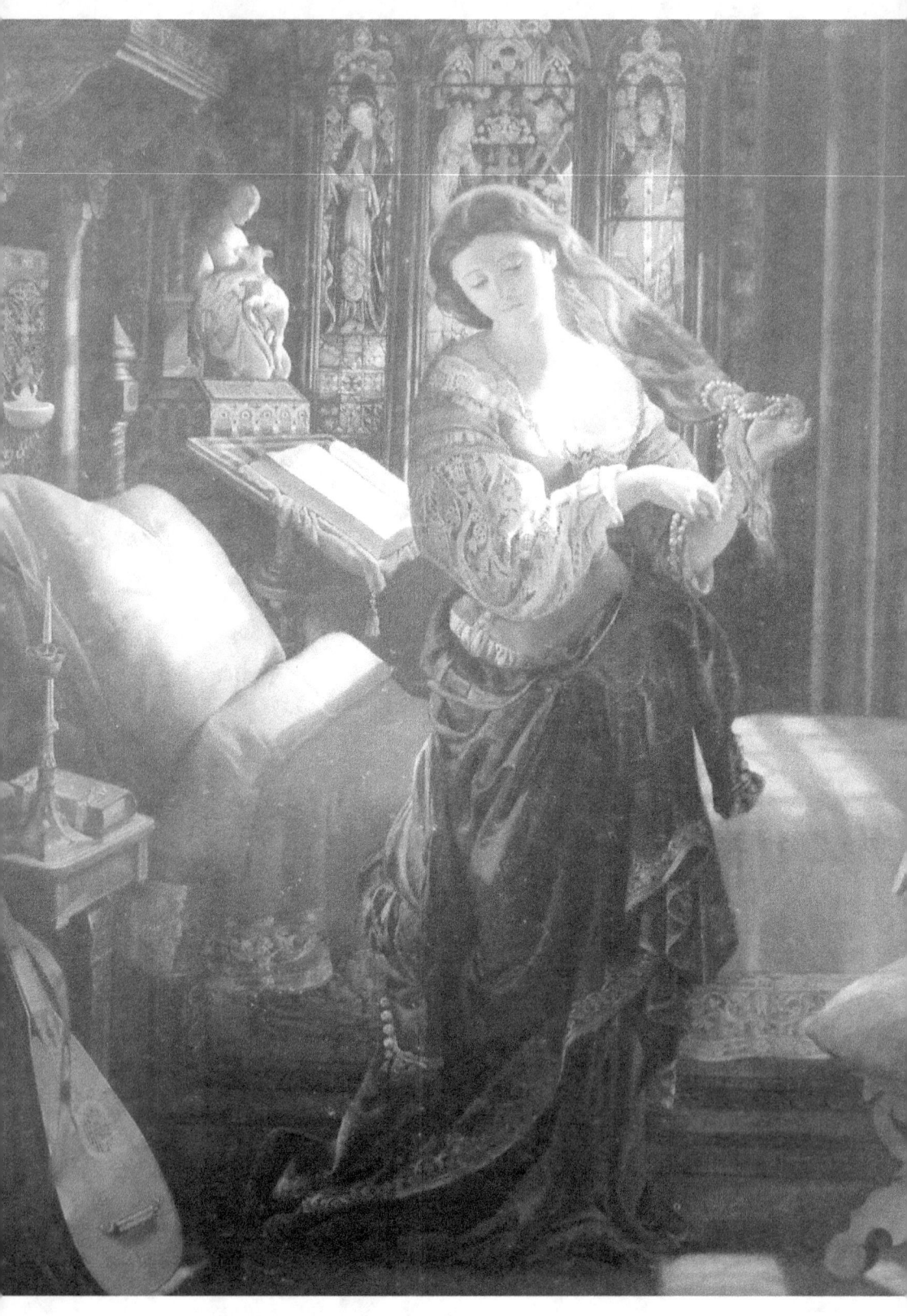

Daniel Maclise, Madeline After Prayer, 1868, Walker Art Gallery

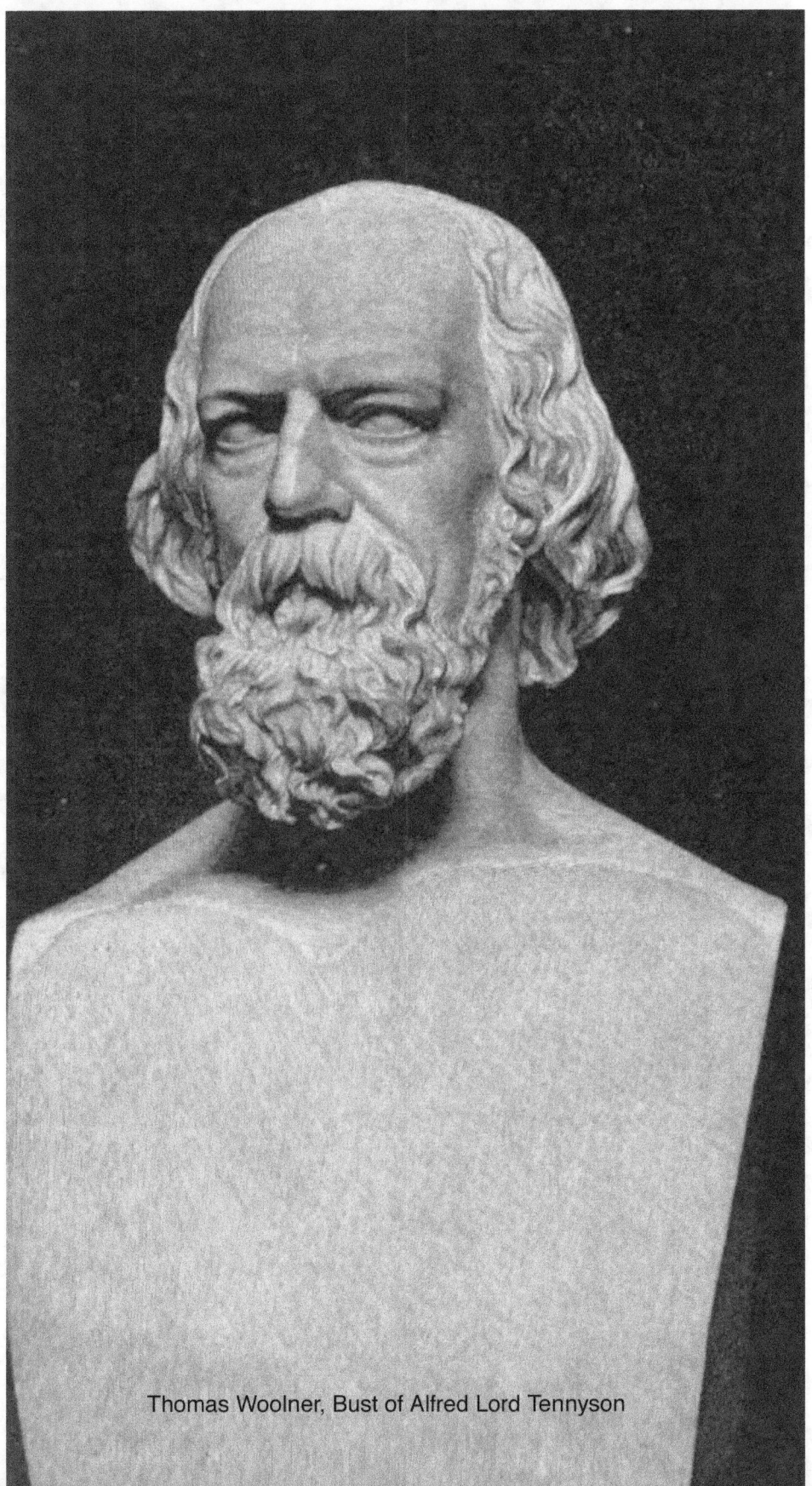

Thomas Woolner, Bust of Alfred Lord Tennyson

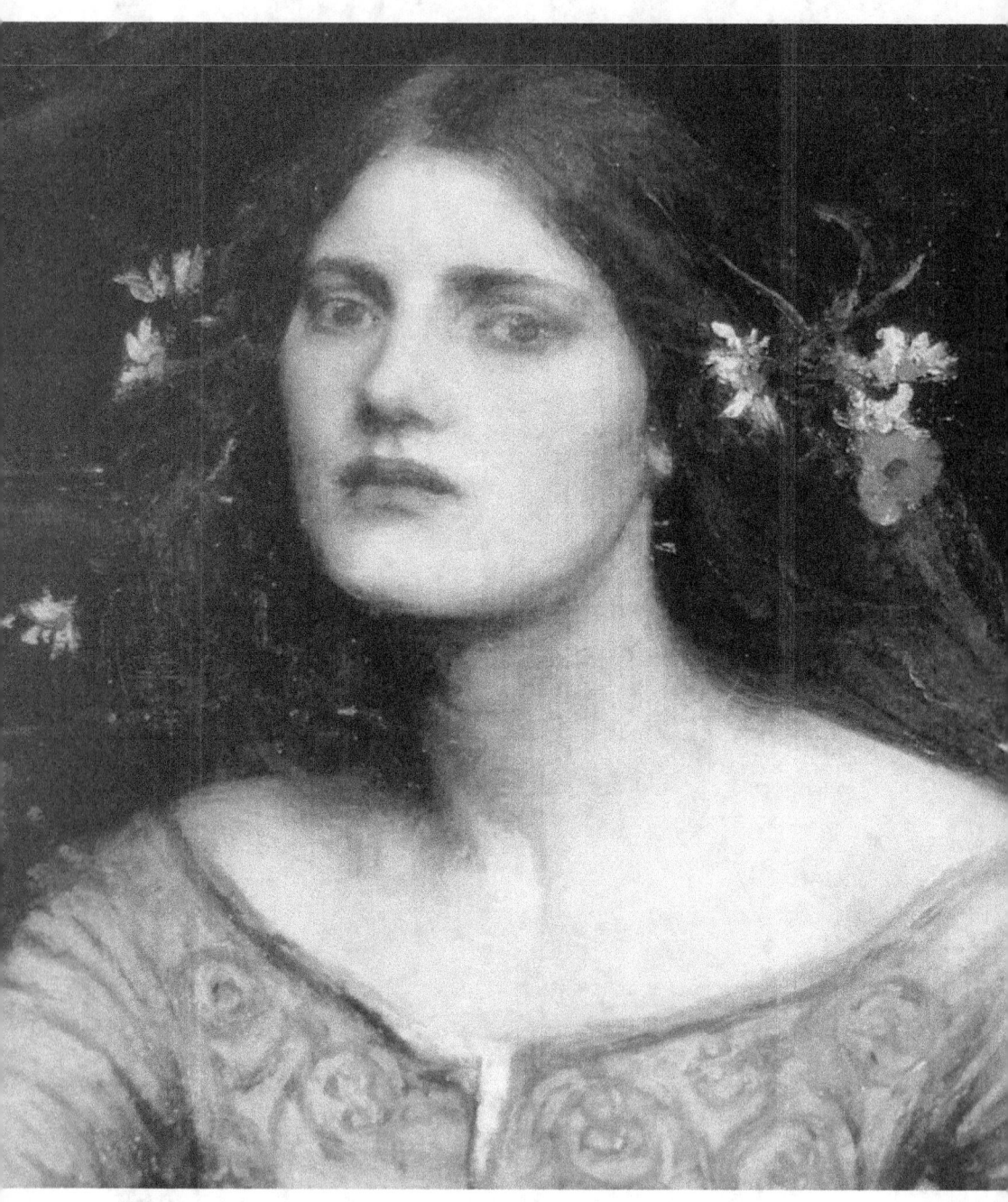

John William Waterhouse, Ophelia, 1910, detail

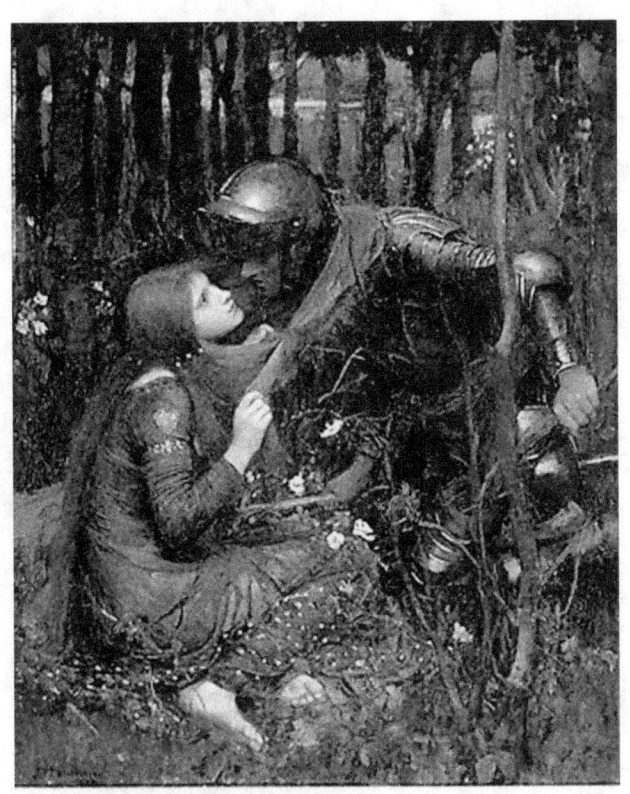

John Waterhouse, 'La Belle Dame Sans Merci'

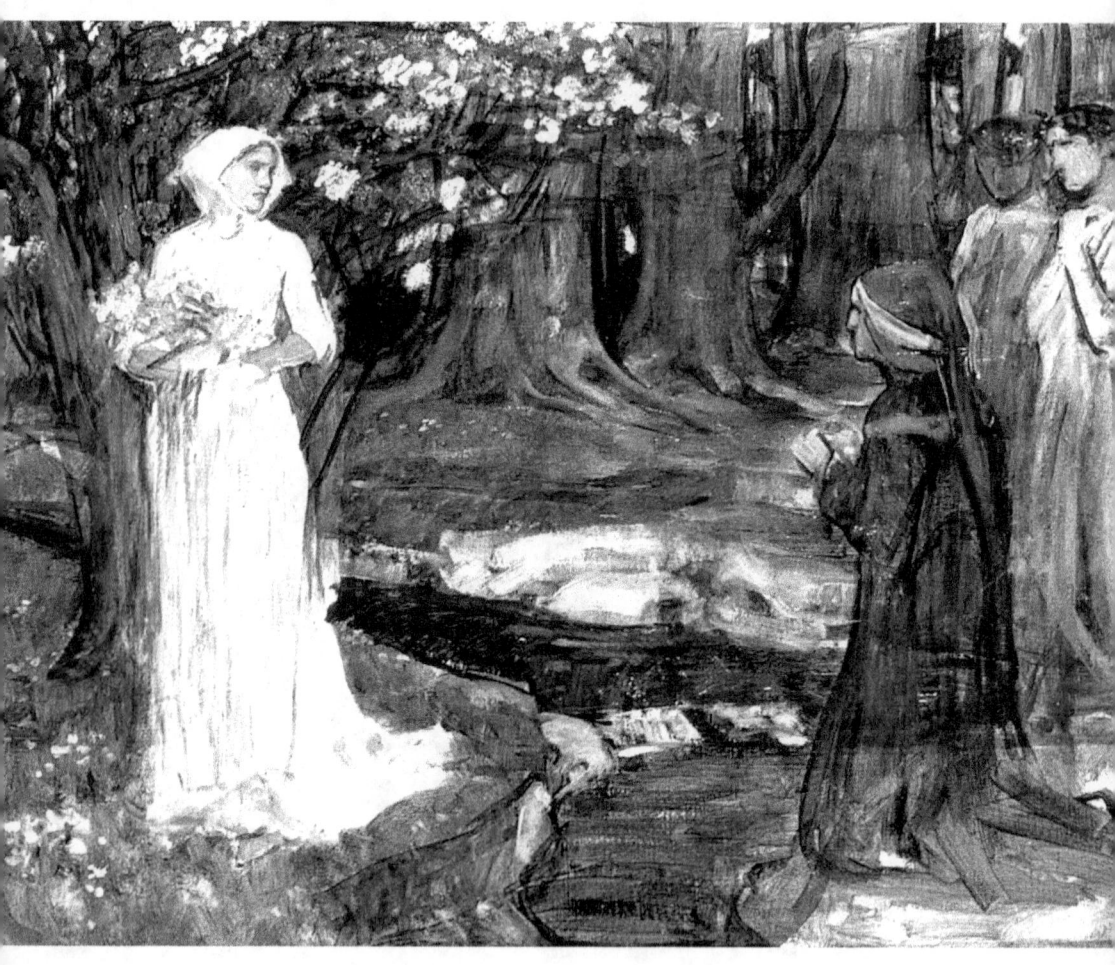

John William Waterhouse, Dante and Matilda, 1915,
Dahesh Museum of Art

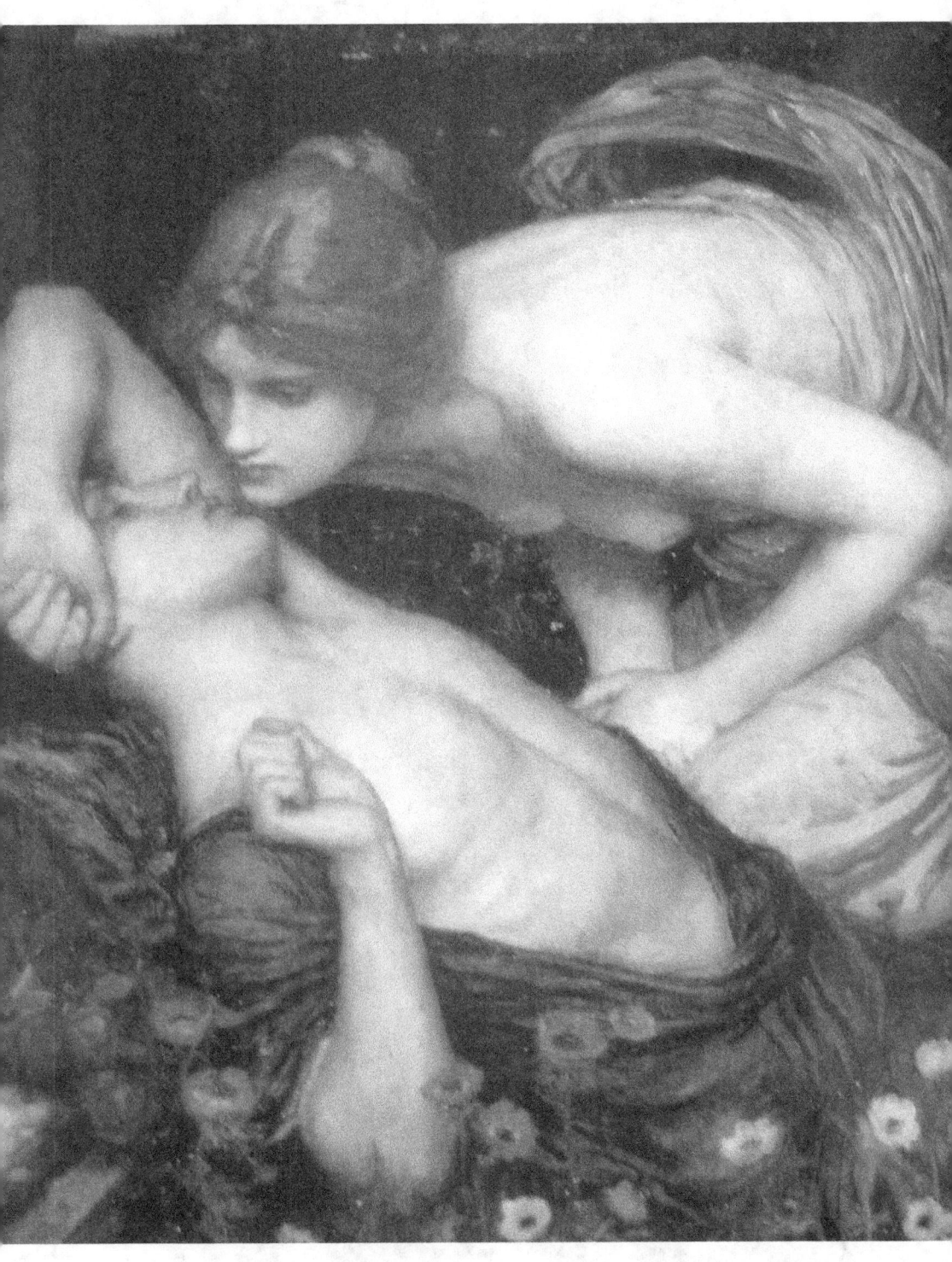

John William Waterhouse, The Awakening of Adonis, 1899, detail

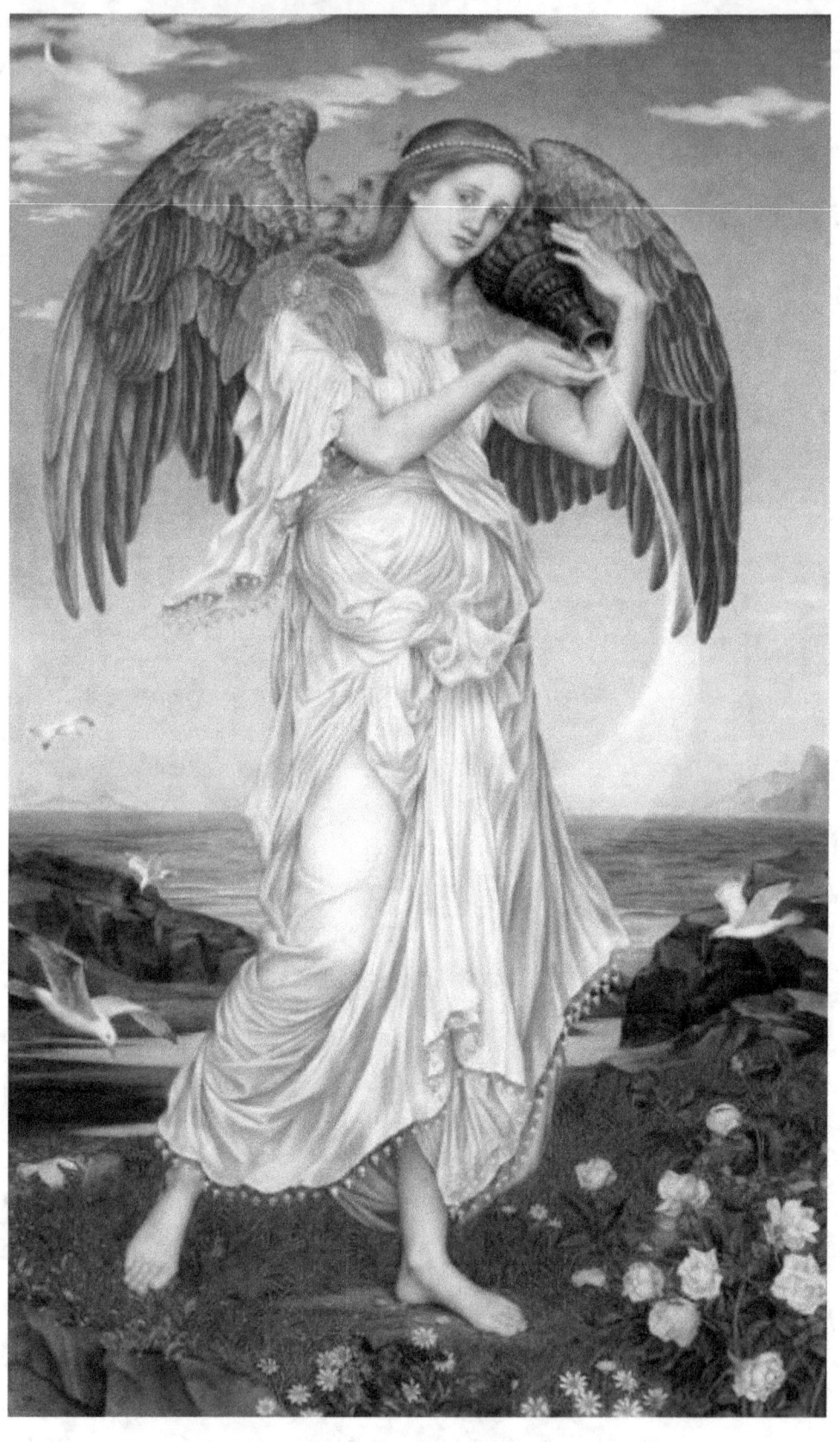

Evelyn de Morgan, Eos, 1895, Columbus, Ohio

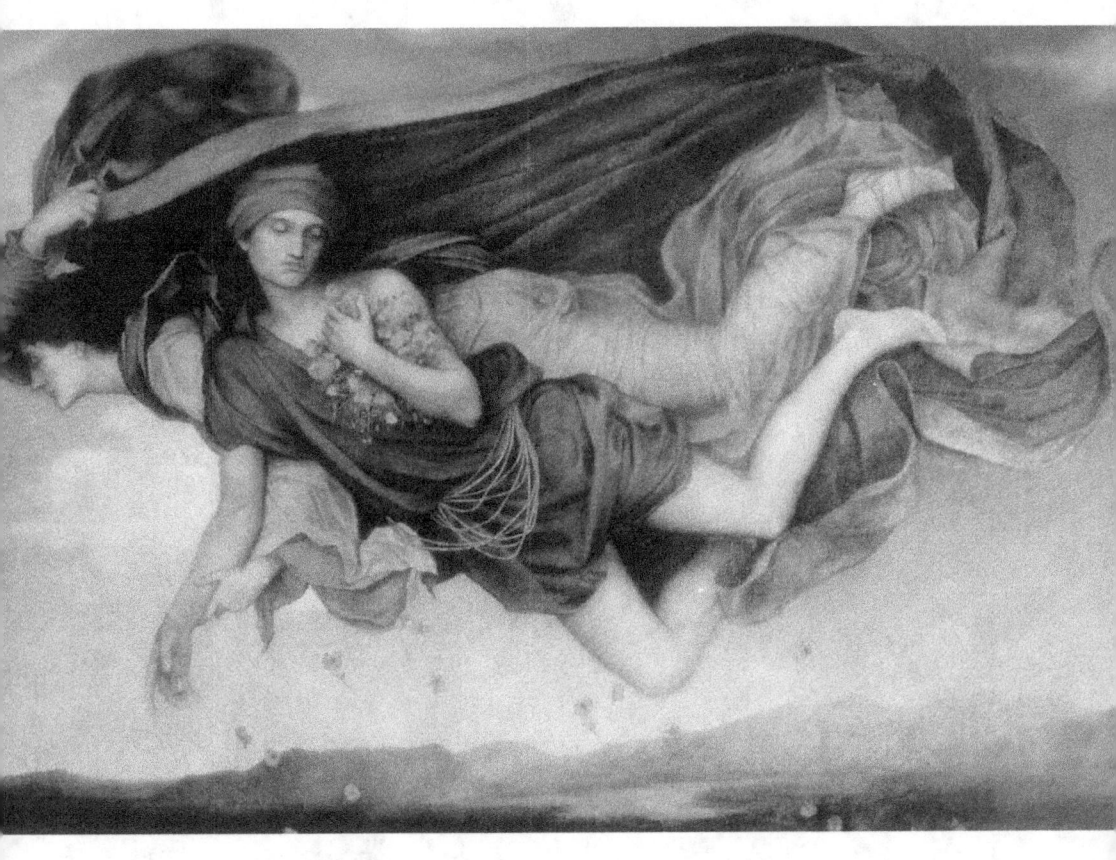

Evelyn de Morgan, Night and Sleep, 1878, Guildford

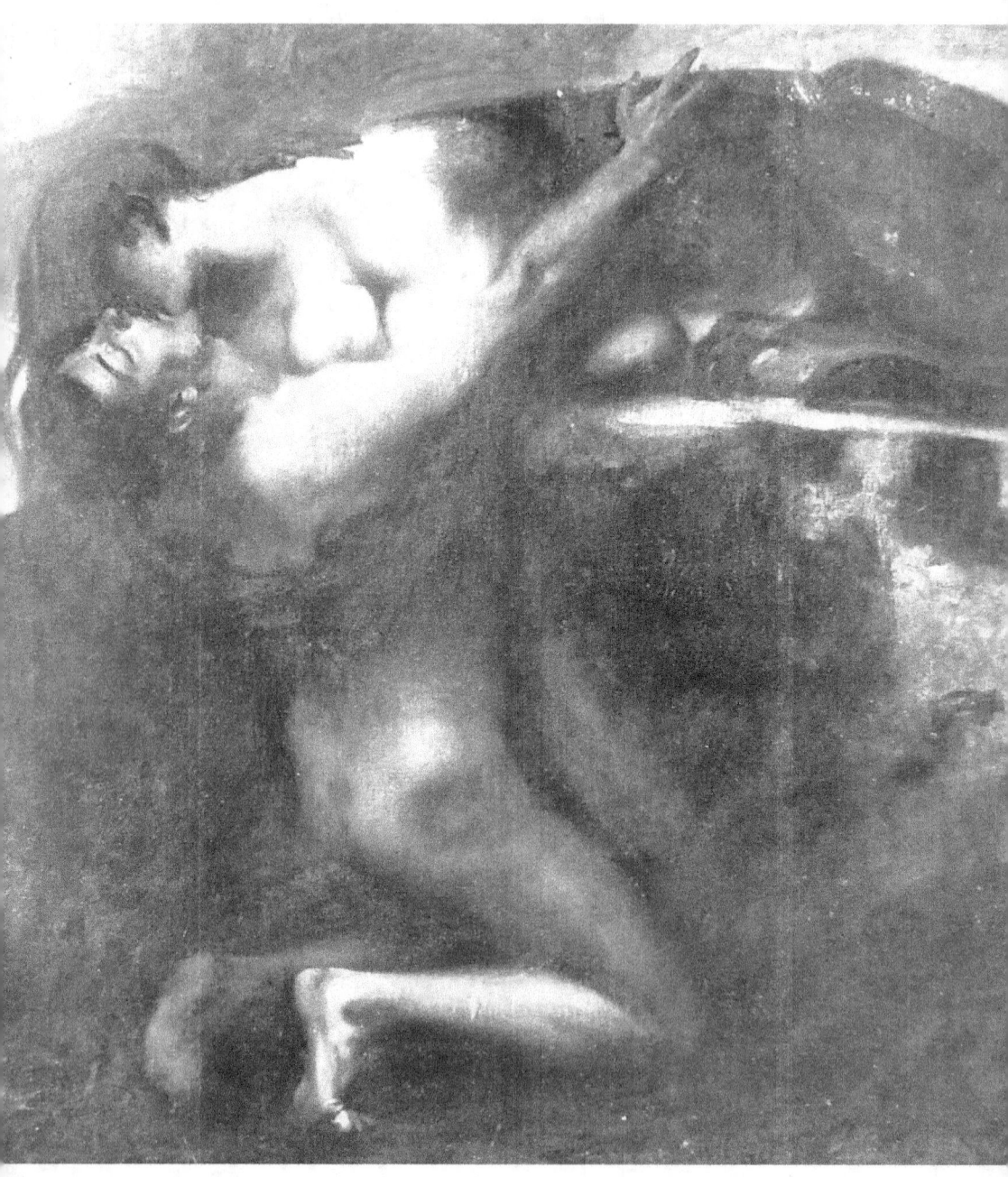

Franz von Stuck, Sphinx

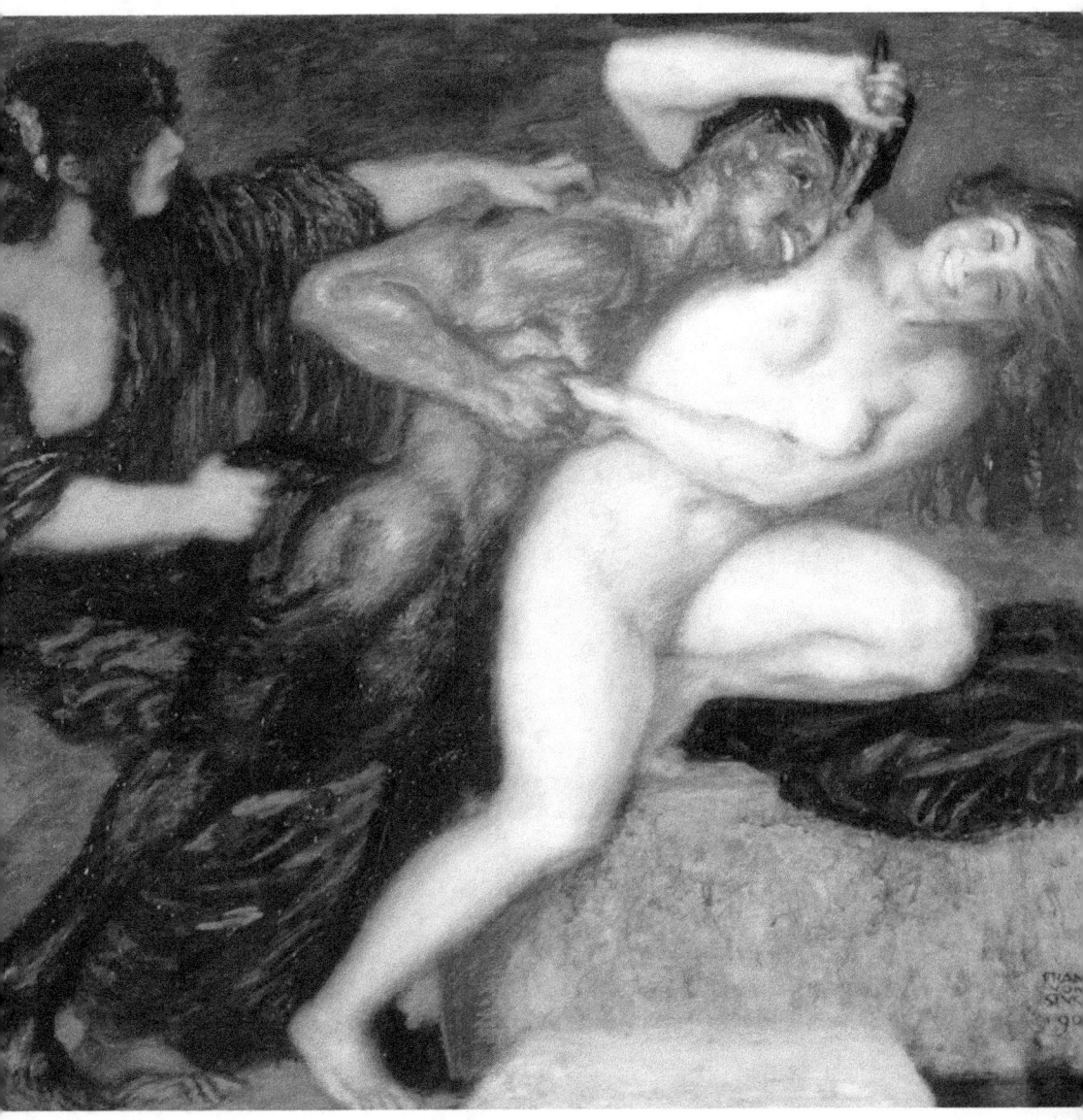

Franz von Stuck, Scherzo

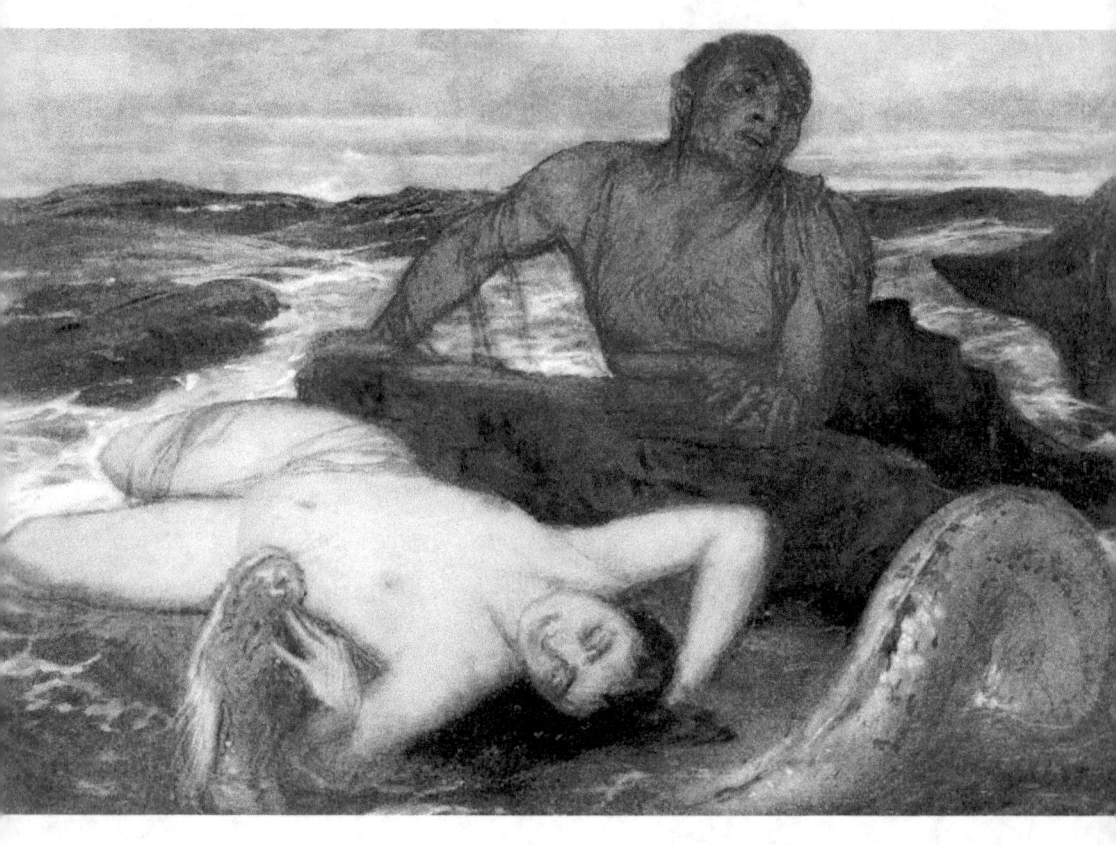

Arnold Böcklin, Triton and Nereid, 1877

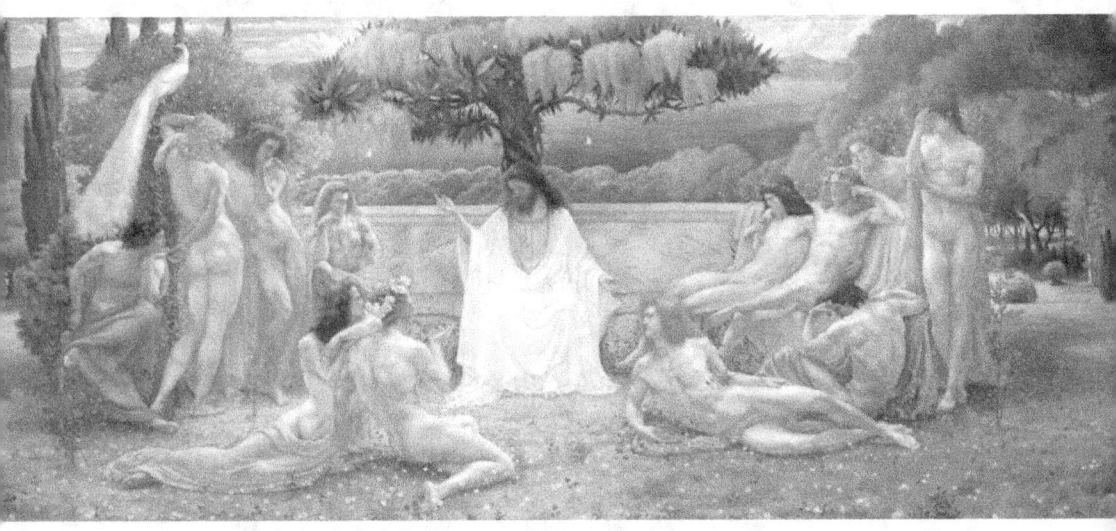

Jean Delville, The School of Plato, 1898

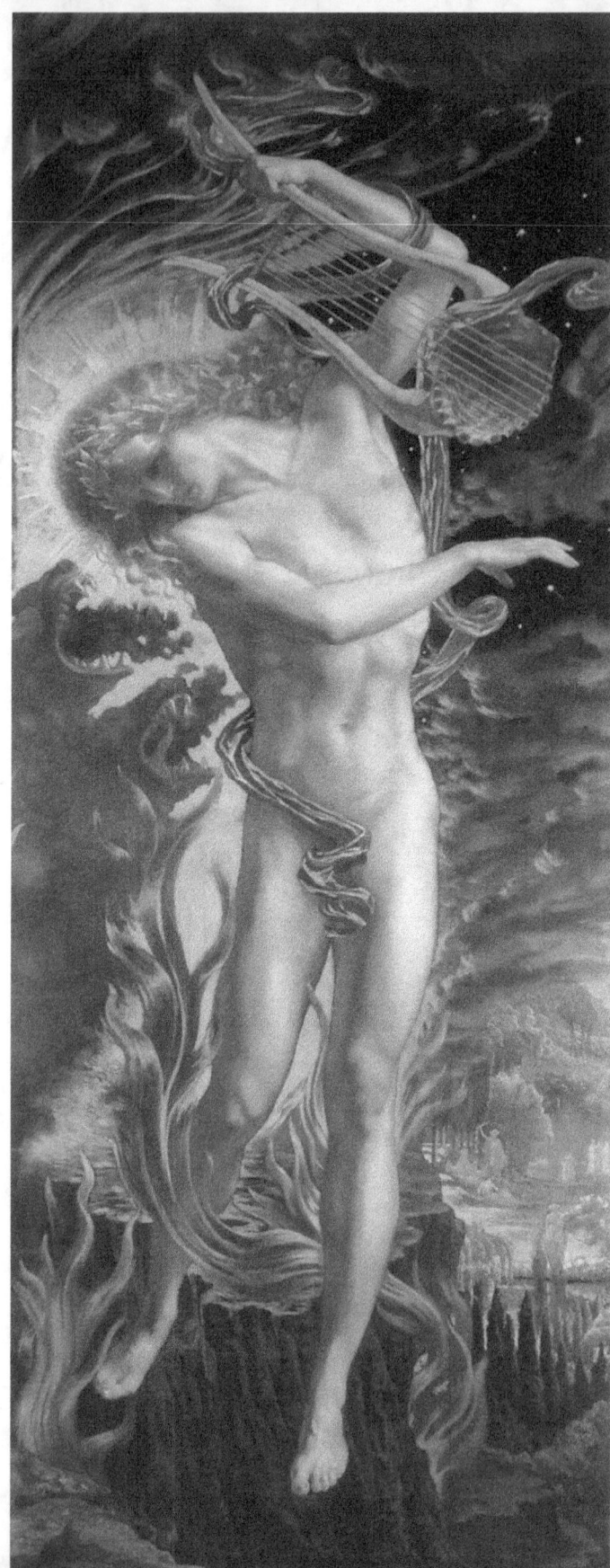

Jean Delville,
Orpheus,
late 19th century

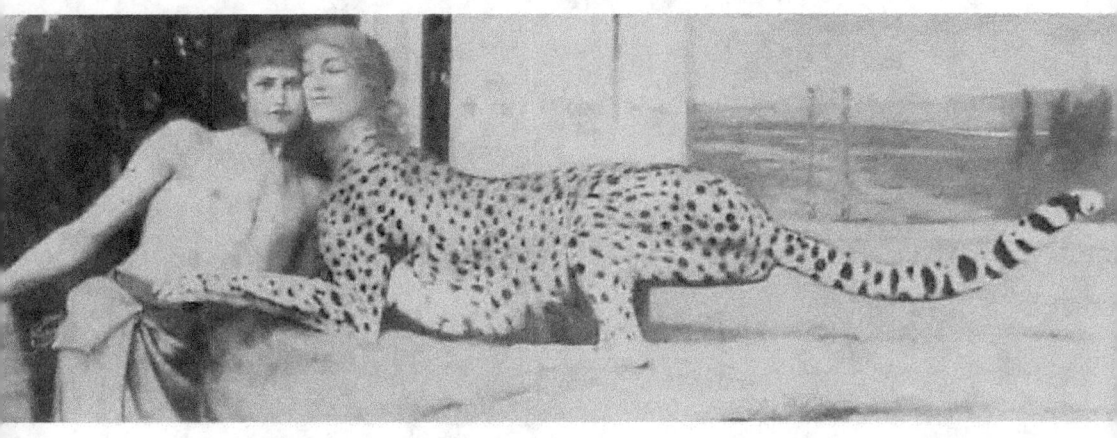

Fernand Knopff, The Caresses of the Sphinx, 1896, Brussels

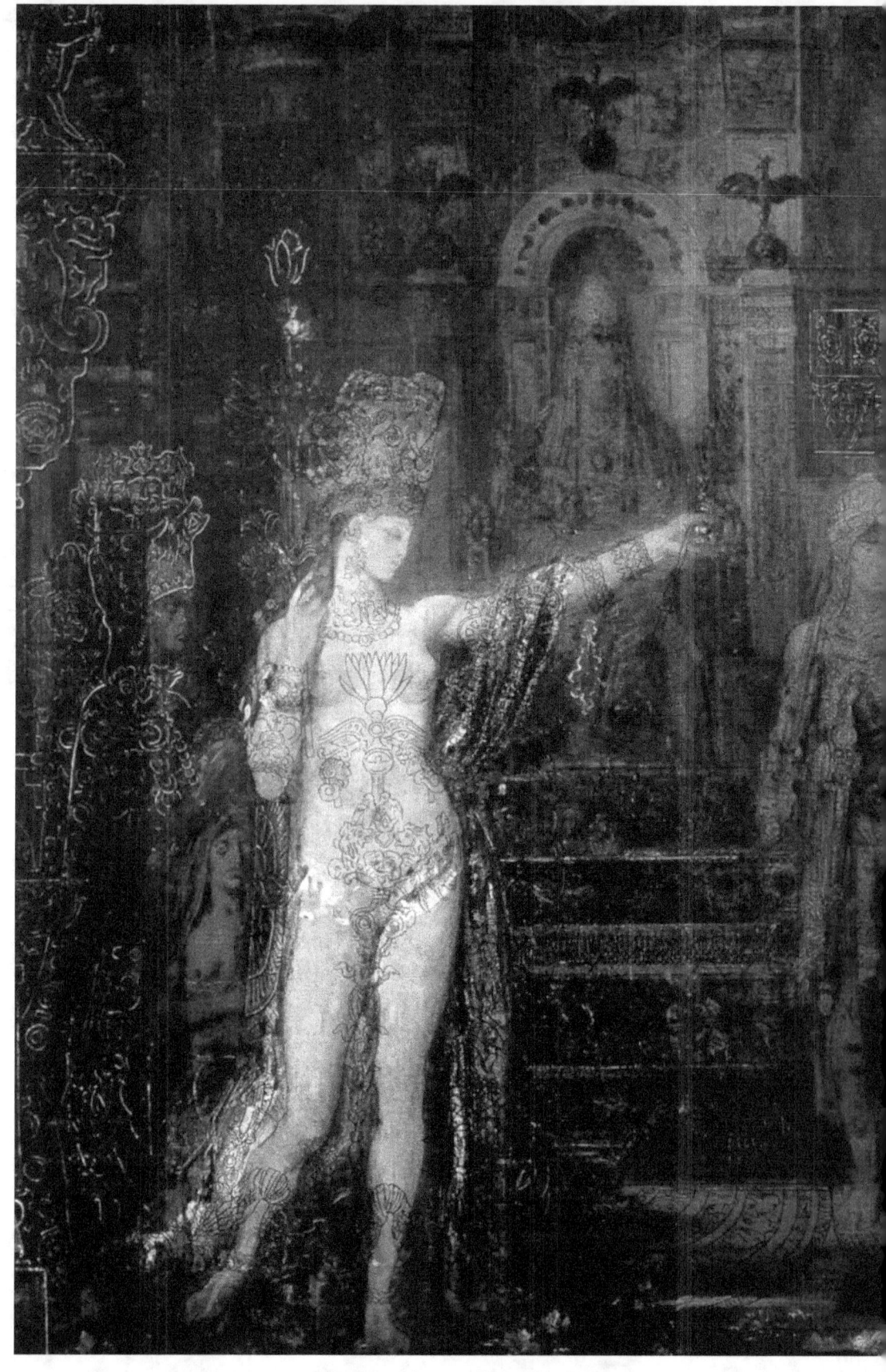

Gustave Moreau, Salomé, 1876

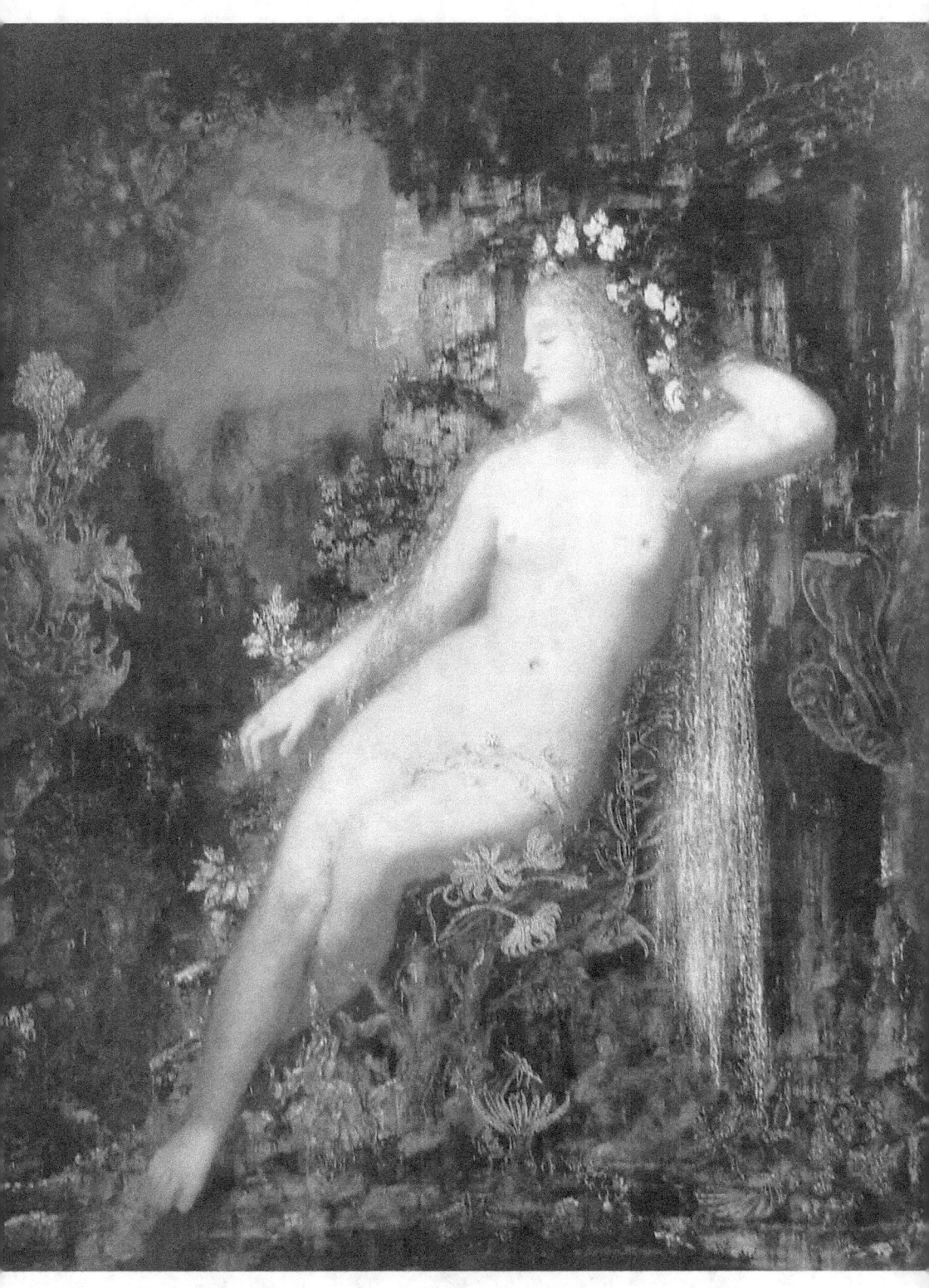

Gustave Moreau, Galatea, 1880

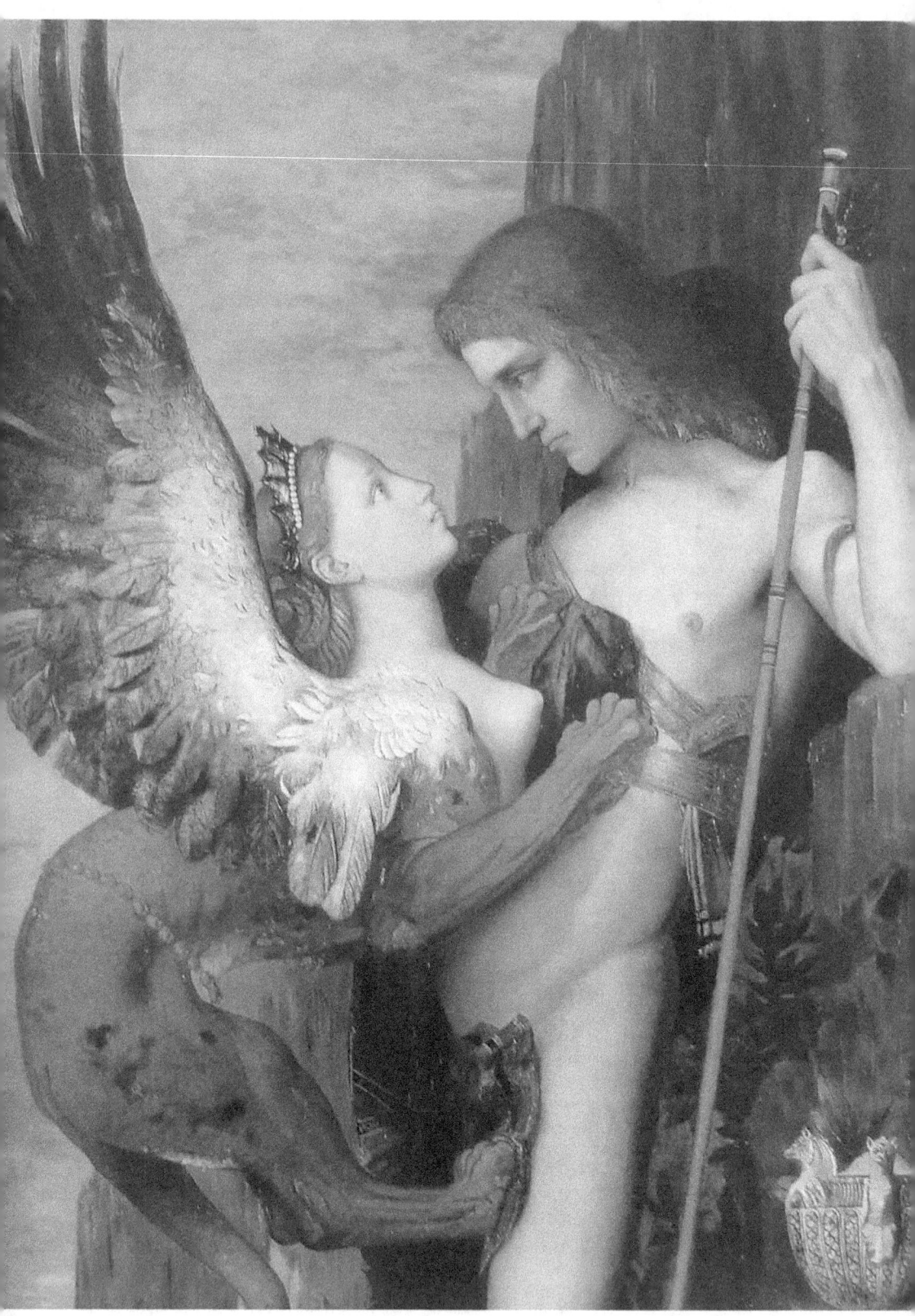

Gustave Moreau, The Sphinx

CHAPTER VI.

TREATMENT OF
RELIGIOUS SUBJECTS.

The Re-birth of Religious Art – "God, Immortality, Duty" – The Pre-Raphaelites and the Reconstruction of Christianity – The Halo in Painting – The Responsibility of Womanhood – The "Girlhood of Mary Virgin" and "Ecce Ancilla Domini" – The Problem of Suffering – "Christ in the House of His Parents," "The Passover in the Holy Family," "The Shadow of Death," "The Scapegoat" – Hunt's Symbolism – "The Light of the World" – Rossetti's Symbolism – "Mary Magdalene at the Door," and "Mary in the House of John" – The Idea of Victory Through Suffering – "Bethlehem Gate" – "The Triumph of the Innocents" – The Spirit of Inquiry – "Christ in the Temple" – The Atonement – "The Infant Christ Adored" – Comparison with Madox Brown and Burne-Jones – "The Entombment" – "The Tree of Life."

"God – Immortality – Duty;" such were the weighty words chosen by one of the greatest women of our century as the text of a now historic conversation in the shadow of St. John's College, Cambridge. The student to whom she spoke has told us with what a tender solemnity she approached the great postulations which those words conveyed, and challenged them in her inflexible judgment one by one; – to her, how inconceivable the first, how unbelievable the second, but yet how imperative and irresistible the third.

The attitude of George Eliot, even in the phase of intellectual scepticism from which she then spoke, was deeply significant of that fundamental change in the constitution of religion, that entire transference of Christian or non-Christian "evidences," from the intellectual to the moral sphere, from the argument to the instinct, which is now largely accepted as the supreme result of modern thought in Europe. For the repudiation of prior conceptions of "God" and "Immortality," so far from precluding a reconstructive faith, rather prepared the way for it; making the belief in unseen goodness a deduction from instead of a premise to the recognition of visible goodness in the present world, and leaving the more scope for that growing reverence for the physical nature of man which, – having its origins in Paganism and its highest sanction in the Gospel of Galilee, and revealing itself in a passionate exaltation of bodily beauty as a symbol of the divine, a resolute acceptance of the laws of nature and destiny, and a strenuous blending of resignation to those laws with conquest of them by spiritual powers, – has inspired the great humanitarian movement of to-day, wherein the faith of the future finds the witness and the justification of its ideal.

To what degree, then, has the Pre-Raphaelite movement in English art affected, or reflected, that momentous revolution? The pictures of Rossetti, Millais, and Holman Hunt have been by turns exalted and condemned by the apologists of contending theological schools, and the painters stigmatized, now as followers of Tractarianism and instruments of Popery, now as leaders of the coarsest rationalism in sacred art, now as apostles of a sensual neo-Paganism brought over from the Renaissance, and credited to hold mystic and sceptic in equal defiance. One clerical critic, indeed, in 1857, sought in an ineffectual volume to prove the essential atheism of all Pre-Raphaelite work. His protest was but typical of that still extant species of mind to which the worship of the body implies the profanation of the soul. It remains to be decided whether such paintings touched the deepest religious principles which underlie all change of creed or ritual, and if so, in what way the art of the Pre-Raphaelites has joined or swayed the general current of humanitarian feeling which is slowly absorbing all forms of religion into a universal spirit and will.

These questions bring us to the great group of pictures in which English artists for the first time have aspired to deal in all simplicity and earnestness with the bases and principles of the Christian religion. It should not be difficult to discern the dominant idea, the moral keynote, so to speak, of the highest utterances of art in an age of such religious revolution as has been suggested by the proposition of George Eliot. The philosophy of "Duty," presented by her in its sternest aspect, but brought more into line with the common heritage of religious thought by Browning, Tennyson, F.D. Maurice, and other contemporaries of the Pre-Raphaelite band, has in fact led in art, as it has led in religion, directly, if unconsciously, to that reverent re-discovery of "God," that transfiguration of the ideal of "Immortality," which the revival of the spirit of romance has made possible to modern England. It has been said that "the romantic temper is the essentially Christian element in art."[*7] Let us rather say that it is the medium through which Christianity itself has been renewed and quickened into a richer and fuller life. The romantic temper, in Pre-Raphaelite art, takes hold of the eternal verities of the Christian faith, and humanizes its whole cycle of history and legend in the atmosphere of the real and present world. It ignores any sort of dividing line between sacred tragedy and the great problems of modern time. It abjures for ever the "glass-case reverence" of relic-worship, the superstition which isolates Christian history as a record of exceptional events, instead of an interpretation of universal experiences. Ruskin justly says that "imagination will find its holiest work in the lighting-up of the Gospels;" but the illumination must have a reconstructive as well as an analytic consequence; must be, as the late Peter Walker

Nicholson expresses it in his fine critique on Rossetti,[*8] *instinctively synthetic* – which is the quality of genius: and all true art is synthetic in its essence and its end. The tendency of modern religious science to discredit the exceptional and the unique, and set the basis of morals in universal and familiar things, – in other words to deduce "God" and "Immortality" from the instinct of "Duty" and not "Duty" from the arguments for "Immortality" and "God," – finds its correlative in the tendency of romantic art to subject the remote specialities of classicism to the test of known conditions and actual character.

Therefore the four gospels, to the Pre-Raphaelite painters, do not stand alone as "religious" history, distinct from the world-wide record of human aspiration and struggle from age to age. They merely afford the supreme examples of man's apprehension of "God, Immortality, Duty," and of his capability of heroic labour and self-sacrifice in the pursuit of an ideal. The Pre-Raphaelites draw their first principle of religion from the beauty and glory of the natural world, and the intrinsic dignity and sacredness of human life. Their Christ is re-incarnate in the noblest manhood of all time; their Virgin Mary lives again in every pure girl that wakes to the solemn charm, the mysterious power and responsibility of womanhood. In humanity itself, with all its possibilities, in its triumphs and in its degradations, its labours and its sufferings, they re-discover "God," – an "unknown God," it may be; "inconceivable," if we will; but evident in the quickened conscience of a growing world, and in the invincible instincts of human pity and love. Millais sees a young Christ in the delicate boy with the wounded hand in the dreary and comfortless carpenter's shop. Hunt sees a crucified Christ in the tired workman, over-tasked and despairing amid the calm sunlight of eventide. Rossetti sees a risen Christ in the noble poet whose great love could conquer death and enter upon the New Life in the present hour. The true Pre-Raphaelitism does not take the halo from the head of the Christ of history; but it puts the halo on the head of every suffering child, of every faithful man and woman since the world began. It is not that the historic Christ is less divine; but that all humanity is diviner because He lived and died.

In such a spirit does Rossetti conceive "The Girlhood of Mary Virgin," – not as a miraculous but an exquisitely natural thing; miraculous, at least, in Walt Whitman's sense of the word, – the sense in which all beauty and all goodness are miracles to man. He shows us the up-growing of a simple country girl, in a home full of the sweetness of family love; remote and quiet, yet with no artificial superiority or isolation from the average world. The maiden in the picture, with an innocent austerity of face, sits at an embroidery-frame by her mother's side. In front of her is a growing lily, whose white blossoms, the symbol of her purity, she is copying with her needle on the cloth of red, beneath St. Anna's watchful eye. The flower-pot rests on a pile of books, inscribed with the names of the choicest virtues, uppermost of which is Charity. Near to these lie a seven-thorned briar and a seven-leaved palm-branch, with a scroll inscribed "Tot dolores tot gaudia," typical of "her great sorrow and her great reward." The lily is tended by a beautiful child-angel, the guardian both of the flower and the girl who is herself, in Rossetti's words,

> "An angel-watered lily, that near God
>   Grows and is quiet."

Around the balcony trails a vine, which St. Joiachim is pruning above; significant of the True Vine which must hereafter suffer "the chastisement of our peace." The dove that broods among its branches promises the Comforter that is to come. The realism of the picture is a realism of the mediæval kind, that takes possession of, instead of ignoring, the spiritual world, and overleaps the boundaries of visible things; depicting the invisible with the daring confidence of imaginative faith. The child-angel with her crimson pinions is as substantial on the canvas as the soberly-clad virgin at her symbolic task.

In the companion-picture, "Ecce Ancilla Domini" ("Behold the handmaid of the Lord!") Rossetti repeats and develops much of the same symbolism in the accessories of the painting, but the universal meaning of the Virgin's call is far more clearly brought out. The design differs from all familiar versions of the Annunciation in that the message is delivered to Mary as she wakes out of sleep, and that she is depicted, not among beautiful and well-ordered surroundings, but in a poor and bare chamber, rising, half-awake, in a humble pallet-bed, and sitting awed before the angel whose presence, perhaps, is but the visualized memory of her dream. The rapt stillness of her look recalls the pregnant line in which Byron speaks of a troubled waking, – "to know the sense of pain without the cause." In Mary's mind there should rather be a sense of joy without the cause; but even in her joy there lies a mystery, a burden of responsibility and foreboded sorrow, that makes it heavy to bear. It is as if some simple girl, waking to the golden glories of a summer morn, should wake at the same time to the thought of the world's pain, and realize, in a sudden exaltation of pity and love, that somehow, by whatever path of grief and loss, her purity, her goodness, must help humanity and bless the race to be. The angel at her side is a girl-child no longer, but a youth, full of strength and graciousness, as if to suggest that the sanctities of manhood are now to be revealed to the maid. In his hand the radiant Gabriel holds the full-grown and gathered lily, whose image is now completed on the embroidered cloth, which hangs near the bed. The dove, the symbol of the Holy Spirit, flies in at the window, and the light is soft and warm from the sun-bathed landscape without.

Once again did Rossetti attempt the subject of "The Annunciation," but only in a water-colour sketch, which found a place, however, in the small but choice collection in the Burlington Club. Here also the lily affords the symbolic keynote of the design, – the Virgin is seen bathing among the water-lilies in a stream; but the singularly fine conception of the angel's salutation gives a special value and interest to the work. The figure that appears before her on the bank assumes for the moment the aspect of a cross; being so enfolded with his golden wings that the Virgin sees not only the glory of her visitant but the dire portent of the message which he brings. "The Annunciation" of Mr. Arthur Hughes is more conventional in spirit, with its veiled Virgin and its stiffly self-conscious Gabriel, and lacks the note of prescience which gives solemnity to Rossetti's designs. Mr. Burne-Jones, on the other hand, gives us a more mature and stately maid. His Mary, nobly simple though she is, seems better prepared for the sacred honour of her destiny, and does not touch us so deeply as the shrinking girl in "Ecce Ancilla Domini," or even as the poor beggar-maiden (for so she appears) in Mr. Hughes's "Nativity," bending timid and reverent on her knees in the straw before the Holy Child.

But the note of prescience, as we have seen, – the prophetic symbolism which brings to mind in every incident of the Saviour's life the whole scheme of sacrifice and redemption, dominates all the greatest Pre-Raphaelite work. The suggestions of the inevitable Cross recur in Rossetti's early picture, "The Passover in the Holy Family," in Millais's "Christ in the House of His Parents," and in Holman Hunt's "Shadow of Death," with a force and urgency that points at once to the universal significance of the history. "The Passover in the Holy Family" shows us the boy Christ carrying a bowl filled with the blood of the newly-slain Paschal lamb, and gazing at it with a mysterious foreboding in his eyes. In the dim background St. Joseph and St. Anna (or, according to Mr. William Rossetti, and as seems more probable, St. Elizabeth), are seen kindling a fire for the ritual. Mary is gathering bitter herbs, and Zacharias is sprinkling the door-posts and lintel with the lamb's blood. The youthful John Baptist is kneeling at the feet of Christ, binding His shoe.

Rossetti, however, does not attempt quite so bold a translation of the Biblical narrative into modern form as does Millais when, depicting "Christ in the House of His Parents," he sets the poor and mean-looking child in the midst of almost wholly English surroundings, in a carpenter's workshop, looking out upon a landscape of thoroughly English meadow-land; – a literalism of method since adopted with more daring fidelity to local colour in their respective fields by such later realists as Fritz von Uhde and Vassili Verestchagin, and others of the German and neo-French schools, but never pursued to the same length in any later experiment from the studios of the Pre-Raphaelite Brotherhood. Critics probably will long be divided as to the legitimacy of such a process, and its success must be judged largely by the intention of the painter, – whether he seeks merely to present an historical incident with vividness and force, and employs familiar scenery to emphasize the hard reality of his narrative, and whether he rather aspires to interpret the universal truth beneath the incident, and to illustrate its bearing upon present life; in other words, whether he desires to impress us (for example) with the reality of the sufferings of Christ, or with the problem of human suffering in all ages, of which the sacred story is at once the type and the key. It can scarcely be argued that the latter object does not come within the scope of art. The point at issue, however, seems to be that the sense of anachronism aroused by the presentation of great historical or legendary figures in present-day garb, amid the surroundings of contemporary life, is apt to endanger the solemnity of the theme, and to some extent defeat the object of the painter, – in which case it may be urged that the failure is quite as likely to lie upon the spectator's side.

But the literalism of Millais's picture is eclipsed by the exhaustive symbolism which he uses in common with his colleagues of the Brotherhood, though never carrying it into the elaborate detail cultivated by Mr. Holman Hunt. The "house" of Christ's Parents is a wooden shed, strewn with shavings and hung with tools. The young Christ has torn his hand on a nail, and St. Joseph, turning from his bench, holds up the wounded palm, which Mary hastens to bind with a linen cloth. John the Baptist brings water to bathe the hurt before she covers it, and the elder woman bends forward to remove the tools with which the boy, perhaps, has carelessly played.

The nail-mark in the palm is an obvious presage of the coming Cross. The rough planks and the half-woven basket convey the idea of unfinished work; and on a ladder overhead broods the ever-present dove. The picture is inscribed from the verse in Zechariah, – "And one shall say unto him, 'What are these wounds in thine hands?' Then shall he answer, 'Those with which I was wounded in the house of my friends.'"

To recover the actual conditions of the early life of Christ – to reproduce the aspect of a Nazarene cottage eighteen centuries ago – and yet to charge the historic figure with a vitality and emotion that brings it home with irresistible significance to the heart of the spectator of to-day, is perhaps a higher triumph of art than could be achieved by Millais's neo-realistic method. Rare as is success in this dual effort – the union of archæological accuracy with profound insight into the eternal meanings of the ancient tragedy – it has been attained beyond question by Holman Hunt in his greatest picture, "The Shadow of Death." Sojourning for four years at Nazareth and Bethlehem (the latter on account of the alleged resemblance of its people to the ancient House of David), the painter equipped himself with knowledge of every detail of domestic life, furniture, custom, and dress that could heighten the literal truthfulness of his work. To that scientific fidelity he added the elaborate symbolism of which he made a studious art, and through that symbolism he poured a wealth of imagination, a dignity of thought and an intensity of feeling which steeped the subject in a moral glow hitherto unknown to English painting. The scene is laid at sunset in the carpenter's shop. The Christ, whose face and form, now grown to manhood, speak utter weariness of body and soul, seems to stand there for all humanity, confronting the whole problem of labour and suffering and death. There is something more than physical exhaustion, though that is paramount, in the drooping figure of the tired workman as He lifts His arms from the tools and stretches them out in the evening sunlight, all unconscious that as He does so, the slant rays cast His

✳ 241

shadow, in the semblance of a crucifix, upon the cottage wall behind, where a wooden tool-rack forms as it were the arms of the cross on which the shadow of His arms is cast; and near it a little window, open to the east, makes an aureole of light around His head. His mother, kneeling on the floor, examining the casket in which she keeps the long-treasured gifts of the Magi – gold, and frankincense, and myrrh, glances up and sees the terrible image on the wall. It is the cross of a daily crucifixion, rather than of the final death, that weighs upon the soul of Christ; – the crucifixion of unhonoured labour in obscurity; the hard, despised routine of toil endured by the uncomplaining workers of all time. He knows both the dignity of labour and its shame; – the dignity, that is, of all honest, healthy, and profitable toil; the shame of that industrial slavery which in any land can make a man too weary to enjoy the sunset glories or to revel in the calm delights of eventide.

In turning to Hunt's earlier picture, "The Scapegoat," we pass from the problem of the slavery of labour to the deeper question of vicarious sacrifice. The solitary figure of the dumb and helpless animal, dying in the utter desolation of the wilderness, the unconscious and involuntary victim of human sin, speaks more eloquently than any words of the reality and pathos of the suffering of innocence for guilt. Seldom if ever has the problem been so directly urged upon us in pictorial art, – Can the law of vicarious sacrifice be reconciled with our highest ideals of moral justice? Can a beneficent and omnipotent God permit one innocent being, without choice or knowledge, to pay another's penalty? Or, on the other hand, can we formulate any other method by which humanity could be taught its own solemn power, and its absolute community and interdependence of soul with soul? The painter's business is to state that problem, not to solve it; and this Hunt does with the utmost simplicity, sincerity, and earnestness. Pitching his tent in the most inhospitable region on the shores of the Dead Sea, the artist painted the actual landscape upon which the ancient victim was cast adrift, to perish slowly in the desert without the camp; and from that strange, wild studio his picture came full-charged with the loneliness and terror of the scene, and the momentous meaning of the scapegoat's sacrifice.

"The Light of the World," frequently regarded as Holman Hunt's greatest work, though more mystical and appealing less directly to common sentiment than "The Shadow of Death," is purely symbolic in design and character; and indeed may be taken to represent the high-water mark of abstract symbolism, as distinct from Biblical history, in the paintings of the Pre-Raphaelite Brotherhood. The circumstances of its execution, partly at Oxford, and partly in his studio at Chelsea by moonlight, have already been referred to. The picture tells no story; deals with no incident or condition of the human life of Christ, but presents the ideal figure in the threefold aspect of prophet, priest, and king. The Saviour appears in the guise of a pilgrim, carrying a lantern, and knocking in the night at a fast-closed door. He wears the white robe of inspiration, typical of prophecy; the jewelled robe and breastplate of a priest; and a crown of gold interwoven with one of thorns. The legend from Revelation, iii., gives the keynote of the work: "Behold I stand at the door and knock. If any man hear my voice and open the door, I will come in to him, and will sup with him, and he with Me." The fast-barred door, with its rusty nails and bolts overgrown with ivy, and its threshold blocked up with brambles and weeds, is the door of the human soul. The light from the lantern in Christ's hand is the light of conscience (according to Mr. Ruskin's well-known description of the picture), and the light which suffuses the head of the Saviour, issuing from the crown of thorns, is the hope of salvation. The lamp-light rests on the doorway and the weeds, and on a fallen apple which gives the suggestion of hereditary sin. The thorns in the crown are now bearing fresh leaves, "for the healing of the nations."

It has been charged against many Pre-Raphaelite paintings that their elaborate symbolism, and the highly subjective development of the designs, require not merely titles and texts, but footnotes also, for their explanation. In the pictures of Holman

Hunt especially, this charge may have some weight; but it may be fairly met by the consideration of the close and deep thought, the prolonged spiritual fervour – unexampled since the Italian Pre-Raphaelites – in which each masterpiece is steeped, and which surely brings a claim upon such intelligent study as would enable all but those wholly ignorant of Christian symbology to interpret the details for themselves. Rossetti said of one of Hunt's pictures that "the solemn human soul seems to vibrate through it like a bell in a forest." That sound, once caught, yields the keynote to the pictorial scheme, and attunes all the latent music to its perfect end.

Rossetti, however, in no case employed the symbolic-figure method, so triumphantly used in "The Light of the World," for his Biblical subjects; but reserved it for the realm of romantic allegory and classic myth. His illustration of the eternal truths of penitence and aspiration, of "the awakening conscience" and the resurrection of the soul, is given us in his beautiful drawing of "Mary Magdalene at the door of Simon the Pharisee." The scene is laid amid the revelry of a village street at a time of festival. Mary, passing with a throng of gay companions, sees, through the window of a house, the face of Christ; and with a sudden impulse leaves the procession and tears the flowers passionately from her hair, seeking to enter where He sits; the while her lover, following, strives to dissuade her, and to lead her back to the mirthful company. The appeal of passion and the answer of the repentant woman, beautiful in her mingled shame and triumph, are best recounted in Rossetti's own words, from the most successful of his sonnets on his own designs:

"Why wilt thou cast the roses from thine hair?
    Nay, be thou all a rose, – wreath, lips, and cheek.
    Nay, not this house, – that banquet-house we seek;
See how they kiss and enter; come thou there.
This delicate day of love we too will share
    Till at our ear love's whispering night shall speak.
    What, sweet one, – hold'st thou still the foolish freak?
Nay, when I kiss thy feet they'll leave the stair."

✳ 244

"Oh loose me! Seest thou not my Bridegroom's face
    That draws me to Him? For His feet my kiss,
    My hair, my tears, He craves to-day: – and oh!
What words can tell what other day and place
    Shall see me clasp those blood-stained feet of His?
    He needs me, calls me, loves me, let me go!"

The face of the Magdalene has been said to present Rossetti's ideal of spiritual beauty, in contrast with the physical beauty of "Lilith" and the intellectual beauty of "Sibylla Palmifera;" but as Rossetti himself afterwards applied the title of "Soul's Beauty" to "Sibylla Palmifera," the distinction can hardly be pursued very far. The head of Christ (for which Mr. Burne-Jones is said to have sat as a model) is of a more peculiar interest and value; being the only serious attempt at the portrayal of the central figure in Christian art which remains to us from Rossetti's hand. Some highly-finished studies were made by him for this head, from one of which the present illustration is taken. Rossetti's Christ differs markedly in conception from that of Holman Hunt. The Christ of the older painter is pre-eminently the "Man of Sorrows," the martyr whose whole life was a crucifixion. Rossetti shows us rather the Galilean dreamer, the peasant poet, the gentle idealist whom women and children loved. The realism of suffering, though delicately suggested by the slightly-drawn brow, the quiet tension of the features, and the bright, glowing depths of the eye, is here in abeyance. Christ is for the time an honoured guest, receiving the hospitality of the Pharisee with a gracious self-possession and an exquisite simplicity of mien. The sole suggestion, in the surrounding objects, of the tragedy that is to come, is given in the vine that trails on the walls of the house, symbolic of the great Sacrifice.

The shadow of the Cross – no longer cast into the future, but abiding on the mourners after the death of Christ – is figured by a device of singular beauty in Rossetti's sketch of "Mary in the House of John." In a small drawing of "The Crucifixion" he had depicted St. John leading the Madonna from the foot of Calvary. Now he shows us the new home, so strangely ignored by painters of the sacred tale, wherein the Mother and the adopted son are together at eventide. Through the window is seen a distant view of Jerusalem, and in the uncertain light the window-bars assume the form of a cross, which thus appears to rest upon the Holy City, and to stand between that quiet household and the outer world. St. John has been writing a portion of his Gospel, and pauses to strike a light, with which the Mother of Jesus kindles a lamp, hanging at the intersection of the bars; so that the light shines from the centre-point of the Cross, where the Head of Christ should be. This delicate emblem gives the touch of hope, the promise of glory through sacrifice, which lightens the darkness of the hour. So fine a use of simple imagery, so perfect an adjustment of the hope to the penalty, admirably illustrates the highest triumph of Pre-Raphaelite art, – the reconciliation of the "crucifixion principle," the essentially Catholic element in religion, with the "resurrection principle," peculiar to Protestantism. Mr. Forsyth, whose essays on the Pre-Raphaelites have already been quoted, makes the suggestive remark, that "In Hunt's technique shadow always means colour as well as darkness: to see colour in shadow is the last triumph of a great painter," and adds that "Rossetti's colour is not merely luminous matter; it is transfigured matter." This conception of the dual truth of Christianity – the necessity of suffering and the assurance of victory – is consistently presented both by Rossetti and Hunt; and it is not merely victory *over* suffering, as Protestantism insists on, which they teach; but rather victory *through* suffering; which is the fusion of Catholic ethics with Protestant faith.

And it is remarkable that the Pre-Raphaelites find as much inspiration for the thought of victory through suffering in the incidents of Christ's childhood as in the story of His martyrdom. Rossetti, in his early picture of "Bethlehem Gate," in which the Holy Family are seen in flight from the massacre of the Innocents, depicts at the side of the Virgin Mother an angel bearing a palm-branch, – the symbol of deliverance and reward. Holman Hunt begins the Resurrection with "The Triumph of the Innocents," applies, that is, the principle of Immortality to universal life; and by the ruddy, healthy faces of his angel-children watching from Heaven over the child-Christ, he insists, as Rossetti insisted in "The Blessed Damozel," that the unknown world must be something intimately related to the one we know, and that immortal life must be something more than the continuance of spiritual being in an immaterial sphere, – must, in short, afford real and eternal activities beyond the grave.

This recognition of the relation of sacrifice to victory leads the painters beyond the reconciliation of the individual man with God to the reconciliation of the social man with man. Something of this idea of "peace on earth" is suggested by Rossetti's picture, "The Infant Christ Adored by a Shepherd and a King," which now forms a triptych in Llandaff Cathedral, – the only picture directly from his hand which occupies a permanent position in an English church. In the left compartment is seen the young David as a shepherd before Goliath; in the right, the psalmist is depicted in old age, crowned as a king before God. In the centre, the Infant Christ appears as the mediator between the high and the lowly, the rich and the poor; the messenger of the "at-one-ment" of all ranks of men, united in a common worship of the Divine Child, and a common love of that Humanity of which He is the type.

A similar interpretation of the childhood of Jesus, as typical of the growth of all humanity, may fairly be drawn from Holman Hunt's picture of "Christ in the Temple," – a work now thoroughly familiar to English eyes, and perhaps the most popular because the least mystical of his masterpieces. The bright, bold, ingenuous face and figure of the boy, confronting with his eager questions the venerable Rabbis of the congregation, seems instinct with the life of the present age, charged with the very essence of the spirit of inquiry – of sceptical inquiry even – before which the apologists of tradition and legalism are dumfounded, and through which, from the dogma of the old world, is wrested the faith of the new.

It would be impracticable here to follow in detail the influence of the Pre-Raphaelites upon the religious paintings of their contemporaries and successors, or to estimate the exact relation of their work to that of their nearest precursor, Madox Brown. But a single example from the last-named artist, and another from the youngest of the Pre-Raphaelite group, but never numbered with the Brotherhood – Mr. Burne-Jones – may serve to illustrate still further the great religious principles of which these painters steadfastly took hold. "The Entombment" remains among the finest works of Madox Brown, and embodies, in its simple austerity, its direct pathos, a spiritual fervour akin to the highest inspirations of Holman Hunt. The dignity of the human body, the solemnity and awfulness of physical death, the tender charm of child life and child innocence, the mystery of immortality, and the apprehension of a "risen" life, – all these things are brought within the range of thought opened up by that sombre and majestic design. Seldom in modern art has the intense realism of death been so delicately handled, and yet with such uncompromising force. The faces of the women bending over the loved corpse are full of grief and perplexity, yet even in the atmosphere of death there is a subtle breath of triumph and of hope, a sense that the body is not all, that what is left is but the shell, the "house of Life;" the true Life is not dead, but gone – whither? The tender light that plays around the mourners, and the contrast of the vigorous little body of the young child with the aged and shattered frame of the dead martyr, seem to voice the eternal protest of the heart against annihilation, the irrepressible demand of the soul for a future life.

Thirty years apart from "The Light of the World" and "Mary in the House of John," but akin to both in motive and spirit, is "The Tree of Life," one of the latest and noblest of Mr. Burne-Jones's paintings. This sombre monochrome, so absolutely original in design, so chastened and restrained in execution, ranks with the highest symbolic work of the Pre-Raphaelites in its grasp of the idea of victory through suffering. For "The Tree of Life" is the Cross. Its roots are in the very foundations of the earth; its branches are fed with the heart's blood of humanity, and its fruit reaches unto Heaven. The Figure that hangs upon it is brooding in benediction over the whole world; the supreme type of that immortal love which fulfils the divine law of sacrifice; embodying in one great symbol the lesson of all history, –

"Knowledge by suffering entereth,
And Life is perfected by Death."

Man, woman and children are gathered beneath the shadow of the Tree. On the one side is a garden of flowers, and on the other a harvest of corn. Along the margin of the earth is the inscription: – "In Mundo pressuram habebitis; sed confidite; ego vici mundum." ("In the world ye shall have tribulation; but be of good cheer; I have overcome the world.") The painting is carried out in a very low key of colour, and a kind of austere and grave conventionalism restrains the sweeping outlines and the sober light. The accessories of the landscape are of the simplest character; no extraneous detail intrudes upon the perfect harmony of the at-one-ment; no over-elaboration mars the calm of that absolute resignation, that unquenchable hope. The Christ upon the Cross is at once the interpretation of the mystery of pain, and the covenant of a complete redemption wherein man at last "shall see of the travail of his soul and shall be satisfied."

CHAPTER VII.

TREATMENT OF MEDIÆVAL
AND MODERN ROMANCE.

The Christian Element in Neo-Hellenism and Romance – "How They Met Themselves" and "Michael Scott's Wooing" – Mediævalism and Romantic Love – "Romeo and Juliet" and "Ophelia" – Millais's Romantic Landscapes – "The Woodman's Daughter," "The Blind Girl," "The Vale of Rest," "Autumn Leaves" – Keats's "Isabella" – Tennyson's "Mariana" and "Idylls of the King" – The Idea of Retribution – "King Arthur's Tomb," "Paolo and Francesca," "Death of Lady Macbeth," "The Awakening Conscience," "Hesterna Rosa," "The Gate of Memory," "Found," "Psyche," "Proserpine," "Pandora" – The Idea of Duty – "The Hugenot," "The Black Brunswicker," "Claudio and Isabella" – Old and New Chivalry – "Sir Isumbras" and "The Rescue" – "The Merciful Knight" – "St. Agnes' Eve" – Ideal and Platonic Love – "The Salutation of Beatrice," "The Boat of Love," "Beata Beatrix," "Dante's Dream," "Our Lady of Pity."

It is but an arbitrary classification that divides the so-called "religious" art of the Pre-Raphaelites from their portrayals of that half historic, half legendary wonder-world we vaguely called "romance." Rossetti, it has been rightly said, "was a pilgrim who had got out of the region of shrines, but who at every cross-like thing knelt down by the force of thought and muscle."[*9] Above all other qualities of Pre-Raphaelite painting, it is the instinctive perception of "cross-like things" that gives nobility and tenderness to the work of Rossetti and his colleagues. By the light of that inward vision do they choose and transfigure every theme. The haunting sense of the mysteries of existence, of the immanence of the supernatural in the natural sphere, and of the divine possibilities of human nature; the apprehension of the moral law, of sacrifice, reward and penalty, and of the consummation of earth's good and evil in an immortal realm; – these abide with the painters when they pass from the holy ground of Judea and Galilee to the Pagan splendours of the Hellenic age, the later glories of mediævalism, and the hard prose conditions of modern life. The same great drama of humanity is set before us, but on another stage, with other players. The ideas which dominate the minds of the artists, the principles by which they interpret alike the history of Jerusalem and the problems of London, are of universal application. A classic myth to them is as rich in meaning as a Christian parable; a legend of chivalrous manliness or heroic womanhood as sacred as if written in a canonical gospel. Holman Hunt's "Awakening Conscience" and "Claudio and Isabella" are as profoundly religious as "Mary Magdalene at the Door;" Rossetti's "Lady of Pity" and "Beata Beatrix" glow with a spiritual fervour as pure as that of "Ecce Ancilla Domini;" the lessons of Burne-Jones's "Merciful Knight" and of Millais's "Hugenot" are as clear as any that "The Light of the World" can teach us; – and this, not that the painters have secularized the highest things, but that they have sanctified the lower; have pierced to the common sources of religious thought and feeling, and have brought into the labour of the present hour the wide and eternal meanings of the past.

In the most naïve phase of romantic mysticism, with its devout faith in the presence of spiritual forces in play at all points upon the human soul, and in the power of the imagination to visualize conjectured things, Rossetti conceived the finest of his early dramatic sketches, – "How They Met Themselves" and "Michael Scott's Wooing;" the former showing the influence of Blake in a more marked degree perhaps than any other drawings of the same period. The lovers that "meet themselves" are confronted, while walking in a wood, with the apparitions of their own persons, reflected, as it were, in the air before them, in exact and startling similitude, – a conception found in the well-known Döppelgänger legends of German folk-lore, which credit a dual existence to every human soul, endowing it with a sort of spectral "double" after the manner of the Buddhistic "astral body," save that the Döppelgänger appear to be independent of the subject's consciousness and will. The sudden terror of the lovers, – the lady sinking to the ground, the knight drawing his sword in her defence against the mysterious phenomenon, yet hesitating, like Marcellus on the ramparts of Elsinore, to "offer it the show of violence," is shown with a force that emphasizes the reality of the vision to those who see it. In this picture, as in Rossetti's treatment of a more exalted theme, "The Girlhood of Mary Virgin," the barrier is over-leaped that separates the visible from the unseen; the outer and inner worlds are merged naturally and imperceptibly the one into the other – an hypothesis in which the previsions of art may yet be vindicated by scientific discovery; and the forms of the spectral lovers are scarcely more shadowy than those who stand aghast before them in the flesh. It has been suggested that the design may typify the meeting of the human soul with its prototype in ages long gone by; the recognition of unknown kinships (as if brought over from a prior existence) through that strange sense of familiarity which sometimes surprises us when we wander in spirit through the dim mazes of the historic past.

In the sketch for "Michael Scott's Wooing," the wizard-hero conjures up, for the entertainment of his lady-love, a magical pageant of Life, Love, and other symbolic figures, which appear before her in a glass. Here the purely subjective nature of the vision is brought out; the lady alone can see the pageant; her attendants are as blind to it as Hamlet's mother to the ghost of the murdered king.

From this initial belief in the potency of the unseen there comes the apprehension of the mystery of fate, of the burden of impenetrable destiny, of the evil powers that assail mankind from within. Something even of the ancient fear of the jealousy of the gods against men's happiness returns in the mediæval awe of human joys or triumphs, and its ascetic suspicion of prosperity, more especially in the field of romantic love. A profound insight of the dualism of nature keeps the romantic spirit in remembrance of the cost of all earthly pleasure, and of the price set by the laws of being upon all aspiration and desire. This it is that gives its subtlest charm to the "Romeo and Juliet" of Madox Brown, with its embracing lovers on the balcony at break of day, full of the passionate poetry of protest against the pitiless caprice, as it seems, of the fate that tears them asunder; and to the "Ophelia" of Rossetti, – now sitting troubled and half-frightened before Hamlet's earnest gaze, now offering him the treasured letters from the casket at her side, now led away in her "first madness," by the hand of Horatio, from the presence of the king and queen; or of Hughes, – singing dreamily to herself as she sits by the waterside on a fallen tree; or of Watts, – gazing down with yearning eyes into the pool beneath the willow; or – best of all – of Millais, floating downstream to her death, with her slackening hands full of flowers, the very embodiment of the pathetic helplessness of weak and isolated womanhood against the tide of the world's strife, – weak, indeed, through the isolation of ages, having never known, in life or ancestry, the bracing discipline of a free and responsible existence. No one of the Pre-Raphaelites has equalled Millais at his best in the landscape setting of the struggle between the human soul and the circumstance that hems it in; and the scenery of "Ophelia" is among the most exquisite of his work. The beauty of the river and its richly wooded banks, its overhanging branches, and its current-driven weeds, gives the greater pathos to the dying girl's face, on which the wraith only of its past and lost beauty lingers to mock the sadness of her end. "The Woodman's Daughter" suggests even more finely the contrast of the unimpassioned glory of nature and the tragedy of romantic love; for here it is not death but life, the complexity of life and duty, that separates the lovers each from each. Between the rough and uncomely peasant girl and the shy young aristocrat who stands so awkwardly before her with his proffered gift of hothouse fruit, there is a gulf fixed which will take a higher civilization than ours to bridge over. And again, in treating of the broader and more common loves and joys of humanity, does Millais set before us the same contrast in "The Blind Girl" and "The Vale of Rest." The Blind Girl is a poor and uncomely vagrant halting by the road-side, wrapping her shawl round her child-guide, who nestles against her in the April weather. But around her is the loveliness of an English village landscape after rain. The warmth of the bursting sun consoles her as she turns her face to its light; the rainbow which she cannot see gives radiance to the humble cottages; the wet grass is cool to her hand, and the peace of resignation seems to fill her maimed and darkened life. But the contrast of her sorrow with nature's joy is very real, though for the moment she forgets it in the little comfort that may yet be hers. The same resignation in the face of the unanswered problem transfigures the mourners in "The Vale of Rest," – the two calm, almost stoical nuns in a convent garden at sunset time. The younger woman is digging a grave; the elder, who sits on a recumbent tombstone hard by, is gazing at the burning gold and crimson of the west, and sees in the midst of its splendour the darkness of the coffin-shaped cloud which, by a widespread superstition, was long deemed the omen of approaching death. The superb "Autumn Leaves," which Mr. Ruskin pronounces "among the world's masterpieces," may perhaps be added to this great group of romantic landscapes, inasmuch as the pathos of its poetry is no less deep, though more subtle, than that of "Ophelia," "The Woodman's Daughter," "The Blind Girl," and

"The Vale of Rest." A group of children are burning dead leaves in the twilight of a mellow autumn day. Oblivious of the changing seasons, realizing nothing of the solemnity of autumn, or the sad significance of the waning year, they revel merely in the bonfire they have made, and are troubled by no fear for the winter, or for the chance of spring.

In the several paintings from Keats's "Isabella" – that favourite subject of the early days of the Brotherhood – the contrast lies mainly in the direction of individual character; the tragedy, in the power of such character to work for evil against the good. Especially in Millais's masterpiece, "Lorenzo and Isabella," are the beauty and graciousness of Isabella and her lover set with a passionate intensity against the icy cynicism and sensuous brutality of the brothers and their guests, and the conflict is felt to be directly between malicious cruelty and innocent love. On the other hand the devotion and self-abandonment of Isabella's thwarted passion find noble expression in the picture by Holman Hunt. The figure of the weeping girl, who has risen from her bed to worship at her strange and terrible shrine, – the Pot of Basil containing her murdered lover's head, is seen in the early light of dawn, that almost quenches, in its pitiless coldness, the more tender light of the lamp that burns in the little sanctuary of secret love. The altar-cloth spread for the sacred relic is embroidered with a design of passion-flowers, and every accessory is symbolic of Isabella's grief and despair. The same unique subject, it may here be noted, has inspired one of the finest paintings of an artist worthily representative of the younger generation of Pre-Raphaelites (if the name may be perpetuated beyond its immediate and temporary significance) – Mr. J.M. Strudwick; whose design, however, deals with the culmination of the tragedy, the theft of the Pot of Basil by the guilty brothers, and the on-coming madness of Isabella.

A stronger moral element is soon perceptible in the work of Rossetti and Millais when they approach the poetry of Tennyson for subject matter, and begin to draw upon the great cycle of

Arthurian legends which he restored in modern garb to English literature. Even outside the "Idylls of the King," in their paintings of Tennyson's "Mariana," the passion and the mystery of romantic love are tempered with the growing consciousness of moral responsibility, of Love's heroic power to conquer destiny – if only the appeals of the lower nature were not so urgent and so sweet. In other words, the lower dualism has given place to the higher; the conflict is not so much between the earthly joy and the misfortune that threatens it in death or any calamity from the physical sphere, but rather between the baser and the better life within. Of such a spirit is the "Mariana" of Rossetti, kneeling and weeping in her dimly-lit chamber in "The Heart of the Night," or of Millais, wearily casting away her unfinished work in the close prison of the "moated grange" – that perfect allegory of modern love, pent in by the mire of indolence and conventionality, and vainly dreaming of an unearned ideal; waiting for the deliverance which, as Mariana scarcely comprehends, must be a self-deliverance into nobler aims and higher standards of duty and of intelligent sacrifice. The sense of a lofty spiritual destiny re-enters at this point into Pre-Raphaelite art; the meaning of the search for the Holy Grail is apparent still more clearly in Rossetti's "Sir Galahad in the Ruined Chapel," and later, in Burne-Jones's more severe and chastened types of the pilgrim-knight. It has been charged against both these painters that the physical beauty and glory of manhood was almost wholly absent from their conception of life. Even in the nearest approach to such a concession, in the latest romantic masterpiece of the younger artist, "The Legend of the Briar Rose," the asceticism learnt at the Arthurian shrines persists, indeed, in the mellowness of his maturity. The heroes of the Pre-Raphaelites are no muscular warriors, as conventional art would portray them. They are concerned with inward conflicts rather than with outward foes. They are the knights-errant of a new chivalry, – to whom moral righteousness is a higher thing than physical courage; self-conquest a nobler triumph than the routing of armies. For they

✳ 256

"wrestle not against flesh and blood, but against principalities, against powers, against the rulers of the darkness of this world, against spiritual wickedness in high places." The whole series of the Arthurian designs, from the illustrations to Moxon's "Tennyson" and the frescoes at Oxford, onward to the latest work of Burne-Jones and his followers, are dominated by this idea of a spiritual pilgrimage, as of beings exiled from a higher realm, which to regain they must needs pass through the lower. "Their sojourn on earth," says M. Gabriel Sarrazin,[*10] "oppresses these Pre-Raphaelites, lost among our pre-occupations of business and of ease."

And further, the sense of the supernatural world, of the struggle between the spiritual and the physical in man, leads onward to the conception of retribution and punishment, "not" (as Hegel puts it) "as something arbitrary, but as *the other half of sin*." The inexorableness of the moral law could hardly be more finely suggested than in Rossetti's treatment of the guilty love of Lancelot and Guinevere. "King Arthur's Tomb," despite its crudity and harshness of drawing, remains among the most superb of his early drawings. The aged queen, now an abbess honoured and revered, is visiting the tomb of the dead Arthur. But not all her long atonement of remorse and piety can avail wholly to blot out the sin of her youth. For even here, as she kneels to pray, the dark and terrible ghost of Lancelot thrusts itself between her and the pure effigy whose marble face she seeks in penitence and tears. The converse of the picture was that of which Rossetti sought to make a fresco on the ill-fated walls of the Oxford Debating Union. The design represents "Sir Lancelot before the Shrine of the Sangrael." He seems to have almost attained the goal of his pilgrimage; the Holy Grail is just within his grasp; but in the hour that might have brought victory, the old sin brings mockery and defeat: the face that looks out at him from the place of his hope is the sad, reproachful face of Guinevere.

With scarcely less of tragic force and direct solemnity does

Rossetti carry this thought of retribution into the world of mediæval Italy, into the cycle of legend and romance that gathers round the name of Dante. The love-story of "Paolo and Francesca da Rimini," recorded by Dante in the "Divina Comedia," has been the theme of poets and painters for many a year, and is the subject of one of the finest water-colour drawings made in Rossetti's transition period. Francesca, the wife of Lanciotto, the deformed son of the lord of Rimini, fell in love with her husband's brother Paolo; and Lanciotto, discovering the two in guilty companionship, put them both to death. In the fifth canto of the "Inferno," Dante describes the terrible sight permitted to him of the condemned lovers in the second circle of Hell. Rossetti's picture is in triptych form, and in the centre are the figures of Dante and Virgil, his guide. Above them is the brief inscription, "O Lasso!" In the left compartment is depicted the fatal embrace of Paolo and Francesca at the moment of the avowal of their love, when in reading together the story of Lancelot, the book suddenly fell from their hands, and, as the narrator simply confesses, "that day we read no more." In the right-hand space are seen the lovers, clasping each other wildly in the darkness and among the furious storms of hell, unable to release themselves from that fixed embrace. The characteristic idea of making the penalty consist in the involuntary perpetuation of the sin, – the guilty love becoming, as it were, its own sufficient punishment, belongs, of course, to Dante, but is worked out with singular power in Rossetti's design. Not only is the stern and relentless fate portrayed with the utmost sincerity in the sequel, but even in the first panel the thought of the coming retribution is finely suggested by the introduction of one sufficient touch at the background of the scene. Beneath the edge of a curtain is seen the foot of the approaching husband, bringing his vengeance and the lovers' doom. The same subject has been more elaborately and completely treated by Mr. G.F. Watts, whose picture shows Francesca telling her sad tale to Dante and Virgil as they pass; and the poet who is said to have known her on earth, and to have written the record quoted from the "Inferno" in the house at Rimini in which she was born, is depicted sinking in a swoon before her, overcome with pity and with awe.

Again, and in a widely different field of dramatic narrative, does Rossetti bring this passionate sense of retribution into play. His drawing for the never-finished picture, "The Death of Lady Macbeth," is full of the same half-pitiful and half-triumphant spirit of righteous vengeance, and the same perception of inexorable penalty. The aged and dying woman crouching on her bed has once been comely and of commanding countenance; and in her last hour the remembered beauty of her face, the lingering majesty of her figure, seem to overawe her attendants, one of whom presses a sponge to her head. In that changed face the conflict between remorse and pride, ambition and terror, is still fierce and strong; but she is dying utterly alone: there is no love, no tenderness, in the ministry of those who gather round the murderess.

Still more clearly and resolutely is this perception of moral issues sustained by the Pre-Raphaelites when they pass from history and legend to classic mythology, to allegorical type, or to the dramatic presentation of modern life. In the "Awakening Conscience" of Holman Hunt, in the exquisitely pathetic "Psyche" of G.F. Watts, in the "Hesterna Rosa," "Gate of Memory," and "Found" of Rossetti, the bitter cost of sin is realized with unfaltering consistency. Rossetti's long-laboured and yet uncompleted "Found" may be taken as the companion, if not the sequel, to his poem, "Jenny." It shows us the last humiliation of a ruined girl who is "found" – dying on the streets of London – by the lover of her youth, – a countryman who has driven in with his milk-cart through the chill light of a London dawn. All the pride and struggle of the past is written on her once lovely face, and she shrinks in shame and terror from his touch.

"Ah! gave not these two hearts their mutual pledge,
Under one mantle sheltered 'neath the hedge

In gloaming courtship? And, O God! to-day
He only knows he holds her; – but what part
Can life now take? She cries in her locked heart, –
'Leave me – I do not know you – go away!'"[*11]

It might almost be the same sad girl that stands at "The Gate of Memory," watching a group of young and innocent maidens at play beside a well.

"She leaned herself against the wall
And longed for drink to slake her thirst
And memory at once."

A more original and striking composition is "Hesterna Rosa" – "Yesterday's Rose." All the weird realism of Rossetti's most mediæval manner pervades this painfully impressive design; – mediæval in spirit, and yet almost Hogarthian in its bold handling of human degradation and debauchery. The motive is taken from "Elena's Song" in Sir Henry Taylor's "Philip van Artevelde," Part II., Act v.:

"Quoth tongue of neither maid nor wife
    To heart of neither wife nor maid,
'Lead we not here a jolly life,
    Betwixt the shrine and shade?'

"Quoth heart of neither maid nor wife
    To tongue of neither wife nor maid,
'Thou wag'st, but I am worn with strife,
    And feel like flowers that fade.'"

The scene is in a tent at early daybreak, amid a group of gamblers and depraved women throwing dice. But one of them is a girl still beautiful, and not yet hardened by the coarseness of her new life. She shrinks from the kiss of the player who bends over her hand. "Yesterday's Rose" is not wholly faded; only her first fresh bloom is gone; she has bartered it irretrievably for her chance in the desperate game of passion, like the vengeful woman in "The Laboratory," offering her pearls to buy poison for her enemy. The contrast between the shamed "rose" and her brutalized companions is emphasized by the tender light of the dawn, which creeps through the orchard trees outside, and makes the lamp within appear more yellow and dull and weak.

Entirely modern in spirit and execution is Holman Hunt's treatment of a similar theme. The "Awakening Conscience" is that of a girl idling with her paramour in a newly and luxuriously furnished room. He has been singing to her, not noticing the change in her face, and his hands still pass carelessly over the pianoforte keys. But the words of the song – Moore's "Oft in the Stilly Night" – have stirred a sudden anguish in her heart; she has started up, tortured with long pent memories and overcome with shame and despair. The utter falsity of her new surroundings seems to strike her as she gazes round the cruelly unhomelike home. A terrible symbolism confronts her on every side; the showy tapestry is woven with a design of ripe corn on which the carrion birds are feeding; the picture hanging above the mantelpiece represents the woman taken in adultery. The tragic intensity of the painting is hardly surpassed by any other of the artist's work.

Far back in the golden ages of classic myth, the ever-significant story of "Psyche" suggests the same stern lesson, – of the irretrievable loss which comes by violation of the moral law or disobedience to the dicta of those "gods" by which the men of old time knew the divine and imperative instincts of the soul. The fall of Psyche has its message for to-day. It was made known to her that the god Eros should come to earth to be her husband. In the darkness of the night he should visit her bed, and there he should vouchsafe to her the sacrament of his love, – but on one condition: that she should never seek to look upon his face, or lift the veil of mystery by which Nature shrouded the sanctities of the godhead from her eyes. But Psyche's curiosity overcame her reverence and trustfulness. In her eagerness to know Love's sacred secrets and lay bare the holiest of holies upon earth, she took a lamp, and would have looked boldly at her visitant. But immediately the spell was broken; the heavenly Eros fled from her, never to return. The widowed Psyche, in Mr. Watts's picture, stands ashamed and broken-hearted, knowing too late the prize that she has forfeited. Her drooping figure is the embodiment of dazed remorse. She has dared to trifle with the divinest things, to be familiar with that which is rare, to probe too curiously into the mystic borderland between earth and heaven. The devout sense of the limitations of man's knowledge, and of the penalty attaching to any impious familiarity with the supernatural world, has thus its roots in Hellenism, but attains its finest flower in the spirit of romance. It is the blending of the sensuous dignity of classicism with the subtle tenderness of romance that gives so fine a pathos to this poor "Psyche," – typical as she is of the modern age, mourning the lost mystery which its own thirst for knowledge at all hazards has dispelled; or again, that places Rossetti's "Pandora" and "Proserpine" in the highest rank of contemporary art. For Proserpine too has eaten the forbidden fruit of the lower knowledge, whereby the higher wisdom is driven away. She has eaten one grain of the fatal pomegranate of Hades, which enchains her to the lower world; and only at rare seasons can her sullied spirit attain the upper air. Her troubled face, as she stands in the picture, in a gloomy corridor of her prison-palace, with the broken fruit in her hand, seems to tell of the long struggle of a soul that, having once tasted the coarser joys, has become less sensitive to the higher, and is torn between the baser enchantment and the pure delights which it longs to regain. A critic already quoted[*12] has pointed out that there is "always in Rossetti's women the kind of sorrow that ennobles affection." The painter never loses the sense of conflict between the dangers of the physical nature and the glories of the spirit which it serves. The sorrow of his great "Pandora," even more than of the beautiful "Proserpine," is the sorrow of a goddess over her own infirmity. She has opened the mystic casket which she was bidden to keep sealed, and now she stands helpless before the witness of her deed. The potent spirits are escaping from the box, and she can never undo the mischief she has done. "The whole design," says Mr. Swinburne, "is among Rossetti's mightiest in its godlike terror and imperial trouble of beauty, shadowed by the smoke and fiery vapour of winged and fleshless passions crowding from the casket in spires of flame-lit and curling cloud round her fatal face and mourning veil of hair."

> "What of the end, Pandora? Was it thine,
>   The deed that set these fiery pinions free?
>   Ah! wherefore did the Olympian consistory
> In its own likeness make thee half divine?
> Was it that Juno's brow might stand a sign
>   For ever, and the mien of Pallas be
>   A deadly thing? And that all men might see
> In Venus' eyes the gaze of Proserpine?
>
> What of the end? These beat their wings at will,
> The ill-born things, the good things turned to ill, –
>   Powers of the impassioned hours prohibited.
> Ay, clench the casket now! Whither they go
> Thou may'st not dare to think: nor canst thou know
>   If Hope still pent there be alive or dead."[*13]

It follows, then, that the earnest apprehension of the spiritual sphere, and of a divine justice and retribution for sin, will give a special power and reality to pictures dealing with a crisis of duty, or a moment of choice between martyrdom and sin. Such a choice, such a responsibility, is the motive of some of the finest work of Millais's transition period, – "The Hugenot," "The Proscribed Royalist," "The Rescue," and "The Black Brunswicker." "The Hugenot" is probably the most popular, as it is the most perfect, of the painter's earlier masterpieces. The story which it tells is explained in its full title: "A Hugenot, on St. Bartholomew's Day, refusing to shield himself from danger by wearing the Roman Catholic badge." "When the clock of the Palais de Justice shall sound upon the great bell at daybreak" (so ran the order of the Duke of Guise), "then each good Catholic must bind a strip of white linen round his arm, and place a fair white cross in his cap." A Catholic lady is beseeching her Protestant lover to wear the white scarf which will preserve him from the coming massacre. Her beautiful face is drawn with anxious terror as she tries to bind the kerchief round his arm, but he, embracing her, draws it resolutely away; the mental struggle is not his, but hers; in spite of the tenderness of his face, there is a certain sternness and solemnity in it which tells that nothing will move him from his purpose; that he is ready, and gladly ready, for martyrdom. The girl's love pleads vainly against his duty and his doom. In "The Black Brunswicker," which formed the pendant to "The Hugenot," the same drama of conflicting love and duty is set forth, though with less convincing fervour and exalted passion than before. The lady seems to be of French family, and is somewhat pettishly delaying the departure of her lover, an officer of the Black Brunswick corps, before the Battle of Waterloo. The converse of the choice of man and woman between disloyalty and death is nobly given us by Holman Hunt in his "Claudio and Isabella" (from Shakespeare's "Measure for Measure"), where the heroism and the devotion lie on the woman's side. Claudio has been condemned to death, and his sister's honour is asked as the price of his release. She visits him in prison, clad in her nun's garb, and Claudio – the human craving for life conquering for the moment his better nature, cries out in a half shamed appeal, "O Isabel, ... death is a fearful thing." But Isabella, standing before him, pressing her hands against his heart, her face full of pity and distress, gives back her resolute answer, "And shaméd life a hateful!"

Together with the conception of duty in its relation to romantic love is linked the ideal of chivalry, – of the immediate glory of duty and its supreme rewards, especially when exercised in championship of the weak, of a defenceless foe, or of womanhood. The splendour of physical courage tends always to give place to the power of moral courage, as in mercy and forgiveness rather than in revenge; or if the physical courage be brought into play, it will, in progress of civilization be applied to deeds of helpfulness instead of cruelty. The nobility of true knighthood, which Rossetti conceived almost exclusively in the mediæval spirit, and presented with exquisite verve and passion in his little sketches of "St. George" and the "Princess Sabra," and of which the converse – the potential knightliness of woman – was suggested both by Rossetti and Millais in their "Joan of Arc" designs, finds full expression in the latter's picture of "Sir Isumbras at the Ford." An aged knight, clad in splendid armour, and bearing with courtly dignity his honours and his years, is fording a river on his war-horse, and pauses to lift up two little peasant children who have asked him to carry them to the other side. The simple graciousness and humility of the act seem to transfigure the old warrior's face, which is further lit by the rich light of the landscape in the setting sun. By the side of this great painting should be set the earlier, but in great measure the companion work, "The Rescue," in which the same artist translates the thought of beneficent chivalry into modern and familiar life. For the knight of "The Rescue" is a London fireman, in the act of saving three children from a burning house. The light that suffuses his calmly heroic face is not the natural radiance of a sunset glow, but the fierce glare of flames around the staircase, down which he brings his precious burden safe and sound. "The Rescue" is a poem of modern chivalry in a great crisis: "Sir Isumbras" celebrates mediæval chivalry in common things. The strong self-possession of the fireman in the midst of imminent peril, beset on all sides by heat, smoke, water, and burning brands, not callous or insensible to fear, but superior to it, gives us, as it were, the other side of that perfect knighthood suggested by the simple kindness of "Sir Isumbras at the Ford." In both these pictures, as indeed in "The Hugenot" and in Hunt's "Claudio and Isabella," the impression conveyed is not merely of a momentary heroism of choice or deed, but of the long discipline which must have gone to produce it, and of what all goodness costs to the life and lives behind it. It is in these aspects that the

Pre-Raphaelites portray, as we have already contended, not merely action but character; not drama only, but the hidden forces of human struggle and circumstance which give the drama its meaning for all time.

But great as are these pictures in thought and emotion, excellent as are most of them in technical quality, they are even surpassed, in the sheer passion of romantic worship, in the purest essence of religious chivalry, by one of the earliest and, technically, crudest paintings of Burne-Jones in what may fairly be called his Rossettian period. "The Merciful Knight" stands apart, in its desperate realism, its mystic exaltation and fervour, its emotional abandonment, from all the ethereal and chastened ideals of his imaginative maturity. It represents a phase of feeling very transitory, for the most part, with the Pre-Raphaelite Brotherhood, – a return to the most devout and ascetic mediævalism, untempered by the larger Hellenic spirit which re-awoke in modern romance. And, full charged as it is with the inspiration of Rossetti in drawing and colour, its religious severity links it rather to the manner of Holman Hunt. It tells the story "of a knight who forgave his enemy when he might have destroyed him, and how the image of Christ kissed him, in token that his acts had pleased God." Low at a wayside shrine bends the Merciful Knight, prostrated by the spiritual struggle between magnanimity and vengeance which he has just passed through. And as he kneels in mingled prayer and thankfulness over his own self-conquest and moral victory, the image of Christ, rudely carved and hanging on a simple cross, bends down, miraculously moved, to kiss his cheek. Rarely if ever have the Pre-Raphaelite painters surpassed in any field the emotional power of this great design. The conflict between loyalty to a cause and charity towards its fallen enemy was for some years a favourite subject with the Pre-Raphaelites of every grade. It yielded the motive, for instance, of Millais's "Proscribed Royalist," in which a Puritan lady secretly conveys food to her lover, a Cavalier, who is in hiding in a woodland oak; of W.S. Burton's "Puritan," where the austere lady, walking with her lover, takes pity on a dying Cavalier, wounded by Roundhead soldiers in a wood; and of W.L. Windus's "Outlaw," similarly hurt and tended in an equally sylvan scene. But in none of these cases is the spiritual struggle of the ministering visitant portrayed with an intensity at all to be compared with the exalted passion that dominates "The Merciful Knight."

Such are the principal stages of thought and feeling through which the Pre-Raphaelite painters pass – in no given order indeed, but with a wholly intelligible sequence of ideas – from the first impulses of romance – the apprehension of the supernatural, of the mystery of fate, of the moral order, and the divine possibilities of human life – to that highest idealism of romantic love, and of its power over death and destiny, which we find in their interpretation of Keats's "Eve of St. Agnes," and supremely in Rossetti's imaginative treatment of the love of Dante for Beatrice. Something of the mystical glory of a pure and lofty passion, and of the power of perfect womanhood to raise, as in Keats's poem, the earthlier elements of love into the very essence of worship, appears in Hunt's early picture, "The Flight of Madeline and Porphyro," and in the triptych of "The Eve of St. Agnes," by Arthur Hughes; but its most complete expression, apart from Rossetti, must be sought in Millais's "St. Agnes' Eve," – in the opinion of many, the greatest of his paintings; the consummation of that wonderful aftermath of poetic genius which followed a full decade later than what seemed to be his prime. For the beauty of Madeline, by a significant paradox, is that she is not beautiful. Her attitude is daringly simple; she is standing by her bed in the moonlight, half-unclad; her gown has slipped from her waist to her feet, and the keen, silver-blue rays creep softly about her slender figure and shed a faint light into the foreground of the deep-shadowed room. Yet with all the mellow tenderness of colour and atmosphere that wrap her round, there is in no detail of her form or gesture, or the aspect of her averted face, the slightest appeal to the sensuous possibilities of the scene. There is about her an extraordinary spiritual loveliness, born of the utter artlessness and sincerity of her pose and the girlish innocence of her look, as if the absolute naturalness of the situation were its own protection from all thought of ill. Everything around her speaks of her simple holiness and purity, and seals, as it were, the pledge of the answering purity of Porphyro's love.

But it is in the presence of the greatest romantic passion known to European poetry – the ideal, immortal love of Dante for Beatrice – that Pre-Raphaelite painting reaches, in the art of Rossetti, the acme of its power to transfigure and interpret the highest experiences of the human soul. With the most chastened symbolism, the finest selectiveness of design and colouring, the loftiest fervour of thought and expression, Rossetti unfolds to us the inmost glories of Platonic love, as Dante knew it, and Michaelangelo; and as our own age vaguely but with increasing aspiration seeks it through many an error and much pain. He leads us in imagination through the sacred course of that all-embracing worship which upheld the soul of Dante through every vicissitude of toil and trial, from the first hour in which the smile of the Blessed Beatrice made the boy's heart tremble for joy, until the solemn moment of resignation when "it was made known to him that his beloved Lady must die." Again and again did Rossetti attempt the unwearying subject of "The Salutation of Beatrice." The most important that remain to us of those efforts, which in one medium or another cover nearly the whole of his artistic career, are the early water-colour sketches in which the scene of the fateful meeting is laid in the portico of a church; the diptych showing in one compartment Beatrice saluting Dante in a street in Florence, while in the other she appears to him in a field of lilies in Paradise ("Il Purgatorio," canto 30); the triptych repeating the same designs, but having in the centre panel a figure of Love holding a dial whereon is marked the date (June 9, 1290) of the salutation; and a much later version in single form, representing Beatrice, walking alone in Florence, within sight of Dante, but watched over by the guardian figure of Love, with crimson robe and wings. Of these works, the triptych is perhaps the most perfect. The left compartment is inscribed with Dante's words, "E cui saluta fà tremar lo core," and the right with those of the salutation in Paradise, "Guardami ben; ben son, ben son Beatrice" ("Behold and see if I am truly Beatrice").

Again we see the gracious lady passing before the eyes of her young lover in a procession through the chapel at Bargello, while above her is depicted "Giotto painting the portrait of Dante," – a portrait actually discovered five centuries later on the chapel wall. Once more, Rossetti pictures Beatrice embarking with Dante in "The Boat of Love." The motive of this work is taken from Dante's sonnet to Guido Calvacanti, his poet-friend (who figures, together with Cimabue, the master of Giotto, in the sketch above mentioned), beginning:

"Guido, I would that Lapo, thou, and I
    Were taken by some skilled enchanted spell,
    And placed on board a barque that should speed well
Through wind and wave, and with our will comply."

With reverent humility and tenderness Dante is leading Beatrice into the enchanted boat of which he dreamed. She yields her hands to him and seems to pause beneath his earnest gaze as she steps down. Around her are the companions of their voyage, – Guido Calvacanti with his lady Giovanna, also known as Primavera, and Lapo degli Uberti and his love.

"Beata Beatrix," – "The Blessed Beatrice," – depicts, not the actual death of Dante's beloved, but rather a mystic trance in which is made known to her the nearness of her end. She sits on a balcony overlooking the city of Florence, which is already shadowed by the coming loss. Before her is a sundial, marking the fatal hour. A dove, flying into her lap, carries a poppy-blossom, the symbol of sleep. The lovely face of Beatrice is upturned, as if to greet the unseen messenger, and full of perfect peace. She seems to have attained the sight of blessedness, and to be yielding her spirit to a deep and sweet content, but the earthly weariness lingers about her brows and on her pale and parted lips. In the background, Dante and the figure of Love are seen passing in the street below. Love holds a flaming heart in his hands, and they both gaze in grief and awe at the rapt countenance which the dignity of the coming death suffuses with exquisite pathos and transcendent charm. In the features of this Beatrice, more than in any other, Rossetti has regained and embodied the thought that found superlative expression in Michaelangelo, – "the notion of *inspired* sleep, of faces charged with dreams."[*14]

A more familiar passage from the "Vita Nuova" is illustrated by the largest, and in many respects the finest, of Rossetti's completed pictures, "Dante's Dream;" dealing with the poet's record of the vision in which "it was revealed to him that the Lord God of Justice had called his most gracious lady unto Himself." "Then feeling bewildered," says Dante, writing of that strange experience, which occurred to him at the age of twenty-five, "I closed mine eyes, and my brain began to be in travail, as the brain of one frantic. And I seemed to look toward Heaven, and to behold a multitude of angels who were returning upwards, having before them an exceedingly white cloud. Then my heart, that was so full of love, said unto me, 'It is true that our lady lieth dead;' and it seemed to me that I went to look upon the body wherein that blessed and most noble spirit had had its abiding place. And so strong was this idle imagining that it made me to behold my lady in death; whose head certain ladies seemed to be covering with a white veil, and who was so humble of her aspect that it was as though she had said, 'I have attained to look on the beginning of peace.'" On a red-draped couch in the chamber of death lies the Blessed Beatrice, clad in white robes, her hands folded on her bosom, and her bright hair spread about her pillow. Her maidens, at her head and feet, are hanging over her a purple pall, filled with May-blossoms, the emblem of the spring-time of her life, in which she died. The floor is strewn with poppies, symbolizing again the sleep in which she takes her unbroken rest; and on the frieze above are roses and violets, suggestive of the beauty and purity of the departed soul. Over the couch hangs a lamp, glimmering with a fast-expiring flame; and high up in air, through an opening in the roof, is seen a flight of angels, garbed in the deep red of a damask rose, – symbolic of the Platonic love which should immortalize the beloved in the sight of all men, – and bearing the white cloud that represents the life that has fled. The crimson doves, of which Rossetti made his constant symbol of heavenly ministries, flutter up and down the staircases on either side of the room. Before the couch stands the figure of Love, with his flame-coloured robes fastened at the shoulder by a scallop-shell, signifying pilgrimage. In one hand he holds a winged arrow – his weapon for the heart – and a bunch of rosemary; with the other he leads Dante, who, clad in the black garb of mourning, tinged with the purple of consecration, advances as if in a dream, and shrinks, dazed and awed, before the beauty of the dead Beatrice. And Love, still holding Dante by the hand, bends forward and kisses the face of the beloved, thus making himself the mediator between Dante and Beatrice, and the reconciler of life with death. It is as though the poet's life-long worship were summed up and presented at the gate of heaven by a higher power than his own, and a benediction wrested for him, by the very humility and devoutness of his passion, from the glorified spirit beyond the grave. The dominant note of the design is one of resignation and hope; the passionate, strenuous, mystical resignation which Platonism brought into Christianity at the dawn of the Renaissance, and hope, born of the quickened fervour and resolution of romantic love.

In two notable subjects Rossetti deals with incidents recorded by Dante of himself after the death of Beatrice. In a early water-colour of singular dignity and elevation of feeling, he celebrates "The Anniversary of the Death of Beatrice." "On that day," says Dante in the "Vita Nuova," "which completed the year since my lady had been made of the citizens of eternal life, I was sitting in a place apart, where, remembering me of her, I was drawing an angel upon certain tablets; and as I drew, I turned my eyes, and saw beside me persons to whom it was fitting to do honour, and who were looking at what I did: and according as it was told me afterwards, they had been there awhile before I perceived them. Then I arose for salutation and said, 'Another was present with me.'" The poet, kneeling at a window overlooking the Arno, absorbed in his memorial task, has suddenly become conscious of his visitors, and is overwhelmed with delicate pride and shame.

Again, among the latest of Rossetti's unfinished works, we have the illustration of another passage in the "Vita Nuova," telling of Dante's mourning for his lady's death. "La Donna della Finestra" ("The Lady of the Window"), better known as "Our Lady of Pity," represents the beautiful woman who looked down on Dante from a window when, as he passed weeping through the streets, and fearing lest the passers-by should mock him, he glanced up, craving for some sign of sympathy, and was consoled by her calm and pitying gaze. Sketches for this design were made in several media, but the head in the unfinished painting at Birmingham is the most perfect of the series, and in fact ranks among the finest of the female heads in all Rossetti's single-figure pictures. The artist has caught with rare felicity the expression so acutely described by the poet:

"Whereupon she, after a pitying sigh,
Her eyes directed towards me with that look
A mother casts on a delirious child."

All the depth, all the tenderness, all the heroic strength of a divine sorrow that sees the end of sorrow, shines in this full-souled face. It is the ideal of the highest womanhood, and indeed of the highest humanity; of the love that has attained to be godlike, redeeming the world by infinite compassion; a love that "hopeth all things and endureth all things," and in whose steadfast courage lies the conquering principle of the life to be. It is the companion picture – and in some respects it is a nobler, healthier version – of "The Blessed Damozel," leaning from the bar of heaven to console the mourner on the earth below. The love that can so take hold of immortality, bring comfort even from the gates of death, and bridge over, by the sweet persistence of its ministry, by the passionate reality of its inspiration, the gulf between the physical and the spiritual world, is the love which of old was the source of the "Vita Nuova," and which springs anew in our own age through "Our Lady of Pity" and "The Blessed Damozel." In such designs Rossetti has restored to us all that was best in the mediæval thought of womanhood, – adding the "ever-motherly" to the "ever-womanly" of the Hellenic model, and the Divine Motherhood to the Divine Fatherhood of the Christian ideal; and enriched it with the whole wealth of psycho-sensuous beauty brought over from the region of romance. And in this consummation is justified the verdict of Ruskin: that "Rossetti was the chief intellectual force in the establishment of the modern romantic school in England."

CHAPTER VIII.

THE POETRY OF DANTE ROSSETTI.

The "Pre-Raphaelite" in Literature – The Complexity of Talent in an Age of Re-birth – The Restoration of Romance in England – The Latin and the Saxon in Rossetti – Latin Diction for the Sonnets as Reflective Poetry – Saxon Diction for the Ballads as Dramatic Poetry – "The House of Life" – Treatment of Romantic Love – Illustrations of Sonnet Structure – Miscellaneous Lyrics – "The Portrait," "The Stream's Secret," "Dante at Verona," "The Staff and Scrip" – The Ballads – "The White Ship," "The King's Tragedy," "Sister Helen," "Rose Mary," "The Bride's Prelude," "The Blessed Damozel" – "A Last Confession" – "Jenny" – Relation of Rossetti's Poetry to his Painting.

The poetry of Dante Gabriel Rossetti lies apart from the main current of contemporary verse, both in its highly specialized quality of thought and language, and in the conditions and circumstances of its production. Inasmuch as he followed openly the profession of a painter, pursuing poetry, for the most part, as a recreative rather than a principal study (though never with less seriousness than his accepted vocation), and publishing his first volume of original poems in his forty-second year, he is exempt to some extent from the standards of criticism applied to him whose creative energies are concentrated in the field of literature. Whether Rossetti's genius, as he himself believed, found its highest and most perfect embodiment in poetry rather than in painting, – whether the essential qualities of his art will be more evident to posterity in the modest volume of his collected poems than in the pictures now dispersed through England and America – is still an open question. It may, however, be admitted that his mastery of the verbal medium was almost always more complete, his discipline in metrical structure more thorough, and his natural habit of diction more facile, than any skill which he attained in brush and pencil. To estimate his final influence upon contemporary thought in the one realm as against the other is yet more difficult than to assess the relative merit of his actual work in either sphere: so intimately was the poet incarnate in the painter; so largely did the painter's vision inspire and dominate the poet.

But it would be a poor analysis that should divide too finely the interwoven threads of a radiant and many-coloured genius. In an age of intellectual re-birth, of artistic and social revolution, the re-adjustment of forces and functions in the ethical and æsthetical realms is apt to produce a strange complexity of talent, not always beneficial to a single art, not always well for the diversely endowed artist, but often tending to the unification of many activities into one effective stream of purpose, moved by the impulse that infused the nation with a Time-Spirit potent for immortal things. Such a combination of talent in single personalities, in a period of rare national fertility in scholarship and creative power, reveals at the same time the basic unity of the æsthetic life and its inseparable interdependence with the moral ideal. Michaelangelo, at the zenith of the Italian Renaissance, standing at the parting of the ways, gathered up, as it seemed, the several arts into his representative genius, and left to the land that was soon to swamp the æsthetic spirit in the mire of a materialistic decadence the threefold heritage of his painting, his sculpture, and his song. Rossetti, at the zenith of the English

Renaissance, drew a twofold inspiration from the struggle of the modern world, and left the double dower of painting and of poetry, to urge the coming generation to the higher issues of fine art, or to stand, the witness of rejected ideals to ages recalcitrant to the vision and the impulse of to-day.

For the first greatness of Rossetti's poetry is that it assumes for ever the reality and the immanence of a spiritual – and more – a moral world. Not that he ever misuses the vehicles of art as tools of philosophy, or stoops to a didactic application of æsthetic truth. But his art is all moral (as Mr. Ruskin would put it) because it is all fine art. And the moral purpose of art is the better secured when art is trusted to effect that purpose in its own way. The consciously didactic poet is less sure to mould the will and character of a people, than he the form and substance of whose utterance are so perfected in truth and virility of thought, in majesty and grace of speech, as to be a fit oblation to his own ideal. Not "how can I best teach others and influence them aright?" but "how can I best express the highest things I know and feel?" is the self-examination of the true artist. Rossetti's poetry is self-expressive, self-revealing to the very heart's core. The ultimate test of poetry is not "what did this man intend to teach us?" but "of what sort is the manhood here revealed? what are the visions by which it lived? what the ideals in which it grew? Is such a soul's experience wide, deep, typical, and profitable to the rest of mankind?"

In applying such a test to the writings of Rossetti, it is necessary to distinguish between what may be roughly termed the "personal" and the "impersonal" poems. In the one class, supremely exemplified by the "House of Life" sonnets, but including also "Dante at Verona," "The Stream's Secret," "The Portrait," and many of the shorter lyrics, the personal note of love or grief, of memory or hope, is wholly dominant; the poet's soul is absorbed with its individual being, and sees in all the life around him the illustration and interpretation of his own. In the other class, in the great romantic ballads, in "Rose Mary" and "The

Blessed Damozel," in "The White Ship" and "The King's Tragedy," in "The Bride's Prelude" and "Sister Helen," the imagination takes a higher and a larger range; the one soul interprets others, waiting not to be interpreted. The art becomes impersonal in this sense only – that the thought of self is merged in the full and immense life of humanity, laying hold of the universal consciousness through its own initiative experience; the heart beats with the world's heart, shares its eternal struggles, contributes to its eternal growth; and the spirit knows itself one fragment of an infinite whole. In such a sphere the art remains the more vitally personal, in that the poet brings the mysteries of existence, the abiding problems and realities of the conscious world, to the touchstone, as it were, of his own spirit, and submits himself thereby to the more crucial test, – of how he can interpret humanity to man, and make more clear the knowledge, more possible the realization, of his highest ideals.

With this general division of the subject-matter of Rossetti's poetry, the classification of its metrical cast and forms of diction will be singularly parallel. Most of his finest compositions might be distinguished as purely Saxon or pre-eminently Latin poems; and it is notable that the more intimately subjective and analytic the thought within, the more persistently does it assume the Latin garb; while as the imagination ranges from the introspection of the hyper-conscious self, and finds, on the heights of common human feeling and aspiration, a larger and a freer air, the mode passes into the more keen and rarified Saxon speech. No other English poet has resolved the breadth and simplicity of the Gothic, and the depth and intensity of the Italian habit of expression, into such distinctive poetic vehicles. But at the same time few have blended the diverse elements of the modern English tongue into the harmony and sonority with which Rossetti's music thrills when he tempers the sharper Saxon with a deep undertone of polysyllabic song; or stirs the languorous pulses of a sonnet with some swift cadence of familiar words. He had the finest perception of national and racial properties of form and rhythm; and discerning the characteristics of the poetry of action in the literature of the north, and the poetry of reflection in the literature of the south, he cast his great historical lyrics in the highest narrative – that is to say, the ballad form; and chose the sonnet – the most remote, chastened, and exclusive vehicle – for the meditative, and yet sensuous, self-delineative love-poetry.

These broad generalizations, however, cannot be closely pressed upon the entire sequence of Rossetti's poems. The exigencies of the English language alone elude their literal application. They will rather serve to illustrate the duality of his endowments, and the singular power of his genius both to conserve and specialize the characteristics of his Italian heritage, and also to waive them in the Saxon mode as utterly as though the latter were more native to his tongue.

Nor does such a superficial distinction affect the spiritual qualities which pervade Rossetti's poetry as a whole. From first to last, in dramatic description or narrative, in sonnet-argument or meditative questioning, his verse remains full-charged with the very essence of romance. As a poet, he is neither less nor more Pre-Raphaelite than as a painter. The vivid and intense simplicity of his Saxon diction, the verbal lightnings of his ballad-style, seem to correspond with the tone and method of his water-colour painting, and the more laboured splendour of the sonnets with the properties of his work in oils. Nor is it difficult to detect an analogy between that stage of his painting in which the pristine lucidity of expression was partially lost in the painful tension of his later thought, and the tendency of some few of his sonnets towards decadence into the over-laborious and the obscure. Yet if by "Pre-Raphaelite" we understand that fusion of the naïve mysticism of romance with austere Platonic Hellenism which we discern in the best Renaissance art, Rossetti never falls in spirit from that standard of beauty and truth; and rarely lapses, through the very richness and fecundity of the language at his command, into the redundant verbiage towards which his sensuous imagery was easily led. It has remained for a brother-poet of the romantic revival to cultivate a more marvellous dexterity of rhyme and rhythm, and to develop the technical resources of our language to the utmost limits of intelligible song. The lyrics of Mr. Swinburne, like the superb decorative extravagances of the later Renaissance, represent that culmination of mastery over the forms of expression wherein to-day, as of yore, the purity of the thought is lost in the splendour of the setting, and poetic power wastes itself in a magic facility of verse.

The poetry of Rossetti, modern as it is in its passionate grasp of human interests, its deep insight into present and perpetual things, links itself nevertheless to an English past; takes up, as it were, the dropped threads of Elizabethan glory; re-inspires the circling breath of life which passed round Europe in the fifteenth century, kindling England from the fires of re-awakened Italy in the golden age of song. It has already been pointed out by one of Rossetti's biographers that "the malign influence over our literature in post-Shakespearean times has been French." It was reserved for a second Renaissance, heralded by Chatterton and Blake, led by Shelley, Keats, and Coleridge, and culminated by Dante Rossetti, to blot out two centuries of foreign tradition and control, and take us back to the broad simplicity and dignity of Shakespeare's England.

Our reiteration, therefore, of the term "Pre-Raphaelite" in approaching Rossetti's work as a poet, leads us to expect, not mysticism merely, but a certain robust sensuousness, as of Pagan origin, in his interpretation of life and destiny. The romantic temper in its highest manifestations, absorbing and transfiguring, rather than conflicting with, the classic ideals, implies much more than receptivity to newer beauty and truth. It has a moral basis and an intellectual range: it apprehends the spiritual world as something closely bound up with familiar things: it finds the human soul striving for expression through material forms: it recognizes the divine possibilities of individual and social life, the force and responsibility of personal character, and the solemnity of the choice between good and evil daily made by man.

✳ 279

But the controversy excited by Rossetti's pictures has been neither more intemperate nor more significant than that which has raged around his poems; – interpreted by one section of his critics as a pæan of sensuality and materialism, by another as the most spiritual and chastened love-poetry of the age. The laureate of the Pre-Raphaelite Brotherhood indeed summed up, in what now affords but one volume of original verse, the inmost vicissitudes of a spirit so rare and rich of vision as to transcend at once the canons of conventional experience. But the personal note, in the self-delineative poems, is struck with a peculiar dignity of reserve; and even while the most sacred depths of individual consciousness are laid bare, the actual *ego* is never intruded upon the surface of the speech, – never portrays directly its own character, seldom describes its own sensations as Byron or Shelley would; but veils itself, even in the profusion of luminous imagery and searching analysis of thought and sense.

The eternal mysteries and sanctities of sexual love, conceived in its highest aspects and known as a revelation and a sacrament, afford the theme of nearly all Rossetti's autobiographic poetry. The conditions of its production were ordained by the stern fate that linked him afar off to Dante among his countrymen, and near at hand to two brother-mourners among minor English bards – James Thomson and Philip Bourke Marston – in the sad fraternity of poets whom death has prematurely robbed of the beloved object that once inspired their song. The exalted spirituality which marks Rossetti's treatment of this theme was doubtless largely due to the influence of Dante, and especially to the fruitful inspiration and discipline of the great literary task of his youth – the translation of the "Vita Nuova" and kindred examples of the early Italian poets – than which Rossetti could have hardly found a better preparation for his work that was to come.

Into his great sonnet-sequence, "The House of Life," Rossetti poured the full passion of his mystic love, – partially inherent in his own sensuous, imaginative, and introspective nature, partially instilled at the feet of Dante; and learned – a bitter and a costly lesson – at the school of experience also; fraught with inestimable joy and sorrow to his own soul. "At an age," says one writing of that hard probation, "when most men have outlived the romances of their youth, Rossetti was laying, in 'The House of Life,' the foundations of a new school of love-poetry." He was in fact re-creating the æsthetic life of a nation; restoring to it, through the alembic of mediæval and Renaissance thought, the lost glory of all that was abidingly precious in the Platonic world. For in this wondrous cycle of sonnets is re-coined the whole language of ideal love. From the last echo of the "Vita Nuova" it takes up the same pure strain, and sings again the song of Dante for the Blessed Beatrice; hymning the very apotheosis of spiritual passion, and harmonizing once more in English poetry the intellectual with the sensuous world. Never, in the superb visions of "The House of Life" – in which the soul of man is pictured sojourning awhile during its solemn and fateful passage through eternity – never does the physical love become the stumbling-block to the spiritual, but always the key to it. The "body's beauty" is only precious as the witness of the "soul's beauty;" the physical bond is nothing if not the symbol of a spiritual affinity, a sacred kinship, fore-ordained, if not eternal, sealed in Heaven and consecrated to the divinest purposes; the sensuous rapture is but a symbolic worship, – "the outward and visible sign of an inward and spiritual grace" which to reject or betray is to profane the inmost sanctuary of the God of Love:

"Even so, when first I saw you, seemed it, love,
    That among souls allied to mine was yet
One nearer kindred than life hinted of.
    O born with me somewhere that men forget,
    And though in years of sight and sound unmet,
Known for my soul's birth-partner well enough!"

Love the revealer of unseen verities, the binder of invisible bonds; Love the deliverer from material trammels, the opener of the gate of life; these are to him the gracious manifestations of the same deity:

"O what from thee the grace, to me the prize,
 And what to Love the glory, – when the whole
Of the deep stair thou tread'st to the dim shoal
 And weary water of the place of sighs,
 And there dost work deliverance, as thine eyes
Draw up my prisoned spirit to thy soul!"

In the large atmosphere of such a worship, seeing all things, as we have said, *sub specie eternitatis*, the poet portrays the sweetest intimacies of communion, soul with soul; questioning, recording, comparing from time to time the recurring phases of joy and hope, memory and regret. "When do I see thee most?" he asks in the exquisite sonnet called "Lovesight":

"When do I see thee most, beloved one?
 When in the light the spirits of mine eyes
 Before thy face, their altar, solemnize
The worship of that love through thee made known?
Or when in the dusk hours, (we two alone,)
 Close-kissed and eloquent of still replies
 Thy twilight-hidden glimmering visage lies,
And my soul only sees thy soul its own?"

"What of her glass without her?" he cries again after the great bereavement which has removed the visible presence of the beloved:

"What of her glass without her? The blank grey
 There where the pool is blind of the moon's face.
 Her dress without her? The tossed empty space
Of cloud-rack whence the moon has passed away.
Her paths without her? Day's appointed sway
 Usurped by desolate night. Her pillowed place
 Without her? Tears, ah me! for love's good grace,
And cold forgetfulness of night or day."

And with what fine insight does Rossetti pierce the tender

subtleties of the woman's responsive heart! Has any other English poet discerned so well that retrospective instinct which clings to the early semblances of pure and non-sexual love?

> – "She loves him, for her infinite soul is love.
> •   •   •   •   •   •
>   With wifely breast to breast
> And circling arms, she welcomes all command
> Of love, – her soul to answering ardours fanned:
> Yet as morn springs or twilight sinks to rest,
> *Ah! who shall say she deems not loveliest*
>   *The hour of sisterly sweet hand-in-hand?"*

In that hint lies the acknowledgment of the Platonic ideal, – that whatever dignifies and ennobles the affections must lie not in the outward conditions but within; that the senses are but the accessories of Love; the temporary channels, not the eternal stream. And this insistence on the spiritual aspects of passion affects the whole tone and temper of Rossetti's poetry; raising it, in moments of intense feeling, almost to the mystic exaltation of a Pascal, and transfiguring all the world of consciousness by the knowledge and memory of an overmastering love. From the first to the last of the hundred sonnets we are shown steadfastly the outlook upon life of one to whom all life has been sanctified by that supreme experience. "Who can read 'The House of Life'" (says Mr. F.W.H. Myers in his essay on "Rossetti and the Religion of Beauty"[*15]) "and not feel that this poet has known love as love can be, not an enjoyment only or a triumph, but a worship and a regeneration?"

In such a spirit does the poet take account of time and opportunity, and recognize the solemnities of passing hour. Life has become more sacred, the man more responsible, the imperative forces of character and destiny more urgent than before. The sense of personal possibilities and shortcomings weighs upon him. "Lost days" and wasted chances oppress his mind. The actualities of evil in his own sphere of being look darker in the face of the recognized good:

"The lost days of my life until to-day,
    What were they, could I see them on the street
    Lie as they fell? Would they be ears of wheat
Sown once for food but trodden into clay?

Or golden coins squandered and still to pay?
    Or drops of blood dabbling the guilty feet?
    Or such spilt water as in dreams must cheat
The throats of men in Hell, athirst alway?

I do not see them here, but after death
    God knows I know the faces I shall see,
Each one a murdered self, with low last breath.
    'I am thyself, – what hast thou done to me?'
'And I – and I – thyself,' (lo! each one saith,)
    'And thou thyself to all eternity!'"

And in a similar strain the poet prays:

"O Lord of work and peace! O Lord of life!
    O Lord, the awful Lord of will! though late,
        Even yet renew this soul with duteous breath:
That when the peace is garnered in from strife,
    The work retrieved, the will regenerate,
        This soul may see thy face, O Lord of death!"

This sense of destiny it is, this keen perception – characteristic
of all true romance – of the reality of the spiritual world, the
transiency of earthly joys and the insufficiency of external things,
that gives the persistent undertone of melancholy to Rossetti's
love-sonnets, and more or less, indeed, to all his poetry. He does
not, perhaps, sustain the peculiar minor key which the resigned
and pensive fatalism of William Morris imparts. His grasp of fate
is firmer, and with all his despair and doubt and grief he keeps a
greater dignity of front than any of his surviving brother-poets.
But his pessimism, if it must be called so, had its source in a
hyper-sensitive and self-conscious personality, and was drawn, as
one has said of Michaelangelo, from "the struggle of a strong
nature to attune itself." It is an absorbing struggle, on which to

look with reverent reserve; carried on within the sorely-shaken spaces of a spirit too proud to vent itself, as Swinburne's, in a broad and vigorous iconoclasm; too isolated to find relief, as the poet of "The Earthly Paradise" was presently to do, in the vanguard of a social revolution promising the heaven of his dreams. Nor could Rossetti's wayward heart find permanent rest in the fervid religious faith which sustained the poetess of the Pre-Raphaelite movement – his sister, Miss Christina Rossetti.

Yet the sadness that tinges Rossetti's verse is nearly always of a kind that chastens without enervating, and strengthens while it subdues. Intimately personal and subtly introspective as it is, it lifts us on to the highest planes of living poetry. We feel that the writer has learnt that first great lesson which indeed Rossetti himself has urged in these sonnets, –

"By thine own tears thy song must tears beget,
O Singer!"

And by that baptism of tears he rises to the rank of those whose individual loss and grief have blessed the world, as the death of Edward King blessed it in Milton's "Lycidas," and in far greater measure the death of Arthur Hallam blessed it in Tennyson's "In Memoriam." For while sometimes the expression of personal pain may be put into such perfect art as to afford in its very poignancy of feeling a sort of æsthetic consolation, the test of the highest poetic grief is that it shall lose the smart of personal injury in a strong sense of brotherhood with fellow-sufferers, and shall translate the revolt against individual pain into a wide compassion with the sorrows of a nation or of all humanity.

Nor can we avoid comparison of "The House of Life" with the two great kindred cycles of love-sonnets in the English language, – the sonnets of Shakespeare, and Mrs. Browning's "Sonnets from the Portuguese;" the one celebrating a hopeless and desolating passion, the other a fortunate and consummated love. Rossetti touches both these precedents, in that he knew alike the depths and heights, the hell and heaven, of that passion of which the poets say, –

"All other pleasures are not worth its pain."

He enjoyed happiness, and suffered despair, not merely in the outward circumstances of his love, but in a more subtle and irretrievable way. The fallacy dies hard, that leads us to imagine that the unvaryingly sad and gloomy natures are the supreme sufferers of the world. On the contrary, the acuteness of pain is measured by its victim's capacity for mirth. And there are some natures so finely organized, so highly-strung, that even joy is almost painful to them. They cannot lose themselves in a moment's rapture, but are beset with contrasts behind and before; are haunted with the cost of every ecstasy, and rarely learn that calm and self-possessing wisdom which is the fruit of the knowledge of good and evil, and through which may come at last, in many channels of temperament, in many forms of faith and duty, the power to subdue the evil to the good. Such were Shelley and Keats, Leopardi and Heine, James Thomson and Philip Bourke Marston: such also was Dante Gabriel Rossetti.

It would be superfluous to dwell at length on the extraordinary richness of Rossetti's metaphor and simile. The imagery in the "House of Life" is for the most part sensuous, fervid, and almost tropical in colour and atmosphere. Here are a crowd of variously portentous spirits, –

> … "Fame, whose loud wings fan the ashen Past
> To signal fires;"
> … "Song, whose hair
> Blew like a flame and blossomed like a wreath;"
> … "Love, smiling to receive
> Along his eddying plumes the auroral wind;"

And –

> … "Life herself, the spirit's friend and love,

Even still as Spring's authentic harbinger
   Glows with fresh hours for hope to glorify;
Though pale she lay when in the winter grove
Her funeral flowers were snowflakes shed on her
   And the red wings of frost-fire rent the sky."

We follow the soul of the lover –

... "where wan water trembles in the grove,
And the wan moon is all the light thereof,"

... "o'er the sea of love's tumultuous trance,"

"Upon the devious coverts of dismay"

across "death's haggard hills"; among

"Shadows and shoals that edge eternity,"

and through

                ... "that last
Wild pageant of the accumulated past
That clangs and flashes for a drowning man."

The superb climax just quoted terminates one of the most vivid and haunting of the "House of Life" series, – "The Soul's Sphere," – illustrative of the vast range of consciousness known to one

"Who, sleepless, hath ... anguished to appease
Tragical shadow's realm of sound and sight
Conjectured in the lamentable night,"

and probes the memory for images whose calm splendour may bring forgetfulness of self. The subject is that of Wordsworth's well-known sonnet, "A flock of sheep that leisurely pass by;" and the contrast between the visions conjured up by the two very diverse poets exactly illustrates the difference of temperament which set them at opposite poetic poles. The mind of Wordsworth rests in the contemplation of familiar things, gains peace in the common incidents of pastoral life, loves Nature best in her ordinary moods, and seeks always the homeliest of consolations, the most universal joys. The mind of Rossetti craves ever for the superlative, the exceptional, the intense, and can find no ease in anything very simple and quiet.

The value of a poet's verdict on his own poems is not always to be measured by his critical faculty when applied to general literature. The friends of Rossetti have been unanimous in his praise as a critic both of prose and of poetry, though his desultory reading and vehemence of judgment led him sometimes into extravagances of worship or condemnation, and blunted his discrimination of relative merits in divergent schools. Hence his persistent and quite explicable antipathy to Wordsworth, and his exaggerated estimate of Chatterton in later life. But in his criticism of his own work it is inevitable that a poet should be somewhat biassed by associations and memories bearing upon its production. It is difficult to take seriously Rossetti's admission to the indiscreet admirer of one of his shorter poems, – "You are right: 'The Cloud Confines' *is* my very best thing." Lyrically unimpeachable indeed it is, though not more so than the exquisite "Autumn Song," "A New Year's Burden," "Insomnia," "Three Shadows," or "Sunset Wings;" and therefore are we fain to take Rossetti's judgment as based largely on technical considerations when, in selecting his own favourites from among the "House of Life" series, he adds to the noble sonnet "Lost Days" (already quoted) the less impassioned but more coherent and melodious "Still-born Love," "The One Hope," and "Known in Vain." These certainly excel in some of the highest qualities of the sonnet form – unity of idea, and the steady set of the rhythmic flow and ebb in motive and application; though in none of these does the sestet conform to the pure Guittonian model on three-rhyme-sounds, blending the first and fourth, second and fifth, and third and sixth lines in a double tercet, as it does with signal success in "Lost on

Both Sides," "The Portrait," and "Hope Overtaken;" and in only one out of his chosen four ("The One Hope") does Rossetti attain what he personally preferred as the most perfect order of sestet rhymes, based upon two terminal sounds, and rhyming the first, fourth, and fifth lines against the second, third, and sixth; thus opening the sestet with a quatrain harmonizing in structure with the octet above, and yet avoiding the rhymed couplet at the close which would remove the whole poem from the Italian mould in which, despite many irregularities, nearly all Rossetti's sonnets are cast. The sestet of "Lost Days" (like several others in the series) exemplifies what is generally held to be the best arrangement of the two-rhymed sestet in the Guittonian form, – that in which the first, third, and fifth terminals chime against the second, fourth, and sixth. Admirable as these four sonnets are, however, in clarity of thought and cumulative power, it is doubtful whether they should rank higher, from the broadest standards of poetry, than "Lost on Both Sides," "Lovesight," "Mid-rapture," or "Supreme Surrender;" in all of which the gathering force of the motive sweeps in a fine torrent – mournful, searching, tender, or triumphant – to its eddying close, and the best tribute to the metrical art of each is that it conveys so perfectly the inmost fulness of the thought. Frequently, indeed, Rossetti ends a sonnet with a rhymed couplet on a new terminal sound, following a Guittonian quatrain, as in "Mid-Rapture," "True Woman," "Her Heaven," and "The Song-Throe;" or in some cases following a Shakespearean quatrain after a Guittonian octet, as, for instance, in "Venus Victrix" and "The Love-Moon." Very rarely does he compose a whole sonnet in the Shakespearean measure, namely, that in which the two rhyme-sounds of the doubled-quatrained octave occur in alternate lines, and the former of them is carried forward with a new rhyme for the similarly alternated quatrain of a sestet clenched with a rhyming couplet on another note, as in "Willow-Wood" (No. III.). The question of the legitimacy of a rhymed couplet at the close of anything but a wholly Shakespearean sonnet has been much debated by conflicting authorities on poetic form. The sonnet is at once the most elastic and the most arbitrary of vehicles for the concise embodiment of a single thought and its accessory similes. From the scholar's point of view, no indiscriminate grafting of one essentially national and historic growth of form upon another is theoretically defensible. But, since no European language is of exclusive stock, the fusion of Latin and Saxon speech in the varied beauty of modern English seems hardly less anachronistic than the adaptation of traditional metres to the new requirements of the poetic faculties of the age.

Akin to the "House of Life" in spirit and substance is "The Portrait;" a reminiscence, after the death of the loved model, of hours which saw the painting of the picture on a stormy summer day. Here the sonnet's long-drawn strain gives place to a quicker measure:

> "But when that hour my soul won strength
>   For words whose silence wastes and kills,
> Dull raindrops smote us, and at length
>   Thundered the heat within the hills.
> That eve I spoke those words again
> Beside the pelted window-pane;
>   And there she hearkened what I said,
>   With under-glances that surveyed
> The empty pastures blind with rain.
> •　•　•　•　•　•
> "Last night at last I could have slept,
>   And yet delayed my sleep till dawn,
> Still wandering. Then it was I wept:
>   For unawares I came upon
> Those glades where once she walked with me.
> And as I stood there suddenly,
>   All wan with traversing the night,
>   Upon the desolate verge of light
> Yearned loud the iron-bosomed sea."

In "The Stream's Secret" the verse assumes a still more lyrical rhythm, as the poet communes with the familiar waters concerning his lost love, and desires –

"The wind-stirred robe of roseate grey
And rose-crown of the hour that leads the day
      When we shall meet once more,"
.   .   .   .   .   .
"As on the unmeasured height of Love's control
      The lustral fires are lit."

The flow of the monologue gleams with such images as these:

"And on the waste uncoloured wold
The visible burthen of the sun grown cold,
      And the moon's labouring gaze;"

or –

"The soul hears the night's disconsolate cry,
      And feels the branches, wringing wet,
      Cast on its brow, that may not once forget,
Blind tears from the blind sky."

In "Dante at Verona" Rossetti portrays in a somewhat diffuse and irregular string of descriptive stanzas, some incidents, historic and imaginary, but always congruous with our best ideals of Dante, – of his exile from Florence and his sojourn at the Court of Verona after the death of Beatrice. The poem lacks balance and unity of plan, but abounds in passages of exquisite feeling, wrought through the keen vision of those significant accessories that make a great, if fragmentary picture of the commanding personality so near akin in many aspects to his modern namesake and disciple, yet strangely removed from him in temperament and character. How far in either case the lover's worship was fulfilled and consummated in a single earthly embodiment of the ideal, or whether such a brief apparent gain served but to feed the fires of the insatiable idealism behind it, is hardly for the historian to estimate. But whatever the actual channels found by the dominant passion of their poetry, however diverse the conditions under which it sought its outlet towards the infinite sea, both Dante and Rossetti may be counted with the isolated band of dreamers, who, as Shelley once said aptly of himself, "are always in love with something or other; their error consists in seeking in a mortal image the likeness of what is, perhaps, eternal." They "have loved Antigone before they visited this earth, and are ever demanding of life more than it can give."

On such a pilgrimage the sombre figure of "Dante at Verona" passes before us, through the palaces and gardens of Can Grande della Scala, ever remote, self-absorbed, austere; "with set brows lordlier than a frown;" and we are shown his vigils, his spiritual isolation among the gross luxuries and corruptions of the table, the chamber, and the hall; and how his presence half won, half awed the women of the court;

> "And when the music had its sign
> To breathe upon them for more ease
> Sometimes he turned and bade it cease."

And he who followed steadfastly the inward vision of the lost Beatrice, to be regained in Paradise, cherished with the more integrity his love for the city of Beatrice, – Florence, that "sat solitary" when Beatrice died, and now seemed lost also. And he answered them that would win back the exiled patriot-poet, –

> "That since no gate led, by God's will,
>   To Florence, but the one whereat
>   The priests and money-changers sat,
> He still would wander; for that still,
>   Even through the body's prison-bars
>   His soul possessed the sun and stars."

Here again is struck the keynote of romance, "the note of resistance and defiance" of external trammels and material bonds; the note of spiritual courage which can pierce through the finite to the infinite life, and "possess" what this world cannot remove or bestow. And in this high strain the personal accent, the autobiographic undertone, loses itself in a loftier music, and "Dante at Verona" is brought within measurable distance of

Rossetti's finest work – his great romantic ballads, "Rose Mary,"
"The White Ship," "The King's Tragedy," "Sister Helen," "The
Bride's Prelude," "The Staff and Scrip," and "The Blessed
Damozel."

"The Staff and Scrip," perhaps, ranks next above "Dante at
Verona," to which it links itself as a kind of companion poem;
celebrating the life-long faithfulness of a lady to her knight-errant,
perished in defence of her cause. Coming as a pilgrim through
her wasted lands, the hero seeks the queen in her dim palace,
where, –

> "The sweetness sickened her
> Of musk and myrrh,"

and dedicates himself to the redemption of the country from
her foe.

> "She sent him a sharp sword, whose belt
>   About his body there
> As sweet as her own arms he felt.
>   He kissed its blade, all bare,
>   Instead of her."

The knight wins in the battle, but dies in the victory, and his
body is brought to the queen.

> "'Uncover ye his face,' she said.
>   'O changed in little space!'
> She cried; 'O pale that was so red!
>   O God, O God of grace!
>   Cover his face.'

> "His sword was broken in his hand
>   Where he had kissed the blade.
> 'O soft steel that could not withstand!
>   O my hard heart unstayed,
>   That prayed and prayed!'"

The exaltation of spirit is more sustained, the diction more finely distilled, the air clearer, the whole balance and setting of the narrative more perfect than in "Dante at Verona." The passion of chivalric love, worship, heroism, loyalty, burns at a white-heat from the first line to the last. Every phrase is purged, chastened, and full-charged; and flies swiftly with its portentous burden of meaning straight to the mark. It breathes the very soul of that romantic chivalry to which the modern world is turning with a shaken conscience and a regenerate will; impelled to a larger application of its principles than the golden ages knew. The glory of true knighthood in its championship of the weak, its resistance of tyranny, its heroic self-sacrifice, its contempt of ease, its defiance of pain, its devotion to principle, is as yet a tardy sunrise brokenly discerned through the long reaches of historic years; an unsteady dawn of world-light clouded by men's lust of private power; a scant and partial gleam of what it must involve for the social life to be.

"The White Ship" and "The King's Tragedy" stand together as Rossetti's sole and supreme achievements in the realm of historical romance. They stand, in fact, alone in conception and treatment among modern English ballads: unequalled even by Tennyson's "Revenge," and crowning the lyric with something almost of the epic quality. The theme of "The White Ship" is found in the familiar story of Henry I. of England, who is said to have "never smiled again" after the loss of the "white ship" in which his son and heir – not mentioned by name in the poem – perished in crossing the channel from Normandy. "The King's Tragedy" relates, through the mouth of Catherine Douglas ("Kate Barlass"), the assassination of James I. of Scotland by Sir Robert Graeme. In neither ballad is the action lifted to an unfamiliar or phantasmal world; in both it is transfused, as it passes across the stage of actual history, with a glow and glamour of supernatural light; brought near to us with a direct realism of incident and detail as convincing as it is transparent, and yet shrouded in an atmosphere of mysticism and reserve, pervaded with a sense of doom and fatality, that holds us in a mingled awe and exaltation such as we feel in the purest Greek tragedy, amid the strivings of the gods with men. The narrative of "The White Ship" is told bluntly, vividly, incoherently, by the humblest of the king's retinue and the sole survivor of the royal train, "the butcher of Rouen, poor Berold;" and the movement seems to gather the more power and sincerity from his untutored lips. Its dominant motives, its finer touches, – the withholding of the hero's name and the allusions to him merely as "the Prince," the emphasis on the manner of the death of the "lawless, shameless youth" who died, after all, for his sister's sake – the emphasis throughout on character rather than on incident – these are true marks of romantic poetry.

But "The King's Tragedy" far surpasses the earlier ballad in sustained and unfaltering dignity of passion, in the tender humanness of the narrative setting, the grandly simple presentation of the climax, and the weird portent of the earlier scenes. None but the two or three who saw the writer in the course of his task can know what the poem cost Rossetti in his dying year, – the last great product of a literary genius still ascendant when obscured by death, and if not the finest of all his ballads, sharing at least the rank of "Sister Helen," "Rose Mary," and "The Blessed Damozel." Never does he use the supernatural machinery with a more masterly restraint or yet with a more powerful effect of dread and presage, than when he brings the aged woman of the sea, like one of the witches of "Macbeth," to confront the King with her fourfold vision of his doom:

"Four years it is since first I met,
    'Twixt the Duchray and the Dhu,
A shape whose feet clung close in a shroud,
    And that shape for thine I knew.

"A year again, and on Inchkeith Isle
    I saw thee pass in the breeze,
With the cerecloth risen above thy feet
    And wound about thy knees.

"And yet a year, in the Links of Forth,
    As a wanderer without rest,
Thou cam'st with both thine arms i' the shroud
    That clung high up thy breast.
.   .   .   .   .   .

"And when I met thee again, O King,
    That of death hast such sore drouth, –
Except thou turn again on this shore, –
The winding-sheet shall have moved once more,
    And covered thine eyes and mouth.

"For every man on God's ground, O King,
    His death grows up from his birth
In a shadow-plant perpetually;
And thine towers high, a black yew-tree,
    O'er the Charterhouse of Perth!"

Then, in strange contrast to the wild scenery of the "black beach-side" in winter, we are shown the king and queen at home and keeping festival in the ill-fated house. The revelry of the halls, and the quiet joy of the hearthside, seem to avert for a time the coming woe. The king takes his harp, and sings to the queen an old love-song which he had written to her from prison long ago. But soon the boded fate falls on them unaware:

"'Twas a wind-wild eve in February,
    And against the casement pane
The branches smote like summoning hands,
    And muttered the driving rain."

The entrance of the traitors, with "three hundred armèd men," urges on the climax of the tragedy, until at last the king, discovered in the vault where he had hastily hidden:

"Half-naked stood, but stood as one
    Who yet could do and dare.
With the crown, the King was stript away, –
The Knight was 'reft of his battle array, –
    But still the man was there!"

The poem ends on a stern note of revenge and retribution, for, when the shameful deed is done, the queen keeps watch for a whole month beside the royal body; refusing to permit the burial till every one of the "murderous league" is put to a more terrible death than his lord.

> "And then she said, – 'My King, they are dead!'
>   And she knelt on the chapel floor,
> And whispered low with a strange proud smile, –
>   'James, James, they suffered more!'"

There is, perhaps, a higher aspect to this passion of revenge, this fierce, imperative, triumphant sense of moral justice and supernatural retribution, than the somewhat partial and personal form which it assumes in mediæval poetry. Beneath the crude worship of arbitrary rule, behind the primitive conception of a Power that for ever vindicates the brave and puts the coward to confusion, lies the germ of that larger sense of divine vengeance which inspires and dominates all great tragedy. Something of this higher strain of feeling, this perception of the futility of merely human punishments and personal judgments, yet mingled with an instinctive acceptance of the human measures as the instruments of the divine, finds expression in the ballad of "Sister Helen." The theme is based upon an ancient superstition to the effect that the death of a wrong-doer could be supernaturally procured by the injured person, by making a waxen image in his semblance and melting it for three days and nights before a fire. Sister Helen's lover has been unfaithful to her, and in her anger against him she melts his image and keeps her dreadful watch relentlessly through the appointed hours, till the spell is completed, and her vengeance achieves its purpose in the death of her enemy. The poem is cast in the form of a dialogue between Sister Helen and her little brother, whose childish wonder at the mysterious process distracts him from his play; and he looks by turns at the fatal fire and at the wintry landscape without.

> "'Why did you melt your waxen man,
>   Sister Helen?
> To-day is the third since you began.'
> 'The time was long, yet the time ran,
>   Little brother.'
>   (O Mother, Mary Mother,
> Three days to-day, between Hell and Heaven!)"

She bids the child watch from the balcony while she, within, proceeds with her incantation. Presently messengers ride hastily up the road, calling upon Helen, and pleading with her for mercy upon the dying man:

> "'But he calls for ever on your name,
>   Sister Helen,
> And says that he melts before a flame.'
> 'My heart for his pleasure fared the same,
>   Little brother.'
>   (O Mother, Mary Mother,
> Fire at the heart, between Hell and Heaven!)"

The contrast between the boy's innocent, eager reports and observations, and Helen's bitter, mocking answers, carries with it all the solemn terror of the Greek, and all the mystic naïveté of the mediæval world. At last the unfaithful lover's aged father, and finally his three days' bride, arrive to add their entreaties for his life, and the lady falls fainting at Helen's inhospitable door.

> "'They've caught her to Westholm's saddle-bow,
>   Sister Helen,
> And her moonlit hair gleams white in its flow.'
> 'Let it turn whiter than winter snow,
>   Little brother!'
>   (O Mother, Mary Mother,
> Woe-withered gold, between Hell and Heaven!)"

It is not until too late that Helen learns that by seeking revenge for her own sorrow she has only doubled the sin. Absorbed in her own heart's bitterness, she cannot know that the only anger worthy to play a part in the divine retribution is that which burns not so much for the sin against self as for the sin against love; which draws from the smart of personal injury a righteous indignation for others' wrongs, a profound and passionate pity for fellow-victims of a too common evil, a too familiar grief. But in Helen's vengeance lies her own despair:

> "'Ah! what white thing at the door has crossed,
>   Sister Helen?
> Ah! what is this that sighs in the frost?'
> 'A soul that's lost as mine is lost,
>   Little brother!'
>   (O Mother, Mary Mother,
> Lost, lost, all lost, between Hell and Heaven!)"

The same thought of reciprocal sin, if we may so express it, – of the mutual responsibility of soul to soul, – that subtle action of the law of vicarious suffering by which every soul that falls short of its own highest and best inevitably drags down some other soul with it, – and the converse thought of individual redemption through mutual love: these afford the motive of "Rose Mary."

> "Shame for shame, yea, and sin for sin:
> Yet peace at length may our poor souls win
> If love for love be found therein."

The story turns upon the magic properties attributed to the Beryl-stone, into which the pure in heart might look and read the future, and be forewarned against all danger or calamity. Rose Mary's mother bids her read the mysterious crystal on the eve of her lover's journey to a distant shrine, whither he rides to seek shrift for his soul before the wedding-day. The mother fears some ambush of foes by the way, and trusts the Beryl to reveal where the danger lies. Unknown to her, however, Rose Mary and her lover have joined in sin; and their sin dispossesses the good spirits from the stone, and yields their place to evil spirits, so that the spell works by contraries, and the oracle speaks falsely; the lover is betrayed and killed on the road at night. But, unknown to Rose

Mary, her lover has been faithless, even to her own love. The sin is threefold, – his with her, hers with him, and his with another; and Rose Mary learns that only by an heroic forgiveness and self-sacrifice which shall cost her very life can she atone for her own and his greater sin, win pardon for both, and cast out the evil tenants from the Beryl stone. The ballad moves throughout at Rossetti's highest poetic level; its majestic rhythm sweeps from verse to verse in a torrent of swift, strong, lyric narrative, almost too cohesive for quotation, save in such descriptive stanzas as these:

> "Even as she spoke, they two were 'ware
> Of music-notes that fell through the air;
> A chiming shower of strange device,
> Drop echoing drop, once, twice, and thrice,
> As rain may fall in Paradise.
> •　　•　　•　　•　　•　　•
> As the globe slid to its silken gloom,
> Once more a music rained through the room;
> Low it splashed like a sweet star-spray,
> And sobbed like tears at the heart of May,
> And died as laughter dies away."

But the imagery from first to last is of extraordinary tenderness and power; as, for instance, in describing the first lightning-flash before a storm, –

> "Ere labouring thunders heave the chain
> From the flood-gates of the drowning rain,"

or when, –

> "The dawn broke dim on Rose Mary's soul, –
> No hill-crown's heavenly aureole,
> But a wild gleam on a shaken shoal,"

and in the past night, –

> "She knew she had waded bosom-deep

Along death's bank in the sedge of sleep."

It is impossible to adequately criticise "Rose Mary" without reference to the question already raised by Mr. Theodore Watts, as to whether in future editions of Rossetti's poems the "Beryl Songs" should not be removed from their present places in the interludes of the poem and relegated to a note at the end. Writing on this point in the "Athenæum," Mr. Watts said: – "The only case in which Rossetti's changes were not improvements was the case of the changes in 'Rose Mary,' made, not after, but before, it appeared in type, – changes which can only be called lamentable. It had lain in its perfect form for years, and although it had been read in manuscript to scores of friends, no line in it had been altered. But when passing 'Ballads and Sonnets' through the press in 1881, at a time when he was out of health, Rossetti called to mind certain remarks upon a supposed lack of clarity in his work which had fallen not only from some critics but from certain friends; and in an evil moment it occurred to him that it would be a gain to 'Rose Mary' if the three parts were knit together by lyrics, and he set to work to write the 'Beryl Songs' which now appear in the ballad. The lyrics themselves are not good, for his endowment of metre was not equal to his other poetical gifts; but had they been as good as the lyrics in 'Maud' the disaster to the poem would have been none the less grievous. A friend whom at that time he consulted upon everything strongly fought against the introduction of these incongruities, but Rossetti was too ill to be persistently opposed, and only became conscious of the mistake when it was too late, the book being then before the public."

It is obvious that the friend here alluded to is Mr. Watts himself, and it must be remembered that inasmuch as every line of the ballad *without* the lyrics had been familiar to him for years, his verdict can hardly be accepted as that of an unbiassed judge. It is, at all events, dubious whether any editor would now presume to disturb the sequence of the poem.

In one other ballad of kindred structure does Rossetti sustain a similar flow of exquisite imagination, in verbal beauty and subtlety of idiom hard to surpass in modern English verse. "The Bride's Prelude" is indeed but a lovely fragment, a delicate vignette, a little character-sketch bathed in the warmest and finest of mediæval colouring; a prelude only, as it modestly claims to be; but, like Chopin's preludes in music, so perfect in its limited range that the ear craves no further melody for a long while after its brief passion has sung itself to rest. It is a bride's confession to her younger sister on her wedding morn; and, taking the form of a broken monologue interspersed with descriptive passages of the highest poetic order, its movement is more deliberate, its ornament more richly wrought, perhaps, than that of the more dramatic ballads. It might almost be said that nowhere else does Rossetti so oppress the reader with the actual feeling of the atmosphere in which the tale is told. The intense and sultry stillness of the chamber at mid-noon, where the two women sit together probing for the first and only time the one dire secret of the past, weighs upon us like veritable glare and burning silence, save for the bride's difficult speech, and the shocked sister's faint answers, and the keen, far-off sounds in the courtyard below, till the last word is said. Every minute detail of sight and sound heightens the effect of warmth and colour in contrast to the bare simplicity and hard tragedy of the narrative.

> "The room lay still in dusty glare,
>   Having no sound through it
> Except the chirp of a caged bird
> That came and ceased: and if she stirred,
> Amelotte's raiment could be heard.
>
> "Although the lattice had dropped loose,
>   There was no wind; the heat
> Being so at rest that Amelotte
> Heard far beneath the plunge and float
> Of a hound swimming in the moat.
>
> "Some minutes since, two rooks had toiled

Home to the nests that crowned
Ancestral ash-trees. Through the glare
Beating again, they seemed to tear
With that thick caw the woof o' the air."

Such fragments afford the merest glimpses of the background, the pure, delicate, ultra-refined, and yet intensely naturalistic setting of the poem.

And indeed it is this highest refinement of naturalism, this perfect idealization of realities, this raising of the simplest and commonest accessories of life into universal beauty and significance, that remains Rossetti's inmost, utmost charm. This it is that sends us back, again and again, from all the splendours of his maturity, from the vivid glories of the ballads and the long-drawn passion of the sonnets, to the primal sweetness and utter simplicity of "The Blessed Damozel;" the easiest to love, the hardest to place in a just order, amid all that came from the hand and heart of Rossetti.

Written in his nineteenth year (though re-touched with important improvements afterwards), while the ballads above referred to were the work of his maturity, – and as remote from them in spirit as in date, the poem is unique among unique poetry. "The Blessed Damozel" is no product of precocity. It has not the laboured archaism, the studied originality, which mark most of the travel-poems of 1849 ("Paris and Belgium," "Antwerp and Bruges," etc.). Superb as are the sonnets of that early period – such noble utterances as "The Staircase of Notre Dame," "Place de la Bastille," and "The Refusal of Aid between Nations" remaining unsurpassed by anything in the "House of Life" series – the irregular lyrics and blank-verse chronicles of those journeys are apt to keep us in mind of those etymological researches at the British Museum by which Rossetti is said to have stored his vocabulary with the purest Saxon, preparatory to ballad-work. "The Blessed Damozel," on the contrary, is the most spontaneous and convincing of all his shorter poems. It seems to have sprung straight from the heart of the boy-poet in a sort of prophetic rapture, ere he knew the sorrow which he sang, and which his song should ease, as the most perfect art can sometimes ease, in other souls, for generations to come. Its strength lies in the very acme of tenderness; its source in the purest strain of common human feeling – the passionate, insatiable craving of the faithful heart for the continuity of life and love beyond the tomb, and the deep sense of the poverty of celestial compromises to satisfy the mourner on either side of the gulf that Death has set between. Here again is the true romantic note – the insistence on the joy and glory of the physical world, the delight in the earthly manifestations of affection, and the awed, plaintive conflict of impatience with resignation under the mystery of parting and transition to an unknown state. It is the same thought which an American poet has expressed in "Homesick in Heaven," – the thought that the beloved departed must in some way share the sorrow of separation, and await the last reunion with scarcely less longing than theirs whom they have left behind. "The Blessed Damozel" is one whom Death has thus removed from her lover's side, and she is pictured leaning out of Heaven, watching with tears and prayers for some sign of his coming. It is the lover himself who sees her thus, as in a dream, and tells us how, –

> "She bowed herself, and stooped
>   Out of the circling charm,
> Until her bosom must have made
>   The bar she leaned on warm,"

and how, on the mystic borderland between earth and heaven, –

> "The souls mounting up to God
>   Went by her like thin flames."

The glories of the upper air have no charm for her until he shares them. Still gazing downward from "the ramparts of God's house," she sees –

"The tides of day and night
        With flame and darkness ridge
The void, as low as where this earth
        Spins like a fretful midge;"

she knows the angels who "sit circlewise" –

"To fashion the birth-robes for them
Who are just born, being dead!"

Her one prayer is for the old companionship, the old, simple, earthly happiness, –

"Only to live as once on earth
        With Love, – only to be,
As then awhile, for ever now,
        Together, I and he."

It was not until many years later that "The Blessed Damozel" afforded the subject of the picture by which Rossetti is most popularly and superficially known to the outer world. It was his habit to inscribe his pictures with some original verse, generally in sonnet form; and some of his best descriptive sonnets, such as "Pandora," "Fiametta," "Found," "Astarte Syriaca," and "Mary Magdalene," had such an origin. "The Blessed Damozel" is said to be only instance of a picture executed after instead of before the correlative poem.

Two important works stand yet apart, alike from what we have classed as introspective and personal poetry, and from the splendid ballads in which consists Rossetti's most immortal contribution to English literature. "Jenny" and "A Last Confession" exemplify his use of the dramatic monologue, and alone among his compositions bear in a marked degree the influence of Browning. Especially is this influence notable in "A Last Confession." The Italy of this wonderful fragment – placed by critics of authority in the front rank of Rossetti's work – is, *par excellence*, Browning's Italy, with all the intense humanness and distinction of character which dominates its furies and its loves, with all the Saxon intellect and reason stamped into and burning through the irresponsible passion of the South. Just as in his ballads and sonnets Rossetti grafted the clean-cut Saxon diction on to the long and languorous habit of the Latin tongue, so in "A Last Confession" does he graft vivid thought and piercing argument upon the deep pathos and terror of the theme. It is a death-bed story told in a priest's ear; a story of passion and crime, and of a girl's shallow laugh that drove her lover to kill her in a frenzy of despair. For he remembered how, awhile before, –

> ... "A brown-shouldered harlot leaned
> Half through a tavern window thick with wine.
> Some man had come behind her in the room
> And caught her by the arms, and she had turned
> With that coarse empty laugh on him....
> ... And three hours afterwards,
> When she that I had run all risks to meet
> Laughed as I told you, my life burned to death
> Within me, for I thought it like the laugh
> Heard at the fair....
> And all she might have changed to, or might change to,
> Seemed in that laugh."

Somewhat akin in spirit (though less dramatic in treatment), in that it deals with the problem of sexual love in its darkest form, is the rhymed monologue entitled "Jenny;" and put into the mouth of one who has followed, half in pity, half in curiosity, a beautiful courtesan to her home, and sits with her in the luxurious chamber which is the purchase of her shame. The poem is to some extent in obvious relation to Rossetti's long contemplated but never completed picture, "Found;" but the latter shows the end of poor Jenny in after years, –

> "When, wealth and health slipped past, you stare
> Along the streets alone, and there,
> Round the long park, across the bridge,

The cold lamps at the pavement's edge,
Wind on together and apart,
A fiery serpent for your heart," –

whereas her visitor in the poem finds her in all her prime and pride, and asks, –

"What has man done here? How atone
Great God, for this which man has done?

.   .   .   .   .   .

But if, as blindfold fates are tossed
Through some one man this life be lost,
Shall soul not somehow pay for soul?"

"Jenny," perhaps, being cast in a more meditative form, lacks the poignancy and fervour of the utterance which comes, in "A Last Confession," from the lips of the sinner himself instead of from the spectator merely, but it surpasses all contemporary studies of its kind in its bold and masterly handling of a difficult theme. Both, however, are distinct from the lyric poems in that their abruptness of movement and irregularity of structure are the abruptness and irregularity of quick dramatic thought, impatient of metrical elaboration, surcharging the poetic vehicle with subject matter; an effect which must not be confused with the ruggedness of the true ballad-form, whose broken music haunts the ear by its very waywardness and variety of rhythm, and gains its end by a studied artlessness the more exquisite for its apparent unconstraint. Nor is the effect of Rossetti's universal preference for assonance over rhyme – a special characteristic of romantic poetry – identical in the ballads, sonnets and monologues just quoted. In the sonnets it relieves the rigid tension of the rhyme-system with an overtone of delicate caprice. In "Jenny" and "A Last Confession" it heightens the suggestion of impulse, and even haste of thought and emotion outrunning the metrical order which it chose. In the ballads, it is the result of the finest workmanship, not of accident or pressure of thought upon speech; it is the rich inlaying of the most highly-wrought woof of imaginative language with the brilliance of a perpetual surprise.

Rossetti is too near to us for a final estimate of his place among the century's poets. Enough has been said to illustrate the range and consistency of his art, as a whole, and the intimate relation of his poetry to his painting. The dominant æsthetic motives are the same in "Dante's Dream" and "The House of Life," in "Dis Manibus" and "The King's Tragedy," in "Beata Beatrix" and "The Blessed Damozel." He was the prophet of a natural idealism, based upon the frank acceptance and pursuit of the highest earthly good, subject only and absolutely to moral and spiritual law. He stood apart, as we have seen, from the intellectual struggles of his day. Philosophical controversies seldom troubled him. To theological speculation and historical discovery he was alike indifferent. But his isolation, his specialism even, are but evidences of the intensity of the new life to which he was awakened, and the reality of the visions which he saw. He sets before us in all its significance the problem of the dual possibilities of womanhood, by the simple, irresistible, pictorial statement of the contrast between the shameful actuality of "Found" and the noble ideal of "Sibylla Palmifera" and "Monna Vanna." His lamentation for the manhood of his age is that, –

> ... "Man is parcelled out in men
> To-day; because, for any wrongful blow,
>   No man not stricken asks, 'I would be told
> Why thou dost strike'; but his heart whispers then,
>   *'He is he, I am I.'*"

Such words are but the reiteration of that moral collectivism, that principle that "soul must somehow pay for soul," which Rossetti maintains unbrokenly as an assumption needing neither emphasis nor reserve. The problem which his work leaves to the next generation lies in the application of that principle to social and national ideals. The task of the twentieth century will be to do for society what Rossetti has done for art, – to restore to it the dignity and glory of a free life, embracing all that nature has to give, under the dominion of associated reason, and conscience, and will. And when Rossetti's genius shall have fulfilled its share in that unification of all knowledge to which the paths of science and poetry, art and scholarship, tend alike in the progress of time, England and Italy may join in worthier recognition of his life-work, whose face was set towards the final triumph of humanity – the reconciliation of the physical with the spiritual world.

THE END.

NOTES

1. F.W.H. Myers, "Rossetti and the Religion of Beauty."
2. "Some Thoughts on the Transition from Paganism to Christianity."
3. "On Pantheism and Cosmic Emotion."
4. "The Magazine of Art," 1888.
5. Gerald Massey: "Lectures on Pre-Raphaelitism," 1858.
6. W.M. Rossetti: "Fine Art; Chiefly Contemporary."
7. Rev. P.F. Forsyth: "Religion in Recent Art."
8. The Round Table Series: "Rossetti," by P.W. Nicholson.
9. William Tirebuck: "D.G. Rossetti; his work and influence."
10. Gabriel Sarrazin: "Poètes Modernes d'Angleterre."
11. Rossetti's sonnet, "Found."
12. Rev. P.F. Forsyth: "Religion in Recent Art."
13. Rossetti's sonnet, "Pandora."
14. Walter Pater, "The Renaissance: Studies of Art and Poetry."
15. F.W.H. Myers, "Essays: Modern."

CRESCENT MOON PUBLISHING

web: www.crmoon.com e-mail: cresmopub@yahoo.co.uk

ARTS, PAINTING, SCULPTURE

The Art of Andy Goldsworthy
Andy Goldsworthy: Touching Nature
Andy Goldsworthy in Close-Up
Andy Goldsworthy: Pocket Guide
Andy Goldsworthy In America
Land Art: A Complete Guide
The Art of Richard Long
Richard Long: Pocket Guide
Land Art In the UK
Land Art in Close-Up
Land Art In the U.S.A.
Land Art: Pocket Guide
Installation Art in Close-Up
Minimal Art and Artists In the 1960s and After
Colourfield Painting
Land Art DVD, TV documentary
Andy Goldsworthy DVD, TV documentary
The Erotic Object: Sexuality in Sculpture From Prehistory to the Present Day
Sex in Art: Pornography and Pleasure in Painting and Sculpture
Postwar Art
Sacred Gardens: The Garden in Myth, Religion and Art
Glorification: Religious Abstraction in Renaissance and 20th Century Art
Early Netherlandish Painting
Leonardo da Vinci
Piero della Francesca
Giovanni Bellini
Fra Angelico: Art and Religion in the Renaissance
Mark Rothko: The Art of Transcendence
Frank Stella: American Abstract Artist
Jasper Johns
Brice Marden
Alison Wilding: The Embrace of Sculpture
Vincent van Gogh: Visionary Landscapes
Eric Gill: Nuptials of God
Constantin Brancusi: Sculpting the Essence of Things
Max Beckmann
Caravaggio
Gustave Moreau
Egon Schiele: Sex and Death In Purple Stockings
Delizioso Fotografico Fervore: Works In Process 1
Sacro Cuore: Works In Process 2
The Light Eternal: J.M.W. Turner
The Madonna Glorified: Karen Arthurs

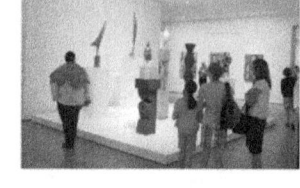
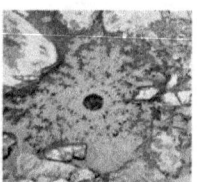
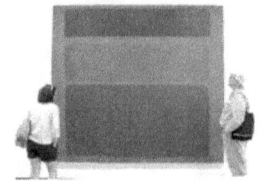
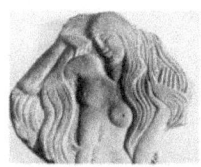
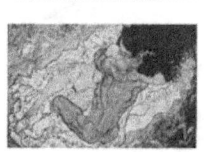
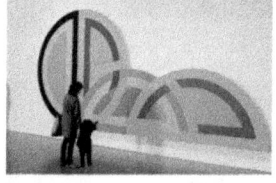
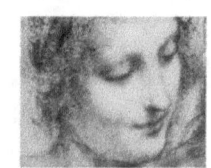
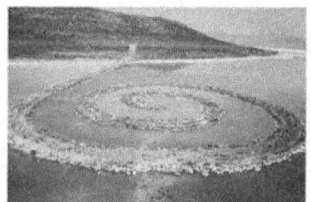

LITERATURE

J.R.R. Tolkien: The Books, The Films, The Whole Cultural Phenomenon
J.R.R. Tolkien: Pocket Guide
Tolkien's Heroic Quest
The *Earthsea* Books of Ursula Le Guin
Beauties, Beasts and Enchantment: Classic French Fairy Tales
German Popular Stories by the Brothers Grimm
Philip Pullman and *His Dark Materials*
Sexing Hardy: Thomas Hardy and Feminism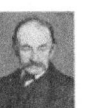
Thomas Hardy's *Tess of the d'Urbervilles*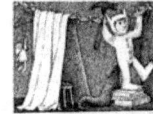
Thomas Hardy's *Jude the Obscure*
Thomas Hardy: The Tragic Novels
Love and Tragedy: Thomas Hardy
The Poetry of Landscape in Hardy
Wessex Revisited: Thomas Hardy and John Cowper Powys
Wolfgang Iser: Essays and Interviews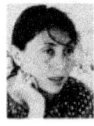
Petrarch, Dante and the Troubadours
Maurice Sendak and the Art of Children's Book Illustration
Andrea Dworkin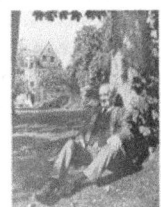
Cixous, Irigaray, Kristeva: The *Jouissance* of French Feminism
Julia Kristeva: Art, Love, Melancholy, Philosophy, Semiotics and Psychoanalysis
Hélene Cixous I Love You: The *Jouissance* of Writing
Luce Irigaray: Lips, Kissing, and the Politics of Sexual Difference
Peter Redgrove: Here Comes the Flood
Peter Redgrove: Sex-Magic-Poetry-Cornwall
Lawrence Durrell: Between Love and Death, East and West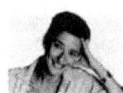
Love, Culture & Poetry: Lawrence Durrell
Cavafy: Anatomy of a Soul
German Romantic Poetry: Goethe, Novalis, Heine, Hölderlin
Feminism and Shakespeare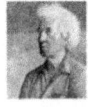
Shakespeare: Love, Poetry & Magic
The Passion of D.H. Lawrence
D.H. Lawrence: Symbolic Landscapes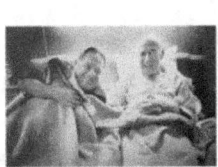
D.H. Lawrence: Infinite Sensual Violence
Rimbaud: Arthur Rimbaud and the Magic of Poetry
The Ecstasies of John Cowper Powys
Sensualism and Mythology: The Wessex Novels of John Cowper Powys
Amorous Life: John Cowper Powys and the Manifestation of Affectivity (H.W. Fawkner)
Postmodern Powys: New Essays on John Cowper Powys (Joe Boulter)
Rethinking Powys: Critical Essays on John Cowper Powys
Paul Bowles & Bernardo Bertolucci
Rainer Maria Rilke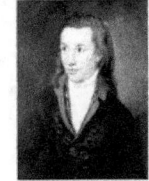
Joseph Conrad: *Heart of Darkness*
In the Dim Void: Samuel Beckett
Samuel Beckett Goes into the Silence
André Gide: Fiction and Fervour
Jackie Collins and the Blockbuster Novel
Blinded By Her Light: The Love-Poetry of Robert Graves
The Passion of Colours: Travels In Mediterranean Lands
Poetic Forms

POETRY

Ursula Le Guin: Walking In Cornwall
Peter Redgrove: Here Comes The Flood
Peter Redgrove: Sex-Magic-Poetry-Cornwall
Dante: Selections From the Vita Nuova
Petrarch, Dante and the Troubadours
William Shakespeare: Sonnets
William Shakespeare: Complete Poems
Blinded By Her Light: The Love-Poetry of Robert Graves
Emily Dickinson: Selected Poems
Emily Brontë: Poems
Thomas Hardy: Selected Poems
Percy Bysshe Shelley: Poems
John Keats: Selected Poems
Joh n Keats: Poems of 1820
D.H. Lawrence: Selected Poems
Edmund Spenser: Poems
Edmund Spenser: Amoretti
John Donne: Poems
Henry Vaughan: Poems
Sir Thomas Wyatt: Poems
Robert Herrick: Selected Poems
Rilke: Space, Essence and Angels in the Poetry of Rainer Maria Rilke
Rainer Maria Rilke: Selected Poems
Friedrich Hölderlin: Selected Poems
Arseny Tarkovsky: Selected Poems
Arthur Rimbaud: Selected Poems
Arthur Rimbaud: A Season in Hell
Arthur Rimbaud and the Magic of Poetry
Novalis: Hymns To the Night
German Romantic Poetry
Paul Verlaine: Selected Poems
Elizaethan Sonnet Cycles
D.J. Enright: By-Blows
Jeremy Reed: Brigitte's Blue Heart
Jeremy Reed: Claudia Schiffer's Red Shoes
Gorgeous Little Orpheus
Radiance: New Poems
Crescent Moon Book of Nature Poetry
Crescent Moon Book of Love Poetry
Crescent Moon Book of Mystical Poetry
Crescent Moon Book of Elizabethan Love Poetry
Crescent Moon Book of Metaphysical Poetry
Crescent Moon Book of Romantic Poetry
Pagan America: New American Poetry

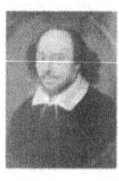
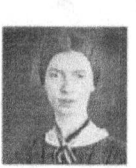
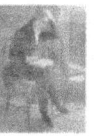
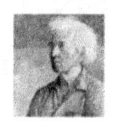
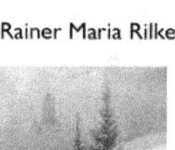
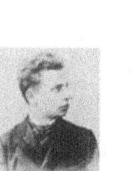
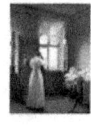
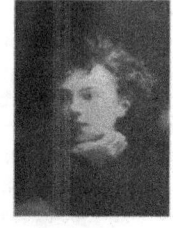
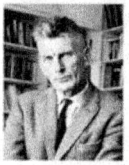
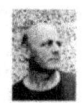
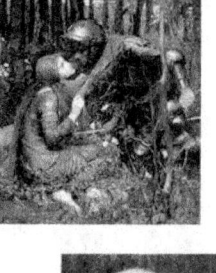
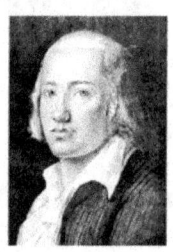
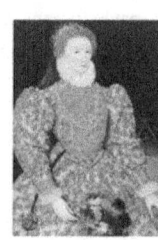

MEDIA, CINEMA, FEMINISM and CULTURAL STUDIES

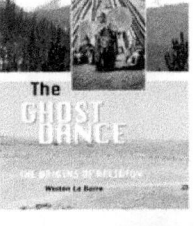
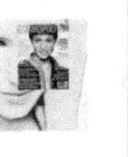

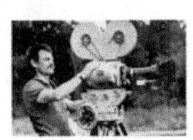
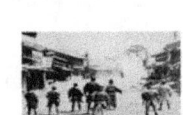
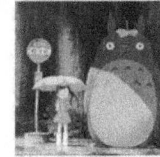
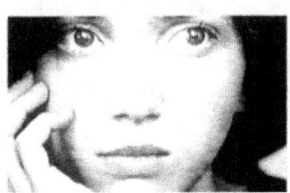

The Light Eternal is a model monograph, an exemplary job. The subject matter of the book is beautifully organised and dead on beam. (Lawrence Durrell)
It is amazing for me to see my work treated with such passion and respect. (Andrea Dworkin)

CRESCENT MOON PUBLISHING
P.O. Box 1312, Maidstone, Kent, ME14 5XU, Great Britain. www.crmoon.com

cresmopub@yahoo.co.uk   www.crescentmoon.org.uk

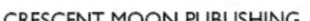

pliance